STAR WARS

THE FORCE UNLEASHED

PRIMA Official Game Guide

Written by

Fernando Bueno

Prima Games
An Imprint of Random House, Inc.

3000 Lava Ridge Court, Suite 100
Roseville, CA 95661
www.primagames.com

Senior Product Manager: Donato Tica
Associate Product Manager: Shaida Boroumand
Manufacturing: Suzanne Goodwin
Texture Maps: David Bueno

A very special thanks to:
Bertrand Estrellado, Ed Tucker, Matt Miller, Dan Wasson, Mark Friesen, Dave Jimenez, Roger Evoy, Stephen Ervin, and Julio Torres.

Please be advised that the ESRB Ratings icons, "EC," "E," "E10+," "T," "M," "AO," and "RP" are trademarks owned by the Entertainment Software Association, and may only be used with their permission and authority. For information regarding whether a product has been rated by the ESRB, please visit www.esrb.org. For permission to use the Ratings icons, please contact the ESA at esrblicenseinfo.com.

Important:
Prima Games has made every effort to determine that the information contained in this book is accurate. However, the publisher makes no warranty, either expressed or implied, as to the accuracy, effectiveness, or completeness of the material in this book; nor does the publisher assume liability for damages, either incidental or consequential, that may result from using the information in this book. The publisher cannot provide any additional information or support regarding gameplay, hints and strategies, or problems with hardware or software. Such questions should be directed to the support numbers provided by the game and/or device manufacturers as set forth in their documentation. Some game tricks require precise timing and may require repeated attempts before the desired result is achieved.

ISBN: 978-0-7615-5916-0
Library of Congress Catalog Card Number: 2008920935
Printed in the United States of America

08 09 10 11 GG 10 9 8 7 6 5 4 3 2 1

Author Bio

Fernando "Red Star" Bueno (aka dukkhah) has been a gamer since opening his first Atari, and has been writing creatively since his early years in high school. During college he combined his loves for gaming and writing and began freelancing for popular gaming websites. The San Diego native found his way to Northern California shortly after high school. After graduating from the University of California, Davis, with a dual degree in English and art history, he was able to land a job as an editor for Prima Games. Though happy with his position as an editor, his life called him to Las Vegas where he now resides. During the move to Nevada, he also made the move to author and has since written a number of game books, including *Naruto Uzumaki Chronicles 2*, *Prince of Persia: Two Thrones*, *Fight Night Round 3*, and *Stubbs the Zombie*.

In his time off he enjoys the works of Hermann Hesse, Johann Van Goethe, Franz Kafka, and EGM. When not writing for Prima, he continues to work on his craft as a poet. We want to hear from you! E-mail comments and feedback to fbueno@primagames.com.

Contents

STAR WARS
THE FORCE UNLEASHED

Dedication

A long time ago in an office building far, far away, there were two people whose knowledge of the Force was strong. Well, okay, one person whose knowledge of the Force was strong, but both people were super awesome. Their names were "Don Vader" Tica and "Shaida Fett" Boroumand. All silliness aside, I treasure these projects where I can work with two of the coolest people I know. Thanks to my lovely Leslie for not slapping me every time I decided to talk like Yoda while working on this project. On her nerves, I'm sure it got.

Last but not least, a million thanks go out to Bertrand Estrellado, Ed Tucker, and all the people at LucasArts for their tremendous support on this project. Without them, this book doesn't happen.

The Story up Until Now...

Surely you've come to know the story of Anakin Skywalker, Jedi Master Yoda, Obi-Wan Kenobi, and the Jedi Order. You may even be familiar with the story of the Rebellion against the Empire or have heard whisperings of a dark organization named the Sith. But for those who need a reminder of where it all began, the following section provides all the background information needed to begin *your* adventure as you unleash the Force.

Star Wars: Episode I The Phantom Menace

During a time of turmoil in the Galactic Republic, a powerful organization known as the Trade Federation engaged in an aggressive maneuver to block trade routes to and from the planet Naboo.

While the Congress of the Republic stalled on resolving the conflict, the Supreme Chancellor of the Republic secretly sent out two Jedi Knights to help resolve the issue quickly and quietly. Unfortunately, both the Jedi Knights and the people of Naboo were unaware that the Trade Federation was being secretly coerced into their actions by a more powerful dark force.

Upon arriving to meet with the Trade Federation delegates, the Jedi were ambushed and forced to flee. In their escape, they rescued Queen Amidala of Naboo and made a dash across the stars. As they fled, Qui-Gon Jinn, the elder of the two Jedi, came upon a small child with an extraordinarily high capacity for the Force—the energy that flows through all living things and that Jedi can harness into unique abilities. Convinced that the child, Anakin Skywalker, was the one prophesied to bring balance to the Force, Qui-Gon Jinn rescued him from slavery and took him on as an apprentice. It was not until after they met with the Jedi Council that Anakin's dark and troubled past was brought into question. Unmoved by the council's warnings, Qui-Gon Jinn continued informally with Anakin's training.

As the Jedi fled from the Trade Federation with Queen Amidala, they found that they were being hunted by a dark figure highly skilled with a lightsaber and shrouded in the dark side of the Force. Upon hearing of the mysterious figure's attack on Qui-Gon Jinn, the Jedi Order realized that the Sith—a dark Order long thought to be extinct—was actually still active. Meanwhile, Senator Palpatine, a two-faced politician with dark ambitions, secretly and successfully schemed to overthrow the Supreme Chancellor and took his place.

In a final move of desperation, Senator Amidala (accompanied by Qui-Gon Jinn, Obi-Wan Kenobi, and Anakin Skywalker) fled back to Naboo to help liberate her planet from the Trade Federation. Though they were supposed to protect Amidala, the Jedi had a second motive for returning. They were to draw out the Dark Lord who attacked them earlier and reveal the existence of the Sith.

In a final confrontation, Qui-Gon Jinn exposed and was defeated by the Sith Lord Darth Maul, who was in turn defeated by Obi-Wan Kenobi. In the end, Palpatine became the new Supreme Chancellor and took control of the Republic, Naboo was liberated from the Trade Federation, Obi-Wan honored Qui-Gon Jinn's final request and took Anakin as his Padawan learner, and the Sith were exposed.

But a question remained: If Darth Maul was a Sith Lord, was he a student or a Master?

Star Wars: Episode II Attack of the Clones

Ten years after the reemergence of the Sith, Obi-Wan Kenobi, Anakin Skywalker, and the rest of the Jedi Knights struggled to keep order in the galaxy. Several thousand solar systems threatened to leave the Republic as they followed a separatist movement led by the mysterious Count Dooku, a former Jedi Knight.

Senator Amidala of Naboo, the former Queen, returned to the Galactic Senate to petition for the creation of an army of the Republic to aid the struggling Jedi. Unfortunately, not everyone shared in her vision, as she was under the repeated threat of assassination.

After another failed assassination attempt, the Jedi Order assigned Obi-Wan and Anakin, whom she'd not seen in years, as her personal bodyguards. While they were on assignment, Anakin's impetuous nature got the better of him and he used the Senator as bait to draw out her assassin.

Still, Amidala's would-be assassin would not relent. She struck once again while Amidala was under the watchful eye of the two Jedi, and the duo chased the assassin down. When they caught her, she was killed by a poisoned dart before she could reveal the name of the person who issued her orders.

While Obi-Wan followed the trail of clues back to a bounty hunter named Jango Fett, Anakin was assigned to protect Senator Amidala while in seclusion on Naboo.

The trail to Jango Fett led Obi-Wan to the mysterious planet Kamino. There he found a race of cloners with an army of soldiers they claimed was commissioned by the Jedi Master Sifo-Dyas, who had died over ten years prior. Though he was perplexed by the development, Obi-Wan didn't have much time to mull it over, as Jango Fett attacked him unsuccessfully before fleeing the planet.

Meanwhile, Anakin and Amidala grew closer while in seclusion. Though Anakin was haunted by the memory of his mother, his love for Amidala grew every day they spent together. Eventually, Anakin's concerns about his mother overwhelmed him, and he was drawn away from the hideout in Naboo. With Amidala in tow, Anakin set out in search of his mother only to find that she'd been captured by a Tusken Raider hunting party. In a failed attempt to rescue his mother, Anakin was briefly reunited with her long enough for her to die in his arms. In a fit of rage, he single-handedly destroyed the entire village of Tusken Raiders.

Meanwhile, Jango Fett led Obi-Wan to the Trade Federation planet Geonosis. There, lying amidst a large concentration of Federation ships, was a large battle droid factory. Obi-Wan infiltrated the factory to discover Count Dooku and his followers secretly scheming to destroy the Jedi and overthrow the Republic.

Before he was captured, Obi-Wan sent out a call to Anakin and the Jedi Order. However, instead of following the Jedi Order's instructions to protect Amidala on Naboo, Amidala coerced Anakin into searching for Obi-Wan in hopes of rescuing him. When Anakin and Amidala arrived at Geonosis, they, too, were captured by Dooku's troops.

STAR WARS
THE FORCE UNLEASHED

Meanwhile, Supreme Chancellor Palpatine issued orders to create a grand army of the Republic, knowing full well that the army was waiting for him on Kamino.

When the Jedi arrived on Geonosis to rescue Obi-Wan, they found that not only was he in danger, but so were Anakin and Amidala. The battle on Geonosis was short but fierce. Just as the Jedi's numbers began to dwindle and all hope seemed to fade, Master Yoda arrived with an army of stormtroopers.

Upon seeing Jedi Master Mace Windu defeat his loyal soldier Jango Fett, Count Dooku fled. Anakin and Obi-Wan followed Dooku and cornered him in a cave where the two Jedi engaged the traitorous Count in heated battle. Dooku's skills were far superior, and he was able to fell Obi-Wan and sever Anakin's arm. Just as Dooku was about to destroy Anakin once and for all, Yoda arrived and rescued the two fallen Jedi. Foiled by his former master, Dooku fled once again—this time successfully.

Though he got away, Dooku did inadvertently reveal that a mysterious Darth Sidious was somehow controlling the Senate. Anakin and Amidala secretly married, but the damage had been done. Anakin had already taken his first step toward the dark side, the dark side of the Force grew stronger, and the Clone Wars began.

The Clone Wars

The Clone Wars spanned about three years, and rapidly spread throughout the galaxy after the Battle of Geonosis. Though Count Dooku seemed the public mastermind of the Separatist strategy, he secretly answered to his Sith Master, Darth Sidious. Military actions were led by the cyborg General Grievous, and Dooku had a cadre of specialized underlings, including the bounty hunter Durge and the dark side warrior Asajj Ventress. Early in the war, Dooku's forces mined the hyperspace routes that connected the Core Worlds to the rest of the galaxy, effectively cutting off the Republic from the bulk of its resources and allowing the Separatists relative freedom of movement in the Outer Rim. To match this maneuver, the Jedi entreated the Hutts to share their control of the Outer Rim, allowing the Republic to move their vessels through Hutt-controlled space.

Over the course of the war, public opinion of the Jedi Order waxed and waned. Their early defeats underscored their vulnerability, and their reluctant adoption of the rank of general caused them to be blamed for many of the missteps in the Clone Wars. Still, there emerged champions like Anakin Skywalker and Obi-Wan Kenobi, respectively dubbed the Hero with No Fear and the Negotiator by an approving public. Heroes arose similarly on the side of the Separatists.

The conflict came to a head with an astonishingly brazen attack mounted by the Separatists on the Republic capital world during the final stages of the Clone Wars. The fierce attack was a cover for General Grievous's daring kidnapping of Supreme Chancellor Palpatine. In the upper atmosphere of the city-planet, starships from the Republic's Fifth Fleet tangled with Confederacy vessels while Grievous returned from the planet's surface to his flagship, Invisible Hand, with his highly prized hostage. Rampant signal jamming from Separatist vessels sowed confusion among the enmeshed fleets. Anakin Skywalker and Obi-Wan Kenobi were once again called upon on a desperate mission to infiltrate the Invisible Hand and rescue the Chancellor.

5

Star Wars: Episode III Revenge of the Sith

As Grievous and his troops attempted to flee Coruscant with Chancellor Palpatine in their clutches, Obi-Wan and Anakin gave chase. Instead of finding Grievous, the duo again faced Count Dooku. The battle was fierce, and Obi-Wan was once more disabled, leaving Anakin to face Dooku on his own.

By then, however, Anakin's powers had grown strong, and he bested Dooku quickly. As Anakin had Dooku in his grasp, Chancellor Palpatine ordered him to execute Dooku in a fit of revenge. Anakin beheaded the evil Count in yet another dark deed. Though Count Dooku had fallen, General Grievous still managed to escape and retained his control of the droid army. The Clone Wars were not over yet.

Once back on Coruscant, Chancellor Palpatine returned to his plotting and scheming, and Padmé nervously awaited Anakin's return. Upon being reunited, Padmé revealed to Anakin that she was pregnant, but their happiness would be short-lived. Again, Anakin would be plagued with terrible, fearful dreams...this time about Padmé.

Back in the shadows, Sidious ordered Grievous to move the Separatist leaders to Mustafar. However, in the broad daylight of Coruscant, Palpatine began playing Anakin against the rest of the Jedi Council. He placed Anakin on the council as his "representative," but Anakin was angered when he was not given the rank of Master as all council members are.

By placing Anakin on the Jedi Council, Palpatine had eyes and ears in the Jedi's business. Similarly, the Jedi wanted Anakin to keep watch on Palpatine, as he was gaining even more executive powers over the Republic. Things grew even more complicated for Anakin as concerns about Padmé began to trouble him. Between the fearful dreams of her death and her own concerns over the Republic, Anakin grew more frustrated and confused.

When Anakin was at his most vulnerable, Palpatine subtly revealed his true motives. He played on Anakin's fear of losing Padmé and turned him even more toward the dark side by promising to teach him a way to cheat death.

As Anakin struggled with his dark side, Obi-Wan tracked down General Grievous to the Utapau system. The general, who had slain several Jedi on his own, was bested by the Jedi Master, thus bringing an end to the Clone Wars. It was then that Anakin revealed to Mace Windu that Palpatine was a Sith Lord.

Windu confronted Palpatine and nearly defeated him, only to have Anakin betray him in a confused rage. Anakin had finally turned to the dark side, and Palpatine, as Lord Sidious, had full control over the former Jedi Knight.

Anakin's first act as a Sith was to execute all the remaining Jedi. Sidious sent Anakin, now dubbed "Darth Vader," to the Jedi Temple to execute

all the Jedi and cripple the Jedi Order. After the Jedi Temple fell, Anakin went to Mustafar and executed all the leaders of the Separatist movement. By doing so, Sidious solidified his hold on the Republic. During Anakin's betrayal of the Jedi, Sidious executed Order 66, which was a secret command sent to the army of the Republic to turn on their Jedi leaders and execute them. The Jedi Knights were now under attack from all sides.

Anakin wiped out the Jedi Temple, the clone army that once fought alongside the Jedi turned on them, and only a handful of Jedi were known to have survived. The end of the Jedi was near.

As Sidious's plans to destroy the last remaining Jedi neared fruition, Yoda and Obi-Wan Kenobi intercepted a fake signal meant to lure all Jedi back to the Temple, where they would be slaughtered. Upon arriving at the Temple to destroy the signal, Obi-Wan and Yoda also discovered that Anakin had slaughtered all the remaining Jedi there, including the younglings.

Obi-Wan revealed Anakin's traitorous actions to Padmé, who immediately set out after her husband. Obi-Wan followed Padmé to Anakin, where he confronted his former student. Convinced that Padmé had deliberately led Obi-Wan to him, Anakin became blinded by rage and attacked his lover. Obi-Wan intervened, but it was too late. The damage was too severe, and Anakin's rage would have horrible consequences.

There, on the planet Mustafar, amidst a river of molten lava, Obi-Wan and Anakin engaged in battle. In the end, Obi-Wan severed Anakin's legs and left arm. As Anakin slowly slipped into the lava river and burned, Obi-Wan left and took the dying Padmé to safety.

Meanwhile, Master Yoda confronted Darth Sidious on Coruscant. Their battle, unfortunately, ended in stalemate, as Sidious escaped once again and Yoda was forced into exile. Sensing that his new apprentice was in danger, Sidious rescued the crippled Anakin from the volatile planet and rebuilt him into a dark menacing being. All that remained of Anakin was Darth Vader.

In a separate part of the galaxy, Padmé gave birth to twins, a boy and a girl, then died. The children were separated to hide their birth line, and Darth Vader was informed that he was responsible for Padmé's death. Though his children would survive, Darth Vader would continue to live tormented by the fact that he was responsible for the death of his love....

Star Wars: The Force Unleashed

And it is here that we begin our adventure. You may know the inevitable outcome of Sidious and the Empire—how the rise of a young Jedi named Luke Skywalker was the demise of Darth Vader and his Master Lord Sidious. But what of the events immediately following Order 66?

Prepare, for it is during these dark days that our adventure will take place. But first you must know the ways of the Four....

How to Use the Force

There are several key elements that will guide you along your journey. Scattered throughout this book are different types of boxes, each containing valuable bits of information.

SITH WISDOM

Sith Wisdom boxes are useful tips. They can often guide you toward a better path, a hidden Holocron, or even direct you in how to use the Force more efficiently. You can skip these if you wish, but they are meant to help hone your skills.

JEDI KNOWLEDGE

Jedi Knowledge boxes are notes. Perhaps it is because they are always mindful of the Force that Jedi have a keen ability to observe the world around them and note what others might miss. These boxes will usually offer a side note on anything and everything, from your adventure to this book.

STAR WARS
THE FORCE UNLEASHED

"I should think that you Jedi would have more respect for the difference between knowledge and wisdom."

—Dex, *Star Wars: Episode II Attack of the Clones*

The final element may not necessarily help you avoid pitfalls, guide you toward Holocrons, or even shed light on the adventure, but they will help you understand the world of *Star Wars*. *Star Wars* quotes, as seen above, are taken directly from the *Star Wars* world. You'll typically find these in places where the quote is particularly relevant. Consider these a way to help you truly grasp the scope of your adventure.

WOOKIEE WARNING

Wookiee Warning boxes are vital cautions. You may be a Sith, but Wookiees are known survivors. They make do with what their land gives them and are as tough as they come. That's why these Wookiee Warnings are so important. If you've ignored the other two boxes, be sure to read these: their sole purpose is to keep you alive.

Achieving Balance

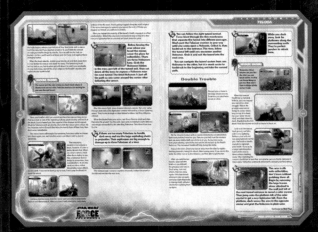

You will find that, much like with the Force, balance can be achieved only by accepting that there are multiple sides to everything. Such is the case with this book. In it you will find different sections dedicated specifically for different versions of *Star Wars®: The Force Unleashed™*. While all text boxes previously mentioned pertain to every section of the book, the Wii and PlayStation 3/Xbox sections will have their own special boxes.

WII WONDERS

Wii Wonders boxes appear only in the section dedicated to the Nintendo Wii version of *Star Wars: The Force Unleashed* and contain Wii-specific tidbits. They help highlight the differences between this version of the game and the others.

ONLY IN...

Only In... boxes will appear in the PS3/Xbox 360 section of the book. The information contained therein will pertain to these three versions of the game. Each box will specify which version of the game it refers to. For example, mention of an Achievement can found in a box that reads "Only In...Xbox 360."

Playable Characters

The Secret Apprentice

A powerful, almost primal Force wielder, Darth Vader's Secret Apprentice has been trained by the Dark Lord of the Sith to hunt down the last of the galaxy's Jedi. Darth Vader discovered his Secret Apprentice on the Wookiee world of Kashyyyk, where he kidnapped the boy after striking down his Jedi father. Vader has spent years personally training the apprentice in the ways of the Sith, but no other Imperials—including the Emperor—know of his existence. The apprentice's training has been harsh and unforgiving; Vader subjected the boy to rigorous physical tests bordering on torture. He first controlled the boy through fear, then taught him to embrace his hatred and other base emotions. As the boy grew older, Vader promised him greater power—through the dark side. Under Vader's relentless tutelage, the apprentice has all but perfected the fine art of lightsaber combat and has learned to wield many fearsome dark side powers.

As his apprentice grew stronger in the ways of the Force, Vader began testing him by sending him on secret missions to dispatch the Dark Lord's rivals and enemies. Vader assigned his apprentice the code name "Starkiller" and provided him with an advanced prototype starship, the *Rogue Shadow*, to aid in his missions. With these early trials complete, the apprentice is now ready to embark on his most dangerous missions yet: the hunt for rogue Jedi. It is Vader's hope that the apprentice will one day fulfill a dark destiny, standing at Vader's side as they confront and destroy the Emperor together.

JEDI KNOWLEDGE

Aside from the Secret Apprentice, you will also be able to control Darth Vader for the first mission.

Nonplayable Characters
Juno Eclipse

Juno Eclipse was born on Corulag, a Core World that would eventually be viewed as a "model" Imperial planet. As a young girl, Juno showed a fascination for alien worlds and cultures, an interest her mother encouraged. Unfortunately, her mother was killed in the cross fire between Imperials and "insurgents" on Corulag, leaving Juno to be raised by her cold and distant father. A fierce follower of Emperor Palpatine, Juno's father instilled in his daughter a belief that the Empire's aims were just. He also chastised her interest in alien cultures. As she grew older, Juno began to feel that she would never earn her father's love or respect. However, he talked endlessly about his great admiration for the "brave men and women" who joined the Imperial academy on Corulag. Hoping to earn her father's love, the serious and intelligent Juno set her sights on the academy. She became an ideal student, but her childhood was lonely and bereft of any real joy.

It did not take long for Juno's incredible academic record to attract Imperial recruiters' attention. At fourteen, Juno was the youngest student ever accepted into the Corulag Academy. There, she worked tirelessly to prove herself to her father. She learned to fly and repair a variety of craft, to maintain droids, and to wield blasters and other weapons with deadly accuracy. Much to her surprise, Juno also proved to be a talented combat pilot. But despite all her hard work, Juno's father never showed her the love she craved. When Juno graduated from the academy, he refused to attend the ceremony. Furious, Juno left Corulag for Imperial service, vowing never to return home. The Empire—particularly her squad mates and fellow pilots—would be her family now.

After graduating from the academy, Juno flew numerous combat missions throughout the Outer Rim as the Empire spread across the galaxy and "brought peace" to war-torn worlds. Her success in battle brought Juno numerous commendations and the admiration of her peers and commanding officers. She was almost happy: She was surrounded by friends, respected (and even feared) for her abilities, and lived a life of high adventure. Juno's record eventually caught Darth Vader's attention. At his command, she led a bombing run against insurgents on Callos, a world in the Outer Rim. This should have been Juno's shining moment—her most important mission, for the Emperor's right hand. Juno handpicked her squadron and launched an unrelenting attack. However, during the strike, Juno realized that the planet's native species had little in the way of offensive weaponry. As Juno began questioning the attack, Vader ordered her to destroy a massive planetary reactor. Unwilling to

8

give up her "perfect life" as an Imperial Officer, she complied. Juno was horrified when she realized that the resulting explosion caused global climate changes, wiping out nearly all life on the planet, including millions of sentient beings and untold thousands of undocumented species.

As a "reward" for her sterling service at the Battle of Callos, Juno received a special assignment from Vader: She became the pilot of the *Rogue Shadow*, an advanced prototype starship reserved for use by one of Vader's mysterious agents, known only to Juno as "Starkiller." After Vader betrayed his apprentice, Juno found herself surrounded by Imperial Stormtroopers, who inexplicably captured and imprisoned the pilot.

After months in a holding cell, Juno was visited by Darth Vader: He revealed that he had killed Starkiller and had branded Juno a traitor to the Empire for her association with his apprentice. The distraught Juno was later transported to Darth Vader's secret laboratory ship, the *Empirical*, where she assumed she would be subjected to horrific Sith experiments. She was ultimately saved from this fate by Starkiller, who was indeed alive and who freed her from the ship during his own escape from the Empire. Together they have set out to find others who might oppose the Emperor, but Juno remains painfully aware that she has left behind the only life she has ever known.

PROXY

PROXY is a prototype holodroid who has been a constant companion to Darth Vader's Secret Apprentice for many years. Although PROXY's origins are unknown, this one-of-a-kind droid is capable of using advanced hologram technology and built-in servos to alter his appearance, becoming virtually anyone. PROXY employs this ability to provide "face-to-face" communication between Vader's apprentice and others (usually Darth Vader himself). Additionally, PROXY has been programmed to act as a training droid, taking the shape of various enemies, including past Jedi, to test the apprentice's fighting acumen. He even harbors several lightsabers within his chassis, which allow him to challenge the apprentice whenever they spar. While PROXY is intensely loyal to Vader's apprentice—who he knows only by his code name, Starkiller—the droid is programmed with a sinister prime directive to kill his master at the first available opportunity. PROXY has spent years ambushing the apprentice in order to fulfill this programming, never realizing that success would end their friendship forever.

JEDI KNOWLEDGE

PROXY also appears as an enemy in the game. Rather than have his own fighting style, however, he emulates other enemies you've fought.

ONLY IN...

The battle with PROXY occurs only in the Xbox 360 or PlayStation 3 versions of *Star Wars: The Force Unleashed!*

General Rahm Kota

Master Rahm Kota is a tough, grizzled Jedi Master who became a respected and feared general during the Clone Wars. Prior to joining the Jedi Order, Kota spent much of his life in the trenches as a solider fighting for freedom on his home world, where he was thrust into battle before his tenth year. When he was 18, Kota met and befriended Mace Windu, who was sent to Kota's planet to negotiate a peaceful resolution to a particularly brutal conflict. Upon completing the mission, Mace decided to bring Kota back to Coruscant with him to hone his powers and finish his training under the watchful eye of Jedi Master Yoda.

Few in the Jedi Order bonded with the gruff Kota, but none doubted his strong commitment to the Republic, his undaunted loyalty to the Jedi Order, or his legendary courage: He often volunteered for the Order's most dangerous missions and never abandoned those in need. But Kota was also viewed as cold and militant. Throughout his long history with the Jedi Order, Kota tended to question the Council's decisions and often advocated a more forceful approach to negotiating treaties and dealing with lawbreakers.

When war broke out between the Republic and the Confederacy of Independent Systems, Kota proved himself a brilliant tactician and cagey commander. He was quickly promoted to the rank of general and led several of the Republic's most successful offensives throughout the Outer Rim. However, Master Kota did not embrace the clone army, believing that nonclone soldiers would be more creative, intelligent, and capable in the field. He recruited and built his own army from local militias, hardened mercenary groups, and even Separatist prisoners of war. His misgivings about the clones saved Kota's life when Order 66 was issued and most of his fellow Jedi were slain by their clone squadrons. Realizing that the Jedi Order had been betrayed, Master Kota and his most loyal lieutenants hijacked a Republic Cruiser and disappeared into the Outer Rim territories. Although believed dead, Kota eventually resurfaced and began recklessly attacking key Imperial targets across the galaxy.

`In one-on-one combat, Kota generally adopts a defensive stance, using his lightsaber skills and mastery of the Force to protect himself until he can launch a devastating counterattack. He often uses the Force to hurl debris or repel his enemies, and he can throw his lightsaber with unerring accuracy.

9

Senator Bail Organa

A decorated war hero from the Clone Wars, Bail Organa is one of the most influential political figures in the galaxy. He is head of the Royal Family of Alderaan, viceroy and first chairman of the Alderaan system, and a respected member of the Imperial Senate who, prior to the rise of the Empire, once commanded the ear of Supreme Chancellor Palpatine. A loyal friend to the Jedi Order, Organa fought alongside generals such as Obi-Wan Kenobi during many conflicts. When Palpatine later betrayed the Jedi Order, Organa secretly helped Jedi Masters Yoda and Obi-Wan Kenobi escape into hiding. He even took one of Anakin Skywalker's twins into his care, raising her as his own daughter, Princess Leia.

Since the Clone Wars, Bail Organa has led Alderaan into an age of prosperity, helping the battle-scarred world recover from the ravages of conflict. At his urging, weapons have been banned from Alderaan to demonstrate the planet's philosophy of peace and life. Meanwhile, he continues to serve as a member of the Imperial Senate, though he disagrees with everything Palpatine has done since his ascent to Emperor. Working alongside senators such as Garm Bel Iblis and Mon Mothma, Organa tries to subvert the Emperor's policies from within. He has also been a vocal critic of the Emperor. While Palpatine does not dare murder the beloved Organa outright, he has attempted to put the Senator and his daughter in harm's way on more than one occasion.

With the Senate's power waning, Organa has begun to consider alternatives to political debate in his effort to overthrow the Emperor. Although a pacifist at heart, he has realized that sometimes great evil can only be defeated through force. Organa also continues to aid the Jedi, funneling information and supplies to Shaak Ti, Rahm Kota, and others whose locations are known only to him. When Kota emerged from hiding, Organa helped the general select key Imperial targets to attack and later ensured that the blinded Jedi Master was safely transported to Cloud City.

When he learned that his daughter was being held hostage by the Empire on Kashyyyk, Bail asked General Kota to arrange a rescue. When the drunk and blind Kota refused, Bail set out in search of Shaak Ti for aid, only to be captured by Maris Brood on Felucia.

Princess Leia

The adopted daughter of Senator Bail Organa, head of the Royal House of Alderaan, Princess Leia has been active in galactic politics nearly all of her life. Although a maverick and tomboy when she was a child, Leia revered her father and sought to emulate his devotion to serving the galaxy. She actively followed Imperial politics and often accompanied her father on his trips to Coruscant. There, she witnessed firsthand the corruption within the Imperial Senate. As the Emperor consolidated his power, passing increasingly fascist laws and regulations, Bail would quietly explain to his daughter how these new policies would hurt the galaxy and its inhabitants. The empathetic Leia began undertaking "mercy missions" on behalf of Alderaan, traveling to war-torn or subjugated worlds to provide supplies and other aid. She quickly gained the love and respect of many systems. By the time she was 14, she had been nominated for numerous political positions, and at only 16 she became the youngest senator in galactic history.

As Emperor Palpatine committed an increasing number of atrocities, both Leia and her father wrestled with their convictions. They desperately wanted to speak out against the Emperor, but they knew that doing so would only put their family and perhaps even their entire homeworld of Alderaan in danger. Bail began quietly gathering support from other senators, while Leia, at her father's insistence, kept her opinions about the Emperor's policies to herself and instead continued to bring aid to troubled systems. When the Emperor created a system of territorial governors who reported directly to him, Bail publicly opposed the plan, claiming that it was a first step toward abolishing the Senate completely. The Emperor was furious but knew that murdering the well-liked Senator Organa would only make him a martyr. Instead, as a threat to Leia's father, he ordered that the princess be sent to Kashyyyk as a "senatorial observer," essentially putting her directly in harm's way. If Bail spoke out against the Emperor again, Princess Leia would meet an untimely end, allegedly killed by berserk Wookiee Slaves....

Mon Mothma

An influential loyalist senator during the final days of the Galactic Republic, Mon Mothma was born on Chandrila and received her political training early in life. Her father was an arbiter-general for the Old Republic, trained to bring peace between clashing species, while her mother served as a planetary governor. The couple taught their daughter the importance of all living creatures and the essential doctrines of strong leadership. With surprising speed, Mon Mothma grasped her parents' teachings and became the youngest person elected to the Republic Senate, an honor she held until the rise of Princess Leia Organa of Alderaan.

On the eve of the Clone Wars, Mon Mothma began to realize that the Old Republic was crumbling. She was one of the first to be wary of Supreme Chancellor Palpatine's policies and began quietly petitioning senators who opposed his rule. She found kindred spirits in Padmé Amidala, Bail Organa, the Corellian Garm Bel Iblis, and others. Together, they plotted to thwart Palpatine's continued rise to power, but his plan to overthrow the Republic was already in motion. Palpatine eventually ascended to the position of Emperor and betrayed the Jedi Order.

When Palpatine created a system of territorial governors to report to him directly, Mothma knew that the Senate would soon be obsolete. Like Organa and Bel Iblis, she continued to quietly oppose the Emperor's rule, despite the very real danger of being branded a traitor. Fearing for her own safety and sickened by the Emperor's evil actions, Mon Mothma began considering more direct action to topple the Emperor and restore freedom to the galaxy.

Garm Bel Iblis

As a young and idealistic politician determined to preserve freedom throughout the galaxy, Corellian senator Garm Bel Iblis was one of the few voices opposed to Senator Palpatine's rapid rise to power. Just prior to the start of the Clone Wars, Bel Iblis argued passionately against the Military Creation Act, favoring planetary security forces over a Republic army funded and controlled by the Supreme Chancellor. He later pulled the Corellia Sector out of the Military Creation Act vote as a symbol of his opposition. Despite this, he did aid the Republic in the Clone Wars. He organized his own militia from Corellian security forces and assembled a formidable fleet of Corellian cruisers to help repel Separatist advances against Mid Rim worlds. He would often act as the cavalry, arriving just in time to rescue an overwhelmed Jedi or provide air cover for Republic commandos. During the Clone Wars, Bel Iblis proved himself a brilliant military tactician, but on the Senate floor, he continued to stand against Palpatine.

When Palpatine ascended to Emperor, a frustrated Bel Iblis could no longer contain his anger. He continually lashed out against the Emperor's policies, opposing the creation of the Imperial war machine, the subjugation of entire planets, and the Imperialization of major corporations. Unwilling to believe that the Jedi had betrayed the Republic, as Palpatine claimed, Bel Iblis frequently evoked the names of the most vaunted Jedi in his speeches. Angered by his constant challenges, Emperor Palpatine ordered Imperial forces to arrest the entire Bel Iblis family. Garm was forced to watch as his wife and children were executed, but he managed to escape the slaughter. The Empire scoured the galaxy for Bel Iblis, who disappeared along with his entire private fleet, but to no avail. His flight from the Empire had been secretly aided by his allies in the senate—Bail Organa and Mon Mothma. Inspired by the mysterious Starkiller, the three have begun to discuss taking more direct action against the Empire.

Master Kento, the Fugitive Jedi

> "Commander Cody, the time has come. Execute Order Sixty-six."
> —Darth Sidious, *Star Wars:* Episode III *Revenge of the Sith*

When the Emperor issued Order 66, the Jedi were all but destroyed. Thousands of Jedi perished when they were ambushed by their own clone soldiers, and dozens of the Order's most powerful members died during Darth Vader's brutal assault on the Jedi Temple on Coruscant. The few Jedi who survived Palpatine's betrayal and Vader's wrath immediately fled into exile. Many disappeared into hiding on remote worlds or turned their backs on the Force and adopted entirely new identities.

Like many Jedi Knights, Master Kento was discovered by the Jedi Order and brought to the Jedi Temple for training at a very early age. Kento was a gifted student, but he lacked maturity. He viewed every mission—no matter how dangerous or disturbing—as just another adventure. While other Jedi were sickened by the horrors of the galaxy—rampant crime, slavery, murder, civil war—Kento saw only another chance to engage in exciting, death-defying heroics.

When the Clone Wars erupted, Kento rushed to the front, where he fought bravely alongside the clone soldiers and other Jedi. However, while battling Separatists on Talus, Kento met a young Jedi freedom fighter named Mallie, and the two fell in love. Kento began seeing the war through her eyes and soon realized that every battle sundered families, devastated communities, and left tragedy in its wake. Even worse, every conflict brought the chance of his or her death, and the possibility that they would never see each other again. Kento and Mallie secretly married but continued fighting for the Republic until Mallie learned she was pregnant.

Torn between their loyalty to the Jedi and their new family, Kento's and Mallie's reservations about the war continued to grow. They began to feel that the war was only sowing seeds of hate throughout the galaxy and that the Jedi were partially responsible for perpetuating the conflict. On the eve of Order 66, Kento and Mallie disguised themselves as medics and slipped away into the Outer Rim, hoping to raise their child far from the raging conflict. When Kento later learned that the clone troopers had turned against the Jedi, he was wracked with guilt but remained with his family as they moved from planet to planet in search of a safe haven.

Kento and Mallie eventually settled on Kashyyyk, where they befriended the fiercely loyal Wookiees, who kept careful watch over their young son. Sadly, Mallie was killed while defending several Wookiees from a group of mercenary slavers, leaving Kento to raise the boy alone. The Emperor's spies learned of the slavers' fight with the Jedi, and Darth Vader was sent to Kashyyyk to hunt down the fugitive. Kento fought bravely against the Sith Lord but was ultimately defeated. Vader discovered and kidnapped the powerful boy, intent on training him as his Secret Apprentice.

JEDI KNOWLEDGE

Though you face Master Kento in battle, you only do so as Darth Vader in the first mission.

Imperial Enemies

Imperial Stormtroopers

Elite shock troops fanatically loyal to the Empire and impossible to sway from the Imperial cause, Stormtroopers wear imposing white armor offering a wide range of survival equipment and temperature controls that allow the soldiers to survive in almost any environment. Stormtroopers wield standard-issue E-11 blaster rifles and attack in hordes to overwhelm their enemies.

Stormtrooper Commanders

The Stormtrooper Commanders patrol hostile battlefields, leading their troops into fierce combat on dangerous worlds such as the fungus planet Felucia. With razor-sharp minds and steely resolve, these highly trained Imperial soldiers continue the reputation established by the Clone Wars' fearsome ARC troopers. Clearly visible in their uniquely detailed armor, the Commanders confront enemies such as the savage Felucians with deadly heavy blaster cannons equipped with a devastating stun setting. They are rewarded for their loyalty with specialized armor fitted with an internal shield generator capable of deflecting nearly any attack save a lightsaber. Most importantly, the Stormtrooper Commanders are entrusted with command over the Empire's elite Shadow Troopers, with authority to call in reinforcements and trigger ambushes without clearance from Imperial high command. Stormtrooper Commanders typically hang back and stun the most threatening enemy, who is then overwhelmed by Shadow Troopers.

Shadow Troopers

The Shadow Troopers form an elite squadron of Imperial Stormtroopers who have been assigned experimental cloaking armor that allows them to disappear in virtually any environment. The Shadow Troopers are trained to use this advanced technology to ambush their enemies, often surrounding victims before they can defend themselves. The unit's standard weapon is a light repeater cannon. Because of the cannon's energy requirements, it must be powered by the shadow armor's energy cells and thus can only be fired when the armor is "uncloaked." In combat, Shadow Troopers typically fire a short cannon burst, cloak and move to a new position, then open fire again. They will almost always try to remain out of range of enemies but will rush a target who has been stunned by a Stormtrooper Commander's stun blast. In addition to their personal cloaking devices, the Shadow Trooper's armor is laced with durasteel

fibers, making it much more resistant to physical and energy attacks than standard-issue Stormtrooper armor. Shadow Troopers are generally powerful reserve units, backing up standard Stormtrooper squadrons and only appearing when a battle turns against the Empire and Stormtrooper Commanders call for reinforcements.

Imperial EVO Troopers

The Imperial EVO Troopers (or "Environmental" Troopers) are trained to survive in the galaxy's most treacherous weather conditions and environments. The EVO Trooper is equipped with advanced survival armor and other gear capable of withstanding hazards such as extreme heat, rivers of acid, and poisonous atmospheres. Each EVO Trooper's FA-3 flechette launcher fires a spread of lethal projectiles that can hit multiple targets and ricochet off surfaces for added carnage. The EVO armor's most formidable feature is its ability to act as a "lightning rod," capable of absorbing sudden energy discharges, including lightning strikes. Once absorbed, this energy can be channeled into the EVO Trooper's flechette launcher to generate a powerful stun blast. EVO Troopers are usually deployed to toxic or inhospitable worlds, which often puts them into conflict with hostile alien species adapted for life on those planets. To ensure ruthlessness in the EVO Trooper ranks, many EVO Troopers are handpicked from Stormtroopers who have displayed a hatred toward nonhumans.

Imperial Incinerator Troopers

Another of the Empire's many Stormtrooper variants, Incinerator Troopers are deployed primarily to raze subjugated planets and incite fear in the local populace. The Incinerator Trooper's primary weapon is a destructive plasma cannon that can quickly turn healthy crops, lush forests, and even vibrant swamps into charred wastelands. Incinerators are typically organized into small squads bolstered by other units, including Scout Troopers and EVO Troopers.

Imperial Jumptroopers

The Imperial Jumptrooper is an air-to-ground attack unit trained to engage airborne, entrenched, or otherwise inaccessible enemies. The Jumptroopers are also trained in hit-and-run tactics, ambushing opponents from above, and often provide other Stormtrooper squadrons with air cover during pitched battles. They are the primary Imperial units deployed to "keep order" on low-gravity worlds and atmospheric platforms such as Cloud City. Equipped with an advanced Imperial jetpack, the Jumptrooper bursts through the air in short spurts and can hover in place for extended periods. The Jumptrooper's long-range rail detonator is far more powerful than standard Imperial-issue weaponry and has no recoil, allowing the Jumptrooper to discharge the weapon without changing his flight path or being knocked off balance while hovering.

Imperial Officer

The legions of Stormtroopers and other soldiers who serve the Empire are under the command of a complex hierarchy of well-educated Imperial Officers. Most Imperial Officers are promoted for their tactical and strategic brilliance, sharp leadership skills, and sheer ruthlessness. While Stormtroopers are the first into battle, the Imperial Officers remain aloof, determining which planet to invade, which species to enslave, and which enemy to crush next. When forced into combat, Imperial Officers wield standard-issue blaster pistols that have surprising accuracy.

Scout Troopers

Lightly armored but highly mobile Imperial Stormtroopers, Scout Troopers are usually assigned to planetary garrisons to patrol perimeters, perform reconnaissance missions, and identify enemy locations. Because their mission profile usually requires long stints away from Imperial resupply, Scout Troopers are trained survivalists who often carry personal survival kits, portable power units, food supplies, microcords, and specialized gear designed for the local terrain. Scout Troopers are known for their self-reliance and ability to operate alone, and the Empire has discovered that these traits make Scout Troopers excellent snipers. Many Scout Troopers are armed with collapsible long-range sniper rifles equipped with powerful scopes and small targeting computers. The Scout Trooper's sniper rifle is deadly and extremely accurate but does emit a brief laser sight beam before firing.

Imperial Purge Trooper

The fearsome Purge Troopers are part of the top-secret Imperial Dark Trooper project, a research and development effort commissioned to create a wide range of advanced battle droids. The Purge Trooper is specifically designed for combat against Jedi and other Force wielders: The droid's armored chassis is protected by refined cortosis, an ore that reduces the damage caused by lightsaber attacks; and its primary weapon is a lethal energy blade. The Purge Trooper is also equipped with a high-powered, short-range rocket launcher and magnetic tractor boots that make it highly resistant to kinetic Force powers such as Force Grip and Force Push.

Imperial Senate Guards

In years past, the well-trained Imperial Senate Guards were dedicated civil servants charged with protecting senators as they traveled the galaxy. Since the rise of the Empire, the Senate Guards have become part of the Emperor's army of ruthless agents. Though they still travel with senators—often to ensure loyalty to the Emperor—they are also stationed on key Imperial installations to protect high-ranking officials, sent on assassination missions, and deployed to hunt down Force wielders. The Senate Guards rely solely on melee attacks using cortosis pikes.

13

Imperial Royal Guard

The Imperial Royal Guard serve the evil Emperor as his personal bodyguards, assassins, and executioners. Clad in crimson robes and sinister helmets, members of the Royal Guard are always at Palpatine's side and remain fanatically loyal to his dark vision. The Emperor has selected each member of the elite Royal Guard from the ranks of only the most successful Stormtroopers. Criteria for admission into the Imperial Royal Guard include great strength and intelligence, along with an unwavering devotion to the Empire. Despite their constant presence alongside the Emperor, very little is known about the workings of the Royal Guard. The unit is so secretive that suggestions as to its numbers have ranged from 50 to tens of thousands. Although trained in the use of many weapons, the Royal Guard typically wield Force pikes, which they combine with hand-to-hand attacks during combat. They are also somewhat resistant to the Force, allowing them to withstand Force powers that would easily dispatch Stormtroopers.

Imperial Interrogation Droid

The Imperial Interrogation Droid was designed by the Imperial Security Bureau for use in questioning prisoners. The black sphere is equipped with a wide range of probes, sensors, and needles, as well as a personal repulsor lift and retractable vibro-blades. They can also emit a low-intensity electroshock that can stun victims. Most frightening is the Interrogation Droid's artificial intelligence, which allows it to analyze each individual's physical and chemical weaknesses. Several Interrogation Droids are used aboard the ISS *Empirical* to monitor and control volatile alien specimens.

Shadow Guards

Few Imperials know the true origins of the mysterious and powerful Shadow Guard. The silent, enigmatic warriors receive orders directly from Emperor Palpatine and are often sent to eliminate suspected Jedi and other Force wielders. The Shadow Guard boast limited Force powers of their own and are capable of wielding lightsaber lances, which has led some Imperials to speculate that the Shadow Guard are, in fact, Jedi who have been captured, tortured, and brainwashed by the insidious Palpatine. Others believe the Shadow Guard are simply loyal members of Palpatine's red-robed Imperial Royal Guard, who have been secretly trained in the basic Sith arts. Whatever the truth, the Shadow Guard command immense respect within the Imperial ranks and often lead elite Imperial Commandos into battle against the Emperor's most hated enemies.

AT-CTs

The AT-CT, or All-Terrain Construction Transport, is an industrial walker designed specifically for use in building Imperial facilities. Designed around the chassis of a standard AT-ST walker, the AT-CT is equipped with small but powerful tractor beams that enable the pilot to easily lift and move heavy metal plates, durasteel girders, and other construction materials. Because of its similarity to the standard AT-ST, the AT-CT is often operated by a trained scout walker pilot and gunner for peak efficiency. In the event an AT-CT falls under attack, the seasoned operators can use the vehicle's tractor beams as an offensive weapon, hurling large objects at enemies.

AT-KTs

The Kashyyyk deployment variant of the AT-ST is designed to root out insurgents and enemy scouts from terrain that offers heavy cover. Rather than acting as an antivehicle platform, the AT-KT (also sometimes referred to as the "Hunter" scout transport, or AT-STh, when deployed on other worlds) is specifically an antipersonnel walker, with heavy weapons designed to fire through foliage, light bunkers, and camouflage. Moreover, the vehicle's weapons are primarily used to stun targets (since dead Wookiees make poor slaves), ensuring that even the most rebellious insurgents live to serve the Empire as laborers.

AT-STs

The All-Terrain Scout Transport (AT-ST) is a vital component of Imperial ground forces due to its speed, maneuverability, and precise weaponry. Each scout walker is manned by a pilot and a gunner, who enter the command pod via a small hatch atop the armored module. Together, the two-man crew uses the vehicle to protect ground troops and provide heavy support fire. The AT-ST's highly maneuverable armored "head" is adorned with a light blaster cannon, a concussion-grenade launcher, and twin blaster cannons, all used to provide covering fire for ground troops. Several variations of the AT-ST chassis are employed through the galaxy, each suited to their unique environments.

TIE Fighters

In order to consolidate power over countless worlds, the Empire has established a massive military war machine. Huge factories have begun to appear in every corner of the galaxy, producing weapons, ships, even armies of Stormtrooper clones. The TIE Fighter, a small and agile single-pilot starfighter, is being mass-produced to form the backbone of the Imperial fleet. This small vehicle, which consists of a spherical cockpit suspended between a pair of immense solar array wings, utilizes advanced twin ion engines and was designed primarily for speed. In order to decrease the vehicle's weight, it has not been equipped with life-support systems, deflector shields, or hyperdrive engines. Armed with only a pair of standard laser cannons, the mass-produced TIE Fighters must rely on greater numbers to overwhelm enemy forces.

Kashyyyk Enemies

Wookiee Slaves

Legendary for their immense strength, the Wookiees are the powerful, hair-covered humanoids native to Kashyyyk. As a species, Wookiees are honorable, fiercely loyal, and very protective of their families. While generally gentle, Wookiees can experience terrifying berserker rages, making them among the galaxy's most fearsome warriors. Wookiee soldiers are typically armed with giant ryyk blades and bowcasters.

Although they speak in a series of growls, grunts, and roars and are often viewed as primitive, Wookiees are actually quite intelligent, capable of designing and building advanced weapons and even starships. Among their most amazing architectural achievements are the sprawling villages they construct in the branches atop Kashyyyk's massive trees.

After the Empire subjugated Kashyyyk, many Wookiees were captured. The Empire relies on the Wookiee's immense strength and stamina to help build its fearsome war machine. Wookiee Slaves have been shipped all across the galaxy and forced into hard labor in dangerous crystal mines, Imperial bases, and space-station construction sites. Although beaten and threatened by the Empire at every turn, many Wookiee Slaves remain defiant and are awaiting their chance to strike back at their captors.

Wookiee Berserkers

Nearly all Wookiees are ferocious combatants, but the Wookiee Berserkers have been trained to channel their strength and legendary Wookiee rage into a viable fighting form. Kashyyyk's first line of defense, Wookiee Berserkers are stationed in villages across the planet. They typically wield enormous ryyk blades and are extremely protective of their kin. When faced with an enemy force, Berserkers will leap into combat with wild abandon; although this tactic initially seems reckless, it is designed to draw enemy fire away from more vulnerable Wookiees, including support soldiers armed with bowcasters.

Wookiee Infantry

Despite their seemingly primitive society, Wookiees long ago learned to design and build a variety of blasters and other ranged weapons. Wookiee Infantry are trained to wield a laser crossbow, commonly known as a "bowcaster." A traditional Wookiee weapon, which requires a Wookiee's great strength to cock and fire accurately, the bowcaster launches deadly energy quarrels. Wookiee Infantry typically attack from a distance, relying on Wookiee Berserkers and other soldiers to slow advancing enemies.

15

Raxus Enemies

Rodian Rippers

The Rippers are the Rodian salvage cartel's excavation specialists. Using sophisticated zero-g lifter devices and a large bladed tool, they can burrow into trash heaps to find the most valuable and useful artifacts. During large-scale salvage operations, the Rodian Rippers tear open starship hulls, allowing Jawa scavengers to enter and dissect the derelict vessels. The Rippers' excavation tools can also be used as formidable weapons, which has become a necessity in the increasingly hostile environment of Raxus Prime.

Rodian Heavy Defenders

Wherever the twisted wrecks of starships can be found, scavengers of many varieties will be close by, looking to make a fast and easy credit by salvaging anything and everything that can be sold to the highest bidder. On Raxus Prime, many salvage operations have made their home among the mountains of refuse. A particularly large cartel of scavengers, composed primarily of Rodians, has established an extremely profitable operation dissecting crashed starships; the cast-off vessels provide them with a seemingly never-ending supply of parts and income. In recent years, as the Rodian salvage cartel's operation expanded, the scavengers have run afoul of Kazdan Paratus, a Jedi in hiding on Raxus Prime. While the Rodians initially suffered heavy losses in their battles with Kazdan and his Force-imbued golems, they have since organized to defend themselves. The large and well-armored Heavy Defenders are the cartel's most formidable soldiers. They wield massive repeater cannons capable of blasting apart any of Kazdan's droids who come within range. During salvage operations, the Heavy Defenders first surround and secure a starship, then protect the vessel as Rodian Rippers tear it open and Jawa laborers enter the ship to surgically remove any usable components.

PRIMAGAMES.COM

Jawas

A mysterious scavenger species native to the deserts of Tatooine, Jawas are particularly adept at dismantling and repairing machinery of all kinds. The Rodian salvage cartel that controls Raxus Prime transplanted a large clan of Jawas to the junk world to help collect valuable machine parts. The Jawas reluctantly work for the Rodians, scavenging through mountains of garbage and cutting apart derelict starship hulls, collecting anything and everything that might still be usable. Jawas are generally timid and pose little threat, but when antagonized, they will use their plasma torches and excavation grenades to lethal effect.

Scrap Guardians

Found on the junkyard world of Raxus Prime, the imposing Scrap Guardians are the core component of Kazdan Paratus's droid army. Composed of detritus and cast-off parts, the powerful golems are actually held together and animated by the Force. This enables them to resist some Force powers, including Force Push, though they are highly susceptible to sudden energy surges, such as those caused by Force Lightning. The sentinels are designed to defend Kazdan against the hordes of opportunistic scavengers and are well suited to battling a Sith, should Darth Vader or the Emperor ever find Kazdan's hiding place. They can also act as his eyes and ears, alerting him to an enemy's approach well in advance.

Scrap Drones

Another of Kazdan Paratus's Force-imbued creations, the Scrap Guardians are devious flying golems designed specifically to combat Darth Vader, who Kazdan knew would one day find him. Capable of creating a powerful negative feedback field, they can attack with a beam that actually drains Force energy from its victims.

Junk Titan

The strongest and most effective of Kazdan Paratus's Force-powered golems, the Junk Titan is a nearly unstoppable juggernaut of incredible power. The Titan's sheer size and strength allow it to crush most opponents with its dense clublike arm or to hurl large pieces of junk at enemies. However, the formidable Junk Titan can also use the Force to repel attackers.

Felucian Enemies

Felucian Warriors and Dark Felucian Warriors

Natives of the immense fungus forest of the planet Felucia, these unusual creatures were long thought to be primitive and savage. While they have not developed any form of advanced technology, the Felucians have survived and even flourished without it, largely because of their innate connection to the Force. While not as powerful as trained Jedi, the Felucians can use the Force to command and control their environment and its creatures, including fearsome Rancors. However, they have often struggled to resist the dark side, and many tribes have descended into violence and madness over the eons.

The entire Felucian species was threatened during the Clone Wars, when large-scale battles left vast portions of their world scarred and uninhabitable. In recent years, the Felucians have managed to aid the forest in its regeneration. When Shaak Ti discovered the Felucians, she began teaching them to use their connection to the Force for both attack and defense. She also encouraged them to resist the temptation of the dark side.

The Felucian species is stratified into a caste system, allowing members of each tribe to perform specialized duties. The Felucian Warriors serve as the backbone of the Felucian tribes, using their innate Force powers for defense and hunting. They can use the Force to generate small spheres of compressed air, which they can hurl to stun and even kill prey. They have also learned to imbue their brutal jawbone weapons with the Force, strengthening them for both increased damage and defense against other weapons, including lightsabers. All Felucians can blend into their surroundings and can crawl along nearly any surface: The Felucian Warriors use these abilities to ambush prey from virtually any vantage point.

When the Felucians allied themselves with Shaak Ti, her influence kept them from slipping to the dark side. When Shaak Ti was murdered, the Felucians succumbed to anger and hatred, eventually embracing the dark side completely. Their strong connection to the dark side has had dramatic effects: The Felucians have physically changed in appearance, their features twisting into hideous masks. They have also become much more vicious and aggressive, recklessly attacking anything they view as a threat. The Felucian Warriors retain their formidable fighting skills and basic Force abilities, but the dark side has made them stronger and much more resilient.

Felucian Shamans and Dark Felucian Shamans

The Felucian Shamans are the spiritual leaders of the Felucian species. They use their Force talents to surround their fellow Felucians in a dangerous aura that will harm any attackers. The Shaman's horn will also call nearby Felucians into battle, summoning camouflaged Warriors from the jungle depths. When pressed into combat, the Shamans will usually attempt to evade or flee, using a combination of the Force and their innate camouflage abilities to seemingly teleport a safe distance away from any enemies.

As with their Warrior and Chieftain brethren, the Felucian Shamans devolve under the influence of the dark side. With their strong connection to the Force, the Shamans retain much of their intelligence and their ability to call hordes of Warriors into battle, but they lose all sense of good and compassion and will send wave after wave of Felucians to their deaths just to satisfy their bloodlust.

Felucian Chieftains and Dark Felucian Chieftains

The Felucian Chieftains are the leadership caste of the Felucian species. Massive and commanding, the Chieftains inspire awe and fear in their followers. Though slower than the Felucian Warriors, the Chieftains are much hardier, with dense flesh that protects them from attacks. They are also incredibly strong and train from an early age to wield a ceremonial staff in combat. A Chieftain can channel the Force through his weapon, drawing on Felucia's web of living energy to create a powerful blast of energy. To increase their effectiveness, many Chieftains also carry sturdy shields that have been constructed using the Force.

With the guiding light of Shaak Ti gone, the Felucians fell to the dark side; the Chieftains devolve the most dramatically under the influence of evil. Originally trained to defend and lead their people, the Chieftains now care only about killing. They rampage across the planet unchecked, blindly attacking anything they encounter.

Rancors and Bull Rancors

Felucians have had some luck in domesticating them for use as combat mounts; like the Nightsisters of Dathomir, the Felucians are inherently Force sensitive, which seems to be critical in the process of training Rancors. Felucians typically paint their Rancors with phosphorescent dyes, which can confuse and frighten prey.

An ancient Rancor monster, the near-mythical Bull Rancor is marked by its pale flesh, elongated tail, and immense horns sprouting from its massive head. The Bull Rancor is generally a solitary creature who guards the legendary "Rancor graveyard" on Felucia. The creature is much more aggressive than its younger brethren, and the Felucians believe it can't be captured or tamed. However, the Force-wielding Maris Brood has formed a strong bond with the ferocious beast. The Bull Rancor is now intensely loyal to Maris and will fight to the death to protect her.

Yerdua Poison Spitters

A semi-sentient plant found on the fungus world of Felucia, the Yerdua enjoys a symbiotic relationship with the native Felucians. Capable of emitting streams of thick venom, the Yerdua is trained by Felucians to protect their villages, ceremonial sites, and travel corridors from wild Rancors and other predators. In return, the Felucians care for the Yerdua, feeding the creatures raw meat and removing parasites from the plants' delicate stalks.

Cloud City Enemies
Ugnaughts and Uggernaughts

Short, stocky humanoids with porcine faces, Ugnaughts are considered loyal and hard-working. They are a major component of the labor force on Bespin's Cloud City, where they have been employed by various corporate interests to construct the massive Tibanna gas-processing plants, carbon-freezing chambers, and majestic skyscrapers of the city proper. The Ugnaughts live on construction platforms surrounding the half-finished Cloud City, where much of the raw materials for the project are produced to be ferried over. Ugnaughts are generally peaceful but can be provoked to violence. In combat, they will grab whatever is handy, from broken bottles to construction-grade plasma torches.

Affectionately referred to as "Uggernaughts," the bipedal construction vehicles the Ugnaughts operate are actually modified electromagnetic load-lifting maintenance exoskeletons manufactured by Bespin Motors. Uggernaughts are piloted by a driver and an operator, who work in tandem to tackle large construction jobs. Equipped with plasma torches and powerful magnetic projectors capable of lifting even the heaviest materials, Uggernaughts are invaluable assets aboard the various construction platforms throughout Bespin. Though the Uggernaught is primarily a vehicle designed for hard labor, it can become very dangerous if operated by angry Ugnaughts!

17

Kota's Militia

When Master Kota was a general in the Clone Wars, he refused to have anything to do with the clone army. Kota never trusted the clones and instead formed his own unique unit of hardened soldiers. He recruited and built this small army from local militias, mercenary groups, and even Separatist prisoners of war. After Order 66, which saw thousands of Jedi assassinated by the clone troops, most of Kota's soldiers remained loyal to their general and accompanied him into hiding. Kota and his men have recently emerged from seclusion, conducting hit-and-run operations against key Imperial targets throughout the galaxy. Though not officially a rebellion, Kota's ragtag group has caused enough trouble to gain Darth Vader's attention.

Militia Elites

Kota's most skilled and proficient soldiers receive the honor of joining his heavy-weapons detail, often providing cover fire for other militia members and defending key positions during raids. Wielding massive repeating blasters, these dangerous enemies can clear entire rooms and cause mayhem and confusion among even the most hardened Imperial soldiers.

Militia Saboteurs

Armed with standard blaster rifles and cylindrical thermal grenades, General Kota's saboteurs form the backbone of his militia. These soldiers maneuver in small tight-knit groups and are well trained in hit-and-run tactics.

Militia Trooper

General Kota has trained some of his loyal soldiers to use energized stun batons, which they employ in close-quarters melee combat in environments filled with explosives and other hazards. These specialized soldiers generally rush their enemies, attempting to surround and overwhelm them before a shot can be fired.

Boss Enemies

Some boss enemies have already been profiled in previous sections. Master Kento, General Kota, and even Shadow Guards, for example, appear as bosses in certain levels but typically double as nonplayable characters or regular enemies.

Kazdan Paratus

As a young Padawan, Kazdan Paratus displayed an uncanny aptitude for technology and an aversion to the rigorous physical training required to become a Jedi Knight. His time at the Jedi Temple would have ended if he had not ingeniously passed the Jedi Trials using his most honed weapon—his intellect. A master machinist and robotics engineer, Paratus used this passion and innovative thinking to outwit his master and succeed where many others had failed in their first attempts. By constructing a sophisticated and deadly combat droid and using his own proficiency with the Force, Kazdan navigated the trials perfectly. The Council was so impressed with his performance that he was immediately bestowed the honorific title of Jedi Knight and was assigned an instructor's position at the School of Padawans.

For many years, Kazdan Paratus remained on Coruscant, creating a veritable army of sophisticated droids to aid in the training of Jedi Knights. Although Paratus rarely fought, he mastered the use of kinetic energies and could animate droids with the Force in remarkably realistic ways. When the Clone Wars began, Kazdan agreed to become a Jedi general, but only so he could fight and study the Confederacy's advanced battle droids firsthand. To ensure he could navigate battlefields easily, the diminutive Jedi cobbled together a harness equipped with several long, spidery legs. This invention gave Kazdan surprising speed and agility, and when combined with his skillful use of his special lightsaber pike, it allowed Kazdan to single-handedly destroy legions of Confederacy droids.

In the waning days of the Clone Wars, Kazdan returned to the Jedi Temple to continue training young Padawans. But when Order 66 brought Darth Vader to the Temple's doors, Kazdan suffered a moment of panic. While other Jedi stood face-to-face with Vader and the clone army, Kazdan fled Coruscant in a nondescript freighter, with only his tools and several prototype droids in tow. Wracked with guilt over his cowardice, Kazdan exiled himself to the remote junkyard planet of Raxus Prime, intent on building an army of droids to one day destroy Vader and the Emperor. However, as the years passed, the reclusive Jedi slowly devolved into a paranoid, frightened, and sometimes delusional hermit. His devotion to the Jedi Order manifested in his obsessive desire to rebuild it—out of the metal scraps and other junk surrounding him. He even constructed a version of the Jedi Temple, complete with replicas of the Jedi Council members. Kazdan's madness has made him a far more dangerous foe. He will fight to the death to defend his rebuilt Jedi Order, using the Force to conjure droid soldiers and to violently repel any perceived threats.

Shaak Ti

A hero of the Clone Wars, Master Shaak Ti is one of the last surviving members of the Jedi Council. She is a Togruta, a humanoid species from the planet Shili. To protect themselves from the dangerous predators of their homeworld, the Togruta band together in dense tribes and rely on their disruptive natural pigmentation patterns to confuse the slow-witted beasts. They also boast hollow montrals on their heads that allow them to ultrasonically sense the space around them. The highly independent Shaak Ti is a notable exception to the communal-minded Togruta, preferring to operate alone. Nonetheless, her heritage is evident in her accuracy and agility when moving and fighting in bustling crowds.

During the Clone Wars, Shaak Ti participated in numerous key offensives. She was among the 200 Jedi who stormed Geonosis to rescue Obi-Wan Kenobi and Anakin Skywalker from Separatist forces, and she later coordinated the defense of the cloning facilities on Kamino. She also fought on Centares and Dagu, and confronted the terrifying Separatist General Grievous in order to protect Emperor Palpatine, who she didn't realize at the time was evil. Soon after, the Jedi discovered that Palpatine was the evil mastermind Darth Sidious. Mace Windu and several others went to arrest him, leaving Shaak Ti in charge of the Jedi Temple's defenses. Shaak Ti was deep in meditation when Darth Vader and his forces stormed the Jedi Temple. She quickly rallied other Jedi and fought bravely to repel the attack, but it was soon obvious that the Temple would be lost. After ensuring that several Padawans and their masters escaped, Shaak Ti reluctantly fled on her own.

While wandering the galaxy in search of other Jedi, Shaak Ti discovered a young Padawan named Maris Brood. Master Ti was initially reluctant to take Maris as her apprentice; she had already trained two Padawans in her career, only to see both fall victim to criminal killers shortly before their graduation to Knighthood. However, Shaak Ti sensed that Maris was tormented by her hatred for Darth Vader and spirited her away to the lush fungus planet Felucia. Shaak Ti became a respected Felucian Chieftain, commanding tribes of Force-sensitive natives. Dedicated to teaching them to control their burgeoning abilities, she hoped they could defend Maris should Darth Vader find her and prevent the barbaric Warriors from slipping to the dark side.

Captain Ozzik Sturn

A child of privilege and wealth, Ozzik Sturn used his family connections to ensure his advancement in the Empire. Born to a long line of celebrated trophy hunters, Ozzik Sturn has carried on the family tradition of hunting down the most exotic and dangerous predators in the galaxy. While his Imperial deployments initially allowed him to travel the galaxy in search of his next quarry, his eventual promotions prevented him from continuing the hunt. He desperately hoped for the chance to pursue a Jedi as part of Darth Vader's Great Purge and was frustrated when sent to a long series of low-profile Outer Rim outposts. While stationed as the chief magistrate on Malastare, he began to clandestinely release prisoners into his own secret hunting reserve, purely for the purposes of stalking intelligent prey. While his private hunting grounds went undetected for some time, its eventual discovery sparked a revolt among the native Dug and Gran populations, which resulted in high casualties for the Empire. Now stationed on Kashyyyk, where he oversees the subjugation of the Wookiees, Sturn has fallen into his old routines, tracking down and killing Wookiee warriors.

Maris Brood

"Fear is the path to the dark side. Fear leads to anger. Anger leads to hate. Hate leads to suffering. I sense much fear in you."

—Master Yoda, *Star Wars: Episode I The Phantom Menace*

Like many of her peers, Maris was discovered by the Jedi as an infant. However, rather than receiving formal training at the Jedi Temple on Coruscant, Maris was tutored by a Jedi warrior aboard the starship *Gray Pilgrim*. When Palpatine issued Order 66, Maris and her master were in the Outer Rim territories and were thus not immediately affected by the initial purge. But her master did feel the ripples in the Force caused by the sudden deaths of so many Jedi. After meeting only silence with every transmission sent to the Jedi Temple on Coruscant, Maris's master took his starfighter in search of answers. He never returned, but his last message revealed that the Jedi Order had been all but destroyed by a villain named Darth Vader. Seeking revenge, Maris set off in search of Vader. However, before she could ever confront the Dark Lord, Maris was discovered by Jedi Master Shaak Ti, who convinced the angry Padawan to disappear into hiding on Felucia. Despite Shaak Ti's positive influence, Maris harbors a strong desire for revenge and is still intent on confronting Darth Vader.

When Vader's apprentice arrived on Felucia, Shaak Ti ordered Maris to disappear into hiding. Although Maris desperately wanted to fight alongside her master, she relented and vanished into the Felucian wilderness. When she later learned of Shaak Ti's death, Maris was grief-stricken and enraged. Over time, her anger and fear corrupted her, and she eventually fell prey to the dark side. When Maris took control of the native Felucians, they, too, embraced the dark side, transforming into hideous monsters that stalk the planet.

Beneath her defiant and wicked exterior, Maris harbors a deep fear of Darth Vader discovering her. When Imperials invaded Felucia and began a bloody war with the natives, Maris was certain that she was about to be exposed. She hid herself from the Imperials, secretly spying on them and watching for any sign of the Sith Lord. A short time later, her Felucian scouts spotted an Imperial transport landing on the planet. Unable to stifle her curiosity, Maris visited the landing site to discover that the pilot was Senator Bail Organa, who had come to Felucia in search of Shaak Ti. Although he knew the trip would put him in great peril, Bail sought Shaak Ti's help in rescuing his daughter from Imperial forces on Kashyyyk. Still believing that Darth Vader would soon arrive on Felucia, Maris recklessly attacked and captured the senator. She held him hostage, hoping to trade him to Darth Vader in exchange for her life.

Although undisciplined and emotional, Maris is a skilled combatant. She is quick and agile, and has mastered a unique lightsaber fighting style that relies on rapid strikes. She has also learned to use the Force to mask herself and become invisible to the naked eye. She uses this ability to vanish for short periods of time before suddenly ambushing her opponents with a vicious attack.

Darth Vader

The personification of evil and fear, Darth Vader is Emperor Palpatine's relentless enforcer. Born Anakin Skywalker, Vader was a spirited and talented child who exhibited strong Force potential. At an early age, he became an expert pilot and was one of the heroes of the Clone Wars, along with his mentor, the general and Jedi Obi-Wan Kenobi. Obi-Wan trained Anakin in the use of the Force, but then-chancellor Palpatine recognized Skywalker's potential and began secretly grooming him to become his own apprentice. Anakin was torn between his loyalty to the Jedi Order and to Palpatine, who promised that Anakin could prevent the deaths of those he loved by mastering the power of the dark side. Skywalker eventually discovered that the chancellor was a Sith Lord but was left behind at the Jedi Temple when Mace Windu and other Jedi set out to arrest Palpatine. Anakin recklessly left the Temple, arriving at Palpatine's quarters just as Mace Windu was about to destroy the chancellor. He lashed out to protect Palpatine, ensuring Windu's demise. The chancellor claimed that Anakin had now become a Sith Lord and dubbed him "Darth Vader."

For his first act as Palpatine's disciple, Darth Vader led a brutal attack on the Jedi Temple, slaughtering most of the Jedi Knights, Masters, and even younglings inside. He then traveled to Mustafar to destroy the remnants of the Confederacy. Obi-Wan Kenobi pursued Vader to the volcanic planet, and the two engaged in a terrible duel that led to Vader's fall into a molten pit. Having declared himself Emperor, Palpatine soon arrived to rescue Vader, who was transformed into a shell of his former self, his shattered body sustained by specially built armor and a breathing apparatus. Despite this, Vader continued serving the Emperor and led the efforts to hunt down and exterminate the remaining Jedi Knights.

Although seemingly loyal to the Emperor, Darth Vader harbors much anger toward his master and secretly plots to overthrow him. As part of his plan, Vader has taken a young apprentice, corrupting the boy and training him in the ways of the dark side, all with the promise that one day they will destroy the Emperor together.

The Emperor (Emperor Palpatine)

"The dark side of the Force is a pathway to many abilities some consider to be unnatural."
—Palpatine, *Star Wars:* Episode III *Revenge of the Sith*

The diabolical Sith Lord who rules the galaxy through fear, Emperor Palpatine ordered the destruction of the last Jedi Knights and corrupted his menacing apprentice, Darth Vader. A conniving schemer, Palpatine first rose to power in the Senate, eventually becoming Supreme Chancellor of the Republic by pretending to be a friend to the Jedi Order and a staunch defender of democracy. But Palpatine secretly plotted against the Jedi and the Republic in his dual identity as Darth Sidious. As Sidious, he trained the Sith Lord Darth Maul, recruited Count Dooku and General Grievous to his side, and masterminded the creation of the Confederacy of Independent Systems and its Separatist army. When the galaxy was faced with the threat of a galactic civil war—a conflict Palpatine/Sidious secretly orchestrated—Palpatine manipulated the Senate into granting him emergency powers that allowed the creation of a Grand Army of the Republic. He quickly took control of the Republic and steered the galaxy into conflict. He continued to profess his loyalty to the Jedi while sending Jedi generals to the front lines and manipulating young Anakin Skywalker into believing that the Jedi Order was corrupt. After the Confederacy's defeat, Palpatine betrayed the Jedi when he issued Order 66; upon his command, the Republic's clone troopers turned against their Jedi generals, slaughtering thousands before they could react. With the Jedi nearly extinct, Palpatine was able to declare himself Emperor, transforming the Old Republic into the first Galactic Empire.

Since declaring the Republic an empire, Palpatine promoted the doctrines of hatred, speciesism, and tyranny. He has violently eliminated all opposition, forcing senators such as Mon Mothma and Garm Bel Iblis to disappear into hiding. He uses Darth Vader as his enforcer and hounds the remaining Jedi Knights, murdering the last of this noble sect to ensure that he will never be challenged. Meanwhile, he has launched a massive military buildup and begun constructing incredibly destructive starships, space stations, and weapons. Under Palpatine's rule, hundreds of worlds have been enslaved or ravaged, dissidents murdered, and entire industries nationalized.

WIELDING THE FORCE
Basic Controls

The following pages will reveal the subtle ways of the Force and how to master the basics. Every great Jedi or Sith began by learning the basics of battle. The Training option in the Pause menu provides equally useful courses on basic controls and provides training challenges. We're listing the basics here so they are by your side as you progress through your journey. We'll also include tips for how and when to use these controls effectively.

Movement

Action	Xbox 360	PS3
Walk	Lightly nudge Ⓛ	Lightly nudge left thumbstick
Run	Press Ⓛ firmly	Press left thumbstick firmly

Before setting out to tackle your foes, you must know how to move. To walk, lightly nudge the left thumbstick in the direction you want to go. The left thumbstick is pressure sensitive, so don't press it too hard unless you want to jump into a sprint. To run, press it all the way in the direction you want to run.

Though you may wonder why it is so important to know the difference between walking and running, keep in mind that it is much harder to block blaster fire while you're running. Fight your instinct to run everywhere. Take your time while navigating through your journey. If you sprint everywhere, you'll risk running headfirst into an ambush.

Jump and Double-jump

Action	Xbox 360	PS3
Jump	Ⓐ	×
Double-jump	Ⓐ, Ⓐ	×, ×

Jumping and double-jumping are staples of level navigation, and they're necessary for combat. Press Ⓐ or × to jump once. To double-jump and reach higher ledges or avoid attacks, press Ⓐ, Ⓐ or ×, ×.

If you time your double-jumps well, you can avoid an enemy's attacks, Force attacks, or even incoming blaster fire. More importantly, use jump during boss battles to land on your feet safely once you've been thrown or hit with a Force Push attack.

Force Dash

Action	Xbox 360	PS3
Dash	LB	L1

Force Dash is a perfect way to sprint away or toward an enemy. While walking or running, press LB or L1 to Force Dash in the direction you're moving. The best use of Force Dash is to travel extra distances after executing a double-jump. While in battle, frequently double-jump and Force Dash to jump over an enemy and gain some distance. This can often be a lifesaving tactic, allowing you to reach distant ledges beyond enemy blaster fire or buying you time to replenish your Force meter.

Lock On

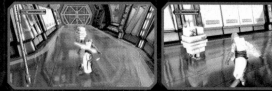

Action	Xbox 360	PS3
Lock on	Press and hold RB	Press and hold R1

One of the most effective tools during battle is your lock-on ability. Press RB or R1 to lock on to an enemy during battle and focus solely on him. You won't be able to target any other enemies directly, so avoid using it while surrounded by enemy groups.

Your movement will also depend on who you're locked on to. Instead of running away, left or right, you'll back away or strafe around your enemy while you remain facing him. To disengage the lock and free your movement, release RB or R1. The lock-on feature is most effective against single or large enemies.

Camera Control

Action	Xbox 360	PS3
Look around	Ⓡ	Right thumbstick
Center camera	Click Ⓡ	Click right thumbstick

Camera control is a valuable tool for players who want to find every hidden Holocron, and it is extremely valuable during battle and while navigating narrow passages. By swinging the camera around a corner, you can get a more detailed view of your surroundings and see what may be waiting just around the bend.

During combat, it is especially useful to string together long combos. As you transition from combo to combo, press in the camera control stick to center the camera and refocus your view.

Lightsaber Combat Basics

Action	Xbox 360	PS3
Lightsaber attack	Ⓧ	■

Not every enemy wields a lightsaber or a melee weapon, so you won't be using your lightsaber in every enemy encounter. Still, your lightsaber is your most important tool. Basic lightsaber combat begins with single slash attacks. Some enemies can be dispatched this way. To execute a slash attack, press Ⓧ or ■.

Though a single slash attack is effective at hurting one enemy, it is not as effective on multiple enemies at once. When a group of enemies surrounds you, string multiple slash attacks to form short basic lightsaber combos.

Basic Lightsaber Combos

Action	Xbox 360	PS3
Lightsaber combo 1	Ⓧ, Ⓧ	■, ■
Lightsaber combo 2	Ⓧ, Ⓧ, Ⓧ	■, ■, ■

Lightsaber combos are the most important part of your combat techniques. The most basic lightsaber combo (double slash attack) is great for swiftly dispatching single enemies. However, you will usually face multiple enemies and will need more than a one-two combo to get the job done. To execute a three-hit lightsaber combo, press Ⓧ, Ⓧ, Ⓧ or ■, ■, ■.

As your lightsaber proficiency grows and you can increase the damage from 'saber attacks, these two basic combos will become the basis of your entire fighting style.

Lightsaber Block

Action	Xbox 360	PS3
Lightsaber Block	ⓛⓣ	L2

Your Sith instincts grant you lightning-fast reflexes. As such, you'll automatically deflect *some* blaster fire. In order to increase the amount of blaster fire you deflect, and even *re*flect some, you must block. When confronted by a wall of blaster fire, press ⓛⓣ or L2. This raises your lightsaber to blocking position and will reflect fire back toward the shooter rather than just deflecting it. Lightsaber block won't reflect all incoming fire, but it will significantly reduce the amount of damage you take while in battle. Of course, you can also use lightsaber block during battle to deflect an opponent's melee attacks.

and slash through the enemy directly in front of you before automatically returning to you. You can also use lightsaber throw to accomplish certain tasks such as cutting distant chains to complete a bonus objective.

Lightsaber Throw

Action	Xbox 360	PS3
Lightsaber Throw	Hold (LT), then press (A)	Hold (L2), then press (■)

Aside from Force Lightning, Lightsaber Throw is your most dependable ranged attack. Force Throw (see below) is great, but if there are no objects nearby to use as projectiles, you won't have anything to throw from a distance. Luckily, you always have your trusty 'saber with you.

To use Lightsaber Throw, hold down (LT) or (L2), then press (A) or (■), respectively. Your lightsaber will travel through the air like a boomerang

Grapple Attacks

Action	Xbox 360	PS3
Grapple attack 1	(A) + (X)	(▲) + (●)
Grapple attack 2	(B) + (Y)	(X) + (■)

Sometimes your enemies will get too close for comfort. If they do, and you don't have the energy to execute a Force Repulse attack, use a grapple to grab nearby enemies and attack them in one fluid motion. After bringing them in for a close-quarters attack, you'll automatically toss the enemy away like yesterday's garbage.

Though tossing your enemy is a great way to remove an immediate threat, it's best to use grapples as a close-quarters combat technique. There are better and more efficient attacks for getting rid of enemies that are breathing down your neck.

Force Attacks

Force Lightning

Action	Xbox 360	PS3
Force Lightning	(Y)	(▲)

Force Lightning is one of your staple Force powers. At its most basic level, it can electrocute an enemy and nearly obliterate them. After upgrading your Force Lightning to higher levels, it can fry one, two, even three enemies at a time for major damage! Press (Y) or (▲) to radiate a devastating current of electricity toward your opponent. Hold it as long as your Force meter has some Force power in it. Once the Force meter is depleted, you can no longer hold your Force Lightning attack.

The most efficient use of Force Lightning is when approaching enemies or as they approach you. Don't wait to use it until the enemy is in range of your lightsaber; use it as a ranged attack to whittle down your enemy's health before they can reach you. Force Lightning is also a great way to stall powerful approaching enemies. By zapping them with your electric current, they'll slow down and grant you the precious seconds you might need to escape, find cover, or even formulate a new attack plan.

Force Push

Action	Xbox 360	PS3
Force Push	(B)	(●)

Force Push is another staple of your Force powers. Much like Force Lightning, it can damage faraway enemies before they're close enough to hurt you with melee weapons. Unlike Force Lightning, it doesn't increase damage with the amount of Force power used. To utilize your Force Push attack and unleash a powerful blast of the Force, press (B) or (●).

Force Push is a great way to hurl enemies away as they approach or to knock them down from a distance. Like Force Lightning, Force Push is also a great way to stall enemies before they can attack. Hit them with Force Push to knock them away and concentrate on a single enemy while the others are on their backs. Force Push also has a great side effect of carrying nearby debris in its shock wave. This attack can throw crates, barrels, and rocks at foes, and it can detonate explosive items. Lead your assaults with Force Push and you'll never go wrong.

Force Grip

Action	Xbox 360	PS3
Force Grip	(RT)	R2
Move gripped object	Left and right thumbsticks	Left and right thumbsticks
Impale gripped enemy	Hold (RT), then press ✗	Hold R2, then press ■
Zap gripped enemy	Hold (RT), then press Ⓨ	Hold R2, then press ▲

Force Grip is a way to manipulate objects. Get near an object or person until your target is surrounded by blue brackets; press (RT) or R2 to grip the object with the Force. Once you have it in the air, you can move it around with the left and right thumbsticks. The left thumbstick moves it up and down in space, while the right thumbstick moves it left, right, forward, and backward.

The best aspect of Force Grip is that it allows you to execute several other attacks while your target is immobile in the air.

Force Throw

Action	Xbox 360	PS3
Force Throw	Hold (RT), move object toward target, then release	Hold R2, move object toward target, then release

While an object or person is in the air, you can use Force Throw. Once the object is in your Force Grip and floating in the air, use the thumbsticks to direct it at a target such as a nearby enemy. When the gripped object gets close to the target, release your Force Grip to throw the object at the target. Use Force Throw to toss enemies into each other and to hurl explosive items.

Counter Force Grip

Action	Xbox 360	PS3
Counter Force Grip	Press Ⓑ repeatedly	Press ● repeatedly

You're not the only one with Force powers. Throughout your journey, you will encounter some of the most powerful Jedi that Order 66 missed. During battle, they'll use their Force powers on you. If your Jedi foe manages to get you in a Force Grip, free yourself by repeatedly pressing the Jump button.

Force Lock and Lightsaber Lock

Action	Xbox 360	PS3
Lightsaber Lock	Press ✗ repeatedly	Press ✗ repeatedly
Force Lock	Press Ⓨ to match onscreen command	Press ▲ to match onscreen command

During your adventure, you will face enemies whose Force and lightsaber skills match your own. When that happens, you must engage them in a Force or Lightsaber Lock at some point during your battle. When you're engaged in either kind of lock, there is only one way to break the lock and win the battle. Once in a lock, several prompts will appear onscreen. If it's a Lightsaber Lock, mash at the Lightsaber Attack button to overpower your enemy.

If you're engaged in a Force Lock, press Ⓨ or ▲ to match the onscreen prompts and thrust the enemy's Force back at them. Do this as many times as you're prompted to win your Force or Lightsaber Lock.

JEDI KNOWLEDGE

You will often have to win several Lock battles to defeat your opponent.

Force Repulse

Action	Xbox 360	PS3
Repulse	Hold (RT), then press Ⓑ	Hold L2, then press ●

Force Repulse is a defensive countermeasure against aggressive enemy groups. This attack unleashes a radiating shock wave of energy from your entire body and knocks back all enemies foolish enough to be in its range. To activate Force Repulse, hold down (RT) or L2, then press Ⓑ or ●, respectively.

You'll then leap into the air, surround yourself in a Force bubble as you gather your energy, and release it, sending all nearby enemies flying backward. Force Repulse won't dispatch many enemies, but it will create breathing room when you're surrounded by waves of foes.

STAR WARS
FORCE
THE
UNLEASHED

Force Shield

Action	Xbox 360	PS3
Shield	Hold (RT), then press **Y**	Hold (L2), then press ▲

Unlike Force Repulse, Force Shield *is* a great offensive attack. Like Repulse, however, it surrounds you in a similar Force bubble of energy that radiates electric currents away from your body and zaps surrounding enemies.

Though it requires all your Force energy, it also temporarily charges your lightsaber with Force Lightning, increasing its damage!

Heads-Up Display (HUD)

1. **Health bar:** This displays how much health you currently have. Once completely depleted, you'll perish.

2. **Level-up bar:** This bar displays how close you are to achieving a new level.

3. **Force meter:** This displays how much Force power you have to use on Force attacks. If it's completely depleted, you can't perform any Force attacks.

4. **Force Point tracker:** When defeated, enemies release Force Points. This display keeps track of your current dispatched enemies and the attack used to dispatch them.

5. **Minimap:** This displays your position on the level as you progress throughout your mission.

Force Power Basics

You've mastered the basics, but in order to truly master the Force, you must learn how to properly handle all your Force powers. These are advanced techniques and lightsaber combos that revolve around your continuing mastery of the Force. Some Force powers require that you use only Force attacks like Push or Lightning while others include lightsaber combos.

Force Abilities

There are three types of Force abilities: Force powers, Force combos, and Force talents. By upgrading different aspects of each ability, you can customize your fighting technique any way you want. Force powers rely on the Force; attacks such as Force Push, Force Lightning, and Force Repulse are all Force powers. Force combos are complex attacks that combine lightsaber attacks with Force powers. Force talents are passive attributes that increase your abilities and are always quietly working in the background. You don't need to activate them like other powers; they're always active.

Depending on your preferred combat style, you can upgrade your Force powers, Force combos, and Force talents to suit your needs. If you're more comfortable with just Force attacks, upgrade Force Lightning and Force Push powers first. If you prefer lightsaber attacks, upgrade Lightsaber Throw and unlock your Force combos.

JEDI KNOWLEDGE

Force talents and Force powers both have three levels to upgrade. Force combos don't have any levels. Once unlocked, they're at maximum power.

While some Force abilities are available at the start of your adventure, you must unlock others as you progress. To activate a dormant power or upgrade an active one, go into the Pause menu and select "Force Upgrades." Cycle through the different types of abilities using the top left and right shoulder buttons (ⓛ and ⓡ on Xbox 360 or ⌐ and ⌐ on PS3). Use the left thumbstick to select different powers, talents, or combos, depending on which ability you've chosen, and press Ⓨ or ⓐ to view their descriptions. After you decide on an aspect to upgrade, press Ⓐ or ⓖ.

As long as you have enough Force Points to upgrade your abilities, you can customize your Force abilities however you see fit.

JEDI KNOWLEDGE

Just as with other lightsaber combos, any of the techniques described below that begin with two- or three-hit lightsaber attacks are considered lightsaber combos.

"Don't underestimate the Force."
—Darth Vader, *Star Wars: Episode IV A New Hope*

Force Points and Upgrade Spheres

There are several different ways to accumulate Force Points. Every time you destroy enemies, the amount of enemies and the method used to dispatch them will translate into Force Points. These will gradually fill your Level-up bar. Once the bar is full, you'll gain a new level and acquire three upgrade spheres you can use toward upgrading your Force abilities—one sphere for Force powers, one sphere for Force combos, and one sphere for Force talents. The more enemies you dispatch in quick succession, the more points each enemy will release. To increase the amount of Force Points you accumulate per battle, build up combos by varying your attacks to dispatch multiple enemies.

Another way to acquire upgrade spheres is by finding hidden Holocrons. These can contain anything from 1,000 Force Points to Force ability upgrade spheres.

Force Combos
Sith Shien

Action	Xbox 360	PS3
Sith Shien	✕, ✕, ✕, ✕	✕, ✕, ✕, ✕

Description: An ancient Sith variation of a classic lightsaber fighting style, Sith Shien focuses on quick and aggressive attacks.

Sith Shien is your most basic Force combo. Much like the shorter two- or three-attack lightsaber combos, Sith Shien is a destructive close-quarters combat technique. It is especially effective against lesser enemies like Stormtroopers and should always be incorporated into lightsaber duels with enemy bosses.

Other enemies armed with swords and skilled in melee combat, such as Felucian Warriors, can often block and counter this attack, making it slightly less effective. When approaching these enemies, first stun them with Force Lightning, then cut them down with Sith Shien.

Sith Saber Flurry

Action	Xbox 360	PS3
Sith Saber Flurry	✕ (pause), ✕ (pause), ✕ (pause), ✕	✕, ✕, ✕, ✕

Description: One of the most difficult lightsaber styles, the Saber Flurry allows you to land multiple blows.

Sith Saber Flurry is a strong lightsaber combo that is as destructive as it is fancy. Best of all, it is extremely effective against small enemy groups. The lightsaber's wide swinging twirl can reach multiple foes and make this a very good attack to begin a string of lightsaber combos.

Dashing Slash

Action	Xbox 360	PS3
Dashing Slash	ⓛⒷ, ✕	ⓛ1, ✕

Description: Your dash culminates with a deadly lightsaber slash, causing severe damage.

The Dashing Slash is a great way to initiate battle with one enemy. By combining Force Dash with a slash attack, you can travel quickly toward an enemy and arrive at his location with a savage blow. This attack isn't effective against multiple enemies, but it is a great way to instantly gain an advantage over one enemy.

Leaping Slash

Action	Xbox 360	PS3
Leaping Slash 1	Ⓐ, ✕	■, ✕
Leaping Slash 2	Ⓐ, ✕, ✕	■, ✕, ✕
Leaping Slash 3	Ⓐ, ✕, ✕, ✕	■, ✕, ✕, ✕
Leaping Slash 4	Ⓐ, ✕, ✕, ✕, ✕	■, ✕, ✕, ✕, ✕

Description: An aerial attack with vicious lightsaber strikes.

Leaping Slash attacks are great for knocking down airborne enemies like Jumptroopers or for inflicting decent damage on large enemies like Rancors or AT-ST walkers. Because this is an aerial attack, it has no effect on enemies on the ground. While you're airborne, you're open to enemy fire and can be knocked out of the air with missiles. Use Leaping Slash attacks solely on airborne or tall enemies.

Leaping Slam

Action	Xbox 360	PS3
Leaping Slam 1	Ⓐ, ✕ (hold)	■, ✕ (hold)
Leaping Slam 2	Ⓐ, ✕, ✕ (hold)	■, ✕, ✕ (hold)
Leaping Slam 3	Ⓐ, ✕, ✕, ✕ (hold)	■, ✕, ✕, ✕ (hold)
Leaping Slam 4	Ⓐ, ✕, ✕, ✕, ✕ (hold)	■, ✕, ✕, ✕, ✕ (hold)

Description: A powerful aerial attack that drives your saber downward, impacting the ground with great force.

Like Leaping Slash, this attack can inflict a great deal of damage on airborne enemies and tall pests. However, Leaping Slam can also wreak havoc on ground forces. Leaping Slam's final blow is a crushing ground-slam attack that radiates a shock wave outward from the ground-slam area and knocks all nearby enemies off their feet.

Saber Blast

Action	Xbox 360	PS3
Saber Blast	⊗, ⓑ	■, ●

Description: A lightsaber attack followed by a powerful Force Push that blasts your opponent away from you.

This two-pronged attack is equally effective for offense and defense. While the slash is a great first blow, it is the ensuing Force Push that makes this attack dangerous for your enemies. The push sends enemies flying away and leaves them open for an additional, possibly more devastating, attack. Use this attack as a defensive countermeasure against enemies when you want to get some breathing room.

Cannonball

Action	Xbox 360	PS3
Cannonball	ⓡ, ⓑ	R2, ●

Description: Blasts your opponent away from you with a powerful push.

Cannonball is a powerful Force Push attack that works in conjunction with your Force Grip. Force Grip an enemy, then hit him with Force Push while he's floating helplessly in your clutches. The blast sends your high-flying foe soaring across great distances.

Lightning Grenade

Action	Xbox 360	PS3
Lightning Grenade	ⓡ, ⓨ	R2, ▲

Description: Envelops the gripped enemy with Force Lightning. The Lightning field then explodes when the enemy is slammed into something.

Perhaps one of the best uses of your Force powers, Lightning Grenade combines the explosiveness of Force Lightning with the velocity of Force Throw. Not only is Lightning Grenade a great way to dispatch an enemy, but it's also the perfect way to turn an enemy on his comrades...as an explosive. This attack is most effective when you encounter a small squad of soldiers but only one is close enough to grip with the Force.

Aerial Strike

Action	Xbox 360	PS3
Aerial Strike	ⓡⓑ (hold) + [ⓐ, ⓛⓑ]	R1 (hold) + [✕, L1]

Description: While locked on to your enemy, you leap into the air and dash toward them with your lightsaber!

This attack is very similar to a Dashing Slash attack. While Dashing Slash keeps you grounded, however, Aerial Strike takes the fight to the air. With this attack, you can safely dash over a target's blaster fire and come down on him from above.

Saber Sling

Action	Xbox 360	PS3
Saber Sling	⊗, ⊗, ⓑ	■, ■, ●

Description: Generates a high-damage lightsaber swing that sends your enemy flying.

Saber Sling is another one of your defensive attacks. Like Saber Blast or Cannonball, this attack can effectively repel enemies that are too close. Saber Sling also has the added effect of dishing out twice the damage of the aforementioned attacks, since it delivers two powerful 'saber slashes before slinging the enemy across the map.

STAR WARS THE FORCE UNLEASHED

Dashing Blast

Action	Xbox 360	PS3
Dashing Blast	LB, B	L1, ●

Description: All nearby enemies are blasted away with a powerful shock wave.

Another dashing attack, Dashing Blast is perfect for breaking up small groups that stand in your way. Dash toward and through them to break up their ranks, then pick them apart as they stagger to their feet. Be careful when you use this attack, however, as it's also a great way to dash headlong into enemy fire.

Sith Strike

Action	Xbox 360	PS3
Sith Strike	X, Y	■, ▲

Description: A quick lightsaber slash that is infused with Force Lightning.

This lightsaber combo is a quick and effective way to demolish large weakened enemies. Sith Strike can even destroy lesser enemies with a single attack. It's fast, easy, and, more importantly, deals decent damage. Sith Strike's best attribute is the temporary stun effect it inflicts on mechanical enemies such as Purge Troopers and large AT walkers! Make Sith Strike a part of your fighting repertoire and you'll never go wrong.

"The Force is what gives the Jedi his power. It's an energy field created by all living things. It surrounds us and penetrates us. It binds the galaxy together."
—Obi-Wan Kenobi, *Star Wars:* Episode IV *A New Hope*

Sith Slash

Action	Xbox 360	PS3
Sith Slash	X, Y, Y	■, ▲, ▲

Description: A quick lightsaber slash that is infused with Force Lightning.

This attack is a longer, more powerful version of Sith Strike. It infuses your lightsaber with Force Lightning to stun enemies and inflict even more damage.

Sith Saber Smash

Action	Xbox 360	PS3
Sith Saber Smash 1	X, X, Y	■, ■, ▲
Sith Saber Smash 2	X, X, Y, Y	■, ■, ▲, ▲
Sith Saber Smash 3	X, Y, X, Y	■, ▲, ■, ▲
Sith Saber Smash 4	X, X, X, Y	■, ■, ■, ▲

Description: Your lightsaber is infused with Force Lightning as you execute a devastating overhand smash.

By far the most destructive of all your Lightning attacks, the Sith Saber Smash is a series of swift 'saber strikes that can dole out serious punishment. Capable of thoroughly destroying single enemies, such as Imperial troopers of all types, this attack is especially useful against Rancor beasts, Junk Titans, and the like. While you strike at your opponent, the lightning-infused 'saber stuns your enemies long enough for you to finish your combo and start a new one. If you time your Sith Saber Smash attacks properly, you can destroy oversized enemies without ever taking any damage!

Lightning Bomb

Action	Xbox 360	PS3
Lightning Bomb	Y, RT	▲, R1

Description: The Force Lightning coursing through the opponent is amplified, soon reaching a critical point that causes the electricity to burst out in an explosion.

Dashing Shock

Action	Xbox 360	PS3
Dashing Shock	(LB), (Y)	L2, ▲

Description: Releases a wave of Force Lightning, damaging all enemies in its path.

Like the other dashing attacks, Dashing Shock is a very good way to get the jump on your opponents. Dash at a small group of enemies and finish your approach by zapping them all with a current of Force Lightning. The blast may be enough to even dispatch a few of the soldiers.

Saber Slam

Action	Xbox 360	PS3
Saber Slam	(X), (X), (X), (B)	■, ■, ■, ●

Description: A slam to the ground that throws your opponent and all nearby enemies into the air.

Make Saber Slam a regular part of your fighting routine. It is the beginning of several other devastating combo attacks that can usually incapacitate a small group while you destroy one of its members. In fact, there are very few situations where Saber Slam is *not* helpful. Aside from using it on large enemies like Rancor beasts, Saber Slam can knock nearly all enemies off their feet.

Aerial Ambush

Action	Xbox 360	PS3
Aerial Ambush	(X), (X), (X), (B) (hold)	■, ■, ■, ● (hold)

Description: After launching your opponent, you jump into the air ready to continue the attack.

This is actually the beginning of several other more powerful attacks. Perfect this assault before attempting any of the following attacks. In effect, all the following are great aerial assaults; they differ only in how you finish off your opponent.

Aerial Assault

Action	Xbox 360	PS3
Aerial Assault 1	(X), (X), (X), (B) (hold), (X)	(L1), (L1), (L1), (R) (hold), (L1)
Aerial Assault 2	(X), (X), (X), (B) (hold), (X), (X)	(L1), (L1), (L1), (R) (hold), (L1), (L1)

Description: Slashes your opponent in midair, causing severe damage.

Aerial Blast

Action	Xbox 360	PS3
Aerial Blast 1	(X), (X), (X), (B) hold, (B)	■, ■, ■, ● (hold), ●
Aerial Blast 2	(X), (X), (X), (B) (hold), (X), (B)	■, ■, ■, ● (hold), ■, ●

Description: Blasts your opponent in midair with a powerful Push attack

STAR WARS
THE FORCE UNLEASHED

Aerial Shock

Action	Xbox 360	PS3
Aerial Shock 1	✗, ✗, ✗, Ⓑ (hold), Ⓨ	■, ■, ■, ● (hold), ▲
Aerial Shock 2	✗, ✗, ✗, Ⓑ (hold), ✗, Ⓨ	■, ■, ■, ● (hold), ■, ▲

Description: Shocks your opponent in midair.

Aerial Throw

Action	Xbox 360	PS3
Aerial Throw 1	✗, ✗, ✗, Ⓑ (hold), [✗ + Ⓐ]	■, ■, ■, ● (hold), [■ + ✗]
Aerial Throw 2	✗, ✗, ✗, Ⓑ (hold), ✗, [✗ + Ⓐ]	■, ■, ■, ● (hold), ■, [■ + ✗]

Description: After launching your opponent, you jump into the air ready to continue the attack.

Aerial Slam

Action	Xbox 360	PS3
Aerial Slam 1	✗, ✗, ✗, Ⓑ hold, [Ⓨ + Ⓑ]	■, ■, ■, ● (hold), [▲ + ●]
Aerial Slam 2	✗, ✗, ✗, Ⓑ (hold), Ⓨ, [Ⓨ + Ⓑ]	■, ■, ■, ● (hold), ▲, [▲ + ●]

Description: After launching your opponent, you jump into the air ready to continue the attack.

Force Talents

As mentioned before, Force talents are passive traits that enhance your abilities; once you unlock or upgrade a talent, it will always be active from then on. Each Force talent has three ranks to upgrade. By upgrading Force talents, you can augment your fighting abilities, buff defensive stats, and even increase your efficiency.

Though you can eventually increase the rank on nearly all your Force talents, the order in which you increase the first few will determine what kind of fighter you become. If you're more defensive minded, increase your Fortitude, Vitality, Resilience, and Defense Mastery. For an offensive-minded build, increase your Combo Mastery, Force Focus, Saber Mastery, and Battle Meditation. If you'd rather keep your talents in balance, augment your Fortitude, Saber Mastery, and Defense Mastery.

Force Talent	Effect
Fortitude	Each rank increases your maximum health.
Force Focus	Each rank increases your maximum Force energy.
Force Affinity	Each rank increases the speed you recover Force energy.
Vitality	Each rank increases the amount of health you regain by defeating your enemies.
Resilience	Each rank reduces the amount of damage you take.
Battle Meditation	Each rank reduces the amount of time it takes to charge your Force powers.
Saber Mastery	Each rank increases the amount of damage you deal with your lightsaber in melee combat.
Defense Mastery	Each rank increases your ability to deflect and reflect blaster fire.
Combo Mastery	Each rank decreases the amount of Force energy it takes to use Force combos.

31

Lightsaber Customization

As we've mentioned before, your lightsaber is the most powerful tool in battle. As such, you can and should customize it to fit your combat style. If you rely more on Force powers like Push and Lightning, equip a combat crystal

that complements one of those attacks. If you're aggressive during battle or while navigating a level during a mission, pick a combat crystal that increases your defensive capabilities, such as blocking blaster fire.

"The crystal is the heart of the blade. The heart is the crystal of the Jedi. The Jedi is the crystal of the Force. The Force is the blade of the heart. All are intertwined. The crystal, the blade...the Jedi. You are one."

—Master Luminara Unduli,
Star Wars: The Clone Wars Volume 1

There are eight combat crystals to choose from, each with its own special attribute:

1. **Ilum combat crystal:** No bonus.
2. **Rubat combat crystal:** Lightsaber deals extra damage.
3. **Ruusan combat crystal:** Force powers cost less Force energy to use.
4. **Lorrdian combat crystal:** Increases ability to deflect and reflect blaster bolts.
5. **Sigil combat crystal:** Lightning based attacks deal extra damage.
6. **Vexxtal combat crystal:** Lightsaber attacks have a chance to corrupt opponents with a damaging aura.
7. **Firkrann combat crystal:** Lightsaber attacks have a chance to deal extra electrical damage.
8. **Katak combat crystal:** Lightsaber attacks have a chance to siphon health from opponents.

Aside from combat crystals, there are also color crystals that change your lightsaber's appearance (but not its performance), adding a depth to your 'saber's customization features.

Training Room Challenges and Tutorial Modules

Training and Challenge Modules are a great way to perfect the skills discussed above. While in-game, go to the Pause menu and select the Training Room option to activate the Tutorials and Challenge Modules.

SITH WISDOM

Save your game before entering the Training Room. If you don't, all unsaved progress will be lost.

ONLY IN...XBOX 360

By completing all the tutorials and challenges, respectively, you'll get two Xbox 360 Achievements!

Tutorial Tips

There are five different Tutorials: Push, Lightsaber Flourish, Grip, Lightning, and Repulse. These are all very easy to complete. The enemies in tutorials don't attack, and there are no time limits, so complete these by following the instructions in each.

SITH WISDOM

In order to have a better chance of successfully completing all Challenge Modules, it is best to wait until you've increased the rank on all Force talents, Force powers, and Force combos. That means waiting until you're nearly done with the main campaign....

Push Challenge

This is perhaps one of the most difficult challenges to complete. Like most of the other Challenge Modules, your other abilities are inactive. You can't use your lightsaber, block, dash, or even jump. In order to complete it successfully, you must be quick, accurate, and make efficient use of your Force energy. There are five Stormtroopers surrounding you with six red-ringed barrels. Begin by locking on to the barrel directly ahead and hit it with one Force Push to hurl it at the trooper behind it.

Immediately turn left and lock on the next barrel. Push it into the trooper behind it. Swivel right and do the same. After weakening each Stormtrooper by Force Pushing them into the explosive barrels, finish them off with Push attacks—trying to hit multiple troopers with each Push—before the time runs out.

Lightsaber Flourish Challenge

This challenge requires you to destroy seven Stormtroopers using only Sith Flurry attacks. To do so, chain your attacks as you move from trooper to trooper. Begin your combo on one trooper and finish your combo on another. If you use a standard attack to destroy a Stormtrooper, the challenge ends in failure.

Grip Challenge

This challenge requires you to use only Force Grip to destroy two glass panels, two Stormtroopers, and several red-ringed barrels within the allotted time. To do so, simply pick up the red-ringed barrels and hurl them at the other objects. By doing so, you destroy two items at once.

Lightning Challenge

This challenge is to merely survive for the allotted time using only Force Lightning. When the challenge begins, focus on the Militia Elite in the room's perimeter. If you let them live too long, they'll shred you with their blaster fire. Run around the room's perimeter and zap them with Force Lightning. By taking them out, you remove a hazard and replenish your health. When only the Militia Troopers are left in the room, either run away from them until the time runs out or zap them with Force Lightning.

Repulse Challenge

You can complete this challenge in much the same way as the Lightning Challenge. Begin by using Repulse to knock away the more dangerous Militia Elite lining the room's walls. Then evade the remaining militiamen. In fact, you can survive this challenge without having to destroy any enemies. When surrounded by foes, use Force Repulse to knock them away and gain a small respite form their blaster fire. Do this enough and they will be on their backs more often than they'll be on their feet firing at you.

SITH WISDOM

The following Challenge Modules do not have time limit or Force Ability constraints.

Stormtrooper Combat Module

To complete this module, use Force Repulse on the troopers lining the room. Dash to the room's left side, dispatch them quickly with Repulse, then dash to the room's opposite side. Dispatch the other troopers along the wall, leaving only a few troopers in the room's center. Either let your 'saber reflect fire back at them or cut them down with it.

SITH WISDOM

Remember that your augmented abilities help you in these challenges. If you haven't increased your Defense Mastery yet, now would be a great time to do it.

Rodian Scavengers Combat Module

Like the Stormtrooper Combat Module, this module has several dangerous enemies lining the room's walls. Focus on them first. Dash to the room's edges and Repulse the Rodian Heavy Defenders off their feet first. Turn on the Rodian Rippers next to replenish lost health, then run your lightsaber through the remaining Jawa at the rear.

PRIMAGAMES.COM

Felucian Combat Module

The Felucian Combat Module has several Felucian Warriors near the room's center and flanking the walls, and two Felucian Chieftains at the room's rear. Ignore the Chieftains at first and focus on the Felucian Warriors. Knock them away with Repulse and finish them off with quick 'saber combos. If they manage to get too close again, use Repulse or Force Throw them at each other. When only one or two Felucian Warriors remain, use them as projectiles against the large, slower Chieftains. Leave the Chieftains for last and decimate them with powerful combos.

Imperial Assault Squad Combat Module

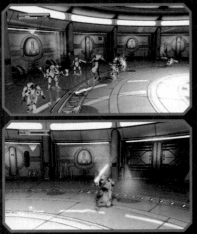

Force Repulse the EVO troopers along the room's left and right sides. Destroy them quickly to avoid being stunned by their blasters. Feed them a steady diet of Repulse attacks, and once they're eliminated, turn on their lesser comrades. Take them out with quick 'saber strikes to complete the module.

Imperial Armed Recon Squad Combat Module

The trick to completing this module is eliminating the troopers in proper order. Begin by running around the room and zapping the Jumptroopers with Force Lightning. Leap into the air and fry them if necessary. With them gone, turn on the other Stormtroopers with blasters. Cut through them with lightsaber attacks, then leave the three Incinerator Troopers for last. Dash around the room to avoid their flamethrowers and wait for them to stop firing at you. When they do, dash at them and use a Force Repulse attack to disable their shields, then slash them to ribbons while they're unprotected.

Imperial Royal Guard Combat Module

This is one of the more difficult Challenge modules. Like the other Imperial Modules, this is best accomplished by eliminating enemies in a certain order. There are three red Imperial Royal Guards and one Shadow Guard in the room. Focus your fury on the red Guards first. Blast them away with Repulse when they get too close, then lunge out at them as they stagger to their feet. Use Lightning-infused 'saber strikes to damage your primary target while stunning any Guards foolish enough to get too close your lightsaber. Afte you whittle down one Royal Guard's health more than the others, focus on that Guard until the onscreen commands prompt you to finish him off.

Move on to the second red Guard. Destroy him and you're left with one red Guard and the Shadow Guard. With only those two enemies left, turn on the Shadow Guard and whittle down as much health as you can before your health takes too much damage. When it does, finish off the red Guard to replenish your health, then turn on the Shadow Guard.

SITH WISDOM

The battle with the Royal Guards can be extremely technical. Use plenty of blocks and counterattacks to limit the amount of damage you take. Also use Repulse attacks only when you're surrounded by more than two enemies.

AT-ST Combat Module

The AT-ST has high-powered blasters at its side, as well as a complement of Stormtroopers and three Incinerator Troopers. You can easily avoid the Incinerator Troopers' flamethrowers, so the real challenge is not being blasted to shreds by the AT-ST. Begin the challenge by immediately zapping the walker with Force Lightning. This stuns it temporarily and disables its blasters. While the walker is stunned, rush at the Stormtroopers on the right and either cut through them or destroy them with Repulse.

Turn back on the AT-ST and stun it again. Dash to the opposite side and destroy the second group of Stormtroopers. This leaves only the walker and three Incinerator Troopers at its feet. Stun the walker one more time, then dash to its feet and immediately unleash a Repulse attack. This knocks the walker off balance and deactivates the Incinerator Troopers' protective shields. Slash the troopers to bits and absorb their health. With them gone, you can take on the AT-ST one-on-one. Strafe around it while zapping it with Force Lightning and slash its legs with Lightning-infused saber attacks.

Junk Titan Combat Module

This module is very similar to the AT-ST module. Instead of Stormtroopers, however, the Junk Titan is accompanied by two Scrap Guardians. Since all three creatures are sensitive to Force Lightning, begin by zapping the Titan to stun him while you take out the smaller Scrap Guardians. Turn to one of the approaching Guardians and cut through it with a Lightning-infused 'saber combo. A Sith Slam attack should be enough to nearly destroy the Guardian with one combo. Turn on the second Guardian and cut through him as well.

When only the Junk Titan remains, strafe around him while you electrocute him. Slowly whittle its health away with Force Lightning so that it can't attack. If it is constantly stunned, it can't attack. Finish it off when the onscreen commands appear.

Kota's Militia Combat Module

Complete this module by first taking out the Militia Elite. Their high-powered blasters are extremely dangerous and even more deadly in numbers. Dash into the Militia Elite's ranks and blast them away with Force Repulse. Follow up your Repulse by dashing at the fallen elites and destroying them with quick combos. If the Militia Saboteurs attempt to stun you with their batons while you finish off their elite comrades, knock them away with Force Push. After destroying the elites, you can easily handle the rest of Kota's men.

Rancor Combat Module

Approach this module just as you did the AT-ST or Junk Titan modules. Knock away the surrounding Felucian Warriors by using Force Repulse. If the Rancor is close enough, the Repulse attack will also stagger him. Dash around the room, letting the Rancor follow you; the Felucians attempt to follow as well. When the remaining Felucians get bunched into a group, dash into the group's center and blast them all with Repulse.

If the Rancor swats at you, there's a good chance he'll hit the Felucians as well. After you eliminate the Felucians, destroy the Rancor just as you did the Titan or AT-ST. Strafe around it while hitting it with Force Lightning and whittle its health. When the onscreen commands appear, finish it off.

Raxus Droids Combat Module

The room is crowded with Scrap Guardians and two Interrogation Droids. If left unchecked, the Interrogation Droids will siphon away all your Force energy. Don't allow them to live. Leap into the air and dash to the room's rear, where the two droids are. Unleash a Repulse attack to knock away the approaching Guardians and isolate the smaller droids. Cut through the droids with Sith Slam attacks, then leap into the air again and dash to the room's opposite side.

Now that the two droids are gone, use Sith Slam and Sith Strike attacks against the remaining Scrap Guardians. The Lightning-infused 'saber strikes will stun them and deplete their health a lot quicker than normal attacks. Stay near the room's edge and use your Lightning-infused attacks to hit multiple Guardians with each assault.

PROLOGUE

A long time ago
in a galaxy far, far away . . . .

The galaxy is on the brink of darkness. The evil GALACTIC EMPIRE has overthrown the Old Republic and now holds countless worlds in the grip of fear.
The Jedi Knights have been all but destroyed. Only a handful have escaped the Imperial forces, disappearing into hiding across the galaxy. The Emperor's spies have located a lone Jedi Knight on the Wookiee homeworld of Kashyyyk. The Sith Lord DARTH VADER has been sent to destroy him....

MISSION DETAILS

Objective
The Emperor has dispatched Darth Vader to destroy a lone Jedi Knight who is in hiding on the Wookiee homeworld of Kashyyyk.

Enemies Encountered
Wookiee Berserker

Wookiee Infantry

Rogue Jedi: Boss

Collectibles Found
There are no Holocrons to collect in the Prologue.

MAP LEGEND

Holocron

STAR WARS
THE FORCE
UNLEASHED

Dark Plans

High above the vibrant blue planet of Kashyyyk, an Imperial Shuttle glides toward the planet's surface. Inside the little ship is Darth Vader. Below, his Imperial troops have been attacking the villages of Kashyyyk in search of a lone rogue Jedi known as Master Kento. With no sign of his men's success, Vader seeks to destroy the troublesome Jedi on his own.

Upon landing, he disembarks his ship and marches down the path toward the nearest village entrance. Ignoring the fallen Stormtroopers at his feet, Vader's gait is strong, confident, and full of resolve. Nothing can stop him now. Not even one of the last remaining Jedi.

On the Hunt

As Darth Vader, march across the short wooden bridge ahead. On the other side are several Stormtroopers engaged in a firefight with Wookiee Infantry.

Approach the large wooden doors barring entrance into the Wookiee village and charge up a Force Push. Unleash it at the doors, bringing them down in a shower of splinters and large chunks of wood. The combined force of the explosion and the resulting debris shower is more than enough to dispatch the troublesome fuzz balls.

If any Wookiees survive, either reflect their blaster fire back at them or use Force Choke to eliminate them.

Storm down the wooded path past several large boulders and tall trees until you reach two abandoned barricades. Several blade-wielding Wookiee Berserkers rush down the path toward you, thirsting for Sith blood. Use your Force Grip to pick up the closest barricade and hurl it at the first wave of oncoming foes.

Calmly continue creeping deeper into the village. Use Force attacks to clear the path of pesky Wookiees, or knock them away with Force Push and toss them over the sides of the village walkways to rid yourself of them quickly.

SITH WISDOM

The Wookiees are no match for your Force powers, so vary your attacks. Familiarize yourself with all of your powers.

Creep between the two large boulders ahead and stop before you run into the Wookiee Infantry ahead. Reflect the Wookiee Infantries' fire back at them and press onward.

The path ahead is clear for a few more paces. When you encounter the first Wookiee watch-post along the cliff to the left, stop and pick up the large gray rock on the right. Use it to bowl over the Wookiees in your way.

WOOKIEE WARNING

Your focus may be on the path ahead and the rogue Jedi at its end, but don't lose sight of enemies nearby. Wookiee Berserkers have tremendous leaping abilities and can leap several yards, pouncing on you from behind!

As you infiltrate the village, Stormtroopers pour in through the cleared path behind you. Allow them to pass you and distract the Wookiees before they attack you. While the Wookiees are distracted, slice through them with swift 'saber strikes.

Several more Wookiee Berserkers try to ambush you once they get past your Troopers, so stay on guard. Lure them to the walkway's edges and engage them in close-quarters combat. There you can cut through them with lightsaber combos and push them over the sides of the pathways.

Resume your warpath through the village and turn left when you reach the small circular platform.

Stop just before setting foot on the bridge and charge your Force Push attack. Wait for several Wookiee warriors to storm across the bridge; unleash a devastating Force Push as they reach the midway point. The blast will destroy the arches over the bridge and dispatch the Wookiees all at once. Toss any surviving Wookiees over the bridge's side as you cross.

Blast down the large wooden barricade at the bridge's end and turn right. Pick up a large gray boulder and maneuver it up the incline on the right, making sure to bowl over all Wookiee warriors in its way.

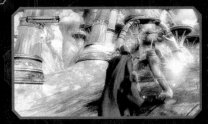

Proceed up the incline and strike down any Wookiees you encounter. There shouldn't be many Wookiees left if your aim is accurate with the boulder.

At the incline's top is a room with an elevator pad. Two Wookiees leap out as you approach. Knock the first one away with a Force Push, then strike down his partner with quick lightsaber combos. Finish off the first Wookiee as he gets back up, then step onto the elevator pad. When the elevator stops, creep up to the exit and locate the Wookiees on the bridge ahead.

Charge a Force Push attack as the Wookiees approach and unleash it on them when they reach the elevator exit. The blast destroys the archway over the bridge ahead and takes the Wookiees out at the same time. Still, the Wookiees are persistent. Several more waves of furry foes will filter through the debris. Greet them with quick lightsaber combos and Force Push.

Slash past the waves of Wookiees as you head up the walkway and turn right at the bridge's end.

JEDI KNOWLEDGE

Don't try crossing the first bridge on the right. As you turn to set foot on the bridge, a rogue TIE Fighter crashes through the bridge and obliterates it!

Turn right onto the second rickety wooden bridge and cut through the first wave of Wookiees. Slash at them with your 'saber or knock them off the bridge with Force Push to take them out quickly. If they leap behind you and try sneaking up, use Force Repulse to repel them and send them flying over the bridge's side.

Stop near the bridge's end and turn right so you can see the near end of the next bridge. Throw your lightsaber across the chasm and cut through the Wookiees approaching the connecting platform between the two bridges.

When the coast is clear, finish crossing your bridge, then turn right at the platform and on to the next bridge.

Just as before, greet the attacking Wookiees with Force Push to knock them away. Don't allow them to leap over you and surround you. Hit them with Force Push while they're in the air. If you miss, repel them with Force Repulse.

Reach the bridge's end and stop before continuing on to the platform ahead. Hold your ground and Force Push away the waves of approaching Wookiees. Turn left at the platform and step onto the final bridge.

Stop near the bridge's midpoint and turn your attention to the small platform just right of the bridge's end. Several Wookiee Berserkers leap from the platform and try to maul you. As they do, hurl them backward with Force Push attacks. Once the Wookiees stop attacking, finish crossing the bridge and arrive at your destination, the rogue Jedi's home.

Rogue Jedi Duel

As you approach the Jedi's small shack, he calmly steps out and approaches. He doesn't seem concerned about his possible demise; instead, he simply tells you to turn back as he Force Pushes a pair of Stormtroopers that have joined you.

STAR WARS
FORCE
UNLEASHED

You're no fool. You know he doesn't stand a chance against your might. Still, he draws his lightsaber and prepares for battle....

Begin your assault on the Jedi by throwing your lightsaber at him and knocking him back. Rush toward him as he reels from your initial attack and lash out with a quick lightsaber combo. Don't allow him to regain his footing after your first attack. Instead, apply pressure quickly by striking first and often.

Force him back against the large rock on the left and pummel him with 'saber strikes. If he tries fighting back, use Force Repulse to knock him off balance before he can launch an attack.

Engage the Jedi in a Lightsaber Lock and follow the onscreen prompts to overpower him.

After successfully winning the Lightsaber Lock and knocking back the Jedi, resume your relentless assault with 'saber combos. Block his counterattacks, wait for him to let up between assaults, then counter with attacks of your own.

If the Jedi surrounds himself in a protective Force sphere, back away to avoid his Repulse attack. Similarly, if he uses the Force to lock on to a TIE Fighter flying overhead, back away immediately to avoid being crushed by it. Wait for the TIE Fighter to explode, then continue slashing at the Jedi with 'saber strikes.

If the Jedi rushes at you, knock him away with Force Repulse. Walk up to him as he lands on the ground and strike him again with your lightsaber.

Once you've nearly depleted the Jedi's Health bar, he will attempt to keep his distance and will attack by using Force Push and by throwing his lightsaber. Block his lightsaber throws and use jump to avoid being knocked back by his Force Push. Turn the tables on him by throwing your lightsaber at him and cutting him down from a distance.

When the Jedi is about to fall once and for all, several onscreen prompts will appear. Follow them to batter the Jedi into submission. Your final attacks knock his 'saber from his hands, thrash him against the nearby trees, then send him flying through the air into his little shack.

Just as you're about to choke the remaining life from the beaten Jedi, you sense a powerful presence nearby. At first you think it might be the Jedi's master, but it's not; you destroyed him years ago. Suddenly, as you raise your lightsaber to finish him off, your weapon inexplicably flies out of your hand!

You turn to find a young boy holding your 'saber. It wasn't the Jedi's master you sensed; it was his son!

You squeeze the remaining life from the Jedi and approach the boy holding your lightsaber as your Imperial Guards arrive. In a split-second decision, you decide to spare the boy's life so that he may suit your own purposes later. If you're to rescue him, however, the Imperial Guards—now witness to his existence—must perish. You take your 'saber from the boy and turn it on the Imperials as they fire on the child. With all witnesses removed, you take the boy and claim his future as your Secret Apprentice.

TIE CONSTRUCTION YARD

MAP LEGEND

Holocron

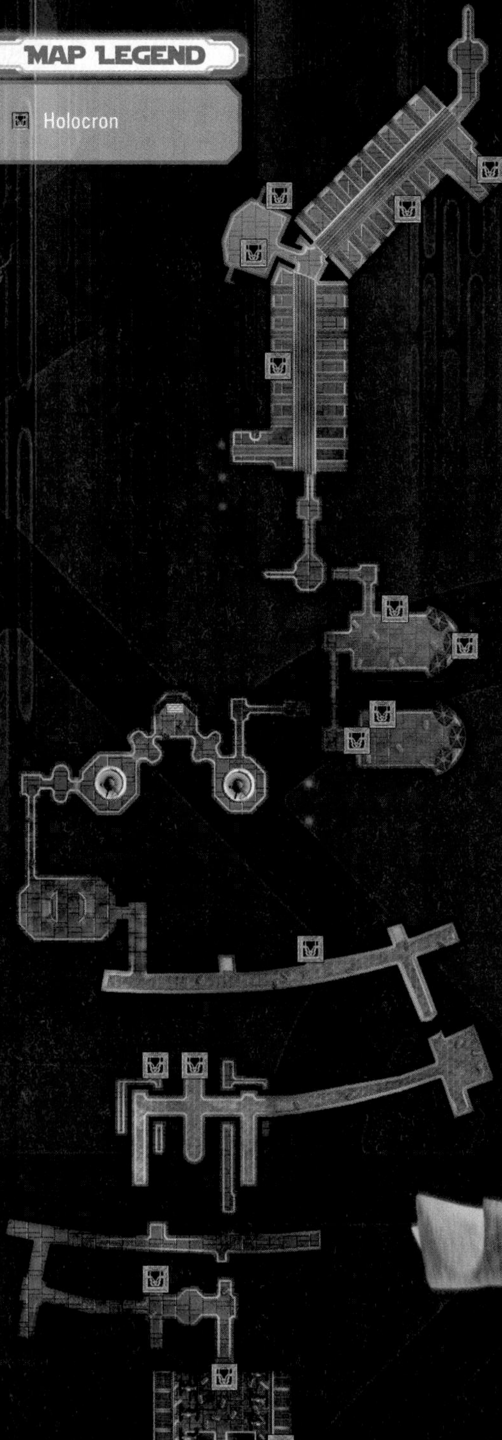

MISSION DETAILS

Objective

Find and eliminate General Kota.

Bonus Objectives

Destroy five TIE fighters

Attain 90,000 Force Points

Locate 15 Holocrons

Enemies Encountered

- Militia Saboteur
- Militia Trooper
- Militia Elite
- Imperial Stormtrooper
- Imperial Officer
- AT-CT
- Rahm Kota: Boss

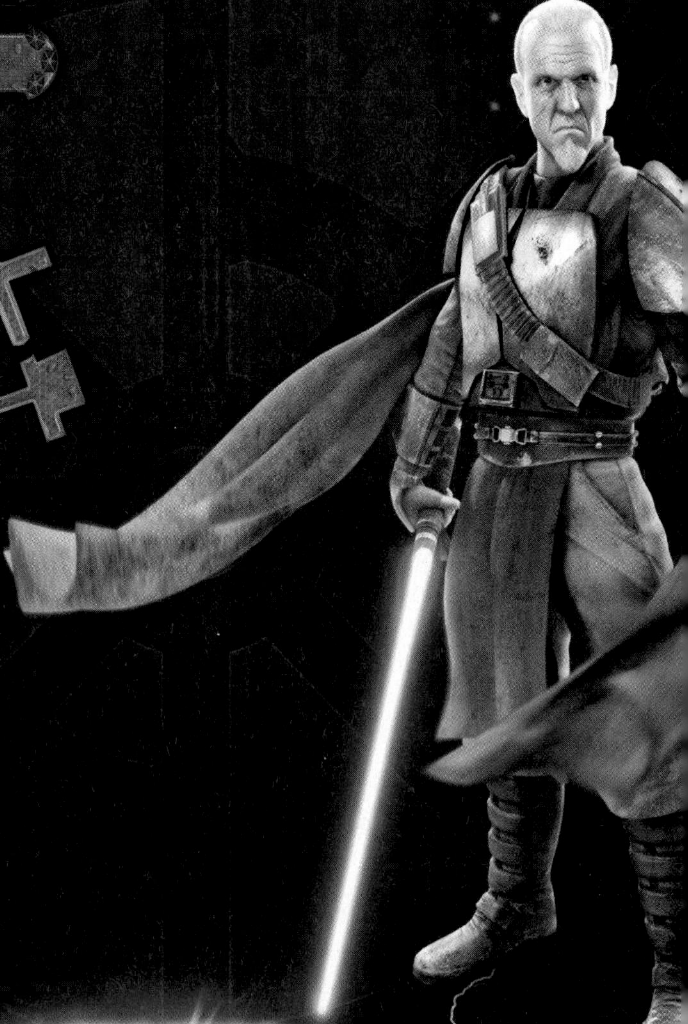

The Secret Apprentice

t is now several years later, and you, as the Secret Apprentice, have been studying the ways of the Force from your master, Darth Vader. You've matured from that brooding child he found on the planet of Kashyyyk into a powerful Sith apprentice. Your years of tutelage under Darth Vader's care have remained a secret even to the Emperor, for your destiny poses a threat to the Dark Lord. However, now it is time to begin your journey in unleashing the full power of the Force....

"Leave No Witnesses."

With your training progressing rapidly, it's time to face your first real opponent. A Jedi named Rahm Kota is attacking a critical Imperial shipyard. You must dispatch him and return his lightsaber to your master. Do this quietly, however, because no one can learn of your existence. This means you must leave no witnesses—Rebel and Imperial forces alike.

On your way to the hangar bay, your personal droid, PROXY, disguised as Obi-Wan Kenobi, lunges out at you and tries to kill you! You deflect his attack and defeat him instantly. With his training exercise complete (and failed), PROXY gets to his feet and updates you on your new pilot as if nothing had happened. According to PROXY's personnel file, Captain Juno Eclipse is a capable, war-hardened, highly decorated combat pilot. But you can see that she is beautiful as well.

JEDI KNOWLEDGE

Prior to setting off on your mission, you stop by the *Rogue Shadow*'s training room to familiarize yourself with your Force Grip abilities.

Juno's piloting skills prove helpful as she manages to infiltrate the TIE construction ship while the battle rages on outside.

Once inside the TIE construction ship, streak down the hallways until you reach the doors leading to the main hangar bay. As you go, use the droids, wall panels, and barrels littered about to practice using Force Grip. Charge your Force Push attack and blast the hangar doors.

Rush down the walkway toward the two Stormtroopers and blast them with Force Push. The shock wave of energy knocks them back and sends the nearby crates flying into them.

 Speed toward the walkway's end and pick up the Sith Holocron.

SITH WISDOM

Defeating the near-endless waves of Stormtroopers in the hangar bay is a great way to fulfill your Force Points bonus objective.

The Sith Holocron grants you unlimited energy for a short period of time. Take advantage of your increased powers! Leap down onto the main hangar floor and use Force Push attacks to knock away the Militia fighters by the bulkhead door, along the hangar's left wall. As they reel from your Force Push, cut them down with quick 'saber combos.

After decimating the Militia Saboteurs by the bulkhead door, turn around and hurl the nearby crates at the Imperial Stormtroopers behind you. They'll emerge from an elevator pad near the hangar's center. As your foes rise, pummel them with crates to dispatch them before they can become a threat.

 Before leaving the main hangar, hop atop the ship at the hangar's center, then double-jump onto the walkway along the far wall. Pick up the Holocron there, then turn around and hop back onto the ship.

Leap atop the ship's rear fin, then double-jump and dash onto the walkway high above the hangar. Head to the walkway's end and pick up another Holocron. Finally, hop back down onto one of the walkways below. From there, Force Grip the TIE fighters hanging on the transporter cranes and bring them down on your enemies below. Destroy five TIE fighters to fulfill your bonus objective.

When the coast is clear, approach the bulkhead doors and use Force Grip to slide the first lock from right to left. Then slide the second lock from bottom to top. The bulkhead doors unlock onto the hallways of the TIE construction ship, where more of Kota's men are engaged with Imperial Stormtroopers.

Dash to the hall's end and rush the two Militia Saboteurs in the alcove there. Use Force Grip to hurl one of their grenades back at them, then run your lightsaber through the second militiaman.

Turn left and speed down the long hall. Stop before running into the three Militia Saboteurs. Launch the grenades back at the grenadier to knock him away, then grip one of the other militiamen and toss him at his comrades.

Blast a hole in the doors on the right to reveal a Holocron. Grab it, then resume searching the TIE construction ship.

Force Push a hole through the next set of doors and continue stalking enemies down the hallways. Use the small red-ringed barrels to blow away the Militia Troopers at the hall's end. Pick up the barrels with the Force, then hurl them down the hall at the group of enemies. Absorb the fallen militiamen's health, then speed down the hall.

Use Force Push attacks to split up the small group of Stormtroopers at the bend in the hall; then slice through them one by one with lightsaber attacks. If the troopers are too far apart from each other to string long lightsaber combos together, use the red-ringed barrels at the hall's rear to blow up distant enemies while you cut up nearby enemies.

Force Push through the doors on the right and enter the large construction room. Turn right and run down the walkway until you reach a connecting walkway leading left. Make a left onto the walkway and stop. Allow the Militia fighters to engage the Stormtroopers in battle farther down the walkway. Keep your distance from the battle and allow them to pare down each others' numbers.

From afar, use the nearby crates and barrels as projectiles against the remaining soldiers; this will either blow them up or knock them off the walkways. When there are less than four or five enemies left, rush at them and finish them off with several lightsaber combos.

At the walkway's end, turn left and blast the doors open. Inside the small chamber are several more soldiers and an elevator pad leading to the second level. Rush inside to the chamber's right and cut down the first Stormtrooper. Turn around and Force Push the crates into the rest of the Imperial soldiers. Finish them off with swift 'saber combos to clear the room.

After you destroy all Imperial Stormtroopers in the chamber, a small squad of Militia fighters comes rushing down the elevator on the right. Greet them with Force Push and several crates to take them out quickly.

Exit the chamber's rear and remove the stacked crates near the walkway's edge. Pick up the Holocron before returning to the chamber.

Ride the elevator up to the second level. As you exit, a Militia fighter manning a turret at the room's rear opens fire on you. Slash past the first Militia Saboteur, then zigzag toward the turret (to minimize taking damage) and cut down the soldier as soon as he's within reach of your 'saber. With him out of the way, turn around and engage the other militiamen in the room.

Force Push the doors on the right to open them. Sneak out and turn left. Remove the stacked crates along the walkway's edge and pick up another Holocron before returning to the elevator room.

STAR WARS
FORCE
UNLEASHED

Blast through the doors on the left and dash out toward the Militia soldiers engaged in battle on the walkway. Sneak up on the militiamen while they are engaged with the Stormtroopers. Toss crates at them from behind, then dash toward them as they recover from your attack. Swing your 'saber at the remaining militiamen, then turn your attention to the troopers farther down the walkway.

Pick up the closest Imperial trooper and throw him at his comrades. Use the crates nearby to push the other soldiers off the walkway.

Speed toward the last group of Stormtroopers at the walkway's end and slice them to ribbons with swift combos. Turn left and approach the small group of militiamen. Toss them over the walkway's side, then make another left at the next intersection.

As you speed down the walkway, another group of militiamen pours out of a small alcove on the right. Run headlong into their ranks and cut your way back out. String together lightsaber combos as you attack each militiaman one by one. By starting a combo on one enemy and finishing it on a second, you can increase the amount of damage you deal, you can cover more ground, and you can reduce the amount of damage you take.

Enter the alcove from where the militiamen appeared to find another Holocron.

Continue down the walkway and eliminate the next group of militiamen as they pop out of the next alcove. Use Force Grip to throw their grenades back at them, then cut them down as they try getting up from the blast.

Make a right through the doors at the walkway's end and enter the control room on the left. Slash through the first enemy as you dash toward the room's center. Grab the Sith Holocron to increase your damage, then turn on the remaining rivals in the room. Circle around the center console as you slice through each of the soldiers with swift 'saber strikes.

Exit the control room via the door on the far right corner. When you enter the hallway, a trio of Militia fighters rushes in from the hall's far end. One of the men is a Militia Elite. Zigzag down the hall toward the elite, targeting him first. Take him out with several lightsaber combos, then finish off the other two men before turning right and entering the next room.

In the next room, dispatch another Militia Elite before turning on his accompanying men.

The next area is an infuser room. Immediately upon entering it, a tall orange laser gate activates. Rush the Militia Elite and eliminate him quickly. Once he's out of the way, Force Grip the large generator nestled in a niche on the left wall and remove it. This deactivates the laser gate. (The generator is behind the laser gate, but you can still pluck it out with your Force powers.)

With the gate down, return to the fight. Lash out at the encroaching enemies and cut them down as they try surrounding you. Link your combos as you go from man to man, attacking each one.

Speed into the next room and immediately target the Militia fighters atop the steps on the left. Pick up the Militia Elite and throw him through the glass window behind him. The resulting outpouring of air into space sucks nearly all the militiamen from the room. The room repressurizes when a large metal hatch slams down and blocks the broken window. When it does, pick up any surviving enemy and throw him out one of the other two windows.

Exit the room via the door on the right and enter a circular chamber crawling with militiamen. Rush the elite on the left and chop him down with lightsaber combos. With him out of the way, the remaining Militia Saboteurs are a lot easier to handle.

Before leaving this room, grab the Sith Holocron in the crevice on the right. It grants you a temporary Health Drain Aura that robs enemies of their health when you're in close quarters.

With your Health Drain Aura active, exit the circular room through the tunnel on the left and run straight into the small squad of Stormtroopers. Don't bother swinging your 'saber; the aura will drain them of their health almost instantly. Simply speed into the center of their squad and stop to drain all of them simultaneously.

On the left, behind the squad, is a platform embedded into the wall. Lock on to the large red circle with your Force Grip and pull the platform out of the wall. Double-jump onto the now-exposed platform and locate the Stormtrooper on a ledge high up on the far wall. Toss the trooper from the ledge, then Force Grip the glowing red panel beneath it. Pull down the panel to create a platform, then double-jump onto the platform to reach the ledge above it.

Leave the ledge and walk to the tunnel's end. Drop into the hallway beneath the tunnel and blast open the doors at the hall's end.

The next room, the wing-assembly chamber, is the location of an intense battle between Kota's men and a large Imperial AT-CT walker. Before engaging the enemies, allow the Militia fighters to whittle down the AT-CT's health. Stand back, away from the firefight, and watch as the two groups nearly destroy each other. When the AT-CT dispatches one of the attacking Militia Elites, join the fight.

Start throwing red-ringed barrels, crates, and any other nearby objects at the walker to further deplete its health. When you do, both the walker and the militiamen will turn their attention to you. Take out the soldiers first, then attack the AT-CT. Dash away from its attacks and counter by throwing objects at it until it's almost ready to fall. When you've nearly destroyed it, follow the onscreen prompts to finish off the Imperial machine.

After destroying the AT-CT, hop atop the wing carriers at the room's rear. Ride the wings up to the highest walkway. Hop off the wing and onto the walkway on the right. Remove the crates at the walkway's far end to reveal a Holocron. Take it, then turn around to locate another Holocron against the far wall.

Jump onto the small ledge along the wall and take the second Holocron before hopping down onto the catwalks just below.

After disembarking the rising wing carrier, follow the walkway into the control room along the far wall. Inside are several Imperial Stormtroopers. Blast them away with a Force Push, then cut them down with quick combos. Enter the hall behind the control room and dash to its end.

Turn right at the hall's end and stop just before entering the next wing-assembly room. Force Throw an explosive barrel into the assembly room and blow up some of the soldiers inside. Dash toward the room's right side and pick up the Sith Holocron. The unlimited energy it bestows will allow you to make quick work of the remaining soldiers.

There are two more Holocrons in this wing-assembly room. The first is on a broken wing against the far wall. The rising wing carrier is busted, so the TIE wings are stationary. Force Grip one of the wings on the floor, lift it, and maneuver it into the first empty slot along the second to last wing carrier on the wall. Hop down to the floor, then use the newly placed wing to jump up to the other broken wing holding the Holocron.

From here, jump and double-jump up the other wings until you're within leaping distance of the walkway on the far right. Double-jump and dash over the broken walkway to reach the second Holocron, then hop back down to the bottom floor.

Exit the wing-assembly room through the tunnel in the room's left corner. Sneak up on the squad of Stormtroopers and hit them with several Force Pushes. Since they're engaged with Kota's men, they don't see you coming and don't put up much of a fight. Dash back and forth across the hall and take down any stragglers with lightsaber combos.

Dash past the defeated troopers and engage the militiamen farther down the hall. Toss crates at them as they arrive on the elevator at the hall's end; finish them off with Force Push attacks or speedy 'saber assaults.

Get on the elevator pad and take it to the next level. Get off the pad and turn left at the corner, then enter the pod-assembly room.

Hurl the first Stormtrooper deep into the room and knock over the other Imperial lackeys on the assembly line. Rather than fight through the enemies on the bottom level of the assembly line, make a right and storm across the walkway along the right wall. Dispatch the grenade-tossing Militia Saboteur, then turn left and use Force Grip to take control of the nearest robotic laser arm.

Turn this on the other enemies inside the pod-assembly room and disintegrate them. As you do, stand behind the arm's large metallic structure so that it protects you from enemy fire. If you can't get a good angle on the enemies firing at you from the bottom floor, scoot up the walkway and take control of the second robotic laser arm to finish the job.

SITH WISDOM

If you choose to take the fight to the militiamen, grab the Sith Holocron near the center of the assembly line to gain a temporary Health Drain Aura.

  With the immediate area clear of all enemies, duck into the small alcove along the bottom floor's left side. Grab the Holocron inside the alcove, then return to the main pod-assembly room.

As you approach the next section of the pod-assembly room, a laser gate activates and blocks the path ahead. Go up the small ramp on the left and slash past the militiamen in your way. The ramp leads to a generator room with several more militiamen. Hurl them at the far laser gate wall to eliminate them quickly.

WOOKIEE WARNING

Be careful when stepping between the large cylindrical generators. If you get too close, they can shock you and inflict a lot of damage.

Carefully step between the two large generators on the left and pick up the Holocron nestled between them. Leave the generators and explore the small niche on the room's right side to find another Holocron.

With the coast clear, approach the laser gate at the generator room's rear and Force Grip the large generator nestled in the wall. Remove it to bring down the laser gates and gain access to the next section of the pod-assembly room.

Jump onto the walkway on the left and destroy the militiamen in your way. Force Grip one of the robotic laser arms below and turn it on the others in the room just as you did before. If any enemies remain out of the robotic laser arm's reach, hop down to the main floor and pick up the Sith Holocron at the room's center. Use your temporary damage increase boost to clear the room of all enemies.

After you eliminate all enemies in the pod-assembly room, check the small niche on the room's right side for a Holocron. The room's far right corner contains a Holocron as well. Pick it up, then continue into the next section of the facility.

Go up the ramp at the far end of the pod-assembly line. Hop onto the elevator pad at the next hallway's end and ride it to the control room where Kota awaits.

Jedi Master Rahm Kota

Apparently, Kota wasn't expecting to see you. The look on his face reveals disappointment. His attacks on the Imperial shipyards weren't meant to get *your* attention, but rather your master's. It doesn't matter; Kota doesn't need to be excited to see you in order for you to destroy him....

Kota is a full-fledged Jedi Master, so be ready to use your lightsaber skills carefully. Leap at the Jedi Master and attack him with a lightsaber combo. He'll probably block your attack and counter. If he does, block his attacks by raising your lightsaber. Kota will often surround himself in a green Force sphere. When he does, leap away to create some distance between you and him. As you do this, he'll hurl his lightsaber at you, so stay on guard.

After you reengage Kota in battle, block his attacks and counterattack with 'saber combos. Engage Kota in a Lightsaber Lock and follow the onscreen commands to overpower him.

Slam Kota with Force Push attacks and streak behind him as he flies into a wall. When he lands, follow up your assault with lightsaber combos to whittle down his health bar.

"The remaining Jedi will be hunted down and defeated."

—Emperor Palpatine,
Star Wars: Episode III *Revenge of the Sith*

When Kota draws in debris toward him, double-jump into the air and prepare to evade his projectile attack. As he begins throwing debris at you, double-jump again and dash out of the way as the debris flies toward you. After firing off all of his debris, Kota's energy will be temporarily depleted.

Take advantage of his wearied state and dash toward him to attack. Unleash devastating lightsaber combos while he's dazed, then back away before he can counterattack.

After taking so much damage, Kota realizes you're more of a threat than he initially anticipated. He uses the Force to unhinge the control room and separate it from the rest of the TIE construction facility! As the control room free-falls toward the planet's surface, he reengages you in battle.

Blast Kota with Force Push and lunge at him as he reels from your attack. Follow your blast with several 'saber strikes, then retreat when he activates his green Force sphere. Leap between platforms so you're in the air during Kota's Ground Slam attack, then reengage him in battle while he's dazed from his missed assault.

As he nears defeat, Kota will attempt to hurl more debris at you. Continue dodging his projectiles and attack only while he's dazed.

WOOKIEE WARNING

If your battle with Kota takes too long, the control room will continue plummeting and will eventually reach the planet's atmosphere. When it does, the room will begin to superheat. The result is a white-hot lavalike glow on the room's floor, which will inflict damage when you step on it.

Once the general's health is depleted to less than 10 percent, a series of onscreen commands will appear. Follow them quickly and accurately to slam him with debris, pound him against the floor, and thrash him about the room. Just as he's about to be destroyed, he foolishly attempts to talk you out of defeating him. He rambles on about your future and how he sees only...himself

It's too late. Your 'saber burns his eyes, and your final attack sends him flying through a window and plummeting toward the planet's surface. You take his lightsaber for your master and leap out of the broken window, landing on the *Rogue Shadow* as it speeds by below you. Your first battle against a Jedi is victorious.

STAR WARS
FORCE
UNLEASHED

RAXUS PRIME

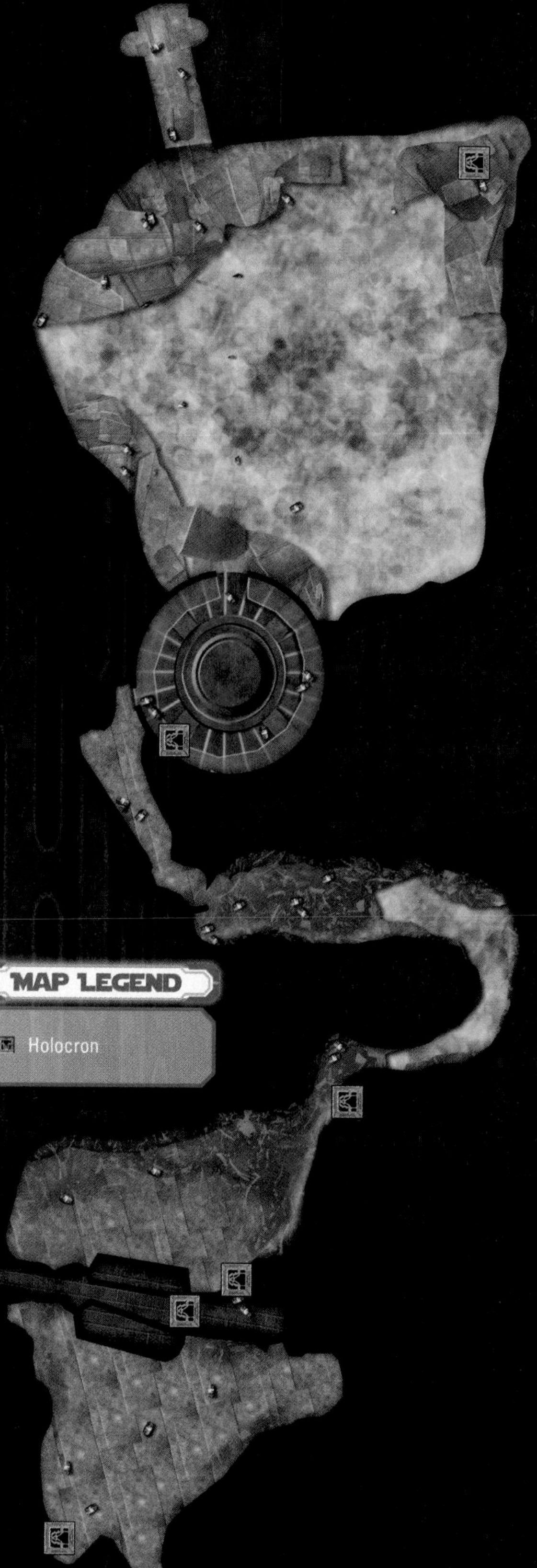

MISSION DETAILS

Objective
Seek out and destroy Kazdan Paratus.

Bonus Objectives
Destroy 10 scavenger skiffs

Attain 150,000 Force Points

Locate 15 Holocrons

Enemies Encountered
Rodian Ripper

Rodian Heavy Defender

Jawa

Scrap Guardian

Scrap Drone

Junk Titan

Kazdan Paratus: Boss

"Where All Droids Go to Die..."

Your hunt for Jedi Master Kazdan Paratus takes you to Raxus Prime, a world whose entire surface resembles the trash heaps and junkyards of Coruscant. From high above the planet, Paratus's home looks much like a Jedi Temple. Once you touch down, however, it is clear to see that this planet is extremely hostile.

The ground is shrouded by a toxic mist that rises from a sulfuric lake of sludge. Meanwhile, transport beams flow overhead like a river of trash.

Take Out the Trash

After disembarking the *Rogue Shadow*, examine the power cell directly in front of you. Use your now-active Force Lightning to power up the cell and send it flying across the sludge lake. The cell spins and sputters directly into a crack in a distant wall.

Hop down onto the lower platform and turn left. Carefully approach the edge and target the sunken circular surface with Force Grip; pull it out of the sludge to create a raised platform.

MAP LEGEND

Holocron

47

PRIMAGAMES.COM

JEDI KNOWLEDGE

After raising a platform from the sludge, it will slowly drop back into the toxic waste over time.

Just behind the first circular platform, underneath a large metal docklike structure, is a Holocron. Double-jump off the platform, then dash into the little alcove to retrieve it. After taking the Holocron, re-raise the platform and double-jump back onto it.

WOOKIEE WARNING

Be careful while leaping from area to area. The sludge is extremely volatile and will drain your health almost instantly!

Double-jump from the platform onto the small docklike structure behind it. Slice through the first Rodian Ripper, then Force Push the other two into the sludge below. As you do, a scavenger skiff swoops in and drops off more enemies. Dispatch them quickly by tossing them into the sludge.

SITH WISDOM

After eliminating the Rodians, immediately turn around and Force Grip a power cell from the transport beam above. Toss the cell at the skiff as it tries to escape and blow it up!
As these skiffs swoop in to drop off enemies, use power cells to blow them up. You can destroy four in this area alone. You can also target the skiffs and zap them with Force Lightning to make them explode.

STAR WARS
THE FORCE
UNLEASHED

Some scavenger skiffs will make return trips, but don't always count on it! You'll need to attack quickly and accurately when trying to blow them up.

Hop down onto the lower platform. As soon as the Rodian Heavy Defenders get off their scavenger skiffs, they'll open fire, so immediately raise your 'saber to block. Fry the nearest Rodian with Force Lightning, then take out the other fiend with lightsaber combos.

SITH WISDOM

Destroy the scavenger skiff before it flies away.

Carefully approach the edge and raise the submerged platform on the right. Jump onto it, then immediately double-jump onto the tilted platform ahead.

Raise another platform from the sludge, jump onto it, then double-jump and dash over the wall of girders onto the next platform just behind them. As you land, pick up the Sith Holocron to gain invincibility, and slash through the Rodians that n a scavenger skiff.

SITH WISDOM

Pick up the power cell near the platform's edge (or use Force Lightning) and destroy the skiff before it escapes.

Leap onto the ledge just beyond your platform and shove the Rodians into the sludge as they disembark their skiff. Destroy the skiff with a nearby red-ringed barrel, then detonate the power cell near the edge. It, too, flies toward the cracked wall and explodes. This time the wall crumbles, creating an entrance into a large cylindrical thruster room.

Follow the ledge on the right toward the hole in the wall. At the ledge's end, jump onto the platform just left and below you, then double-jump onto stable ground in front of the hole in the wall.

Venture into the large thruster room and confront the Jawa on the right. Sidestep his explosives as you approach him, then cut him down with a short lightsaber combo.

Circle around to the right, cutting down Jawas. The little trash mongers are not particularly resilient, so a simple combo or Force Push will dispatch them quickly. Hop onto the small ledge on the right and take out the three Jawas, then turn right again.

Jump up the series of ledges to the right and ascend the thruster room. Reach the two Rodian Heavy Defenders and engage them with a quick combo. Begin your lightsaber combo on one Rodian, and finish the combo on the second. This keeps them from opening fire on you and blasting your Health bar to bits. Force Push one of the Rodians off the ledge, then finish off the other with quick combos.

There is a Holocron in the thruster room, but it can be tricky to reach. Begin by dropping down onto the spinning rotor in the room's center. From the rotor, leap onto the small ledge on the left. Follow it to the series of brown pipes leading up and across the room to another ledge.

Jump onto the raised area on the left, then double-jump onto the tiny ledge on the large spinning rotor. Follow the ledge as it circles around the rotor, then double-jump and dash onto the ledge along the far wall. Land and immediately dispatch the two Jawas and claim your Holocron. After picking up the Holocron, jump back down to the ledge just below you.

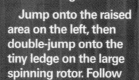 

Go through the hole in the wall and drop into the long trash tunnel. Follow the path and fry the two Rodian Rippers you encounter. Near the tunnel's end is a metal wall with an X-shaped tear in it. Blast the X with your Force Push to widen the tear and step through.

Eliminate the Jawas on the other side with short bursts of Force Lightning and quick combos, then leap atop the rising ledges just ahead. Before you leap back down to the ledges' other side, stop and locate the Rodian Heavy Defenders farther down the path.

Use the red-ringed barrel nearby to blow up the Rodians on the far right ledge, then double-jump and dash at the Rodian Heavy Defender on the far left ledge. Cut him down with 'saber strikes before he can open fire on you.

With the two Rodian Heavy Defenders no longer perched at high sniper positions, it's safe to jump down onto the bottom floor and take the fight to the Jawas and Rodians. First destroy the Heavy Defenders, then slash through the Rippers. As you do, let your combos also strike the nearby Jawas.

Leave the fallen trash mongers behind and use the Force to create protective cover overhead by bending the metal panels above you. The falling sparks drop harmlessly on the metal canopy, allowing you to continue to the path's end. When you reach a small river of sludge, double-jump onto the far ledge, then leap onto the small metal walkway leading right. Follow the next tunnel to its end and turn left.

 Make a sharp left at the tunnel's end and grab the next Holocron.

There is a crashed starship crawling with Rodians in the next area. As you approach, they're engaged in battle with Scrap Guardians. Stay on your perch before dropping down and joining the battle. Wait for a scavenger skiff to pull up just below you and to the left. Force Grip a nearby power cell from the trash transport beam and hurl it at the skiff to destroy it, then blast the Rodian Heavy Defenders below with Force Lightning.

Though you help the Scrap Guardians by taking out the Rodian Heavy Defenders, that doesn't stop them from teleporting behind you on your ledge. Turn on them and finish what the Rodians started. Cut through the walking trash monsters with several strong lightsaber combos. Drop to the bottom floor and pick up the Sith Holocron near the area's center.

The Sith Holocron temporarily grants you unlimited energy. Take advantage of this and unleash Force Lightning, Force Push, and Force combos on the remaining Rodian Heavy Defenders and Scrap Guardians. If your boost runs out before you demolish all enemies, retreat back to higher ground and assault them from above.

 After defeating all the enemies near the crashed starship, examine the niche behind the rear engine covering to find another Holocron.

With the area clear, approach the large metal structure at the crash site's far end. Use Force Grip to lift it out of the ground, then hop onto it and turn toward the crashed ship. Double-jump from your structure to the large glowing cone on the ship's right end. To remove the cone, hit it with Force Lightning or with the maglane engines you can grab as they float by. Finally, double-jump into the hole in the starship left by the cone.

Inside the ship are several Rodian Rippers. Hurl explosive canisters at them, then lunge at them with your lightsaber swinging! Dice them to bits before turning your attention on the Heavy Defender at the chamber's far end. Fry him with Force Lightning, then finish him off with your 'saber.

Exit the chamber through the hole at the ship's rear and join the battle between the Scrap Guardians and the Rodians. Throw large pieces of scrap metal at your enemies as they fight each other, then rush in behind your projectiles and slice them up.

 Grab the Holocron near the cliff's far right edge before leaving this area.

STAR WARS THE FORCE UNLEASHED

Decimate the Rodian Heavy Defenders in the area first. If they are out of your 'saber's reach, use Force Push and Force Grip to toss them over the cliff. Next, turn on the Scrap Guardians and engage them in battle. String your combos together as you jump from one Guardian to another. Don't allow them to surround you, but if they do, use Force Push to blast them away.

With the coast clear, approach the circular hatch doors near the far left corner and blast them open with Force Push. Dash inside and turn left. Follow the tunnel, blasting Jawas out of your way.

At the tunnel's end, before leaping up into the tunnel's second level, Force Push the circular hatch and split the hatch doors open. Behind them is another Holocron; grab it before proceeding.

Leap onto the tunnel's second level and follow it to its end. You emerge high above a wide-open chasm guarded by a Heavy Defender. Pick him up with Force Grip and toss him into the chasm. Hop to the level below and grip the barrels on the chasm's edge. Maneuver them across the gap and slam them into the Rodian Heavy Defenders guarding the left and right sides of the metal grates bridging the canyon.

Dash across the grates to the canyon's other side and zap the Heavy Defender in your way. Engage the Rodians with quick lightsaber combos. String them together as you move from Rodian to Rodian until you reach the Heavy Defender at the rear of the pack. Target the tower near the right wall and crush it with a Force Push to destroy the Rodian perched on top.

Force Grip the large gates at the far end and swing them open.

The next area is flooded with Rodian Heavy Defenders. If you speed in carelessly, they'll shred you to pieces in no time. Instead, take cover behind the pillars nearby and target the closest defender with Force Grip. Zap him with Force Lightning while he's floating helplessly in the air,

then toss him at the Rodians to the right. Rush into the large steeple-like structure on the right, blow up the two Rodians with an explosive barrel, and grab the Sith Holocron inside. The Sith Holocron increases your damage, so quickly leap out of the structure and lunge at the Rodians on the right.

Cut through as many as possible while your damage is increased, then take cover behind the large scrap-metal pieces to avoid taking damage yourself. Wait for the Heavy Defenders to reload; dash out of cover and fry the rest with Force Lightning. Clear the area's right side before exploring the far left side. You'll encounter two or three more Rodians. Hurl them off the cliff to clear the area of all enemies.

After dispatching all enemies, explore the area. Begin by crossing the long bridge on the far left side. Grab the Holocron there. Then, walk over to the far right corner of the area to find another Holocron.

A laser gate blocks the path into the next area. Walk into the tunnel on the area's right side and take the elevator down one level. At this area's center is a large electrical power supply guarded by several Rodian fighters and a few Jawas. Slice and dice the Rodians as you approach the power supply, and blast the Jawas with Force Push to eliminate them quickly.

Shove the Rodian Heavy Defenders at the rear of the power supply off the cliff. Return to the power supply and use Force Grip to move the large rectangular switch on the power generator. This turns off the laser gate on the first level.

Before returning to the first level, check the garbage skiff behind the power supply. Another Holocron is sitting on top of it. Then, explore the left corner to find another Holocron just as you did in the first level.

Return to the first area, where several more Rodian fighters have entrenched themselves. As you exit the elevator tunnel, dash away from their fire and take cover behind the steeple-like structure at the area's center. Circle around the structure and sneak up on the Heavy Defenders. Thrash them with Force Grip, then rush into the area where the laser gate once stood.

Follow the tunnel as it wends into a large wide-open chamber with a cliff at the far end. Blast the Scrap Drones with Force Lightning; they're not tough to bring down, but if you leave them alone for too long, they'll lock on to you with a vacuum beam that sucks away your Force energy.

Take a minute to examine the area below before dropping into it. At the chamber's far end is a cliff with a large metal beam hanging precariously above the chasm. To the left and right are ledges where several Scrap Guardians stand watch. At the room's center is a large deactivated piece of electrical equipment. Hop down to the right ledge and destroy the first Scrap Guardian.

 Pick up the Holocron on the right ledge as you fight the Scrap Guardian.

Leave the Sith Holocron at the right ledge's end and leap down to the center area. Use short 'saber combos to take out the Scrap Guardian, and jump onto the left ledge where a Scrap Drone and a Scrap Guardian wait. Destroy the Drone with a blast of Force Lightning before turning on the Guardian.

Walk up to the final Guardian by the engine and toss him off the cliff. Don't engage him near the engine or you'll risk being thrown off the cliff too! After dispatching the Scrap Guardian, target the engine on the left and hit it with Force Lightning. The engine comes alive and begins to melt the large piece of metal hanging over the chasm.

Return to the chamber's center area. A large Junk Titan has appeared and is now towering over you. Dash past him and streak onto the far right ledge again.

From the safety of your ledge, grab the power cells nearby. As you throw the cells toward the Junk Titan, light them up with Force Lightning to inflict extra damage. Stay on the move to avoid his attacks. The Titan will pound on the ground, sending a shock wave that burrows into the ground and erupts beneath you. When the ground begins turning bright orange, dash away to avoid the ensuing explosion.

Stay on the ledges as you fight the Titan. Hit him with surges of Force Lightning to whittle his health even more. Continue to dash away from his attacks and pelt him with power cells until he is nothing more than a pile of scrap metal.

JEDI KNOWLEDGE

There are several ways to destroy the Junk Titan. You can also stay on the ledges and periodically activate the large firing beam at the chamber's center by blasting it with Force Lightning as the Titan lumbers underneath it.

If you want to get close, pick up the Sith Holocron at the right ledge's end and increase your damage. Dash at the Titan while your damage increase is active and slash away at him. Once he is ready to fall, a series of prompts will appear onscreen. Match them to finish off your foe.

Edge out to the right ledge's end and Force Grip the large beam on the chasm's other side. Bring it down with the Force and create a bridge. Carefully hop down onto the bridge and speed across. At the first stop, deal with the Scrap Guardians by crushing them with strong lightsaber combos. Take out the first wave of Guardians, then use Force Push and Force Grip to shove the other Guardians over the edge.

Creep to the ledge's end and grip the large curved piece of metal hanging on the right cliff side. Bring it down to create a platform and hop onto the piece of metal. Double-jump and dash onto the next ledge.

 Stop at the second ledge and examine the girders on the left. There's a Holocron beyond them  on a distant platform. To reach it, first use Force Push to destroy the girders, then use Force Grip to lower another curved piece of metal next to the platform. Back away from the wall of girders and blast them with Force Push to bend them out of the way.

Lower the piece of metal attached to the girders to create another platform; creep out onto it. Double-jump and dash onto the second metal platform (the one you lowered first) then double-jump and dash onto the platform containing the Holocron. Backtrack to return to the main path.

Turn right at the girder wall and head down the path. When you encounter a group of Scrap Drones and Guardians, take out the Drones immediately. Blast them with Force Lightning to fry them, then string together several combos to scrap the Guardians.

Just before you reach the doors into the next area, a large Junk Titan appears directly in front of you. Circle around him and repeatedly hit him with Force Lightning to whittle down his health. Keep your distance as you circle around him, and dash away from his burrowing attacks. If he begins swinging his boulder hand, double-jump into the air to avoid it and hit him with Force Lightning while in midair. To crush the beast once and for all, follow the onscreen commands as they appear.

Force Push the doors behind the Junk Titan.

There are three Holocrons behind the large doors. The first is on the left. The second is floating above the center of the path ahead; position an AT-CT head underneath to reach it. The third is in the far right corner, on top of the right platform. Leap from the AT-CT head to the platform and grab the Holocron.

Get on the elevator at the path's end to reach Kazdan Paratus's lair.

Paratus and His Puppet

The elevator takes you to Kazdan Paratus's hiding spot—a nostalgic, if not sullen, re-creation of the Jedi Temple on Coruscant. Not only has the cowering Jedi re-created the Jedi Council chamber, but he's also sculpted many of the Jedi Council members out of trash. Lock on to the speedy Jedi and attack!

Lunge at him with several quick lightsaber combos and block his counterattacks. Engage him in a 'saber lock and overpower him. As he stumbles away from your assault, dash toward him and hit him with more combos.

Kazdan Paratus doesn't use many Force powers, but his lightsaber skills are extremely dangerous. Keep him at bay by blocking his 'saber attacks, then counter with your own.

Follow the Jedi as he speeds about, and occasionally hit him with Force Lightning blasts. If you engage him in a Force Lock, time your button presses with the onscreen prompts to overpower him. When Paratus's health drops to about two-thirds, he'll retreat to a pillar outside the arena, far beyond your reach. From there, the cowering Jedi will summon a Junk Titan to fight for him. Defeat this Titan just as you did the previous one. Strafe around the beast as you scorch him with Force Lightning blasts, and avoid his boulder and burrowing attacks.

When the Titan begins stomping his feet, leap into the air to avoid being knocked down by the tremors. Once you've destroyed the Titan, Paratus will begin throwing objects at you from his pillar. Wait for him to lock on to an object and leap away from the projectile. If you try dashing out of the way too early, he'll hit you as you stop.

After you dodge Paratus's projectile attacks, he'll leap back into the middle of the arena and resume the fight. Mix up your attacks—if he's close, use 'saber combos. If he backs away, switch to Force attacks like Lightning blasts and Force Push. When engaged in Force Lock or 'saber lock battles, follow the onscreen commands as they appear and overpower the pint-sized Jedi.

Eventually, after losing nearly two-thirds of his health, Paratus retreats to his pillar again and summons a second Junk Titan. Destroy the Titan as you did before, then dodge the Jedi's projectiles to lure him back into the arena. Once there, finish him off by following the final series of commands that appear.

As the Jedi lies defeated on the floor, he sighs his last words: "I'm sorry, Masters. I've failed you again...." And with that, a bright blue beam of light shoots out of his body and into the air. The mysteries of the Jedi....

MAP LEGEND

⊡ Holocron

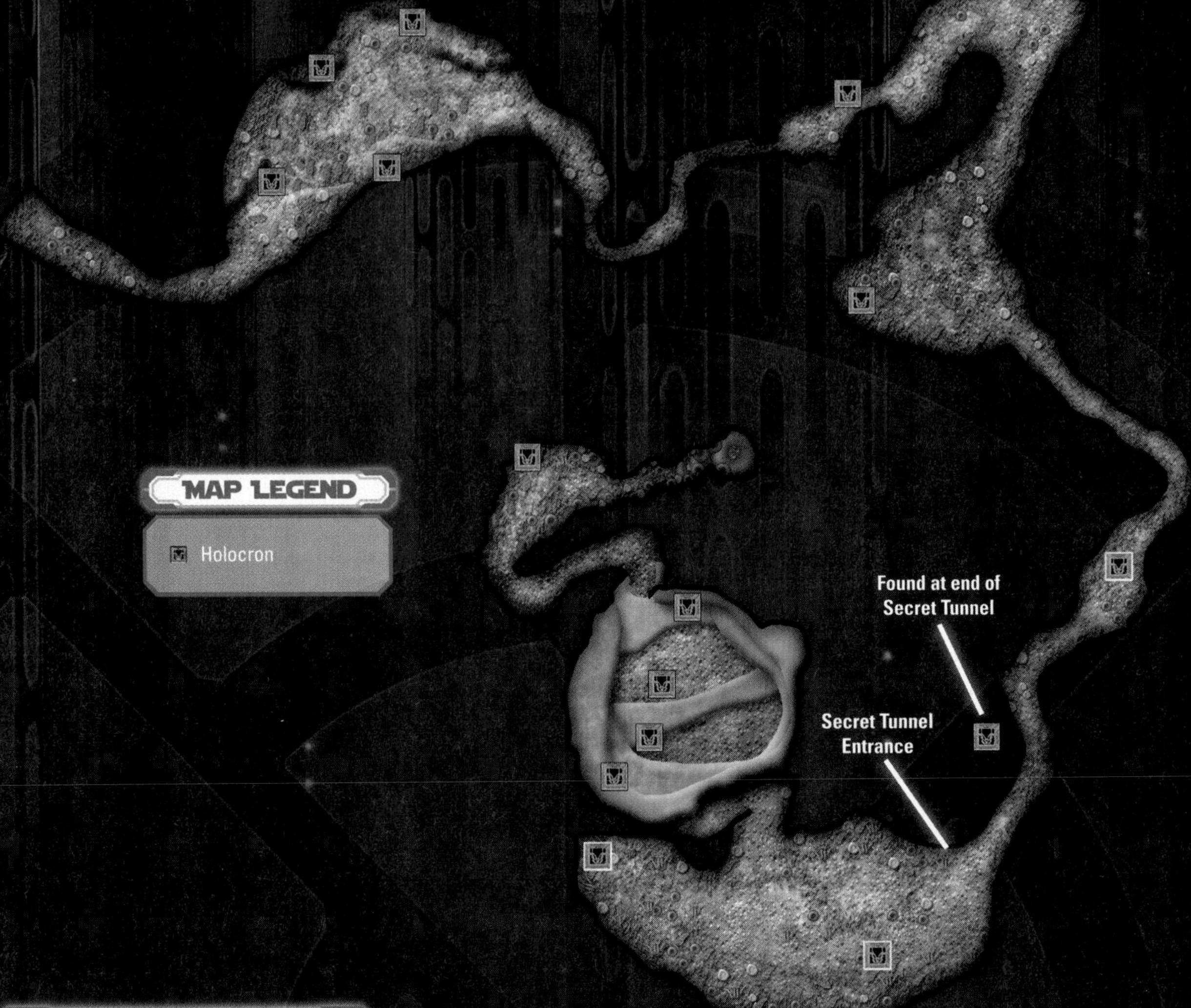

Found at end of
Secret Tunnel

Secret Tunnel
Entrance

MISSION DETAILS

Objective
Hunt down and destroy Shaak Ti.

Bonus Objectives
Destroy four Rancors

Attain 250,000 Force Points

Locate 15 Holocrons

Enemies Encountered
Felucian Warrior

Felucian Shaman

Felucian Chieftain

Felucian Slug

Yerdua Poison Spitter

Rancor

Saddle Rancor

Shaak Ti: Boss

STAR WARS
THE FORCE
UNLEASHED

"Then There Is but One More Test."

As you meditate on your victory over another Jedi, your master interrupts. The 'saber you were building falls to pieces, and Darth Vader storms up to you. He dismisses your victories over both Jedi, claiming they were nothing more than "an old man and an outcast." He has one more test for you before you can fulfill your destiny by his side.

Your next test is against a true Jedi Master, one of the last of the Jedi Council. You're to fly to Felucia and hunt down Jedi Master Shaak Ti.

Juno deftly pilots the *Rogue Shadow* toward the fertile planet of Felucia. Meanwhile, on the planet's surface, Shaak Ti and her apprentice anticipate your arrival. Maris Brood, Shaak Ti's Padawan, is eager for a fight. She's not pleased when her master sends her away. There's a hint of darkness in Brood, and Shaak Ti knows this.

JEDI KNOWLEDGE

You automatically learn Force Repulse at the start of this mission.

Speed though the vibrant Felucian forest until you encounter the first of many Felucian Warriors. They're highly skilled with the sword, so block their attacks before countering with Force Lightning and 'saber combos.

Check the small alcove on the right, just off the main path. Pick up the Holocron before returning to the main path.

Continue stalking down the path. When more Felucian Warriors come speeding around the corner, detonate the large bulbous plants to inflict major damage on them. Slash at the Warriors as they attempt to get back on their feet, then speed past their demolished bodies.

Electrocute the next group of Felucians with Force Lightning. If they surround you, use Force Repulse to create some breathing room, then resume your 'saber assault.

At the main path's end are a Felucian Warrior and a Yerdua Poison Spitter plant. Pick up the Warrior, toss him at the plant before it can spit poison at you, then enter the tunnel ahead. This leads into the interior of a huge mushroom.

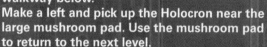

Before proceeding up the mushroom, carefully edge out to the spiral walkway and drop onto the walkway below.
Make a left and pick up the Holocron near the large mushroom pad. Use the mushroom pad to return to the next level.

Turn right and follow the curving pathway as it spirals upward. Block the Felucian Warriors as they attack, then counter with 'saber combos. Use Force Push and Force Grip to toss the Felucians over the walkway's side, sending them down the center of the mushroom structure.

Reach the large connecting bridge crossing the structure's center and take it up to the next level. At the bridge's top, turn so that the other bridge is just below you and to the left. Carefully hop down onto the bridge below.

Hop down onto the second bridge, leap over the Sith Holocron near the midway point, then jump onto the ledge just behind it.
Pick up the Holocron on the left before returning to the bridge containing the Sith Holocron.

Speed up the bridge and pick up the Sith Holocron. Make a right and use your increased damage to easily slice through the Felucian Warriors.

Turn right onto the small bridge and leap over the Poison Spitter's attacks. Dash up to the spitter and zap it with Force Lightning.

Go through the tunnel at the walkway's end and emerge in the Felucian wilderness. Exit the tunnel and make a beeline toward the Felucian Shaman. Dash past the other Felucians and concentrate on the Shaman first—it is much harder to eliminate the other Felucians while the Shaman is alive.

With the Shaman down, take out the other Felucians with strong lightsaber combos. String combos together to make one long, seamless assault on the Felucian pests.

From the small bridge, turn right and locate the Holocron hanging on the nearby pad. Double-jump and dash to grab it before returning to the little bridge.

As you emerge from the tunnel, make a sharp right. Pick up the Holocron behind the large curved spike before returning to the main path.

Finish walking up the little bridge and make a left. Head up the winding ledge and shove your Felucian foes over the ledge's side until you reach the Sith Holocron. Pick this up to gain a Health Drain Aura, then dash toward your next victim. Cut him down with a combo as your aura does its job.

Take advantage of your temporary boost and allow the Felucian Warriors to get near. When they do, string together a chain of combos and take them all out.

Fight past the next wave of Felucian Warriors using quick 'saber assaults. The area here is wide open, so you're more likely to get surrounded. If this happens, use Repulse to knock enemies away, then use Force Push or Force Throw to send foes flying into nearby walls and poisonous pits.

Farther down the path is another Felucian Shaman. Dash toward him, past his lackeys, and stop when you're within throwing range. Rip one of the nearby spikes from the ground and hurl it at the Shaman as you approach. As he tries to get up, fry him with Force Lightning, then turn on the other Felucians behind you.

Stop near the walkway's midpoint and turn left. Locate the Holocron high along the series of hanging pads. You can't jump from the first pad to the second, so double-jump onto the small forked structure on the ledge and immediately double-jump and dash onto the second highest hanging pad.

From there, jump up the series of pads until you reach the Holocron, then jump back down to the spiral ledge.

WOOKIEE WARNING

Don't step on the pustules on the ground as you navigate the Felucian wilderness. If you do, they'll blow up and inflict damage. Similarly, the pits in the ground are full of poisonous gas, so don't fall in!

SITH WISDOM

Keep an eye out for a Sith Holocron near the path's far right edge. It temporarily grants you unlimited energy.

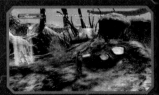

56

STAR WARS
FORCE
UNLEASHED

Hidden in a tunnel just off the path's far left side is another Holocron. Grab it and return to the main path. Before leaving this area, remove the large Sarlacc tooth by the exit tunnel to locate another Holocron.

Streak into the next tunnel and slam the Felucians with Force Push. Use Force Lightning–infused 'saber assaults to cut through your enemies.

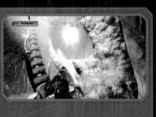

While in the tunnel, stop near the fork in the road. Leap through the broken wall at the center of the split path and grab the Holocron floating overhead.

Leave the tunnel and sprint down the path toward the next group of Felucians. Dash past the first few Felucian fiends and furiously fling yourself at the Felucian Shaman at the group's rear. Strike him down first.

After finishing off the Shaman, focus on the Chieftain. He's dangerous if left unchecked. Use 'saber combos and short bursts of Force Lightning to eliminate him.

Drop down into the next area—a pit where a Rancor beast waits. Blast it with Force Lightning as it trundles toward you, then dash away before it gets too close. Speed past the Felucian Warriors in your way. You can deal with them after you take down the Rancor.

Grab the Sith Holocron near the pit's center, and turn on the Rancor while your damage is increased. Hit it again with Force Lightning, then furiously slash away at its legs until you destroy it.

JEDI KNOWLEDGE

This is the first of four Rancors you must destroy to meet your bonus objective.

With the Rancor destroyed, take the fight to the Felucian Warriors in the pit. They're no match for you while your damage is increased, so have at them! Cut through them with your 'saber and clear the area of all hostiles.

There is a Holocron floating near the far left wall of the Rancor pit. Grab it before leaving.

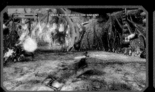 

Leave the Rancor pit and storm down the path at the far end. When the attacking Felucian Warriors lunge at you, speed past them and their Chieftain. Lock on to the Felucian Shaman at the rear of the pack and Force Push him away from the others. After you destroy him, turn on the rest of the Felucians and strike them down with a string of combos. The remaining Felucian Warriors can easily surround you, so use Force Repulse to shove them away.

Stop before entering the next tunnel and use Force Lightning on the Poison Spitter in the entrance's top left corner. Grab the Sith Holocron as you enter the tunnel to gain unlimited energy for a short time. Use Force Lightning to eliminate all enemies in your path as you speed through the tunnel.

Pick up the Holocron floating on the path's right fork, near the tunnel's midpoint.

Exit the tunnel in a long narrow chamber flanked by several large ledges. Inside this chamber are three more Rancors and plenty of Felucian fighters.

There are several Holocrons in the narrow chamber. Grab the first two by jumping onto the ledge on the far right.

As the first Rancor approaches, dash toward the ledge on the right wall. Lure it toward you and take cover behind the ledge's upward-turned lip. When the Rancor gets within striking distance, unleash a series of Force Lightning attacks. As your energy regenerates, fend off the Felucian fighters that come flying at you.

Knock them off your ledge with Force Push or Repulse, then resume your Lightning attacks on the Rancor beast. If the Rancor lifts its hand to swipe at you, double-jump high into the air to dodge the beast's assault.

Double-jump across the chamber onto the ledge along the far left wall. Dash toward the Felucian Shaman on the nearby precipice and crush him with 'saber strikes.

From here, lock on to the second Rancor and zap him with Force Lightning, just as you did the other. Fend off more Felucian fighters while your energy regenerates, and double-jump to avoid the Rancor's projectile attacks. Whittle down the Felucians' numbers before hopping down onto the main floor.

Lure the Rancors and remaining Felucians toward the large plant at the center of the chamber. Dash around the plant and let your enemies form a short line behind you. When they do, turn toward the plant's base and zap it with Force Lightning. This stimulates the plant's reflexes, and its curled arm lashes out at the nearby enemies!

Continue whacking the Rancor and Felucians with the plant's curled-up arms until you eliminate all foes.

JEDI KNOWLEDGE

After defeating the three Rancors in this narrow chamber, you've completed your first bonus objective.

With the first section of the narrow chamber clear, collect the Holocron on the far ledge. Double-jump onto the farthest ledge along the left wall and pick it up before continuing.

Pick up the Sith Holocron as you speed into the next area. There's another large whack plant near the area's center. Lure enemies toward it, then activate its thwacking reflexes to destroy them.

Pick up the final Holocron resting atop the base of the second whack plant.

The Last of the Council

In the next area, you find the Jedi Master meditating in front of a large open chasm containing a Sarlacc creature. Just as you approach for the final battle, Shaak Ti senses your presence and draws her 'saber. She's ready for you.

Immediately run up to Shaak Ti while blasting her with Force Lightning, then strike at her with your lightsaber. Avoid the pustules on the ground as you attack. If you step on them, you'll take damage and leave yourself open to Shaak Ti's attacks as you stumble back.

Dash away if she lunges toward you, then resume your assault with Force Lightning.

When Shaak Ti leaps into the air to execute a Ground Slam attack, leap into the air and dash to avoid her shock wave. Lunge at her immediately upon landing and hit her with several 'saber combos.

Block her counterattack, then zap her with Force Lightning again until he attempts to retreat. If she tries attacking you with her lightsaber, block again and back away to allow your energy to regenerate.

After taking some damage, Shaak Ti will summon a few Felucian fighters to fend you off. Focus on fighting these fiends first. Once they're gone, resume your assault on the Jedi.

If Shaak Ti surrounds herself in a red Force sphere, back away immediately. She creates a second Force sphere above her; leap away as she launches this at you. Sprint and dash around the arena until she stops hurling Force spheres at you, then dash toward her and hit her with Force Lightning again. If you engage her in a Force Lock, follow the onscreen commands to overpower her.

After taking even more damage, Shaak Ti will summon more Felucians. Fend off her second wave of Felucian fighters.

Eventually, Shaak Ti decides that she needs a change of scenery, so she leaps off the ledge's side and lands on the Sarlacc pit's bottom level. There she'll use the Sarlacc's tendrils as weapons, so be careful!

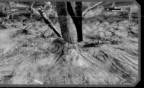

Resume the battle just as you did on the previous level. This time, however, Shaak Ti adds a new attack to her repertoire—she fires an underground tremor at you that surges along the ground like a shock wave. Leap over them just as you did her other attacks, then dash away.

Watch for the large Sarlacc tentacles to start flailing about. When they begin slamming down on the rest of the pit, dash away to either side and avoid their crushing attacks.

Continue attacking Shaak Ti and her Felucian comrades with Force Lightning and saber assaults until the onscreen prompts appear. Match the first few prompts to engage Shaak Ti face-to-face.

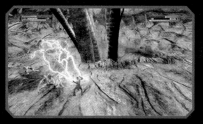

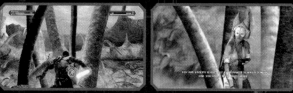

Realizing that she's about to perish, she leaps atop an overgrown tentacle whipping around in the background. Follow her onto this and block her attacks. Continue following the onscreen prompts until you bring down the final member of the Jedi Council. As expected, the defeated Jedi attempts to dissuade you from destroying her. Just as the Jedi before her, she tries convincing you that you could be so much more than a Sith Lord and Vader's puppet. Her words fall on deaf ears, and she falls into the chasm. Your job here is done.

MISSION DETAILS

Objective
Rejoin Darth Vader, challenge the Emperor, and fulfill your destiny.

Enemies Encountered
None

Collectibles Found
None

This chapter is a bridge between Acts 1 and 2 of *Star Wars: The Force Unleashed* and, more importantly, is a bridge between the prequel trilogy and the original trilogy. During Act 1, you were tasked with hunting down Jedi in accordance with Order 66, thus bringing a tidy end to the first three episodes of the *Star Wars* saga. During Act 2, you'll take part in setting up the last three episodes of the saga.

"We Will at Last Control the Galaxy!"

Having just defeated Jedi Master Shaak Ti, you communicate your success to Darth Vader via PROXY. He seems pleased—about as pleased as Darth Vader can seem, at least—and commands you to rendezvous with him on his flagship.

You can now stand together against the Emperor…and destroy him!

Betrayal!

You fly back to Vader's flagship to discuss the next phase of your plan. Little do you know that the Emperor's spies have followed you! All of Darth Vader's efforts to keep you a secret from the Emperor were wasted, as your existence has been discovered. Shortly after your arrival on the flagship, the Emperor's ship arrives, only it was not Vader who summoned him….

Just as the Emperor enters the chamber, Vader runs his lightsaber into your back. You've been betrayed! Still alive, you plead with your master to let you live. What of your plans to destroy the Emperor together?

Still, the Emperor's hold on Lord Vader is stronger than the sound of your pleas. The Emperor issues Vader an ultimatum: Either Vader destroys you to prove his loyalty or the Emperor will eliminate you both. Without hesitation, Lord Vader sends you through a glass pane and into the darkness of space….

"It Is Done."

Once the Emperor is satisfied that you're no longer a threat, he returns to his ship and departs. Little does he know that Vader's treachery is boundless. As he departed, the Emperor failed to notice a small droid zip out into space toward your lifeless floating body.

Moments later, the darkness begins to fade. You wake up on an operating table—alive! Lord Vader salvaged your body and rebuilt you.

Now that the Emperor believes you're history, you can resume your path to fulfill your destiny. Only this time, you and your master must alter the plan. The Emperor's sudden arrival proves that he cannot be easily deceived. If you and Vader are to destroy him, you must divert his attention away from your machinations. Your new task is to provide a large enough distraction to keep the Emperor preoccupied. Lord Vader believes that only a rebellion could sufficiently do this. Before you and Vader strike, you must raise an army. A rebel army. You must form a Rebel Alliance….

As always, PROXY is there by your side. He's pleased that you've survived, but only because he can continue to try and destroy you himself…to fulfill his programming, of course. He scuttles off to prep the *Rogue Shadow* for departure, but you're going to need a pilot.

With your next mission in hand, you must rescue Juno from captivity. Even in her weakened state, she's a better pilot than anyone else you can find. Besides, she's much more than a pilot to you.

EMPIRICAL LAB

Objective

Escape the ISS *Empirical*.

Bonus Objectives

Destroy all six remaining escape pods

Attain 150,000 Force Points

Locate 5 Holocrons

Enemies Encountered

Imperial Stormtrooper

Imperial Officer

Imperial EVO Trooper

Imperial interrogation Droid

Stormtrooper Commander

Shadow Trooper

Imperial Purge Trooper

MAP LEGEND

🔲 Holocron

61

As PROXY scampers off to prep your ship, you're left to escape the main lab and rescue your pilot, Juno. Before exiting the large glass chamber you're trapped in, look to the lab's right. Locate the large generator, located nearby in one of the room's niches; then use a Force Push to shatter the glass and escape the chamber. The lab immediately begins filling with deadly gas!

Speed through the gas toward the generator. Lift it out of the ground to deactivate the gas.

Pick up the Holocron in the small corridor leading out of the main lab.

Rush out of the main lab, through the small corridor, and into a long tunnel. Pick up the first Stormtrooper and hurl him at his squad mates. There are several more Stormtroopers down the hall to the right.

Turn right in the hall and use quick 'saber combos to slash past the Stormtrooper squad. Lightning-infused 'saber attacks and Force Push attacks are both extremely effective here. If any Stormtroopers remain out of reach, hit them with Force Lightning to clear the hall.

Make a right at the hall's end and enter the specimen lab.

Follow the catwalk as it wends right, and Force Push the three Imperials ahead. Lock on to the Imperial EVO Trooper at the room's rear and fry him with Force Lightning. His blaster is equipped with a special type of shock ammunition. If he blasts you with it, he can temporarily stun you and leave you defenseless. Cut him down, then leap onto the top of a specimen jar nearby.

On the bottom floor are more EVO Troopers. Lock on to them as they pass underneath you and stun them with Force Lightning. Jump down to the main floor of the specimen lab and engage the troopers with swift 'saber strikes. If an Imperial Interrogation Droid buzzes up to the battle, grip it and toss it at the troopers.

While in the specimen lab, go to the room below and pick up the Holocron to the entrance's left. Shatter the glass specimen container near the lab's far left corner and pick up the second Holocron before proceeding.

Force Push the lab's exit doors and enter another short hall. Make a left, then a right into a longer hallway occupied by more Stormtroopers. Wait at the entrance to the long hall and allow one of the Imperial EVO Troopers to get close. When he does, pick him up and throw him at the other troops down the hall.

If you miss the Trooper manning the turret down the hall, zigzag down the halls, dashing past the turret's blaster fire, then slash him to ribbons.

Follow the hall into the escape pod room. Use Force Lightning to activate all six pods. The active pods skitter into the closed hatch doors and get stuck. They soon burn out and explode, leaving no pods for the troopers to escape in.

The sixth pod reveals a Holocron after it's been activated. Grab it before you leave the room.

STAR WARS
THE FORCE UNLEASHED

Blast down the escape pod room's exit doors and pick up the Sith Holocron in the next passageway to replenish your health. Speed down the passage and zap the troopers with Force Lightning as you approach them.

Dash toward the hall's end and detonate the barrels next to the Stormtrooper Commander. If the blast doesn't destroy him, finish him off with quick combos. As you approach the hall's end, a Shadow Trooper appears. He'll probably disappear before you can reach him. Wait for him to reappear, and Force Grip him before he vanishes again. While he's in your grip, thrash him about to dispatch him.

Grab the Holocron in the corner of the hall. The barrels you previously detonated hid it.

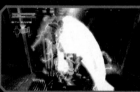

Backtrack to the hatch doors on the passage's right. Behind them are two EVO Troopers and one very large Imperial Purge Trooper. Force Push through the door and rush in. Don't try to use Force Lightning on the EVO Troopers; they'll immediately shield themselves. Use your lightsaber and other Force attacks to take them out.

Quickly finish off the two EVO Troopers, then turn on the Purge Trooper. He's much harder to take down than any other Imperial Trooper. Lash out at him with Lightning-infused 'saber attacks and Force combos.

WOOKIEE WARNING

While you fight in this room, stay away from the large electrical generators. If you touch them, they'll inflict major damage!

Force Push the doors at the end and enter Juno's holding room. Dash out to the intersection of the walkway ahead and use lightsaber combos to take out the nearest EVO Trooper.

Backtrack to the walkway's center and use Force Repulse to knock away the other soldiers. Destroy them as they attempt to get up, then dash to the walkway's far end, toward the last EVO Trooper. Slice him up, then drop to the level below.

Dodge the two large Purge Troopers on the bottom floor, then rush into the small room on the right. Eliminate the troopers in the room with Lightning-infused 'saber attacks, then take the fight to the two Purge Troopers outside.

Run out of the room and zap the Purge Troopers with Force Lightning. This stuns them and allows you to execute 'saber combos without fear of retaliation. Isolate one Purge Trooper while the other slowly lumbers toward you. As he does, use swift Lightning-infused 'saber attacks. If he raises his red shield, back away and hit him with Force Lightning to stun him again.

Pound away at the Trooper until you're facing the other Purge Trooper one-on-one. Dispatch him with electrified 'saber strikes and Force Lightning.

With the coast clear, lift the two large cylindrical reactors out of the ground to deactivate the laser gates on the level above.

Double-jump back up to the first level and rush into Juno's holding area. Decimate the Imperial Officers nearby and approach your pilot.

She's weak but alive. Even though Vader told her you were dead, she held on to hope. Hope that you were still alive. Hope that you would come for her. And you did.

6

MAP LEGEND

🔲 Holocron

MISSION DETAILS

Objective
Escape Cloud City with General Kota.

Bonus Objectives
Freeze 10 Imperials in carbonite

Attain 200,000 Force Points

Locate 5 Holocrons

Enemies Encountered
Imperial Senate Guard

Ugnaught

Imperial Stormtrooper

Imperial Jumptrooper

Scout Trooper

Uggernaught

Shadow Guard: Boss

"I'm no Jedi now. Not since...this."

Cloud City is not as vibrant as Felucia, but it is teeming with life nonetheless. Unfortunately, the life there is drunk and angry. General Kota is somewhere among the scum and villainy in the bars of Cloud City.

Meanwhile, on the distant planet of Kashyyyk, Captain Ozzik Sturn stands at high attention to welcome his newest prisoner. Princess Leia Organa, daughter of Senator Bail Organa, arrives and is taken into custody.

STAR WARS
THE FORCE UNLEASHED

"You will never find a more wretched hive of scum and villainy. We must be cautious."

-Obi Wan Kenobi,
Star Wars: Episode IV A New Hope

You arrive at the Cloud City bar and find Kota to be a shadow of his former self. His blind eyes have been bandaged, and he's drunk himself into a stupor. While you attempt to coerce him into joining you in creating a rebellion, an Imperial squad arrives.

Bar Fight!

Don't wait for the Stormtroopers to come to you. Instead, rush out into battle. Your mission is to get General Kota, so if he falls, you fail. Dash away from him to take on the Imperials by yourself. He'll follow behind you, but in his current state, he won't be as quick to join the battle.

The bar rests on a series of platforms; use these to your advantage. Toss the first Imperial Senate Guard over the platform's side to dispatch him quickly. By the time he hits the floor, other Imperials will practically be on top of you. Greet them with a string of lightsaber combos.

Double-jump onto the platform above the bar to find your first Holocron.

Before storming up to the bar's second area, break the glass advertisement on the right and carefully leap up to grab a Sith Holocron just beyond it. This increases your damage temporarily, so move quickly! Rush up to the next level and destroy the Guards there.

JEDI KNOWLEDGE

The Ugnaughts scuttling about the bar don't really pose much of a threat, but if you get rid of them, they'll count toward one of your Xbox 360 Achievements. If you really want to make things a bit more fun, try using Sith Punt attacks on them.

SITH WISDOM

As you stalk your prey throughout the facility, Force Grip the carbonite hoses and turn them on approaching enemies. Hit the floor fans with Force Lightning to send your enemies flying sky-high.

A Holocron is hidden in the center steam vent on the upper platform. Leap into the vent to retrieve it.

Walk into the hall on the second level and turn left. Blast the Imperial Senate Guard and Stormtrooper with Force Lightning. This should be enough to defeat the Trooper, but not the Senate Guard. Finish him with a combo or two before continuing down the hall.

The hall exits into a large circular walkway. Edge out to the hall's end and throw your lightsaber at the approaching Senate Guard. The lightsaber throw doesn't defeat him, but it slows him down and inflicts damage. Engage him with your 'saber to finish him off. While you do, Kota takes on a second Senate Guard that approaches from the left.

JEDI KNOWLEDGE

Kota will follow behind you through this entire mission, but if he dies, your mission is over.

Walk up the right path and follow it as it curves upward. Upon reaching the top, Force Throw the barrels along the walkway's edge at the approaching Imperials. The barrels contain carbonite, and they freeze the Imperials upon explosion.

Follow the walkway around and make a right down the far ramp. Fry your foes as they approach and trundle down to the wide-open area containing two large fans.

Examine the area's far right corner to find another Holocron.

Speed up the far ramp onto the walkways above the fan area. Dash down the catwalk and blast the enemies ahead with Force Lightning. The Stormtroopers don't stand much of a chance against your Lightning attacks, so weaken them with electricity and finish them with your 'saber.

65

After destroying the first two Stormtroopers on the catwalk, turn left and locate the Holocron floating high over the fan area. Double-jump toward it and dash above it so that you grab it as you fall back to the fan area below. After grabbing it, return to the catwalk.

When the second Uggernaught prowls toward you, back away and allow the surrounding Imperials to get close to it. As soon as they're all bunched up together, rush in and slash them all with Force Lightning 'saber strikes.

If the Imperials surround you while you crush the Uggernaught, dash away from the action to gain some distance, turn back on the group, and hit them all with Force Lightning. Approach them while they're stunned, then string together several combos to dispatch your remaining rivals.

Continue down the catwalk, passing under a large beam, and electrocute the Stormtroopers on the circular walkway ahead with Force Lightning. Dash at them with your 'saber swinging, then turn to the Imperial Jumptroopers floating nearby. Their jetpacks allow them to hover over the action and usually keep them safely away from your 'saber strikes, so lock on to them and fry them with Force Lightning to bring them within reach.

After destroying the second Uggernaught on the loading docks, a transport shuttle arrives with a whole new batch of bothersome bullies. A Shadow Guard appears with a small complement of Stormtroopers. Run into the niche in the docks' far left corner and grab the Sith Holocron inside. With your energy now temporarily unlimited, rush out toward the Shadow Guard and greet him with a Lightning combo.

After clearing the catwalk, backtrack to the large beam overhead. Double-jump onto it, then dash to the far end to find another Holocron. Be quick about it, though: There's a large thruster that slides back and forth along the beam. If you're in its way, it'll take you out.

Focus solely on the Shadow Guard while you energy is maxed out, and take full advantage of your temporary boost. Knock the Shadow Guard to the floor, then zap him with Force Lightning as you approach.

Carefully approach the second circular walkway and toss the first Stormtrooper over the catwalk's side. Dash at the Scout Trooper next and cut him down with a 'saber combo. Circle around the catwalk to make sure you've removed all foes. If any remain, they'll make life very difficult for you in the next area as they pepper you with blaster fire from above.

Run down the ramp to the loading docks and turn left immediately. The docks are swarming with Imperials. Jumptroopers, Senate Guards, Stormtroopers, and Scout Troopers are all joined by a new foe, the AT-ST-like Uggernaught. Dash left and meet the first Uggernaught head-on. Fry it with Force Lightning, then bring it down with Lightning-infused 'saber attacks.

The Jumptroopers eventually arrive and attempt to join the action. When they do, use Force Lightning again to bring them down. Eliminate them with combos, then turn back to the Shadow Guard.

Continue to zap and pound on the Shadow Guard until the onscreen commands prompt you to finish him off. Follow these as they appear onscreen and lay the final assault on your now-frail foe.

After taking down the first Uggernaught, turn on the Jumptroopers. Bring them down with Force Lightning and finish them off with combos. With the Jumptroopers dispatched, use Force Throw to hurl carbonite barrels at the approaching Senate Guards. The barrels dispatch them quickly and help complete your first bonus objective.

With the battle over, General Kota still tries to convince you that defeating the Empire is a fool's errand. Unmoved by his doubt, you insist that the Empire must be opposed. Reluctantly, Kota decides to help.

STAR WARS
THE FORCE
UNLEASHED

KASHYYYK

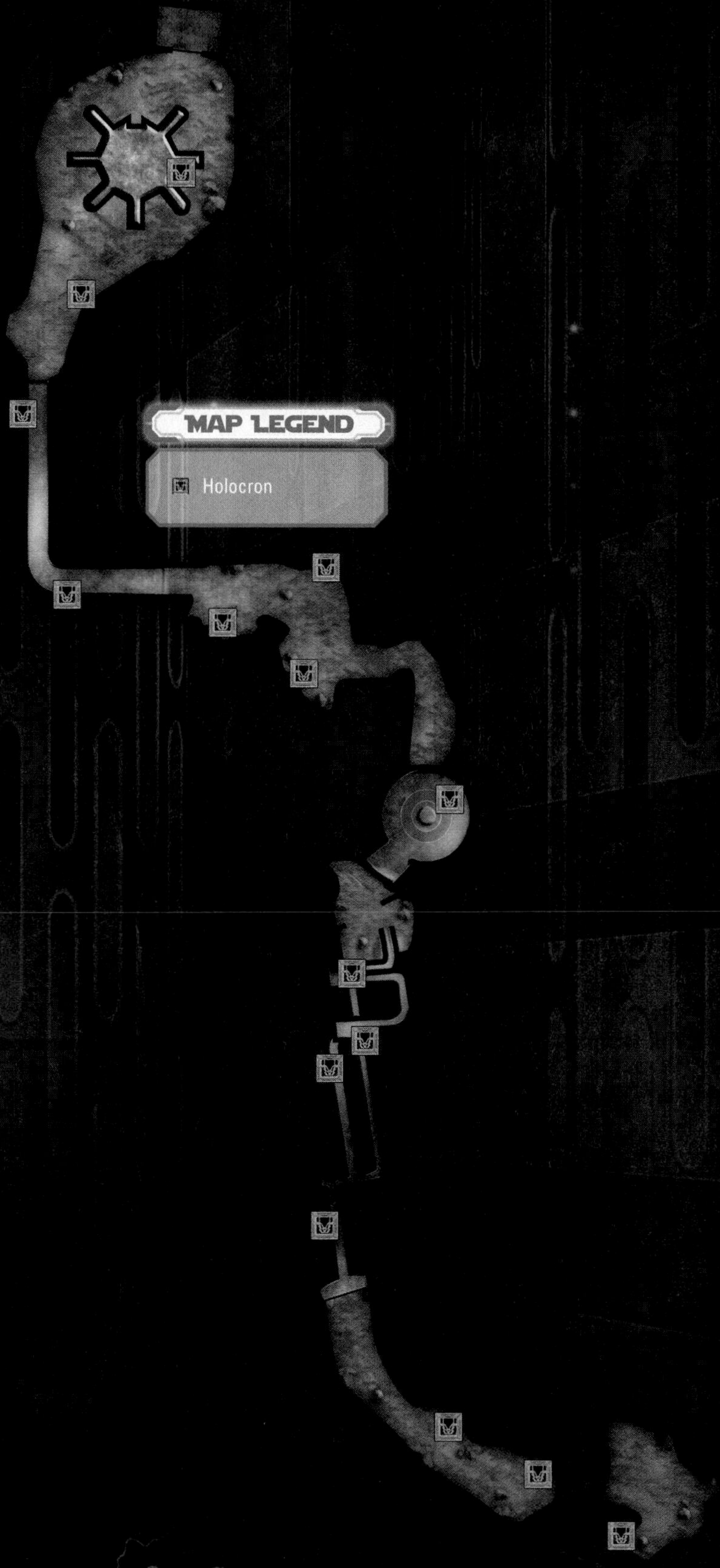

MISSION DETAILS

Objective
Prove yourself to Kota's Senate contact by retrieving a mysterious object on Kashyyyk.

Bonus Objectives
Destroy the Imperial Comm Tower

Attain 300,000 Force Points

Locate 15 Holocrons

Enemies Encountered
Imperial Stormtrooper

Imperial Incinerator Trooper

AT-KT

Shadow Trooper

Stormtrooper Commander

Scout Trooper

Imperial EVO Trooper

Imperial Jumptrooper

Imperial Senate Guard

Imperial Royal Guard

Imperial Purge Trooper

Imperial Interrogation Droid

Captain Ozzik Sturn: Boss

MAP LEGEND

 Holocron

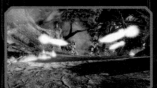
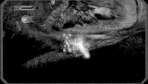

Back on the *Rogue Shadow*, General Kota's drunken stupor has started to wear off. As his haze fades, one of his contacts in the Senate sends a communication. He doesn't say much other than the name of your new destination. Your next stop is Kashyyyk.

While you approach the planet, Kota remains tight-lipped about the purpose of your trip to Kashyyyk. He mentions that his contact in the Senate needs something from the Wookiee planet. If you get it, he might be persuaded to help you against the Empire. But the question still remains....

"Get What?"

There's no sense in standing around wondering what you're looking for. The war-torn Kashyyyk landscape sprawls out ahead of you, inviting just one more fighter, you, into battle.

Before leaving your landing area, turn left and locate the Holocron sitting behind the large tree stump. Grab it, then venture forward.

Just ahead, you come across a small dilapidated hut. Its walls are decorated with a strange symbol resembling a bird inside a circle. Fires rage just outside the hut, but amid the chaos and destruction, you sense something familiar. Something dark. Something sad.

You ignore Kota's warnings and allow your curiosity to get the better of you. Rather than press on into Kashyyyk as Kota suggests, you step inside the hut, where you're surrounded by a familiar force. Then he steps out of the shadows. His face is hidden by a low cowl, but his voice is familiar. "I never wanted any of this for you," he says. "I'm sorry, son." And with that, he fades back into the hut's ruins.

"For over a thousand generations, the Jedi Knights were the guardians of peace and justice in the Old Republic. Before the dark times, before the Empire."

-Obi-Wan Kenobi,
Star Wars: Episode IV A New Hope

Your father's apparition shakes you up a bit, but you're able to continue. Ahead you can see three Imperial Incinerator Troopers burning down what's left of the Kashyyyk wilderness. When they see you, they activate their protective shields and make a beeline for you.

Their shields protect them from Force Grip attacks, so use Lightning-infused 'saber strikes to cut through their shields. After you burst their protective bubbles, unleash a series of combos to decimate the fiery fiends.

WOOKIEE WARNING

Do not allow these fiery foes to surround you! If they do, you'll be Apprentice flambé!

After destroying the incinerator troops, examine the hollow tree trunk on the path's right side. A Holocron sits behind it, and another Holocron floats high above a stump on the path's right. Hop onto the stump, then double-jump to grab the Holocron.

Farther down the path, an AT-KT walker guards the entry into the Imperial fort ahead. Zigzag past the walker's blaster fire as you run up to it. When you're within striking distance, unleash a devastating current of Force Lightning and stun the overgrown mechanical monstrosity.

Creep between its legs and lash out at them with Lightning 'saber swipes to chop down the AT-KT. After weakening it, the final assault prompts appear. Follow them as they appear onscreen to scrap the meta giant.

With the metal monster minced, the fort's main gates are easily accessible... after you destroy the two remaining guards manning turrets, and a small complement of Stormtroopers. Zigzag up to the gates to avoid the blaster fire and pick up the Sith Holocron on the path's left side.

STAR WARS
THE FORCE
UNLEASHED

The Sith Holocron augments your damage temporarily. Take out the oops on the ground first, then dash to the path's sides to fry the troopers anning turrets. Lock on to them and unleash a blast of Force Lightning dispatch them quickly.

Open the fort gates with Force Grip, then creep into the Imperial ronghold.

Follow the walkway until you reach a small incline with several red crates scattered on it. Toss the Stormtroopers over the catwalk's side or detonate the red crates to release the steam jets on the unsuspecting troopers.

Dash past the Imperials at the intersection at the walkway's end and pick up the Sith Holocron on the right. With the Sith Holocron's invincibility buff, turn on the remaining troopers and go berserk! They can't hurt you, so don't worry about performing careful combos. Just demolish them!

Immediately after entering the fort, carefully hop onto the strut ledge on the left. Edge out to the strut's end and pick up the Holocron.

The Sith Holocron on e immediate left of the trance will replenish ur health. If you're w on health, grab it. not, save it for later. se the small force-field rricades to cover ur approach down e ramp. As you sneak behind the barricades, use Force Push to knock emies off the ramp.

There are two Holocrons located on the upper catwalks. Once you collect the Sith Holocron, turn around to see the Holocron hidden behind the pipe. Another Holocron is hidden behind the large pipe at the end of the ramp. Leap off the catwalk to get the Holocron.

SITH WISDOM

To complete your primary bonus objective, zap the two grates along the center comm tower with Force Lightning. The first is high up on the tower, you'll only be able to reach it from the top right catwalk. The other is low on the tower. Reach it from the low, left catwalks.

SITH WISDOM

There's a sniper on a high, far ledge on the fort's left side. Force Throw him off his perch to dispose of him. Otherwise, he'll pick you off from his ledge as you penetrate the fort.

There is another Holocron on the left strut farther down the path. Double-jump onto the large beam above the catwalk, then carefully hop onto the strut on the left. Creep to the strut's end to grab the Holocron, then backtrack to the main catwalk.

Force Grip the doors and swing them open, then dash inside toward the small force fields. Force Push the soldiers in your way, then get cover behind the force field. Edge away from the field to get a better angle on the soldiers, then, from the safety of your cover, electrocute them with Force Lightning.

Dash out from behind your cover and strike down the remaining Imperials.

69

Double-jump to get the Sith Holocron floating above the entrance to the next room, then enter. Run into Ozzik Sturn's personal quarters and throw your lightsaber at the Imperial Royal Guard inside. Sprint up to him after your 'saber returns and slam him around the room with Force Push attacks and Force Throw.

Zap him with Force Lightning when his health is nearly depleted, and a series of onscreen commands will appear. Follow them to finish off the Imperial Royal Guard.

There is another Holocron in one of the glass trophy cases.

Enter the next room to find what you're looking for. As you do, you spy a young woman with a droid by her side. She stares out into the Kashyyyk wilderness as if looking for something or someone. When she hears you enter her room, she assumes you're one of the Emperor's assassins.

The young lady is Leia Organa. Even though you're there to rescue her, she's unwilling to leave the planet while it is under Imperial occupation. She's concerned that if the Empire completes the Skyhook transport, it will begin to shuttle Wookiee slaves off the planet. If you promise to destroy the Skyhook, however, she'll willingly leave. Your next task is clear....

After being automatically lifted to the forest floor, slowly venture down the path ahead. Imperial snipers perched on nests flank the path. Pick up the Sith Holocron to gain temporary invincibility, then dash forward. Slash through the soldiers with Force Lightning 'saber combos, then use the Wookiee cage on the right to double-jump into the first nest and destroy the sniper there.

Before leaving the first sniper nest, pick up the Holocron inside.

From the safety of the sniper nest, use Force Lightning attacks to whittle down the number of soldiers on the ground. Jump back to the forest floor and release the Wookiees from their cage. Strike down any remaining soldiers nearby, allowing the Wookiees to move ahead without you.

Stalk down the trail, behind the freed Wookiees, and destroy the next sniper nest with Force Grip. Free the batch of Wookiees from the cage or the trail's right.

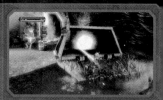

Free the Wookiees from the third cage, then grab the Holocron inside.

Let the Wookiees engage the remaining enemies while you focus on eliminating the sniper in the final nest. As your furry friends fight their foes on the forest floor, double-jump into the air, lock on to the sniper, and fry him with Force Lightning.

Once the coast is clear, move a large boulder into place just below the last nest. Use it to double-jump into the nest and grab the Holocron inside.

Carefully approach the sliding doors at the trail's end and let the Wookiees storm into the hall. Pick off the Stormtroopers while the Wookiees work on the Shadow Guard. After you eliminate the other soldiers, join the Wookiees in destroying the Shadow Guard.

 SITH WISDOM

The prison containment fields are just as deadly as laser gates. Throw enemies into these to fry them instantly.

STAR WARS
FORCE
UNLEASHED

To remove the containment field, Force Grip and pull the cable running down the hall's left side.

Before running out into the Skyhook perimeter, grab the Holocron on the trail's right side, just above a large tree branch.

To dispatch the Stormtrooper manning the turret, quickly Force Push him into the next containment field, then detach the cable on the left to remove the field. In the next area, toss the nearby crates at the enemies farther down the passage. Dash toward them as they try getting up and finish them off with your lightsaber.

Continue down the passage until you encounter a Purge Trooper. Rush him while stunning him with Force Lightning and cut into him with Lightning-infused 'saber attacks. He's got a mean, and deadly accurate, arm cannon. If you approach him without stunning him first, he'll unload on you and keep you pinned to the floor with his booming blasts.

To deactivate the Skyhook's tractor beam, you must remove seven traction hooks surrounding the building. Unfortunately, they're all guarded by Stormtroopers and Purge Troopers. Rather than try removing the traction hooks (which resemble long lightning rods) while the troopers pick you off, remove the troopers first. Zigzag toward the closest traction hook and zap the Stormtroopers with Force Lightning. Then Force Throw the Stormtroopers at the Purge Troopers.

With the surrounding troopers gone, focus on the Purge Trooper. Slice him up with Lightning-infused 'saber strikes to bring him down swiftly. If he attempts to counter your attacks, back away and stun him with Force Lightning, then resume your assault.

SITH WISDOM

If you're having a hard time against the Purge Trooper, dash past him and pick up the Sith Holocron. This grants you unlimited energy. Use it to fry the overgrown Trooper.

After you remove the enemies in the immediate vicinity of the traction hook, use Force Grip to lift the traction hook out of its slot to destroy it.

Destroy the turret near the next field with a blast of Force Lightning, then deactivate the field like you did the others. Hurl the nearby crates at the next Purge Trooper to deplete his health, then speed up to him with your Lightning unleashed. Finish off the Trooper with Lightning 'saber strikes, then exit the passage.

There is another Holocron floating near the Skyhook building's far right wall. Nab it as you move from traction hook to traction hook.

There are two Holocrons hidden in prison cells in the Slave Halls; there's one in the first section, and one in the second section.

The next area is home to the Skyhook building. The large, circular area is extremely well guarded by several Purge Troopers, Jumptroopers, and an AT-KT walker.

After you remove the first hook, Captain Ozzik Sturn decides to take matters into his own hands. He exits the Skyhook facility in a large walker and opens fire on you. Luckily, you're much faster than the mechanical menace, so speed away and repeat the hook removal process—destroy nearby enemies, then safely remove the hook—with the remaining six hooks.

SITH WISDOM

Use the Sith Holocrons littered about the area to augment your abilities while you speed from hook to hook. The temporary boosts will make things much easier on you.
You can also release the Wookiees from their cages to help you fight off the Imperials.

After removing all traction hooks, engage Sturn in his walker. Use any remaining Sith Holocrons to augment your abilities, such as unlimited energy, and blast the AT-KT with a surge of Force Lightning. Even if you're out of Sith Holocrons, use your Force Lightning as you circle around the machine and keep its blasters from locking on to you. If you run out of energy while you zap it, dash away from it and allow your energy to replenish.

Return to the fight once your energy is full and assault it again. Continue picking away at its health like this until you can unleash your final assault by matching the onscreen commands, finishing it off.

With the traction hooks destroyed and Sturn out of the way, the Skyhook facility breaks down and the Wookiees are once again free.

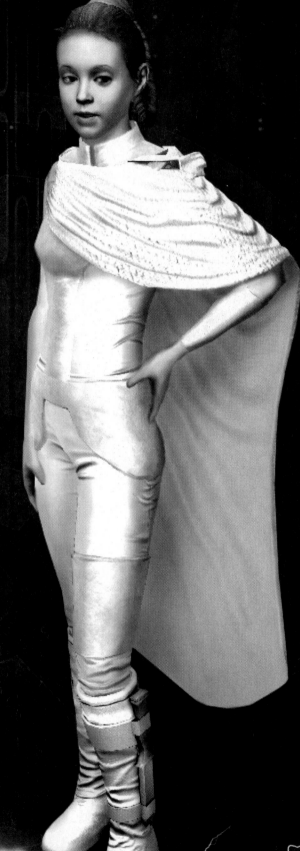

STAR WARS
THE FORCE
UNLEASHED

IMPERIAL FELUCIA

MISSION DETAILS

Objective
Find and rescue Senator Bail Organa.

Bonus Objectives
Release the Sarlacc

Attain 375,000 Force Points

Locate 15 Holocrons

Enemies Encountered
Imperial Stormtrooper

Imperial EVO Trooper

Imperial Purge Trooper

Imperial Incinerator Trooper

AT-ST

Dark Felucian Warrior

Dark Felucian Shaman

Dark Felucian Chieftain

Rancor

Yerdua Poison Spitter

Bull Rancor: Boss

Corrupted Maris Brood: Boss

MAP LEGEND

Holocron

73

A

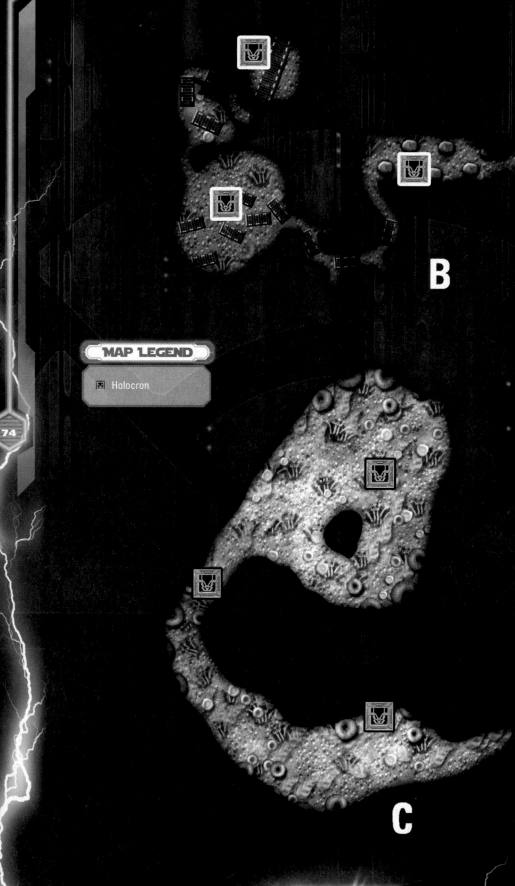

MAP LEGEND

Holocron

B

C

"Your master would be disgusted...."

Down on the Felucian surface, all is not well. Senator Bail Organa is being held captive by Jedi Master Shaak Ti's old apprentice, Maris Brood. Since her master's demise, Brood has become a dark, angry creature. She's resigned herself to giving in to the dark side, and she holds Organa as a prize for Darth Vader should he ever visit Felucia.

She tells Organa that if he attempts to escape, she'll feed him to her new pet—a monstrous Bull Rancor beast!

Return to Felucia

You land on Felucia to find that Brood's Felucian Warriors are fiercely engaged in battle with the Imperials at the Imperials' base camp. Watch the action for a bit. Let them pummel each other before you leap into battle.

Drop into the Imperial base camp and rush the Imperials on the left. Dash into their ranks and assault the group with a lightsaber combo. Leap onto the shuttle's top and take cover behind its fin. From there, use Force Lightning to fry the enemies or throw them into the explosive pustules on the floor.

After destroying the Imperials nearby, hop down and put 'saber to Felucian flesh. Slice through the small group of Felucian Warriors that appear, then use Force Lightning 'saber attacks to crush the Imperial Purge Trooper near the bridge.

There are three Holocrons in this area. One is floating high above a Sarlacc tooth; use the stacked crates to reach it. Another is hidden inside a Sarlacc tooth near the bridge to the next area. The final Holocron in this area is hidden at the end of a side path to the right of your starting point.

Slowly creep up the bridge and unleash a blast of Force Lightning at the Stormtroopers manning the turrets. Stalk across the bridge and throw the red-ringed barrels at the enemies ahead. Use the small protective force fields to shield you from incoming fire as you cross the bridge.

Toss troopers over the bridge's side until you reach the Purge Trooper near the end. Edge out to the side of a force field and zap the Purge Trooper with Force Lightning. Rush out from your cover and swat at the stunned Trooper with several Lightning-infused 'saber strikes.

Take out the final Purge Trooper at the bridge's end, just as you did the other—stun him with Lightning as you approach, then cut through him with Lightning-infused lightsaber attacks.

Before jumping down into the next area, locate the Holocron floating over a mushroom pad high along the right cliff. Jump up the mushroom pads to reach it. From here, carefully jump out to the flower pads on the left, then double-jump and dash to the Sith Holocron (invincibility) on the area's far left side.

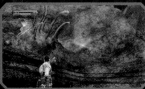

Drop to the area below and take advantage of your temporary invincibility. Dash around the bottom floor while invincible and cut through all enemies. Their attacks can't hurt you, so feel free to stay out in the open as you hack away.

With the ground floor clear, locate the troopers on the far right cliff. Lock on to them and pull them down from their perches.

As you approach this area's far end, a rock slide blocks the path ahead and an Imperial support ship drops an AT-ST behind you!

Before taking on the AT-ST, double-jump from the left ledge to the right ledge, where a Holocron can be found next to the rock slide. Follow that ledge back through the tunnels until you reach the second Holocron high on the cliff side.

Jump onto the tower and slice up the three troopers at the top. With the coast clear, lock on to the stabilizer generator at the tower's rear and hit it with Force Lightning to charge it.

While here, stand just in front of the reactor and turn around to face the Sarlacc. Shimmy up the connecting cable a bit, then double-jump and dash toward the Holocron at the cable's other end. There's another Holocron on the other side of this tower.

Turn on the AT-ST and fry its circuits with your Force Lightning. Circle around it as you blast it, then creep between its legs and thwack at them with your Lightning-buffed lightsaber. Dash away from the machine to avoid its stomp attack, then resume your electric attacks once your energy is fully replenished. Follow the onscreen commands as they appear to unleash a series of final blows that will destroy the oversized tin can.

If the battle with the AT-ST doesn't dislodge some of the rubble and open a pathway under the rock slide blockade, use Force Push on the wall to progress. Go through it and into the next area where another AT-ST awaits. Rush the machine and short-circuit it with a Force Lightning blast. Dash past the stunned walker and use two quick blasts of Force Lightning to eliminate the Poison Spitters near the area's rear.

With the Spitters out of the way, return to the AT-ST and assail it with Force Lightning attacks. Finish if off with a final assault, then enter the next area.

Carefully approach the Sarlacc pit and turn right. On the far right is an Imperial stabilizing tower; to the left is a long narrow bridge. Move left to lure out the Stormtroopers near the stabilizing tower. When the ground units charge you, either stand behind one of the force-field generators or move beyond reach of the fire coming from the stabilizing tower—just don't allow the ground forces and the troopers on the tower to combine fire on you!

Allow them to reach you and greet them with quick combos. Use the force fields to protect you from their incoming fire while you demolish the attacking troops. After defeating the first wave, move from field to field, cutting through enemies until you reach the stabilizing tower.

To release the Sarlacc and complete your first bonus objective, step onto the ledge at the tower's front and lock on to the chains attached to the Sarlacc's tentacles. Throw your lightsaber at the chains to cut them—one on each stabilizing tower—and free the Sarlacc.

Leave the stabilizing tower and dash back to the bridge. Use the force fields to cover your approach. Allow the squad of troopers to cross the bridge and approach you while you wait behind the force field closest to the bridge. When the troopers get close enough, pick them up with the Force and throw them into the Sarlacc pit.

Dash across the bridge to the connecting platform at the center of the Sarlacc pit. As you go, use powerful 'saber attacks to knock enemies into the pit.

Turn right at the connecting platform and cross the bridge. Destroy the soldiers on your way to the tower and charge the generator just as you did before. Return to the connecting platform, cross the third bridge, and do the same with the third and final stabilizing tower.

STAR WARS
THE FORCE UNLEASHED

Return to the connecting platform and hop onto the elevator pad inside. Ride it down into the Sarlacc's body.

Before you take the elevator, collect the Holocron above the bridge to the left of the elevator. Walk out onto the bridge, turn around, and jump above it to reach the Holocron. As soon as you get off the elevator, pick up the Holocron on the path's right.

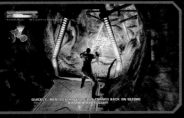

Follow the path deeper into the Sarlacc's stomach. Ignore the Sarlacc hairs; they'll glance off you harmlessly. When you come upon a Sarlacc trap (one of the large holes in the wall), seal it by activating a nearby Imperial stand with your Force Lightning.

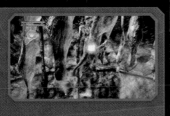

At the end of the hairy path is a large pit with a Holocron floating high overhead. Double-jump into the air and dash at the Holocron to get it.

Drop into the pit and through the hole at the bottom to enter the Sarlacc's lung room. Once again, carefully navigate the hairy tunnels, stopping only to activate the Imperial sealing stands.

WOOKIEE WARNING

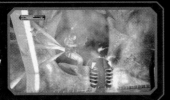

If you don't stop to seal the holes in the tunnel, they'll suck you in and chew you up before they spit you out.

Rush out of the hairy tunnel and into the breathing chamber. The Sarlacc's breaths can create long gale-force gusts of wind. If you step into the chamber while it exhales, you'll be thrown against the far wall. Wait for the Sarlacc to inhale, then rush into the chamber and hide behind one of the pillars there. Stay in the lit area to avoid being blasted with a gust of wind.

Stay behind the pillar, fighting off Felucian Warriors as they approach, then hold position while the wind blows. When the wind dies down, rush out of your cover and up the chamber to another well-lit pillar. Hold position there until another inhalation, then dash to the next pillar.

7

Use Force Repulse to float in place while hiding behind the pillars. When the wind dies down and Felucians come to attack, unleash it!

Dash right as you move from pillar to pillar, and pick up the Holocron along the far right wall.

At the end of the breathing chamber is the lung cavern. Step inside and a gust of wind will blast you out of the Sarlacc and into a Rancor graveyard.

The graveyard is crawling with Felucians. Fend off the first wave of foes, then locate the Felucian Shaman nearby.

Focus your fury on the Felucian Shaman and eliminate him quickly. That will make the other remaining Felucians easier to destroy.

Use the mushroom pads on the right to reach a Holocron floating high above the ground.

Trek deeper into the graveyard until you reach an ornery Rancor beast. Stand clear of its destructive path and Force Grip some of the explosive plants nearby; hurl these at the beast. Follow your plant-pelting by rushing the beast and frying it with Force Lightning.

Circle around behind the beast, zapping it with Force Lightning, then leap into the air and bombard it with Force Lightning and 'saber attacks.

Weaken the animal, then finish it off when the onscreen commands appear.

After destroying the Rancor, leap up to the highest steppe. Use the steppe as a platform from which to do a double-jump dash to reach the Holocron floating overhead.

Storm up the trail and speed past the two Felucian Chieftains. Electrocute the two poison-spitting plants on the path's right with Force Lightning, then turn back on the nearest Chieftain and zap him with Force Lightning.

Pick him up while he's stunned, then throw him at the other Chieftain. Carefully approach the two entangled Felucians and finish them off with a string of lightsaber combos.

The next area is home to another Rancor. Strafe around the beast while you zap it with Force Lightning, and destroy it just as you did its comrade.

With the Rancor gone, the only enemies left are a few Felucian forest dwellers. They're no match for a few quick 'saber combos. String your attacks together and use Repulse to knock them away if they attempt to surround you.

Veer left and examine the area behind a large plant. There you'll find another Holocron.

Before running headlong into the next tunnel, stop to eliminate the poison-spitting plants on the tunnel's left entrance. Rush into the tunnel with your Force Lightning leading the way and take out the Felucian Shaman.

STAR WARS
THE FORCE
UNLEASHED

Once he's down, turn on his cronies and stun them with Force Lightning. While stunned, take your 'saber to them and cut through them with lightning-infused 'saber attacks. Clear the tunnel and follow it to the end.

The Battle with Brood...

In the next area, you find Senator Organa. But he's not alone....

Though she may have been only an apprentice, Maris Brood is highly skilled with her light-tonfas. As you enter her arena, she appears behind you with her pet Bull Rancor by her side. The battle with Brood will not be easy. It won't be fair either, as you'll have to face her and her pet at the same time.

Focus on the beast while Brood is invisible. Hit it with Force Lightning and lure it toward you. Dash away when it begins to slowly lumber toward you, and speed to one of the arena's far walls.

Allow the Bull Rancor to rush you. When it gets close, dash out of the way and let its momentum deliver it into the arena's wall. This temporarily stuns the beast and grants you an opportunity to circle behind it and slash at it with your lightsaber.

While behind it, use Lightning-infused 'saber strikes to inflict maximum damage. If Brood appears nearby, dash away before she can pounce on you, then lure the Bull Rancor away again.

 ## SITH WISDOM

Don't bother trying to fight Brood while her Rancor is still alive. You'll waste energy and time and will leave yourself open to Rancor attack.

Continue luring the beast away from its master and leading it into the arena walls. While it's stunned, pummel away at it until the onscreen commands appear; then deliver your final assault.

After you defeat her pet, Brood decides to come out and play. The battle with her is pretty straightforward. You'll need to block her attacks, counter, and move around the arena evasively. If Brood disappears, raise you lightsaber to blocking position. When she reappears and attacks, her blows will automatically be deflected.

After deflecting her blows, seize the opportunity and counter with combos of your own.

If you engage her in a Lightsaber Lock, rapidly follow the onscreen command to overpower her, then run your 'saber through her while she's on the ground.

Continue blocking Brood's attacks and countering with attacks of your own. If she moves away, raise your block to deflect her tonfa toss, then resume your assault. Once she's been damaged enough and her health is nearly at 50 percent, use Force Lightning and Force Shield to deplete her health even faster.

Follow the commands as they appear onscreen to lay down a series of final blows. With Maris Brood under your lightsaber, it becomes clear that she can still be saved. Rather than strike her down for good, you decide to let her go.

Reunited with General Kota, Senator Organa expresses his concerns over waging war against the Empire. Organa knows another Senator who has spoken out against the Emperor, but in order to rally troops, you must show them that the Emperor is vulnerable and must instill a sense of hope in the dissidents. Organa sets off to meet with his Senator comrades while you decide which Imperial facility to target first.

IMPERIAL RAXUS PRIME

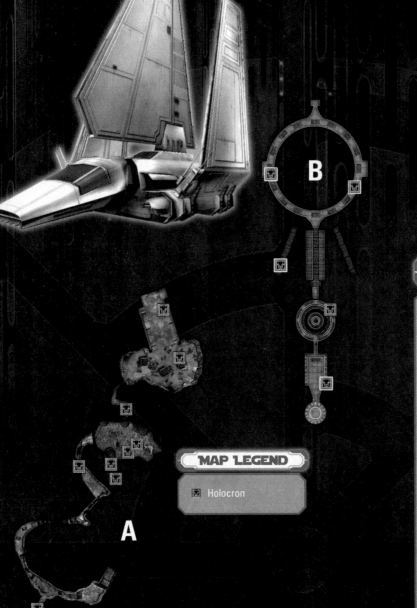

B

C

A

MAP LEGEND

🔲 Holocron

MISSION DETAILS

Objective
Destroy the Orbital Shipyard.

Bonus Objectives
Destroy the Imperial tractor beam tower

Attain 430,000 Force Points

Locate 15 Holocrons

Enemies Encountered
Rodian Heavy Defender

Rodian Ripper

Jawa

Imperial Purge Trooper

AT-ST

Imperial Stormtrooper

Scout Trooper

GNK Power Droid

Imperial Officer

Imperial EVO Trooper

Imperial Jumptrooper

Stormtrooper Commander

PROXY: Boss

Imperial Star Destroyer

TIE Fighter

STAR WARS
FORCE
UNLEASHED

"You Still Serve Me."

ack on the *Rogue Shadow,* you communicate your success with Darth ader. Though he's satisfied with your progress, he senses conflict in ou. Your feelings for your new allies grow while your allegiance to the ark side remains. Juno walks in on you while you seek Vader's counsel, nd though she's disappointed in you for remaining loyal to him, she emains loyal to you.

Perhaps she sees good in you still. Perhaps she sees through your old exterior and sees the feelings you have for her. Regardless, she nows that sooner or later, *you* will decide the fate of the Rebellion, ot Darth Vader. And when you do, she wants you to remember her truggles. For now, however, Darth Vader has given you the information you need to rally the Rebels. Your next target is the Star Destroyer onstruction facility on Raxus Prime....

Take advantage of your Health Drain Aura and run up to the Rodians. Allow your aura to suck the life out of them, then finish them off with your 'saber. After striking them down, use Force Push to bend the girders blocking the path ahead.

A Rodian Heavy Defender opens fire on you when you pass the twisted metal, so zigzag-dash past his fire and run your 'saber through him. Two quick combos should do the trick. Approach the other Rodians on the path ahead and use Force Push or Force Throw to knock them off the ledge.

Return to Raxus Prime

Once on Raxus Prime's urface, hop down to e lower level and mmediately destroy the odian Heavy Defender your way.

Double-jump and dash across the broken bridge ahead and keep your sights locked on the enemies on the other side.

Immediately upon landing, knock the Rodians off the cliff with a strong 'saber combo or Force Push attacks. Double-jump at the Rodian Heavy Defender on the far ledge and do the same. The faster you eliminate them, the less damage you will take from incoming fire.

Double-jump onto the ledge on the right, then double-jump and dash to the far left ledge. Turn right on the ledge, into a small passage and down a short shaft. Take the Holocron from the Jawa inside, then hop back out.

SITH WISDOM

If you've taken damage from the Rodians' assaults, pick up the Sith Holocron on the fallen beam to replenish your health.

Storm down the trash-riddled path and crush the Ripper in your way. Veer left and pick up the Sith Holocron to get a Health Drain Aura.

Dash across the fallen beam to the next ledge, far across the chasm. Sith Punt the Jawa and decimate his Rodian friend with quick 'saber combos.

Go into the cave on the path's left to find another Jawa guarding a Holocron.

While on the ledge with the Jawa and Rodian Ripper, hit the metal wall with Force Push blasts to bring it down. Behind it is another Holocron—and another Jawa.

Drop to the left ledge and destroy the Rodian there. Turn to the transportation tunnel surrounded in a blue glow, then double-jump and dash inside.

The next Holocron is floating in the center of the tunnel entrance. You get it as you enter.

At the tunnel's end is a large wide-open area with Rodians and Imperial Purge Troopers engaged in fierce battle. Platforms line the battleground's curving right wall; several Rodians are stationed at key positions throughout the grounds.

As you exit the tunnel, grab the Sith Holocron on the immediate left and drop down into the battlegrounds. Take advantage of your unlimited energy and dash up the platforms on the right, blasting enemies with Force Lightning.

Drop to the main battleground floor and engage the three Purge Troopers there. Blast them all with Force Lightning, then dash away before they can slam you.

There are three Holocrons in this area. Two are readily visible from the ground floor. They're floating above the surrounding platforms; you can easily reach them by double-jumping and dashing. The third is hidden inside a small cave that is accessible only after the Rodian reinforcements storm out of it.

Let the Rodians wear down the Imperials, then dash to the Sith Holocron near the left corner of the main battleground floor. It sits just behind the AT-ST walker that drops in from above. Use the Sith Holocron's invincibility to finish off the Purge Troopers and savagely slash away at the AT-ST's legs.

Use short bursts of Force Lightning and Lightning-infused 'saber strikes to deplete the walker's energy. When the onscreen prompts appear, follow them immediately to crush the infernal machine.

As you fight the walker, an Imperial drop ship lands near the far cliff side. Hurl the Imperial Stormtroopers over the cliff, then turn around and hop up the series of metal planks lining the area's left wall. Turn right into the tunnel.

Pick up the Holocron in the tunnel as you go.

The next area is similar to the previous battleground. Platforms line the area's surrounding wall, and a large Imperial drop ship sits on the far left. As you drop to the platform below, grab the Sith Holocron to gain invincibility for a short period of time. While invincible, drop to the main battleground floor and eliminate the Purge Trooper. As you fight him off with Lightning-infused 'saber attacks, also string combos to destroy the Stormtroopers at his side.

After you destroy the Purge Trooper and your invincibility wears off, dash back to the area's far left corner and pick up another Sith Holocron. This one increases your damage. Double-jump onto the platform directly above you, destroy the Scout Trooper, then dash toward the area's far right side. As you approach the next Purge Trooper, zap him with Force Lightning to destroy him.

Double-jump onto the far right ledge and destroy the Purge Trooper perched there. If your damage increase wears off while you fight him, strafe around as you electrocute him with Force Lightning to avoid taking damage. Continue moving up the platforms on the right, decimating Stormtroopers as you go.

There is a Holocron floating high above the center junk tower. Double-jump to reach it.

STAR WARS
FORCE
UNLEASHED

After you clear the battleground of all enemies, the drop ship opens to reveal an AT-ST walker and a large group of Imperial soldiers. Grab the Sith Holocron on the arena's far right end and gain a damage-increase boost. While your damage is increased, speed out toward the AT-ST walker lumbering from the drop ship and blast it with Force Lightning.

One sustained Force Lightning blast should be enough to prompt the final assault commands. Finish off the walker, then dash toward one of the remaining Sith Holocrons. Pick up the Sith Holocron nestled against the wall directly across from the drop ship to gain invincibility.

Enter the facility and head to the central ring. Dash to the ring's rear and throw the Stormtroopers into the nearby laser gates.

Drop down from where you got the Sith Holocron, speed into the drop ship, and crush the Purge Troopers inside. Inside the drop ship is another Sith Holocron. Wait for your invincibility to wear off, then pick it up to gain unlimited energy. Use it to fry the rest of the troopers inside the drop-ship bay.

SITH WISDOM

Use Force Grip to remove the large circular cogs from the generators behind the laser gates. After removing the laser gates, you can pick up a Sith Holocron to gain a damage increase.

Double-jump onto the catwalk on the left. Follow it right, destroying the Scout Trooper as you go, and pick up the Holocron on the far catwalk.

Circle around the ring and go up one of the flanking ramps to the ring's upper level. From there, double-jump and dash to the tower in the ring's center and immediately cut through the Stormtroopers on the tower.

Walk around the tower and use Force Lightning to destroy the five tractor conduits surrounding it. This destroys the Imperial tractor beam and completes your first bonus objective.

At the drop ship's rear, take the elevator to the top, where a small shuttle lands and drops off more Stormtroopers. Before they can disembark, you force them off the ship and commandeer the shuttle! The shuttle twists, turns, and careens over an Imperial ore-collection facility just as you jump off.

While on the ring's upper level, use Force Push to destroy the wall and reveal the hidden Holocron.

The few Stormtroopers guarding the ore facility's entrance are no match for you; quickly dispatch them with Force Push attacks or simple lightsaber combos. Enter the facility, take the elevator up to the next level, and destroy the few Imperials in your way.

Go into the tunnel at the rear of the ring's lower level and take the elevator down. As the sliding doors open, unleash a Force Push blast down the catwalk to knock away the attacking troopers. Exit the elevator onto the walkway, and fry the troopers with Force Lightning. The Jumptrooper's pack ignites from the Lightning, and he spins uncontrollably before exploding.

There are two walkways (and several soldiers) just below and to each side of the main walkway. From your elevated position, use either Force Lightning or Throw on the soldiers to dispatch them quickly. There is a Sith Holocron floating over the main walkway. Double-jump to grab it and attain temporary invincibility. While invincible, drop to the lower left walkway and hurl one of the nearby barrels at the sniper perched on the beam at the chasm's far end.

There is another Holocron on the far left beam across the chasm. The beam tapers near the wheel puzzles. From the left wheel, double-jump and dash to the beam, then run along it to collect the Holocron.

Use the Force to lift the two large locking mechanisms on both sides of the doors and enter the next area.

The next area is another large ring. Take either the left or right path to your ultimate destination. Several Stormtroopers guard both paths. As you move around the ring's perimeter, string together long lightsaber combos and cut through all the enemies in your way.

There are two Holocrons in this ring, one on each opposing path. Grab one, then backtrack to the ring's other side and grab the other.

Take the elevator to the next and final area. There, a Shadow Guard ambushes you. Strike at it with Lightning-infused 'saber combos. After a few short 'saber exchanges, the Shadow Guard backs away defensively and reveals himself to be...PROXY?

Your clever training droid's tactical computer suggested that this would be the best time for him to attack you. He was programmed, after all, to kill you. By doing so, he serves his purpose as a training droid. In order to complete your mission, you must defeat PROXY. After revealing himself as your attacker, he quickly transforms into Maris Brood!

PROXY is a skilled combatant. Not only has he learned from failed training exercises with you, but he also programmed himself with the combat abilities of many people you've already faced. And one you haven't.

Approach the battle with PROXY just as you did with the combatants he imitates. If he appears as Brood, block and counterattack.

After defeating one of his avatars, he'll temporarily revert into a Shadow Guard. When he does, hit him with Force Lightning, block his staff attacks, and wait until he's done attacking. Counter with Lightning-infused 'saber strikes and knock him back.

When he switches to Kota, he'll become very elusive and possibly leap away from you. Use lightsaber throws to strike him from afar, then dash toward the imposter and lash out at him with Lightning combos. If he evades and traps you in his Force Grip, follow the onscreen commands to free yourself and throw your 'saber at him as you land. Keep attacking him like this until you defeat PROXY's version of Kota.

If PROXY emulates Shaak Ti, defeat her like you did her apprentice. Block attacks effectively and counterattack only when she leaves herself open. If you engage her in a Lightsaber Lock, follow the commands onscreen to overpower her.

SITH WISDOM

There are plenty of open electrical currents and explosive barrels to use against PROXY.

After defeating all of PROXY's impersonations, he'll transform into one you haven't seen in combat before—Darth Maul.

The fight against Darth Maul is tough. You must rely heavily on your lightsaber combos and evasive techniques. Begin your assault on Maul with Lightning-infused 'saber strikes. Lash out and stop only to block when he counterattacks. Use strong combos like Saber Slam to knock Maul into the air and follow up with combos as he lands.

STAR WARS
FORCE
UNLEASHED

Dodge his amplified lightsaber throw (which cannot be blocked), block his whirling 'sabers, and wait patiently for him to offer you an opening. When he does, unleash your own combos on him.

Continue pummeling away at Darth PROXY until he can take no more.

When PROXY's health is nearly depleted, a series of onscreen commands will appear. Follow them to finish off your training droid. You then get on the nearby elevator and take it to the next area.

Force Push down the doors and dash out onto the walkway. Double-jump onto the large circular platform and engage the small Stormtrooper squad guarding the rail-gun tracks. Destroy the turret troopers with 'saber strikes, then fry the floating Jumptroopers nearby with Force Lightning.

With the area clear, turn to the middle power generator at the platform's center and overload it with Force Lightning. Circle around the walkways and overload the other three rail-gun tracks in the same manner.

JEDI KNOWLEDGE

You must backtrack all the way around at one point, because one of the connecting walkways is broken.

Overloading the four rail-gun tracks redirects a blast from the ore cannon up to the orbital station. All you must do now is bring down the Imperial Star Destroyer.

In order to do this, you must first destroy the attacking TIE Fighters. Get cover behind one of the two large lighting fixtures. From there, Force Grip a power cell as it floats by in front of the walkway. Maneuver the power cell into the TIE Fighter's path and let the fighter simply fly into it. You can also fry the TIE Fighters with Force Lightning as they fly by.

The TIE Fighters alternate flight patterns but usually stick to two paths: They'll either swerve to the lower right or to the upper right. The easiest way to destroy the attacking TIE Fighters is to get cover behind the light support on the right and grab the power cells as they emerge on the platform's right. From here, you can even grab a TIE Fighter if your reflexes are quick enough. Destroy all six TIE Fighters to safely walk onto the platform's center and Force Grip the massive Star Destroyer.

Grip the Star Destroyer and follow the onscreen commands to slowly turn the ship toward you using both analog sticks. Once it is facing forward, use the two analog sticks to pull it straight down. As you begin pulling the ship down, more TIE Fighters come swooping in from underneath the Destroyer.

SITH WISDOM

As you turn the Destroyer toward you, carefully watch for the TIE Fighters to appear beneath it, then release the Destroyer when the fighters open fire!

You won't be able to bring down the ship on the first try. When you release it from your Force Grip, the momentum you've created will continue to turn the Destroyer. If the ship turns too far in one direction, you must undo the momentum and turn it back toward you the next time you can Force Grip the behemoth.

Because of this, you must act *very* quickly in destroying the second wave of attacking TIE Fighters. Destroy the fighters as you did the first wave—with explosive barrels or by ramming one fighter into another. Then quickly return to the Star Destroyer and yank it down with your Force Grip.

It takes several attempts, but if you maneuver the ship efficiently and react quickly when destroying the TIE Fighters, you'll bring the ship down with minimal damage to yourself.

With the Imperial Star Destroyer grounded for good, you're free to return to the *Rogue Shadow*. Before you leave Raxus a second time, a shadowy figure stumbles out of the wreckage and falls at your feet. PROXY sustained some damage and is no longer capable of executing his program to full capacity, but he's still your droid and you can't leave him behind. You take him under your wing and haul him back to your ship...

MISSION DETAILS

Objective
You've contacted all the allies you can find who are opposed to the Empire. Now is the time to act. Go to Corellia and meet with them to plan a course of action.

Enemies Encountered
None

The following is not a standard walkthrough, as there is no player-controlled action during this chapter.

"One day, the galaxy will indeed be free."

You've come a long way from that day on the beach of Kashyyyk years ago. Your journey began in Kashyyyk's warm, lush jungles, and now you're in the icy, snow-covered landscape of Corellia. You touch down on the planet and meet with your contacts.

Standing around the table are Senator Organa, his daughter, Senator Bel Iblis, Kota, you, and Mon Mothma. Everything has fallen into place, and the Rebel Alliance is taking shape.

Betrayal!

Just as Organa makes an official declaration of rebellion, the room begins shaking as if it's being bombarded with blaster fire. Everyone scatters when the meeting-room doors are blasted open and Darth Vader comes storming in. His men make short work of the Rebel soldiers guarding the senators.

You've been betrayed again. Rather than allow the Rebellion to flourish and challenge the Emperor as planned, Darth Vader betrayed you and is taking the leaders of the Alliance as prisoners.

Kota draws his lightsaber but is unable to do anything as Vader tosses him aside like a rag doll. It is up to you to save the Rebellion!

You stand there, stunned at Vader's betrayal. Before you can react, he uses the Force to hurl a table at you, knocking you out onto the snowy Corellian mountain peaks. Vader confirms your greatest fears: He's been lying to you since the very beginning. He never planned to destroy the Emperor with you. You were just a tool to gather the Emperor's enemies together to destroy them all at once.

He picks you up and tosses you once more. This time you fall helplessly over the ridge but manage to hold on by your fingertips. Just when it seems you're about to slip and fall to your doom, Vader is attacked! A Jedi with shaggy brown hair and a full beard comes leaping out of the Corellian meeting room. It's Obi-Wan Kenobi!

"I've been waiting for you, Obi-Wan. We meet again, at last. The circle is now complete. When I left you, I was but the learner; now I am the master."
—Darth Vader, *Star Wars:* Episode IV *A New Hope*

The battle doesn't last long. Kenobi strikes and Vader strikes back. A short exchange of flashing 'sabers ends with Vader's lightsaber running through Kenobi's chest. The Jedi Master falls to the floor. Kenobi's body disappears, revealing PROXY's fallen form. It wasn't the Jedi Master after all! It was your trusty PROXY droid all along.

He knew that he was no match for Vader, but his surprise attack bought you enough time to drop down from the cliff's edge to a ledge along the cliff side. Juno swoops in to rescue you there. Not all is lost.

STAR WARS THE FORCE UNLEASHED

DEATH STAR

MAP LEGEND

▣ Holocron

MISSION DETAILS

Objective

Find General Kota and the Founders of the Rebel Alliance.

Bonus Objectives

Attain 450,000 Force Points

Locate 15 Holocrons

Enemies Encountered

Imperial Stormtroopers

Scout Troopers

Imperial Purge Troopers

Imperial EVO Troopers

Shadow Guard

Imperial Royal Guards

Imperial Jumptroopers

Imperial Incinerator Troopers

AT-CT

AT-ST

Darth Vader: Boss

The Emperor: Boss

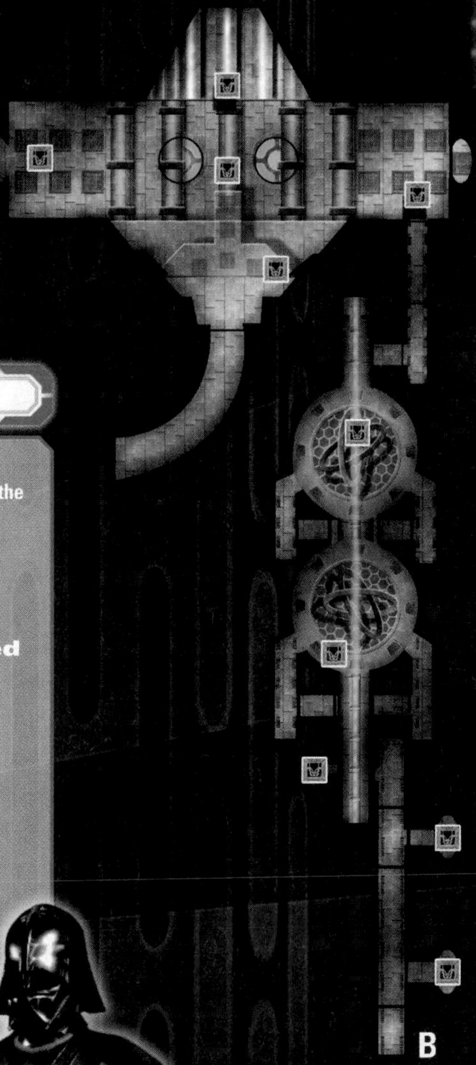

A

B

8

"I've never been a Jedi before."

The *Rogue Shadow* is much quieter now without PROXY and General Kota on board. As you speed away from Corellia, Juno makes an eye-opening observation: Darth Vader betrayed you multiple times in spite of your loyalty. But now that he's taken the leaders of the Rebellion prisoner, the fate of the Alliance rests with you.

You decide to go after Darth Vader and rescue the Rebels. But first you must figure out *where* to go. Juno pilots the *Rogue Shadow* while you sit in the navigator's seat meditating.

You've never been a true Jedi before, but somehow your meditation pays off. You see visions of Kota and a large space station still under construction. There's something wrong with General Kota....

You set course for the Outer Rim and find Vader's Death Star. Juno carefully navigates the *Rogue Shadow* into the Death Star and docks. You order her to raise the ship's cloak after you disembark and orbit the space station just out of scanner range. Realizing that this might be the last time she sees you, she finally reveals her true feelings...with a kiss.

Assault on the Death Star

You leap off the *Rogue Shadow* and land in a hangar bay far below. As soon as you land, the hangar bay comes alive with blaster fire. Scout troopers fire on you from the walkways above, Purge Troopers open fire from the main hangar floor, and, to make matters worse, an AT-CT walker stomps around the hangar bay. Dash out of the blaster rain and make a beeline for the small room on the hangar's far left.

Hide behind the room's center wall panel and blast the Purge Troopers with Force Lightning as they approach. Lure them into the room and finish them off with Force Lightning 'saber strikes as they lumber into your trap. With one Purge Trooper out of the way, shimmy out from behind the center wall to get a better view of the AT-CT walker in the main hangar. Electrocute it with Force Lightning as it stomps around outside your shelter.

When you deplete your energy, retreat back into the cover of your small room. Use the barrels there as projectiles to further damage the walker or the approaching Purge Troopers.

After whittling down the machine's health, you can finish it off just as you have other walkers. Follow the onscreen prompts as they appear and crush the mechanical menace. Unfortunately, destroying the AT-CT only prompts an AT-ST to appear from the hangar's floor elevator. Defeat it just as you did the first—whittle it down from behind your cover and only pop out to finish it off.

Destroying the AT-ST prompts several more Troopers to arrive. Three Purge Troopers and three EVO Troopers join the battle with blasters blazing. Lure the speedier EVO Troopers into your room and decimate them with 'saber combos.

Purge troopers are much slower than other troopers. After destroying the EVO Troopers, lure the Purge Troopers toward you and fry them with Force Lightning. Before they can counterattack, rush out of your small room. Dash across the hangar bay, picking up the Sith Holocron to replenish your energy; then turn on the Purge Troopers. Blast them again with Force Lightning, then dash away.

This time, dash to the hangar bay's other side. If you're low on health, pick up the second Sith Holocron to replenish it. Lock on to the Purge Troopers as they approach your room from across the hangar. Continue blasting them with Force Lightning and finish them off once they reach you. Destroy the troopers with Lightning combos to clear the bay of all enemies.

Use either of the two elevators (found in opposite corners of the hangar) to reach the upper walkway. There are two Holocrons up here, one on each side of the bay. Grab them both, then hop back down to the main floor.

Back on the main hangar floor, walk onto the glowing blue trapdoors near the hangar's center. Use Force Repulse to blast them open and fall into the Death Star's tunnels.

STAR WARS
THE FORCE UNLEASHED

You land in a huge firing tube and narrowly dodge a green beam as it fires off. Wait until the beam stops firing, then dash up the firing tube. Force Push the green glass at the tube's end, dash to the other side, and break through the second glass pane. When the firing sequence begins to spool up again, dash into the niche along the firing tube's left side.

The niche is well guarded. As you speed in there for cover, lead with your lightsaber swinging. Slash through the Stormtroopers inside and use Force Repulse to keep them from surrounding you. Once the laser stops to recharge, go into the next firing tube.

Storm up the firing tube and use Force Lightning to blast the small gun turrets that pop out of the ground. After destroying them, continue up the tube and turn right into the next small niche. Cut through the soldiers in there, then throw any surviving soldiers into the firing beam.

There is a Holocron hidden behind the sliding doors in this niche.

Wait for the firing beam to stop, then dash back into the firing tube and make a right. Break through the two green glass walls and speed into the passage on the left.

Make a right in the passage and zigzag toward the cannon turret at the hall's end. When you're within striking distance, fry it with Force Lightning, then move past it into the small control room at the hall's end.

Demolish the turret in the control room with a quick combo, then turn right. Wait for the beam to stop again, and crush the small ground turrets in the firing tube. Cross the tube and use quick combos to dispatch the incendiary troopers in the next control room. Grab the Sith Holocron (Health Drain Aura) floating above the control room's center to aid your battle against these troops.

If the firing beam reactivates while you're fighting the incendiary troopers, hurl them into the beam to dispatch them quickly.

There are two Holocrons above the second control room. To reach them, use the elevator pad on the first control room's far left and ride it up to the catwalks above the control center. Double-jump onto the walkways above the second control room and pick up the Holocrons before dropping back into the second control room.

Use your Force Grip to unlock the sliding doors and enter the next hallway. At the far end are two Purge Troopers. Dash up the corridor as you evade their fire and take cover behind the small niches along the passage.

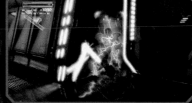

From your cover, throw the nearby crates and barrels at the Purge Troopers at the corridor's end. Hit them with Force Lightning and weaken them before rushing out and finishing them off with a few Lightning-infused 'saber attacks. Once they're eliminated, turn on the remaining soldiers in the hall.

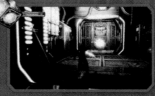

Sneak into the small room on the right and go through the sliding doors to find a Holocron. Continue throught the next set of doors and continue right through another pair of sliding doors to claim a second Holocron.

Go through the doors at the hall's end and make a left into the next sliding doors.

Directly across from the sliding doors is a small alcove with a Holocron. Grab it before turning right and going up the laser tube.

In the tube's next section, align the rings in the next pulsarium. Once they're aligned, dash across the bridge and into the passage on the right.

At this tunnel's end is a large spherical room with three pulsarium rings gyrating around the room's perimeter. The rings align only to initiate a laser firing sequence, at which point a small bridge extends through the room's center. In order to proceed, you must align the rings while the laser is not firing and force the small bridge to extend through the room's center.

As you cross the bridge, grab the Holocron floating above in the second pulsarium.

Duck into the small room on the right and take the elevator down to the lower level. Turn right down the tunnel and enter the spherical room's bottom level. Grab the Holocron on the right, then backtrack to the top level. On the way, use a series of quick combos to dispatch the Imperials standing in your path.

Follow the tunnels to the convergence chamber. There aren't many enemies in here, but the chamber is a tall complicated room to navigate. On the left is a tall chamber housing eight firing tubes arranged in a large circle. At the center of the eight tubes, about halfway up the tall chamber, is a platform leading to the Emperor's observation dome.

Drop into the bottom of the tall chamber on the left and immediately stun one of the two AT-ST walkers with Force Lightning. Dash away from the two mechanical beasts and take cover in the large tunnel on the far right. Lure the walkers toward you and stun them repeatedly with Force Lightning. While stunned, dash between their massive legs and assault them with Lightning-infused 'saber attacks.

Back in the firing tube, wait inside the elevator room for the laser to cease firing. When it does, edge out toward the tube's end so that you can see the pulsarium rings spinning around. Use your Force Grip to grab the first ring and move it into place—align it so that it stands upright, touching the room's top and bottom. Align the second and third rings to force the small bridge to pop out, then dash across it to the second small tunnel ahead.

After destroying both AT-STs, use Force Grip to shove the large reactor surrounded by yellow lights back into the wall. This activates the two blue elevator tubes embedded in the floor. Step into the blue transport beam to ride it up the tall convergence chamber.

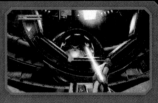

WOOKIEE WARNING

Whatever you do, don't touch the firing beam! It may look like it's far enough above your head to dash underneath it, but it's not. If you touch it, you'll be zapped into dust!

There are several Holocrons in this area. One is floating in the center of the lowest firing tube. Use the blue elevator tubes to launch yourself into the air. Come down on the lowest firing tube, carefully double-jump onto the tube's lower beam, then leap into the ring's center to grab it.

STAR WARS
FORCE
THE
UNLEASHED

There is another on the highest firing tube; ride the elevator up to it. Double-jump and dash to the support strut on the room's rear end, then walk up the strut to the Holocron.

Collect an additional Holocron on the top level above the convergence chamber entrance. Yet another Holocron appears on the opposite side of the room, on the third floor platform.

Drop onto the platform at the chamber's center and prepare for battle. As soon as you land on the platform, a Shadow Guard arrives with a full complement of Imperial Royal Guards.

Knock away the Royal Guards with powerful Force attacks. Don't let them pin you against the railing! Dash away from the small group to create some breathing room. As the Royal Guards give chase, turn around and slash away at the closest one. When the others get close, retreat evasively to avoid their light-staff attacks.

After destroying the first of the Royal Guards, dash right and pick up the Sith Holocron to gain a Health Drain Aura. Use this to weaken the remaining Guards while you thrash them and finish them off. Turn on the Shadow Guard while your Health Drain Aura is active, and hit him with Lightning combos.

There is a Holocron nestled in the control panel on the left. Pick it up as you fight the Guard.

Continue pounding away at the Shadow Guard until he tries using his Force techniques on you. If he grabs you with Force Grip, follow the onscreen commands to free yourself. Finish him off with a quick grapple by matching the prompts onscreen; then use Force Grip to rotate the large door lock on the circular hatch at the platform's end. Enter the tunnel to your final destination.

The Reckoning

As you approach the Emperor's room, he and Darth Vader interrogate the founders of the Rebel Alliance. The Emperor calmly sits at his throne as Vader stands by and watches his master. The Emperor, sure of himself and his power, insists that the Rebellion will fail. But he fails to sense what Kota is immediately aware of—you.

You storm toward the Emperor's control room with your lightsaber ready, but the Emperor leaves his dirty work to Darth Vader. It's time to confront your former master. Darth Vader calmly charges and confronts you in the passage before you reach the Emperor's chamber.

Lock on to Vader and hit him with Force Lightning. Engage him in lightsaber combat. Use multiple attacks of Force Push to stun Vader. Follow up with 'saber combos to deal damage to the stunned boss. If he  surrounds himself in a red Force Shield, double-jump into the air to dodge the ensuing blast of the Force.

As you land, hit him with Lightning-infused 'saber combos. If he attempts attacking with his lightsaber, block his attack, then counter with quick, short combos. As you fight, Vader will lift you into the air with his Force Grip. Free yourself by following the onscreen commands, then resume your attack.

Move evasively around the hall, dodging Vader's Force attacks and dashing behind him. Strike him from behind to inflict major damage and reduce the risk of him counterattacking.

Once you've depleted Darth Vader's health to about 50 percent, he retreats to an antechamber to the Emperor's room. There, Vader stands on a small circular platform at the room's center, while the area around the platform is surrounded by a red perimeter.

Throw your lightsaber at Vader from the safety of the room's surrounding ledges. If you attempt getting onto his platform without stunning him, he'll simply swat you away. Instead, stay on your ledges and use Force Grip to grab the explosive barrels lining the wall and throw them at your former master.

While he's stunned from the explosive barrel, double-jump onto his platform and unleash devastating combos to further deplete his health. When he comes to, leap back to the surrounding platform.

Continue pummeling Vader with barrels to stun him, then leap onto this platform to ravage him with 'saber strikes.

Rather than give away the two possible endings, the following section provides tips on how to defeat the Emperor and Darth Vader. You must choose which side to align yourself with. Will you join the light side by defeating the Emperor and freeing the Rebels, or will you join the dark side by destroying Darth Vader and taking his place next to the Emperor?

Tips for Defeating the Emperor

- The Emperor doesn't wield a lightsaber; his attacks are all Force power–focused. Lightsaber combos will be more effective against him than Force attacks.
- Attack him repeatedly with lightsaber combos until he attempts to hurl barrels at you.
- Hide behind the control panels to keep him from getting a clean shot at you with the barrels.
- Stay on the move while he's surrounded by his purple Force Lightning shield.
- Focus solely on his Imperial Guards when he summons them. Don't bother trying to hurt the Emperor while they're in the battle arena.
- After he misses you with Force Lightning, use your own Lightning attacks to damage him.
- Jump to avoid getting knocked off your feet by exploding barrel attacks.
- Don't stand too close to the blue force field while fighting him.

Tips for Defeating Darth Vader

- Vader relies less on the Force than the Emperor. The majority of his assaults are lightsaber attacks.
- Keep your lightsaber in blocking position at all times to block his 'saber slashes.
- As soon as he stops swinging his 'saber, counter his attacks with 'saber combos.
- Don't rely too much on one attack. Mix up your lightsaber combos with Force Push and Force Lightning strikes.
- Use your strongest lightsaber combo after successfully defeating Vader in a Force Lock.
- Stay mobile and avoid standing toe-to-toe with him.
- If he corners you against a wall, double-jump to leap over him.
- Double-jump and dash over his Force Push attack. When he begins charging his Force, dash away and prepare to jump.

Be mindful of Vader's Force Throw ability. If you jump into the air while Vader isn't attacking, he will most often pluck you out of the air with his Force Grip. If you can't loosen yourself from his grip, he'll toss you across the room!

When Vader is ready to fall, he'll leave his platform and take the fight to you, on the surrounding ledges. Block his attacks and counter with assaults of your own. Engage him in a Force Lock and overpower him by matching the onscreen commands.

Your final attack destroys Vader's protective mask and sends him flying into the Emperor's chamber. There, the Emperor prepares to execute the leaders of the Rebel Alliance. You've got other plans, though.

A Choice

As you stand over Darth Vader's body with your 'saber drawn, ready to finish the job, the Emperor's scratchy voice urges you to do it. Destroy Vader and you'll rightfully replace him at the Emperor's side.

General Kota tries to keep you from striking down Vader and crossing completely to the dark side, but the Emperor stops him. Suddenly, things change. Vader is still at your mercy, but the Emperor is destroying Kota! You have a choice: Eliminate Vader and take your place by the Emperor's side, or defeat the Emperor to free the Rebels.

What will you do?

SITH SECRETS

The following pages were ripped from secret scrolls known only to the Sith. They reveal the locations of all Holocrons and how to attain all Xbox 360 Achievements.

Holocron Locations

The Holocrons are listed in order as you progress through the level. Use that knowledge to identify specific locations listed below.

TIE Construction Yard

MAP LEGEND

▣ Holocron

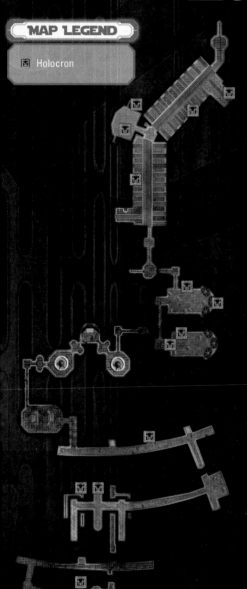

Sector	Holocron Number	Reward	Location
Hangar	1	Force Points	On the catwalk on the opposite side of the entrance
Hangar	2	'Saber Crystal: Yellow	High on the catwalk above the TIE Fighter
Hangar Hallways	3	Force Points	Behind right-hand side of destructible doors; requires Force Push to acquire
Chasm Area	4	Force Combo Sphere	Behind stacked crates at edge of upper platform
Chasm Area	5	Force Talent Sphere	Behind stacked crates on skiff at lower platform
Chasm Area	6	Force Points	In second upper catwalk alcove
Wing	7	Force Points	Behind crates on upper catwalk inside first wing room
Wing	8	Force Points	On top of control room in first wing room
Wing	9	Force Points	Use TIE wings to create platforms to reach Holocron placed on broken TIE wing
Wing	10	'Saber Crystal: Damage	On high catwalk in second wing room
Assembly Room	11	Force Points	Inside alcove beside laser arm in first section of assembly room
Assembly Room	12	Force Points	Inside alcove beside laser arm in second section of assembly room
Assembly Room	13	Force Points	Inside alcove in generator room
Assembly Room	14	Force Sphere	In center of quad-generators in generator room
Assembly Room	15	Force Points	In corner of laser arm room

93

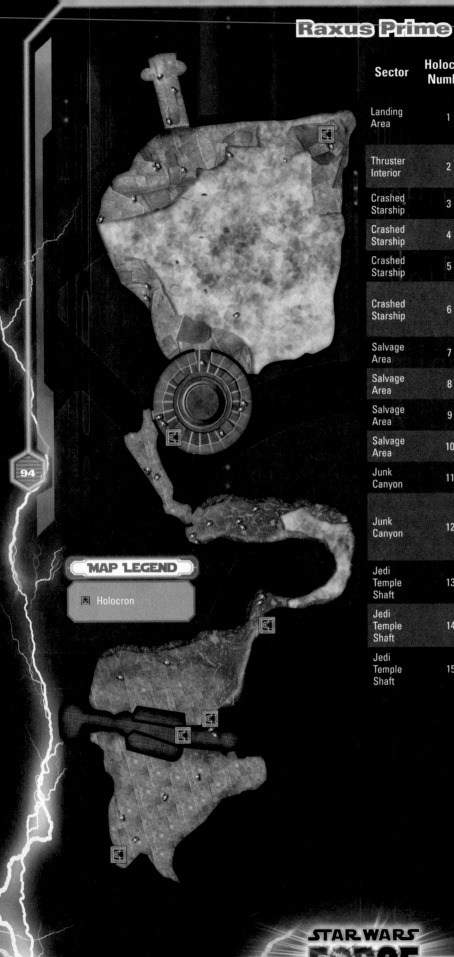

Sector	Holocron Number	Reward	Location
Landing Area	1	Force Points	Right past the first Force-raised platform, underneath large metal docklike structure
Thruster Interior	2	Force Power Sphere	On high platform inside thruster, protected by two Jawas
Crashed Starship	3	Force Points	To the left, as you exit the tunnel into the crash site
Crashed Starship	4	'Saber Crystal: Compressed Red	Behind rear engine covering
Crashed Starship	5	Force Points	Cliff edge in second landing area
Crashed Starship	6	Force Points	Behind door at end of crashed starship interior; use Force Push to open door
Salvage Area	7	'Saber Crystal: Gold	End of the long dock in top level
Salvage Area	8	Force Combo Sphere	Corner of the top level
Salvage Area	9	Force Talent Sphere	On garbage skiff in lower level
Salvage Area	10	'Saber Crystal: Compressed Yellow	Corner of lower level
Junk Canyon	11	Force Points	Right side junk canyons
Junk Canyon	12	Bonus Costume: Sith Robe	Through a wall of girders and pipes, located on a distant platform that requires a double-jump and dash to reach
Jedi Temple Shaft	13	Force Points	Inside destructible pillar base
Jedi Temple Shaft	14	Force Points	Out in the open in the corridor
Jedi Temple Shaft	15	Power Crystal: Firkrann	Use AT-ST head to jump up to reach

MAP LEGEND

Holocron

94

STAR WARS THE FORCE UNLEASHED

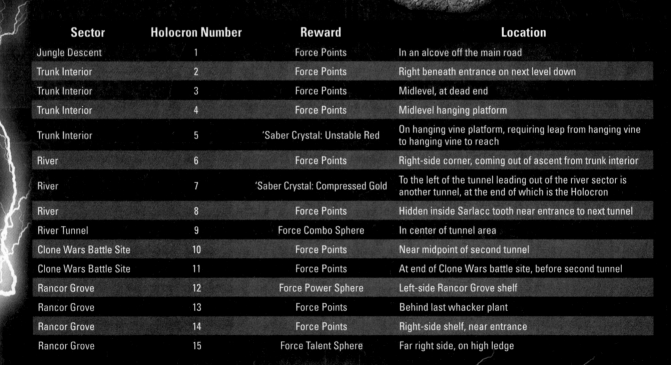

MAP LEGEND

 Holocron

Sector	Holocron Number	Reward	Location
Jungle Descent	1	Force Points	In an alcove off the main road
Trunk Interior	2	Force Points	Right beneath entrance on next level down
Trunk Interior	3	Force Points	Midlevel, at dead end
Trunk Interior	4	Force Points	Midlevel hanging platform
Trunk Interior	5	'Saber Crystal: Unstable Red	On hanging vine platform, requiring leap from hanging vine to hanging vine to reach
River	6	Force Points	Right-side corner, coming out of ascent from trunk interior
River	7	'Saber Crystal: Compressed Gold	To the left of the tunnel leading out of the river sector is another tunnel, at the end of which is the Holocron
River	8	Force Points	Hidden inside Sarlacc tooth near entrance to next tunnel
River Tunnel	9	Force Combo Sphere	In center of tunnel area
Clone Wars Battle Site	10	Force Points	Near midpoint of second tunnel
Clone Wars Battle Site	11	Force Points	At end of Clone Wars battle site, before second tunnel
Rancor Grove	12	Force Power Sphere	Left-side Rancor Grove shelf
Rancor Grove	13	Force Points	Behind last whacker plant
Rancor Grove	14	Force Points	Right-side shelf, near entrance
Rancor Grove	15	Force Talent Sphere	Far right side, on high ledge

STAR WARS
THE FORCE
UNLEASHED

Empirical Lab

Sector	Holocron Number	Reward	Location
Vader's Lab	1	'Saber Crystal: Blue	Floating in exit doorway to lab
Specimen Lab	2	Force Combo Sphere	Inside specimen "jar"; use Force Grip/Throw to smash glass to acquire Holocron
Specimen Lab	3	Force Talent Sphere	Inside enemy spawn closet below and to the left of the specimen lab's entrance
Escape Pod Room	4	Force Power Sphere	Hidden inside final escape pod; light the pod to activate it and reveal the Holocron
Corridor 3	5	'Saber Crystal: Lorrdian	Hidden behind barrels, guarded by Imperials, right before final hallway to the bridge

MAP LEGEND

▣ Holocron

MAP LEGEND

■ Holocron

Sector	Holocron Number	Reward	Location
Vapor Room	1	'Saber Crystal: Unstable Orange	Hidden in center steam vent on upper platform
Vapor Room	2	Power Crystal: Ruusan	Hidden on platform above bar
Landing Platform	3	Force Points	Hidden behind exploding barrels near ramp exiting the landing platform area
Landing Platform	4	'Saber Crystal: Unstable Yellow	Hidden on rail above landing platform. Player must double-jump from catwalk up to rail
Landing Platform	5	Force Combo Sphere	High in air between two carbonite containers. Use Lightning on second propeller fan, allowing player to float up to Holocron, or double-jump and dash off walkway to next section

STAR WARS THE FORCE UNLEASHED

Kashyyyk

MAP LEGEND

☒	Holocron

Sector	Holocron Number	Reward	Location
Intro Area	1	'Saber Crystal: Compressed Blue	Resting to the left of the starting spawn point, between the large tree's roots
Intro Transition	2	Bonus Costume: Kento's Robes	Hidden behind wreckage, behind your spawn point
Intro Transition	3	Force Points	On the path's right side, behind a large branch overhead (requires a jump)
Imperial Fort	4	Force Points	Left side, on a strut ledge next to the main ramp
Imperial Fort	5	Force Points	Left side, on a strut ledge farther down, near a huge pipe
Imperial Fort	6	Force Combo Sphere	Hidden behind large pipe at the end of the ramp leading to the fort's upper catwalks; leaping off the catwalk is required
Imperial Fort	7	Force Points	Hidden behind large pipe on the first ramp
Commander's House	8	Force Points	Inside one of the glass trophy cases
Hunting Grounds	9	Force Power Sphere	Hidden in the first sniper nest
Hunting Grounds	10	Force Points	Hidden in the last sniper nest before the exit to the slave hall
Hunting Grounds	11	Force Points	Hidden inside last Wookiee cage, near door leading to the slave hall
Slave Hall	12	Force Talent Sphere	Held in one of the slave cells, protected by Interrogation Droids
Slave Hall	13	Force Points	Contained in one of the last slave cells before the slave-hall exit that leads to the Skyhook
Skyhook	14	'Saber Crystal: Purple	Atop tree branch on the right as you enter Skyhook area
Skyhook	15	Force Points	Against the side of the Skyhook building

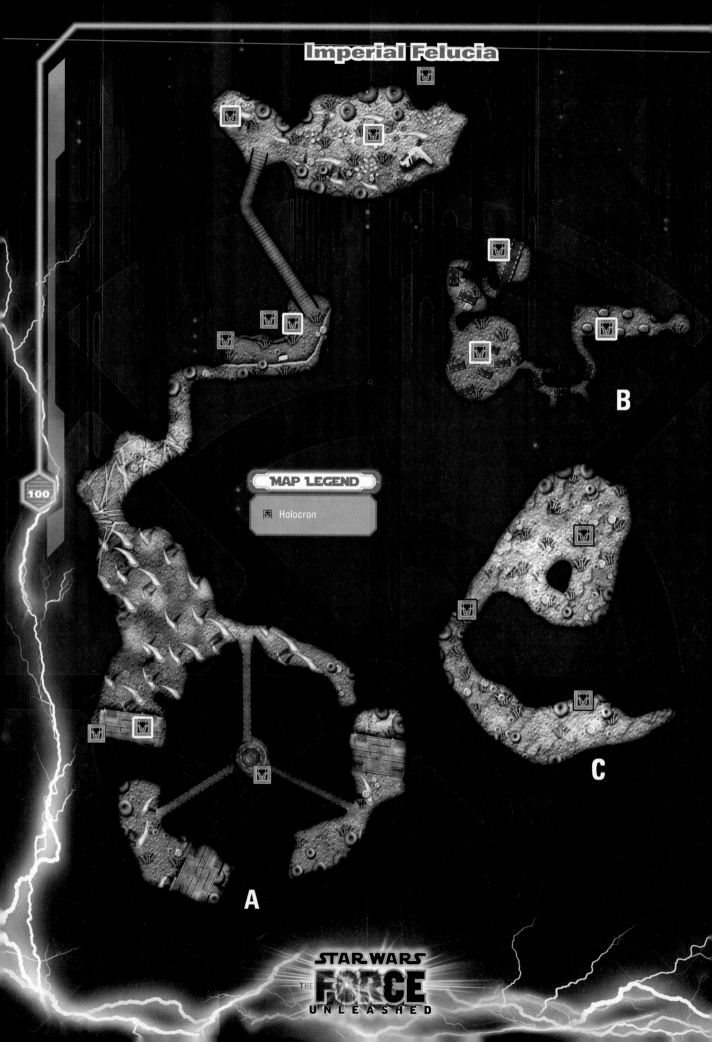

MAP LEGEND

Holocron

100

A

B

C

Imperial Felucia (continued)

Sector	Holocron Number	Reward	Location
Jungle Descent	1	Force Talent Sphere	Above large Sarlacc tooth; must use a crate to stand on and then double-jump to acquire
Jungle Descent	2	Force Points	Hidden inside Sarlacc tooth, near bridge to next area
Jungle Descent	3	'Saber Crystal: Green	Located deep in a tunnel beneath your starting location
Sarlacc Surface	4	'Saber Crystal: Compressed Purple	After you cross the Imperial walkway, guarded by Imperials, you reach a drop-off leading down into the Felucian jungle. To the drop-off's right is a series of mushroom pads; atop the highest one is the Holocron
Sarlacc Surface	5	Force Power Sphere	In upper ledge, past two turret gunners
Sarlacc Surface	6	Force Points	Back ledge leading to the tunnel and ledge that has the Force Power Sphere
Sarlacc Mouth	7	Force Points	Far corner, behind one of the Imperial tank structures
Sarlacc Mouth	8	Force Points	Above one of the three bridge structures
Sarlacc Mouth	9	'Saber Crystal: Vexxtal	Atop one of the stabilizer towers; requires a very tricky double-jump dash to reach
Sarlacc Stomach	10	Force Points	The Holocron is right on the level start
Sarlacc Stomach	11	Force Points	In the large chamber leading to lung room
Sarlacc Stomach	12	Force Points	Inside lung room
Jungle Descent	13	Force Combo Sphere	Holocron is placed high, requiring you to use nearby mushrooms as jumping platforms
Jungle Descent	14	'Saber Crystal: Unstable Blue	Placed high; to reach the Holocron, you must use the highest step as a platform from which to double-jump dash
Jungle Descent	15	Force Points	On the left path near the exit to the Bull Rancor fight

Imperial Raxus Prime

Sector	Holocron Number	Reward	Location
Camp Ruins	1	Power Crystal: Sigil	Soon after the starting area, walk through a narrow passage with ledges to the left and right. Jump on the right ledge, then double-jump and dash to the left ledge. Hop down the passage on the right to find the Holocron guarded by a Jawa
Camp Ruins	2	Force Points	Small dead end, right before the first girder wall
Mountain Pass	3	Force Power Sphere	Past the girder bridge, a metal barricade blocks a short passage; use Force Push on the barricade to enter the passage and recover the Holocron
Mountain Pass	4	Force Points	At the entrance to the tunnel leading to the Imperial battle zone area
Battleground	5	'Saber Crystal: Compressed Green	On a platform on the battleground's right side
Battleground	6	Force Points	End of tunnel where Rodian reinforcements arrive
Battleground	7	Force Points	Along the region's left-hand side is a series of platforms. Jump on them to reach the catwalks that jut out from the junk wall. Double-jump and dash from one of these catwalks; the player can jump/dash to reach the Holocron floating in midair over the battleground
Secret Passage	8	Force Points	Inside tunnel leading to Imperial drop-ship area
Imperial Battle Zone	9	Force Points	Dropbase exterior, high above one of the junk towers
Imperial Battle Zone	10	Force Talent Sphere	On the high catwalk above the AT-ST inside the drop ship
Ore Factory: Hangar	11	Force Points	Upper catwalk of arrival hangar

Sector	Holocron Number	Reward	Location
Ore Factory: Collection	12	'Saber Crystal: Unstable Purple	Hidden in a hallway on the collection area's upper level; use Force Push to destroy the metal doors blocking the way
Ore Factory: Underground	13	Force Combo Sphere	Hidden on the left-hand catwalk; requires a bit of tricky jumping to reach
Ore Factory: Control Ring	14	Force Points	Left side of ring
Ore Factory: Control Ring	15	Force Points	Right side of ring

MAP LEGEND

Holocron

B

C

A

STAR WARS
THE FORCE
UNLEASHED

Death Star

MAP LEGEND

▣ Holocron

A

B

Sector	Holocron Number	Reward	Location
Hangar	1	Force Points	On far left of an upper catwalk alcove
Hangar	2	Power Crystal: Katak	On far right of an upper catwalk alcove
Firing Tube	3	Force Points	Inside a spawn closet at the firing tube's far end
Subway	4	'Saber Crystal: Unstable Green	Above the path of the firing tube is a catwalk of pipes. Leap onto the pipes and to a narrow passage where the Holocron is located
Subway	5	Force Points	Located in the same area as the previous Holocron
Second Subway	6	Force Talent Sphere	Inside a spawning closet at the front end of the firing tube's hallway
Second Subway	7	Force Points	Located in a nook inside the firing tube, right before the first pulsarium
Second Subway	8	Force Points	Inside a spawning closet at the far end of the firing tube's hallway

Pulsarium Chamber 1	9	Force Power Sphere	Bottom floor of the first pulsarium chamber
Pulsarium Chamber 2	10	Force Points	In the center of the second pulsarium; pick it up as you cross second pulsarium bridge
Convergence Chamber	11	Force Points	There are eight laser tubes converging in this chamber. Holocron is at the lowest one, floating in midair in a focusing ring's center. Wait until the laser stops firing before it's safe to acquire the Holocron.
Convergence Chamber	12	'Saber Crystal: Black	Of the eight laser tubes, this Holocron resides at the very top, above a rail, near the chamber's far end
Convergence Chamber	13	Force Points	Far side, second level
Convergence Chamber	14	Force Points	Highest level, above where you enter the convergence room (behind closed doors)
Convergence Chamber	15	Force Combo Sphere	Near the chamber's exit, on the platform containing the large circular door leading to the Emperor's throne room; the final Holocron is in the center of a console cluster along the platform's edge

 JEDI KNOWLEDGE

There are 115 Holocrons to collect in total.

Xbox 360 Achievements

Achievment Name	Gamerscore	User Requirements
Corellian Star	10	Complete all bonus objectives on one level
Holocron Collector	75	Collect all Jedi Holocrons in the game
Vapor Room	10	Complete Level: Cloud City, act 2
Empirical	10	Complete Level: Empirical, act 2
Jedi Hunt	10	Complete Level: Felucia, act 1
Infestation	10	Complete Level: Felucia, act 2
Revenge	25	Complete Game: Dark Side
Apprentice	75	Complete Game: Apprentice difficulty
Sith Master	100	Complete Game: Sith Master difficulty
Redemption	25	Complete Game: Light Side
Sith Warrior	75	Complete Game: Sith Warrior difficulty
Sith Lord	100	Complete Game: Sith Lord difficulty
Skyhook	10	Complete Level: Kashyyyk, act 2
Invasion	10	Complete Level: Prologue
Junkyard	10	Complete Level: Raxus Prime, act 1
Destroyer	10	Complete Level: Raxus Prime, act 2
Insurrection	10	Complete Level: TIE Construction Yard, act 1
Sith Trials	20	Complete all Training Room challenges
Sith Training	20	Complete all Training Room lessons
The Harder They Fall	15	Defeat 10 AT-STs or AT-KTs
PROXY Won't Be Happy	15	Destroy 35 droids
Rebel Leader	15	Defeat 500 Imperials

Xbox 360 Achievements (continued)

Achievment Name	Gamerscore	User Requirements
The Bigger They Are	15	Defeat 6 Rancors
Cannon Fodder	15	Defeat 150 Stormtroopers
Red Five	15	Destroy 20 attacking TIE Fighters
Bully	15	Defeat 25 Ugnaughts or Jawas
Bossk	15	Defeat 200 Wookiees during the Kashyyyk Prologue level
Legend	25	Earn 600,000 Force Points on a single level
Expert	10	Earn 500,000 Force Points on a single level
Skilled	5	Earn 250,000 Force Points on a single level
Force Grip Mastery	20	Defeat 500 enemies with Force Grip
Gripped	5	Defeat 100 enemies with Force Grip
Force Lightning Mastery	20	Defeat 500 enemies with Force Lightning
Shocked	5	Defeat 100 enemies with Force Lightning
Force Push Mastery	20	Defeat 500 enemies with Force Push
Pushed	5	Defeat 100 enemies with Force Push
Force Repulse Mastery	20	Defeat 500 enemies with Force Repulse
Repulsed	5	Defeat 100 enemies with Force Repulse
Lightning Shield Mastery	20	Defeat 500 enemies with Lightning Shield
Stormed	5	Defeat 100 enemies with Lightning Shield
Grappled	10	Defeat 100 enemies with a grapple move
Launched	15	Defeat 100 enemies with a launcher move
Lightsaber Throw Mastery	20	Defeat 500 enemies with Saber Throw
Impaled	5	Defeat 100 enemies with Saber Throw
Sith Lord Frenzy	20	Get a Frenzy x12 bonus
Sith Frenzy	15	Get a Frenzy x8 bonus
Frenzy	5	Get a Frenzy x4 bonus
Worst Day-Shift Manager Ever	10	Kill 12 Stormtroopers as Vader during the Prologue
Total:	1000	

STAR WARS®

THE FORCE UNLEASHED™

PRIMA Official Game Guide

Written by
Fernando Bueno

Prima Games
An Imprint of Random House, Inc.

3000 Lava Ridge Court, Suite 100
Roseville, CA 95661
www.primagames.com

Senior Product Manager: Donato Tica
Associate Product Manager: Shaida Boroumand
Manufacturing: Suzanne Goodwin
Texture Maps: David Bueno

A very special thanks to:
Bertrand Estrellado, Ed Tucker, Matt Miller, Dan Wasson, Mark Friesen, Dave Jimenez, Roger Evoy, Stephen Ervin, and Julio Torres.

ISBN: 978-0-7615-5916-0
Library of Congress Catalog Card Number: 2008920935
Printed in the United States of America

08 09 10 11 GG 10 9 8 7 6 5 4 3 2 1

Author Bio

Fernando "Red Star" Bueno (aka dukkhah) has been a gamer since opening his first Atari, and has been writing creatively since his early years in high school. During college he combined his loves for gaming and writing and began freelancing for popular gaming websites. The San Diego native found his way to Northern California shortly after high school. After graduating from the University of California, Davis, with a dual degree in English and art history, he was able to land a job as an editor for Prima Games. Though happy with his position as an editor, his life called him to Las Vegas where he now resides. During the move to Nevada, he also made the move to author and has since written a number of game books, including *Naruto Uzumaki Chronicles 2*, *Prince of Persia: Two Thrones*, *Fight Night Round 3*, and *Stubbs the Zombie*.

In his time off he enjoys the works of Hermann Hesse, Johann Van Goethe, Franz Kafka, and EGM. When not writing for Prima, he continues to work on his craft as a poet. We want to hear from you! E-mail comments and feedback to fbueno@primagames.com.

Contents

2

The following pages reveal the subtle ways of the Force and how to master the basics. Every great Jedi or Sith began by learning the basics of battle. It is only from there that one can become a master of the Force.

SITH WISDOM

The Tutorial option in the Main menu provides an equally useful course on basic controls. We're listing these controls here so they are easily accessible as you progress through your journey. We also include tips for how and when to use these controls effectively.

Movement

Before setting out to battle your many foes, you must know how to move. To walk, lightly nudge ◎ in the direction you want to go. The control stick (◎) is pressure sensitive, so don't press it too hard unless you want to jump into a sprint. To run, press ◎ all the way in your desired direction.

Keep in mind that it is much harder to block blaster fire while you're running. Fight your instinct to run everywhere. Take your time navigating the halls of Imperial ships and the lush Felucian wilderness. If you sprint everywhere, you'll risk running headfirst into an ambush.

Jump and Double-Jump

Jumping and double-jumping are staples of level navigation, and they're necessary for combat. Press Ⓑ to jump once. To double-jump and reach higher ledges or avoid attacks, press Ⓑ, Ⓑ.

If you time your double-jumps well, you can avoid an enemy's shoulder slams, Force powers, or even incoming blaster fire. More importantly, use Ⓑ during boss battles to safely land on your feet once you've been thrown or hit with a Force Push attack.

Force Dash

Force Dash is a perfect way to sprint away or toward an enemy. While walking or running, press Ⓐ to Force Dash in the direction you're moving.

If you want to dash sideways or backward, press ◎ in the direction you want to dash, then press Ⓐ to Force Dash in that direction.

The best use of Force Dash is to evade an enemy. While in battle, frequently use Force Dash to sprint away from your foe and gain some distance. This can often be a lifesaving tactic, allowing you to reach bacta tanks quickly or buying you time to replenish your Force meter.

JEDI KNOWLEDGE

You can also perform Force Dash in midair.

SITH WISDOM

Force Dash backward to execute an evasive backflip.

Lock-on Camera

One of the most effective tools during battle is the lock-on camera. Press ✚ to lock on to an enemy during battle and focus solely on him. When locked on, you can't target any other enemies directly, so don't use it while surrounded by enemies.

Your movement will also depend on who you're locked on to. Instead of running away, left or right, you'll back away or strafe around your enemy while facing him at all times. To release the lock-on, press ✚ again. The lock-on camera is most effective against single or large enemies.

WOOKIEE WARNING

If you maintain a lock on large enemies such as rancors at all times during battle, you won't be able to run away from them when they come barreling down on you!

JEDI KNOWLEDGE

A red aura around the enemy means that you're locked on to them or, if you're holding an object with Force Grip, that you can throw the object at them. A blue aura means they're within targeting distance but you're not locked on.

First-Person Camera

The first-person camera is a valuable tool for players who want to find every collectible. By activating first-person, you can get a more detailed view of your surroundings. Press and hold ✛ to activate first-person view, then use ◎ to look around.

While in this mode, you can't move and block, so don't use it while in combat unless absolutely necessary.

Lightsaber Combat Basics

Not every enemy wields a lightsaber or melee weapon, so you won't always need to use your lightsaber. Still, this is your most important tool, so the basics of lightsaber combat are important. Basic lightsaber combat begins with single slash attacks. Some enemies can be dispatched this way.

The sideways slash attack is effective at hurting multiple enemies at once. To execute this attack, swing the Wii Remote from side to side. When a group of enemies surrounds you or stands in line directly in front of you, use a sideways slash to run your 'saber across their chests.

To execute a down ward slash, swing the Wii Remote down. This attack is most useful against single enemies and often works best as a finishing attack or as part of a lightsaber combo.

WII WONDERS

Only the Wii's motion-sensing controls allow you to use the Wii Remote and Nunchuk controllers to truly emulate battle with the lightsaber and Force powers.

Lightsaber Combat Advanced

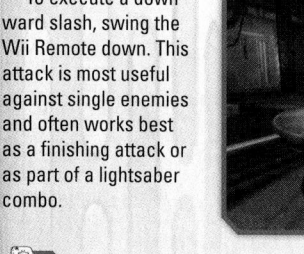 

To reach distant enemies with your 'saber, use lunge attacks. Simply thrust the Wii Remote forward as if poking the air to lunge at enemies directly in front of you. Because the attack is more like a stab than a slash, it will not carry momentum easily into other lightsaber combos. You can, however, transition from lunge attack to upward slash.

Execute an upward slash by swinging the Wii Remote upward. You'll perform an uppercut-like slash and cut deeply into your enemy. Link the two attacks (lunge and upward slash) to formulate your first lightsaber combo!

Lightsaber Block

Your Sith instincts grant you lightning-fast reflexes. As such, you'll automatically deflect *some* blaster fire. In order to deflect even more blaster fire, and even *re*flect some, you'll need to block. Tilt (don't swing) your Wii Remote sideways so that ✛ is facing your Nunchuk. This raises your lightsaber to blocking position and will reflect fire back at the shooter rather than just deflecting it away.

Use lightsaber block when you're slowly navigating long hallways, approaching distant enemies, or even when you're taking too much fire from multiple foes. Lightsaber block won't reflect all incoming fire, but it will significantly reduce the amount of damage you take while in battle.

JEDI KNOWLEDGE

Pale blue blaster fire is significantly more dangerous and difficult to block than red blaster fire.

Lightsaber Combo

Lightsaber combos are the most important part of your combat techniques. The most basic lightsaber combo (lunge and upward thrust) is great for swiftly dispatching single enemies. However, you'll usually face multiple enemies and will need more than a one-two combo to get the job done.

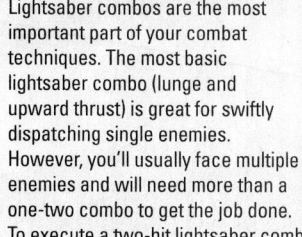

To execute a two-hit lightsaber combo, swing from left to right, then left again. To execute a three-hit lightsaber combo, swing the Wii Remote from left to right, then left, then right again in one fluid motion.

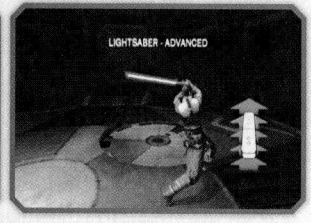

Remember both the two-hit and three-hit lightsaber combos, as they are the basis for every other lightsaber combo.

Lightsaber Throw

Aside from Force Lightning, Lightsaber Throw is your most dependable ranged attack. Force Throw (see below) is great, but if there aren't any objects nearby to use as projectiles, you won't have anything to throw from a distance. Luckily you always have your trusty 'saber with you.

To use Lightsaber Throw, hold down Ⓐ then swing your Wii Remote downward as if performing a downward slash. Your lightsaber will travel through the air and slash through the enemy directly in front of you before automatically returning to you like a boomerang.

Force Attacks
Force Lightning

Force Lightning is one of your staple Force powers. At its most basic level, Force Lightning can electrocute an enemy and nearly obliterate them completely. After upgrading your Force Lightning to higher levels, it can fry up to three enemies at a time for major damage! Press Ⓒ to radiate a devastating current of Force Lightning toward your opponent. Hold Ⓒ until your Force meter is depleted, at which point you can no longer maintain your Force Lightning attack.

Force Lightning is most efficient when used as you approach enemies or as they approach you. Don't wait to use it until the enemy is within lightsaber range; instead, use it as a ranged attack to whittle down your enemy's health before they can reach you. Force Lightning is also a great way to stall powerful approaching enemies. Your blast will slow them down, granting you time to escape, find a bacta tank, or even formulate a new attack plan.

Force Push

Force Push is another staple of your Force powers. Much like Force Lightning, it can damage faraway enemies before they're close enough to hurt you with melee weapons. Unlike Force Lightning, it doesn't increase damage with the amount of Force power used. To use Force Push to unleash a powerful blast of the Force, thrust the Nunchuk forward (much like a lunge attack with your lightsaber) as if you're pushing the air.

Force Push is a great way to hurl enemies away as they approach or to knock them down from a distance. Like Force Lightning, Force Push is a great way to stall enemies before they can attack. Knock them away with Force Push and concentrate on a single enemy while the others are on their backs. Force Push also has a great side effect of carrying nearby

debris in its shock wave. Force Push can throw crates, barrels, and rocks at foes, and it can detonate explosive items. Lead your assaults with Force Push and you'll never go wrong.

Force Grip

Force Grip is another way to manipulate objects. Get near an object or person until a blue aura surrounds whatever you're targeting; then press Ⓩ to grip the object with the Force. Once you have it in the air, move it around with ⓞ.

The best aspect of Force Grip is that it allows you to execute several other attacks while your target is immobile in the air or to use other objects (even enemies) as weapons!

Force Throw

While an object or person is in the air, you can use Force Throw. Once the object is in your Force Grip and floating in the air, use ⓞ to direct it at a target such as a nearby enemy. When the targeted enemy becomes surrounded by a red aura, release Ⓩ to throw the object at the target. Use Force Throw to toss enemies into each other and to hurl explosive items.

Force Slam

Force Slam is an effective way to slow down an enemy and deal major damage while he's in your grip. Pick up your rival with Force Grip, then swing the Nunchuk downward to slam your captive into the ground. Of all Force attacks, this is one of the quickest and easiest to execute. It deals moderate damage and instantly incapacitates your enemy.

Force Pummel

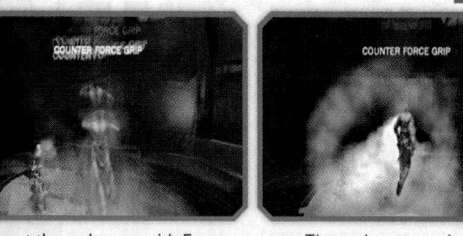

Force Pummel is another attack you can execute while someone is in your Force Grip. Like Force Throw, it is a way to damage enemies by throwing objects at them. Instead of throwing an object at a distant enemy, you can Force Grip a foe, then hurl nearby objects at him while he's in your grip. To do so, pick up an enemy with Force Grip. While your enemy is floating in the air, wave the Wii Remote from right to left as if you're performing a sideways slash.

This attack is only effective when there are nearby crates and other debris to use as projectiles against your captive.

Counter Force Grip

You're not the only one with Force powers. Throughout your journey, you will encounter some very powerful Jedi that Order 66 missed. During battle, they'll use their Force powers on you. If your Jedi foe manages to get you in a Force Grip, free yourself with Force Push or Force Lightning. It's as simple as fighting fire with fire.

Force Lock and Lightsaber Lock

During your adventure, you will face enemies whose Force and lightsaber skills match your own. When that happens, you must engage them in a Force or Lightsaber Lock at some point during your battle. When you're engaged in a lock, there is only one way to break it and win the battle. Once in a lock, several prompts will appear onscreen. If

it's a Force Lock, rotate the Nunchuk to match the angle shown in the onscreen prompts, then shove the Nunchuk forward to thrust the enemy's Force back at them.

If you're engaged in a Lightsaber Lock, turn the Wii Remote to match the angle shown in the onscreen prompts, then shove the Wii Remote forward to nudge your 'saber into your opponent. Do this as many times as you're prompted to win your Force or Lightsaber Lock.

> **JEDI KNOWLEDGE**
>
> You will often have to win several lock battles to defeat your opponent.

Force Repulse

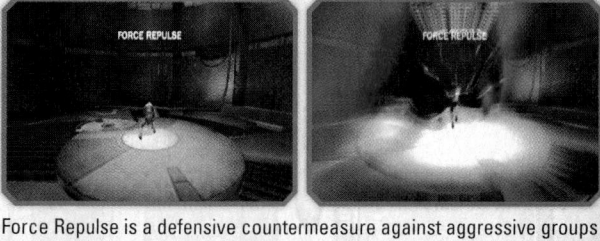

Force Repulse is a defensive countermeasure against aggressive groups of enemies. This move unleashes a radiating shock wave of energy from your entire body and knocks back all enemies within range. To activate Force Repulse, hold down Ⓑ and Ⓩ then swing both the Wii Remote and Nunchuk in a downward motion at the same time.

You'll leap into the air and send all nearby enemies flying backward. Force Repulse won't dispatch many enemies, but it will create breathing room when you're surrounded by waves of foes.

Force Maelstrom

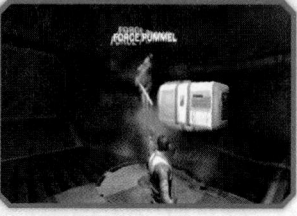

Unlike Force Repulse, Force Maelstrom *is* a great offensive attack. Like Repulse, however, it unleashes a shock wave of energy that radiates away from your body and knocks back surrounding enemies— but this attack does it with all the charged-up power of the Force and is capable of inflicting major damage to surrounding foes.

Activate Force Maelstrom by holding down Ⓐ, Ⓑ, Ⓒ, and Ⓩ to focus your Force, then swing both the Wii Remote and Nunchuk in a downward motion simultaneously.

Heads-Up Display (HUD)

Health bar: This displays how much health you currently have. When it's completely depleted, you'll perish.

Minimap: This displays your position on the level as you progress throughout your mission.

Force meter: This displays how much Force power you have to use on Force attacks. If it's empty, you will be unable to perform Force attacks of any kind.

Force Point tracker: When defeated, enemies release Force Points. This display keeps track of your current Force Points, enemies defeated, and total accumulated Force Points.

Collectibles tracker: This appears only when you've obtained a collectible item. It shows how many you've already collected and how many remain.

Current Goal meter: Sometimes you must defeat a certain amount of enemies to proceed. When you do, this meter will appear and empty as you defeat whichever enemies are listed above the meter.

BECOMING THE SITH
Force Power Basics

You've mastered the basics, but in order to truly master the Force, you must learn how to properly handle all your Force powers. These are advanced techniques and lightsaber combos that revolve around your continuing mastery of the Force. Some Force powers require that you use only Force attacks like Push or Lightning while others include lightsaber combos.

Upgrading Force Powers

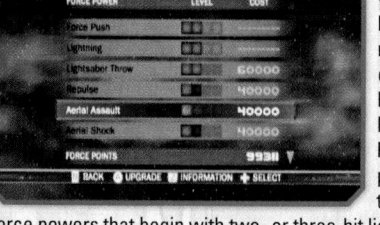

Depending on your preferred combat style, you can upgrade your Force powers to suit your needs. If you're more comfortable with just Force attacks, upgrade Force Lightning and Force Push only. If you prefer lightsaber combos, then upgrade only the Force powers that begin with two- or three-hit lightsaber attacks.

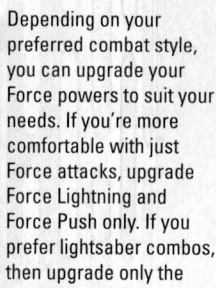

JEDI KNOWLEDGE

Just as with other lightsaber combos, any of the techniques described below that begin with two- or three-hit lightsaber attacks are considered lightsaber combos.

Every Force power has four levels to upgrade. While some are available at the start of your adventure, you will have to unlock others as you progress. To activate a dormant power or upgrade an active one, go into the Pause menu and select Force Powers. Choose the power you want to upgrade and press Ⓑ. As long as you have enough Force Points to upgrade your powers (20,000 to activate, then 40,000, 60,000, and 100,000 to upgrade each subsequent level), you can customize your Force powers however you see fit.

Force Points

To accumulate Force Points, you must dispatch enemies. Every time you destroy an enemy, he'll release small blue clouds of light that you will automatically absorb. These blue clouds are Force Points. The more enemies you dispatch in quick succession, the more points each enemy will release. To increase the amount of Force Points you accumulate per battle, build up combos by varying your attacks to dispatch multiple enemies.

Force Powers

Aerial Assault

Description: Jump into the air and thrust a powerful wave of the Force toward your target. Press Ⓑ then Force Push.

Aerial Assault is a great tool for knocking down airborne enemies like Mandalorians or stormtroopers with jet packs, or for inflicting decent damage on large enemies like rancors or AT-ST walkers.

In addition, it is effective against ground forces. There are several ways to get yourself out of a bind when surrounded by the enemy. Leap into the air and launch an Aerial Assault on the group below to blast a hole through their ranks.

Aerial Shock

Description: Jump into the air and electrocute your target with a powerful lightning attack. Press Ⓑ then Ⓒ.

Like Aerial Assault, Aerial Shock is a great attack to use against large groups of flying foes. Using it on ground troops is not much different than using standard lightning attacks while on the ground, so don't count on it too much while facing ground forces. If you must use it on ground forces, use it against faster, more aggressive enemies like Felucian warriors.

Force Choke

Description: Grip your opponent in the air and choke them with the invisible fingers of the Force. Hold ⓩ then turn the Nunchuk upside down.

Force Choke is, by far, one of your most underrated powers. Capable of dispatching single enemies with one attack (after being upgraded a bit), this maneuver is best used in one-on-one situations. You are defenseless when using Force Choke, so don't use it while surrounded by enemies!

To make effective use of Choke, defeat the majority of enemies in a group, leaving only one or two alive. Knock one away so that you're facing only one enemy, then Choke them.

Sith Strike

Description: Slam your enemy into the ground with the Force. Perform a two-attack lightsaber combo, then Force Push.

This lightsaber combo is a quick and effective way to demolish weakened enemies. In its upgraded state, Sith Strike can destroy lesser enemies with a single attack. It's fast, easy, and, more importantly, deals decent damage.

Use this attack when approached by three enemies or less. If you try to use Sith Strike while surrounded by foes, you'll be open to counter-attack from other nearby enemies.

Storm

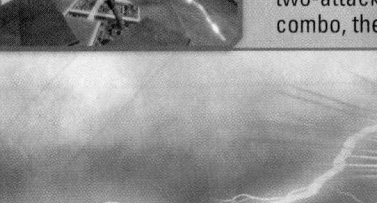

Description: Infuse your lightsaber with the power of lightning and unleash it in an explosive burst of the Force. Perform a two-attack lightsaber combo, then press ⓒ.

Of all lightsaber combos, Storm is one of the most impressive. The initial two-hit lightsaber attack can damage multiple enemies if they're sideways slashes, but the most potent part of the attack is the final lightning surge you release.

The explosive burst of electricity can inflict major damage on surrounding enemies. Upgrade Storm to gain one of the most effective attacks against small groups of enemies.

Detonate

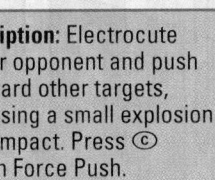

Description: Electrocute your opponent and push toward other targets, causing a small explosion on impact. Press ⓒ then Force Push.

Explosives are some of the best methods for dealing with large enemies or small groups. Unfortunately, there won't always be explosive barrels or blinking bombs nearby to hurl at your opponents. That's where Detonate comes in.

As long as there is one opponent within range of your Force Lightning, you'll always have a bomb handy. Use Detonate to turn enemies into bombs and blow up groups from a distance. Because Detonate sends your initial target flying, you can use this Force power as an effective ranged attack.

Ground Slam

Description: Slam your lightsaber into the ground, creating a powerful shock wave. Press Ⓑ then swing the Wii Remote downward.

Of all your Force powers, Ground Slam is one of the most effective methods to disperse small groups while inflicting damage. Execute Ground Slam attacks to send enemies flying with a radiating shock wave of energy.

Use this attack as a lead-in when approaching small groups. Leap into the air and come down on the group's center with Ground Slam to knock them all away at once. Follow this up with lightsaber combos of your choice.

Saber Assault

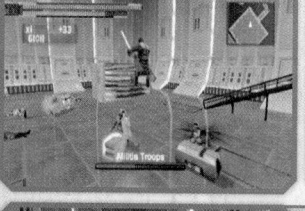

Description: Slam your lightsaber into the ground and send a powerful burst of the Force outward. Press Ⓑ, Ⓑ then swing the Wii Remote downward.

Like Ground Slam, Saber Assault is perfect against crowds. Upgrade this attack to dole out major damage.

Saber Whirlwind

Description: Dash forward and slam your lightsaber into the ground, creating a powerful shock wave. Press Ⓑ then Force Dash and swing the Wii Remote downward.

Saber Whirlwind is much like Ground Slam or Saber Assault. However, this attack is much better suited toward rushing enemies. By leaping into the air and dashing away, you can soar over enemies as you approach distant foes and crush them with your Ground Slam.

Dark Rage

Description: Charge up with the power of the dark side and increase the damage of your lightsaber. Perform a three-attack lightsaber combo, then press Ⓐ.

Dark Rage may be a lightsaber combo, but it's the aftereffect that deals the most damage. After activating Dark Rage, your lightsaber attacks will increase in damage and the damage you receive will decrease.

Take full advantage of your Dark Rage power while facing bosses and large groups of enemies. The increased lightsaber damage will help cut through foes quickly, and the decrease in damage incurred allows you to get close to enemies and execute devastating lightsaber combos. As you defeat foes while in Dark Rage, your Force meter will slowly refill. Once it's completely full again, your Dark Rage will dissipate.

SITH WISDOM

If your preferred style of combat is lightsaber-heavy, the Kaiburr lightsaber crystal is a perfect complement to this Dark Rage.

Sith Barrage

Description: Cast a destructive bolt of lightning toward your target. Perform a three-attack lightsaber combo, then press Ⓒ.

Like Storm, Sith Barrage is a destructive lightsaber combo that combines Force Lightning with multiple lightsaber slashes.

Sith Scorcher

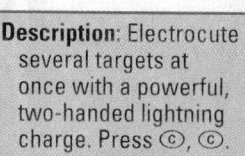

Description: Electrocute several targets at once with a powerful, two-handed lightning charge. Press Ⓒ, Ⓒ.

By far the most powerful Force power, Sith Scorcher can destroy multiple enemies with one strike. Upgrade this power to maximum to become one of the most destructive forces in the galaxy.

Rather than sting your opponents with simple Force Lightning attacks, you can use Sith Scorcher to fry groups of foes with a single burst. When approaching groups of enemies, begin your assault with Sith Scorcher to whittle down their numbers before finishing them off with lightsaber combos. More importantly, Sith Scorcher is an effective way to quickly deplete the Health bars of large, dangerous enemies like AT-STs or rancor beasts. If you upgrade only one Force power, make it this one.

Power Slam

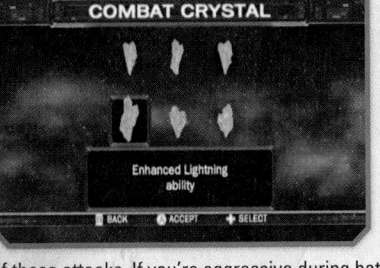

Description: A massive surge of Force that launches any nearby target into the air. Perform a three-attack lightsaber combo, then Force Push.

Power Slam is a good lightsaber combo when you're facing one foe while several others approach from a distance. The initial three-hit lightsaber attack can dish out decent damage on one foe and may even destroy him, but the Force blast that follows is where the attack's real power is.

After cutting down the first foe, the enemies following him take the Force blast and are knocked away like bowling pins. Use this attack when you're heading into thick waves of enemies.

Sith Seeker

Description: Send your target flying, followed by an explosive ball of lightning. Force Push, then press ©.

Like Detonate, Sith Seeker is a devastating attack that creates a powerful surge of Force energy capable of destroying multiple targets. This attack, however, doesn't rely on using one opponent as a bomb but rather transports your Force Lightning in a Force shock wave.

The result is a traveling Force bomb that detonates on impact. Like Detonate or Sith Scorcher, this attack is also extremely useful against large enemies.

Lightsaber Customization

As we've mentioned before, your lightsaber is the most powerful tool in battle. As such, you can and should customize your lightsaber to fit your combat style. If you rely more on Force powers like Push and Lightning, equip a combat crystal that complements one of those attacks. If you're aggressive during battle or while navigating a level during a mission, pick a combat crystal that increases your defensive capabilities, such as blocking blaster fire.

"The crystal is the heart of the blade. The heart is the crystal of the Jedi. The Jedi is the crystal of the Force. The Force is the blade of the heart. All are intertwined. The crystal, the blade...the Jedi. You are one."

—Master Luminara Unduli, *Star Wars: The Clone Wars Volume 1*

There are six combat crystals to choose from, each with its own special attribute:

1. **Kaiburr combat crystal:** increases Force Push strength.
2. **Qixoni combat crystal:** increases Force Choke strength.
3. **Opila combat crystal:** increases Lightsaber Throw strength.
4. **Dragite combat crystal:** increases Lightsaber Damage.
5. **Firkrann combat crystal:** increases Force Lightning strength.
6. **Damind combat crystal:** Greatly increases strength of lightsaber damage.

Aside from combat crystals, there are also collectible lightsaber hilts and color crystals to change the look of your lightsaber. Though the hilts and color crystals don't change the way the lightsaber performs, they do add depth to your 'saber's customization features. As you progress throughout your adventure, you'll also unlock new abilities for your lightsaber that are applied automatically.

PROLOGUE

A long time ago in a galaxy far, far away . . . .

The galaxy is on the brink of darkness. The evil GALACTIC EMPIRE has overthrown the Old Republic and now holds countless worlds in the grip of fear.

The Jedi Knights have been all but destroyed. Only a handful have escaped the Imperial forces, disappearing into hiding across the galaxy. The Emperor's spies have located a lone Jedi Knight on the Wookiee homeworld of Kashyyyk. The Sith Lord DARTH VADER has been sent to destroy him....

AREA 4

AREA 3

AREA 2

AREA 5

AREA 1

MISSION DETAILS

Objective

The Emperor has dispatched Darth Vader to destroy a lone Jedi Knight who is in hiding on the Wookiee homeworld of Kashyyyk.

Enemies Encountered

Wookiee Berserker

Wookiee Infantry

Rogue Jedi: Boss

Collectibles Found

20 Holocrons

MAP LEGEND

🗃	Bacta Tank
🔹	Color Crystal
⊚	Force Holocron
◆	Health Holocron
▦	Holocron
➘	Lightsaber Hilt

13

There are 200 Holocrons to collect in *Star Wars: The Force Unleashed*. Some are pretty easy to find, so they won't be covered in the following walkthrough. If you're interested in collecting all 200 Holocrons, look for these Holocron boxes to give you tips on obtaining some of the trickier ones. Holocron locations are always given on the map at the beginning of each area, and a checklist of all 200 Holocrons and their locations can be found in the "Sith Secrets" chapter at the end of this guide.

Dark Plans

As battles rage in the lush jungles of Kashyyyk, an Imperial fighter touches down on one of the planet's besieged villages. Darth Vader arrives in time to take control of his befuddled stormtroopers. They've struggled long enough against the troublesome Wookiees, and he's intent on handling the lone Jedi on his own.

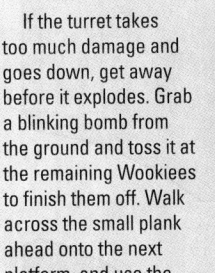

Upon disembarking the Imperial Lambda-class shuttle as Darth Vader, slowly approach the stormtrooper manning the turret behind the nearby barricade. Familiarize yourself with your powers by using either the Force Push to destroy the barricade or the Force Grip to rip the turret from its supports. Ripping the turret won't do you much good now, since there are no enemies to mow down, but this is a good chance to get used to a power you'll be using frequently in upcoming missions.

SITH WISDOM

By using Force Grip on a turret, you gain a powerful ally in battle: It will temporarily float to your left, firing on enemies as you complete your mission.

Walk up the bridge beyond the barricade and rendezvous with Triton Squad. When you arrive, they're busy fending off a wave of Wookiee Berserkers but quickly finish them off...for now.

Lead Triton Squad down the path on the right, past the large fire. As you approach, two more Wookiee Berserkers emerge from the smoky path ahead. Force Grip one and quickly toss him over the ledge on the right. Then turn your attention to the second Wookiee and assault him with a double-slash attack. As soon as he is down, Force Grip the Wookiee Infantry on the platform ahead and choke him.

Continue ahead until you encounter two more Wookiee Berserkers and a turret. Quickly Force Push the two rushing Wookiees or slash them to ribbons, then raise your lightsaber to deflect the turret's incoming fire. Slowly creep toward the barricade and throw your lightsaber at the Wookiee manning the turret.

Once you clear the immediate area of foes, Force Grip the turret and move ahead until the next batch of Wookiees come into view. Let the turret blast them to bits while your lightsaber deflects incoming fire.

If the turret takes too much damage and goes down, get away before it explodes. Grab a blinking bomb from the ground and toss it at the remaining Wookiees to finish them off. Walk across the small plank ahead onto the next platform, and use the Force to choke the lone Wookiee. If you've taken any damage, pick up the Bacta tank near the platform's far edge.

Turn left and Force Grip the turret on the neighboring platform. With the turret in tow, traipse across the next plank with your lightsaber in blocking position. The turret will make short work of the Wookiees ahead while your lightsaber deflects incoming fire. Finish off the last of the Wookiee Berserkers on this platform and forge ahead.

Stop at the plank before reaching the Wookiee building on the next platform; demolish the Wookiee squad in your way. Force Push the squad to spread them apart, then pick them off one by one. Either lift and toss them over the ledge or slash them with your lightsaber. When only the Wookiee manning the turret remains, use the Force to steal his turret and turn it against him.

Surely the Wookiee squad dealt *some* amount of damage. If so, pick up the Bacta tank at the bridge's end, just left of the building's entrance. If that Bacta tank isn't enough to replenish all your health, there is another Bacta tank in an alcove inside the building.

Enter the building and carefully round the hallway as it circles left. Charge your Force Push and destroy the barricade in your way. Force Grip the Wookiee waiting behind the demolished wall and choke him. As his lifeless body hits the floor, raise your lightsaber and fend off the Wookiee Berserkers in the corridor. If they inflict damage, pick up the Bacta tank on the balcony ahead.

Upon reaching the building's exit, turn left and raise your guard. Several Wookiees with guns wait outside. Reflect incoming fire and slowly step toward the glowing cube on the bridge ahead. The glowing cube is a Holocron. You'll find these scattered throughout your adventure, so keep your eyes peeled and your senses sharp. In the meantime, walk across the bridge while reflecting incoming fire and steal the turret away from the attacking Wookiee. Once the turret is floating beside you, continue onto the next platform and let it destroy the remaining enemies.

Just beyond the demolished turret, to the left of the bridge, is another Holocron. Snatch it up before you do an about-face and continue tearing through the Wookiee city.

Turn back around and continue trekking into the Wookiee city. Stop when you reach a wide, open platform with several bombs littered around a lone barricade. The area is deserted, but there are two Holocrons here. One is hidden under the small pointed statue at the center. Use Force Grip to remove the statue and grab the Holocron; then claim the other Holocron, hiding behind the large metal drum near the wall on the right. After claiming the Holocrons, turn left and head toward the next pair of Wookiee warriors holding position on a nearby platform.

Two Wookiees await you on a platform. Lure the Wookiee Berserker toward the left ledge and engage him in combat. Block his incoming attack, and once his guard is down, grab him with your Force Grip and toss him over the side. With him out of the way, you can easily choke the remaining Wookiee waiting in the next area.

After choking the Wookiee, examine the area beneath the walkway, just left of the next platform. Grab the Holocron hiding there. On the platform's far edge, remove another small pointed statue to reveal yet another Holocron.

Walk across the bridge on the left and into the next area. Shove the Wookiees aside. Once they are down, rush toward the closest Wookiee and wait for him to get up. As he does, run your 'saber through him with two or three quick slashes. Then turn toward his partner and launch your lightsaber at him to finish him off. Pick up the Bacta tank on the floor before entering the next area.

In the next area's center is a barricaded turret. Use Force Push to demolish the barricade, then steal the turret from the Wookiee and turn it against him. Turn your 'saber toward the other Wookiee and unleash a flurry of attacks. Slash at the hairy beast until he's a pile of singed follicles, then lead the turret onto the next platform.

Hold your 'saber high to reflect Wookiee fire, and allow your turret to do most of the work.

Lead the turret as far into the Wookiee defenses as possible. Once the turret is disabled, use lightsaber combos to finish the job. If more than two Wookiees remain, use Force Push to split them up and pick them off individually. Focus on Wookiee Berserkers first, as they pose the greater threat. Leave Wookiee Infantry for last.

With the Wookiee Berserker out of the way, you can quickly choke the Wookiee Infantry from afar.

Once you clear the area of all enemies, examine the crevice behind the large brown drum to find another Holocron.

Each step brings you closer to the lone Jedi Knight. Trample past the fiery rubble, across the bridge, and onto the next platform. At its center is another Wookiee-manned turret. Creep up to the turret and deflect fire. Pounce on your enemy when you're close enough to attack.

Either destroy the turret with Force Push or rip it away and strike down the hairball with your 'saber. Continue deeper into the Wookiee city.

Take advantage of the blinking bombs littered about. In the following area, when you see the next group of Wookiees, pick up a bomb and hurl it at them. A single bomb can instantly rid you of several hairy headaches.

WOOKIEE WARNING

Even though the blinking bombs are plentiful, don't be careless with them. If you detonate one near you, it can cause extensive damage and take sizable chunks out of your Health bar.

Follow the walkway on the right, between the huge tree trunk and the holographic emitter, and press onward until you encounter a group of Wookiees.

Rip apart the small pointed statue at the walkway's center to find a Holocron.

Let the Wookiee Berserkers approach and blast them back with your Force Push. As they stumble back, Force Grip a piece of rubble and hurl it at the downed Wookiee. Pick up the second Wookiee and toss him over the edge, then finish off the third Wookiee by either slashing him with your lightsaber or choking him from afar.

Carefully navigate the planks ahead and continue moving forward.

Remove the small pointed statue on the first circular platform and claim the Holocron.

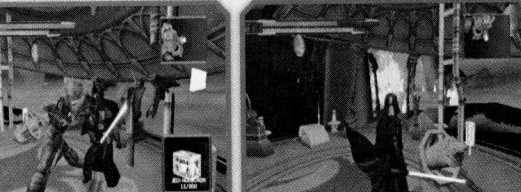

When two more Wookiee Berserkers appear, deflect their slashing attacks and counter with a combo. Fell one bothersome beast, then Force Push the other one down. As he lies helpless on the floor, pick him up and toss him over the edge.

While still on the first circular platform, pick up a nearby blinking bomb and hurl it at the turret on the platform to the left. If you miss with the bomb, grab a large piece of debris and toss it at the turret: Use the debris as a shield by positioning it between you and the blaster fire as you move toward the turret. Once you're close enough, hurl the debris at the turret to destroy it.

In the next area, use Force Push to detonate a blinking bomb near the two Wookiees in your way.

Just around the bend, past the now-crispy Wookiees, are three more furry foes. Slash past the first, then pick up the second and hurl him at the third. Be quick, as all three carry blasters and can quickly decimate your Health bar. Force Grip the turret at the next area's center and lead it around the walkway to the right. Let it blast through the next Wookiee fighter while your 'saber blocks incoming blaster fire.

Turn left and go into the building. Just inside the building is an elevator pad; ride the elevator down to the Kashyyyk beach.

Beachfront Battle

The once-peaceful Kashyyyk beach is now the scene of a brutal battle. Giant AT-AT walkers splash along the shore as they fire down on Wookiee warriors. Meanwhile, a hooded figure watches the battle from a perch high above the sand. It is the rogue Jedi Master, and his Wookiee forces are holding tight. They swarm over the stormtroopers and overwhelm the Imperial forces—that is, until you arrive, of course.

STAR WARS
FORCE
UNLEASHED

When you reach the bottom floor, rush out of the passage and onto the beach. Charge at the Wookiees head-on, and tear them apart with swift 'saber strikes.

> After defeating the Wookiees, make a sharp left at the passage exit and hug the cliff walls as you go. Collect the three Holocrons (one inside a burning ship and two more among several trees), then turn your attention back toward the beachfront battle where several more Wookiees await.

Grab the turret near the downed ship, and use it to whittle down the Wookiee forces. Lead the turret down the beach toward a second turret near the shore. By the time you reach the second turret, the first is ready to give out. Claim the second turret, then use it until it, too, gives out. After exhausting both turrets, use your lightsaber to cut down the remaining Wookiees. Stay by the beach's far edge, near where the AT-AT walkers approach, so that you can quickly grab a Bacta tank (should you take too much damage).

Just as the last Wookiee falls to your 'saber, the Jedi Knight comes out of hiding. He's safe in a large hut perched high on the cliffside...until you use your Force powers to bring it crumbling down.

Rogue Jedi Duel

The rogue Jedi manages to navigate the crumbling debris and lands safely on the beach. He takes out his lightsaber and prepares for battle. It's time to strike down the arrogant fool!

The Jedi has several attacks that can inflict moderate damage. When the duel begins, raise your lightsaber to block his attack. He'll throw his lightsaber at you when your guard is down, so keep your guard up to block his ranged attack. When he comes in close and raises his weapon to attack, use quick two-hit combos with your 'saber to whittle down his health. If he hurls objects at you, either jump over them or block them with your weapon.

Maintain pressure on him by being aggressive. You're a Dark Lord, after all. Stay on the attack and continuously press forward as he backs away. As you approach, maintain your guard. Counterattack only after you've deflected his attacks.

If the rogue Jedi uses Force Push to launch you back, jump while in the air to land safely on both feet. Once you're back on the ground, the Jedi will continue his assault. He's extremely fast and can quickly circle around you and attack in one fluid motion, so stay alert!

After whittling down the Jedi's health and knocking him off guard, use your Force powers to finish him off. Carefully follow the six onscreen prompts to quickly strike. Wait for each to show up and shake the corresponding control (Wii Remote or Nunchuk) to activate your attack.

First you'll deflect the Jedi's attack, then rob him of his 'saber and use it against him. Finally, after crushing his will, you'll hurl him around the beach and send him crashing helplessly onto the sand.

Just as you're about to crush the life from his body, you sense a being far more powerful than this rogue Jedi. At first, you think it's his master, but he claims you destroyed his master years ago. Just then, as you're about to run your 'saber through him, the lightsaber flies out of your hand and into the hands of a child! You turn to find that it was not his master you sensed, but his son.

Rather than let the child perish at the hands of the Imperial forces or, worse, the Emperor, you resolve to make him your secret apprentice. You slay the encroaching stormtroopers and quickly sneak him off Kashyyyk without anyone noticing....

17

TIE CONSTRUCTION YARD

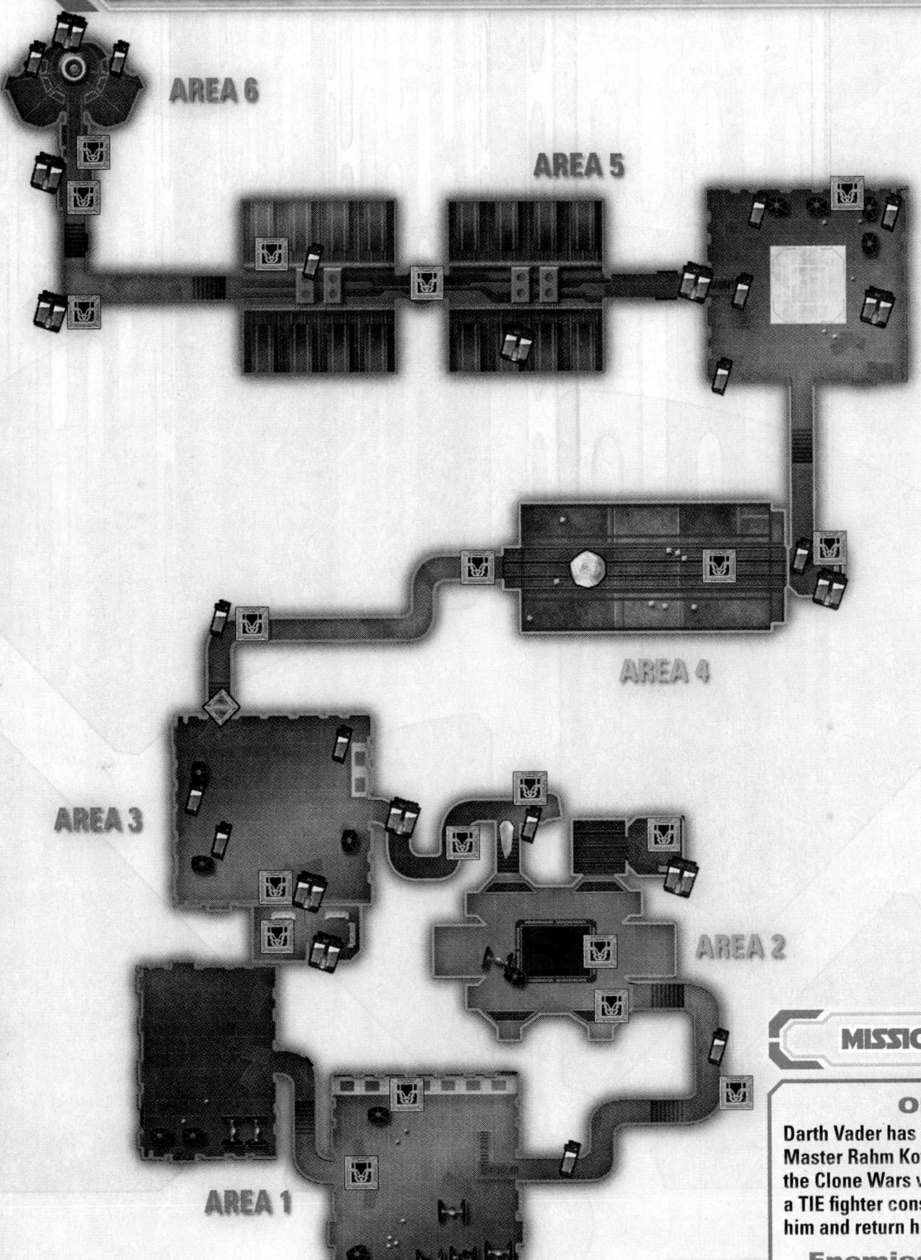

AREA 6

AREA 5

AREA 4

AREA 3

AREA 2

AREA 1

MAP LEGEND

- 🛢 Bacta Tank
- 🔹 Color Crystal
- ⚙ Force Holocron
- ◆ Health Holocron
- ▦ Holocron
- ✎ Lightsaber Hilt

MISSION DETAILS

Objective

Darth Vader has sent you to defeat Jedi Master Rahm Kota, a respected general of the Clone Wars who is leading an attack on a TIE fighter construction facility. Destroy him and return his lightsaber to Lord Vader.

Enemies Encountered

Militia Elite

Militia Trooper

Militia Saboteur

Imperial Stormtrooper

AT-ST: Minor Boss

Rahm Kota: Boss

Collectibles Found

20 Holocrons

Color Crystal

Force Holocron

Health Holocron

STAR WARS
THE FORCE UNLEASHED

The Secret Apprentice

It is now several years later, and you, as the Secret Apprentice, have been studying the ways of the Force from your master, Darth Vader. You've matured from that brooding child he found on the Kashyyyk beach into a powerful Sith apprentice. Your years of tutelage under Darth Vader's care have remained a secret even to the Emperor, for your destiny poses a threat to the Dark Lord. However, now it is time to begin your journey in unleashing the full power of the Force....

"Leave No Witnesses."

With your training progressing rapidly, it's time to face your first real opponent. A Jedi named Rahm Kota is attacking a critical Imperial shipyard. You must dispatch him and return his lightsaber to your master. You must do this quietly, however, as no one should learn of your existence. This means you must leave no witnesses—eliminate Rebel and Imperial forces alike.

At the hangar bay, your personal droid, PROXY, updates you on your new pilot. According to PROXY's personnel file, Captain Juno Eclipse is a capable, war-hardened, highly decorated combat pilot. You need no more than a glance to see that she is beautiful as well.

Juno's piloting skills prove helpful as she manages to infiltrate the TIE construction ship while the battle rages on outside. When your ship drops you off, dash to the hangar bay's right side and raise your lightsaber to reflect blaster fire from Kota's men. When the Rebels rush in to attack, greet them with two lightsaber combos.

Get a better view of your enemies by jumping atop a TIE wing container. From there, you can locate the rest of the Rebels in the hangar and even pick them off with Force Grip. Grab the nearest Rebel and choke him.

After clearing the hangar bay of Rebel scum, hop down and trundle into the corridor at the bay's far end. Just before the stairs at the bend in the corridor, use your Force Grip to rip a panel off the wall and toss it at the enemy forces gathered on the stairs. Edge closer to the steps, then grab the small blinking bomb at the base of the stairs. Throw it at the men gathered atop the steps and blow them up!

If you missed any of the Rebels atop the steps, rush up to them and finish them off with a Force Push. They've taken a lot of damage by now and should fall quickly.

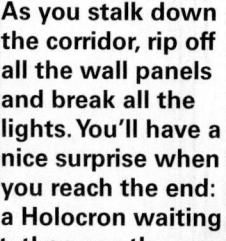 As you stalk down the corridor, rip off all the wall panels and break all the lights. You'll have a nice surprise when you reach the end: a Holocron waiting for you in the hangar. Grab it, then use the crates to jump to the balcony above the main hangar door. There you'll find one more enemy trooper and another Holocron.

Charge your Force Push at the corridor's end and release it once it is fully charged. The blast tears down the sealed hatch at the passage's end and sends several or Kota's men flying onto their backs.

The next hangar is swarming with militia troops. In order to proceed, you must destroy enough militia to deplete the Militia Troops bar at the screen's bottom. Unfortunately, they're all extremely well armed and can cut you down with blaster fire in no time. Immediately bring up your lightsaber to reflect their fire and rush for cover behind one of the large TIE wing crates on the hangar's right.

Stalk the militia in the hangar by staying near the walls and out of the open. Weave in and out of the crates and the large TIE fighter parts while you whittle down the militia's numbers.

After taking down nearly half the troops, rush out to the turret at the bay's rear and steal it from the Rebel. Turn it on the remaining militia troops and clear out the rest of the hangar. If you can't get close enough to rip the turret from its supports, use Force Grip or Force Push to hurl a large cylinder at it.

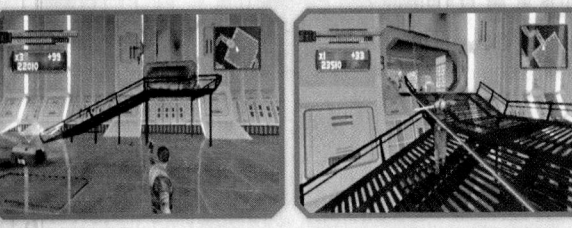

With the hangar clear of militia troops, the door along the left wall opens to reveal a heated battle between stormtroopers and Kota's men. Wait for them to spill onto the walkway in front of you, and use your Force Grip to toss them aside. While the soldiers are down, rush the downed troops and finish them off.

Now that the first wave of troops are out of the way, the soldiers inside the next corridor aim their laser sights on you. Carefully creep up the walkway leading to the next corridor and raise your lightsaber to protect yourself. The 'saber won't block fire from the blasters with laser sights, but you can deflect incoming fire from enemies deeper in the corridor. As soon as you reach the passage's entrance, unleash a Force Push and knock the enemies back.

Slowly walk deeper into the hallway with your lightsaber raised, and reflect the troops' fire back at them, knocking them out one by one. When you're close enough to strike, unleash your lightsaber and cut the saboteurs down. Use your Force Lightning to fry the next wave of militia, then dash deeper into the corridor until you reach the next set of stairs.

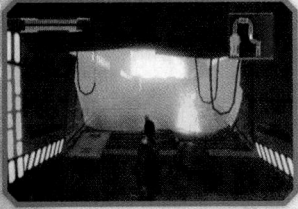

Stop at the steps where an electrical field is going haywire and wait for the field to dissipate. Use Force Grip to pick up and hurl the nearby blinking bomb down the corridor and blast the militia waiting to ambush you. Creep up and grab the turret just atop the steps. Lead the turret into the hallway and let it do most of the work.

Keep your guard up as the turret blasts your enemies, and use Force Lightning to finish off any stragglers the turret missed. If the troops are too far to reach, unleash a Force Push and knock them down. Your blast should also shake loose several wall panels, which you can hurl at the downed enemies.

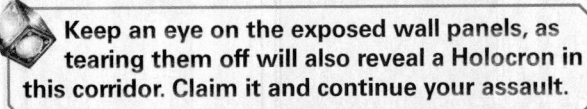

Keep an eye on the exposed wall panels, as tearing them off will also reveal a Holocron in this corridor. Claim it and continue your assault.

At this corridor's end is another set of stairs. Unfortunately, there are five or more militia soldiers waiting for you here. Approach the steps, but stay outside of striking range. Reflect their blaster fire as you approach and unleash a torrent of Force Lightning as soon as you're close enough to fry them. You may get only three or four of them with your Force Lightning, so dash at the remaining militiamen and strike them down.

Go up the steps and through the next hatch. The following room is a tall, wide-open area where several TIE fighter wings are being transported to the next phase of construction. Raise your guard and approach the soldiers inside the facility. Immediately edge left upon entering the area and take cover behind the large metal pillar. From there, use your Force Push to knock away approaching enemies, then rush out and slice through them as they get up.

Near the room's center is a large blue force-field floor panel. Even though it appears otherwise, it's perfectly safe to step on. Approach the TIE fighter wings lying near the corner of the blue floor panel; use the Force to hurl them upward. (Just follow the onscreen prompts for this.) As they fly upward, the wings get stuck along the wall, creating a series of ledges.

Jump from wing to wing and leap through the next blue force field.

After leaping through the blue floor panel, immediately engage the group of fighters waiting to blast you to pieces. Jump into the air, high above them, and land squarely at the group's center. As soon as you land, unleash a horizontal slash attack to cut through several soldiers with one strike.

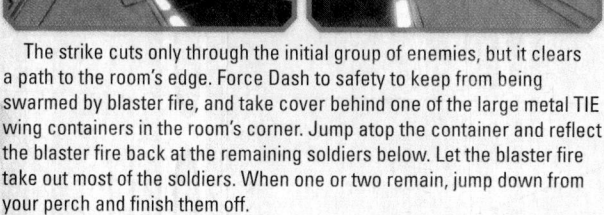

The strike cuts only through the initial group of enemies, but it clears a path to the room's edge. Force Dash to safety to keep from being swarmed by blaster fire, and take cover behind one of the large metal TIE wing containers in the room's corner. Jump atop the container and reflect the blaster fire back at the remaining soldiers below. Let the blaster fire take out most of the soldiers. When one or two remain, jump down from your perch and finish them off.

Explore the room's other side and locate a large, closed hatch.

> If you remove the large metal cylinder in the corner, it exposes another Holocron. From there, the hatch is directly behind you.

Use Force Push to blast the hatch open, then grab the turret near the now-open hatch. Lead the turret inside and lay waste to the stormtroopers inside. Keep the lightsaber up to guard yourself, then dash at the last of the stormtroopers and fry him with your Force Lightning. If you take too much damage, grab the Bacta tank near the control console to replenish, then backtrack to the main area with the blue force-field flooring.

Locate another pile of TIE fighter wings and use the Force to toss them up and create another series of ledges. Use the ledges to leap all the way to the next level.

> As you climb the ledges, stop on the second wing and look atop the tall crate in the corner. A lone Holocron sits here. When the robotic arm along the wall

begins transporting another TIE fighter wing, jump atop the moving wing, then double-jump onto the crate to get the Holocron. Be careful not to cross the next blue force field.

Upon reaching the next level, immediately dash toward the corner with the burning rubble. Run past the militiamen and rip the nearby turret from its supports. Use the high-powered blaster to tear through Kota's men, then use Force Push to detonate the blinking bomb in the corner. The bomb should completely wipe out any remaining militiamen.

Behind the explosion is another open hatch door. Go through to find your first lightsaber color crystal. Grab it on your way into the next corridor.

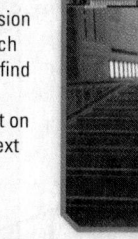

Immediately upon entering the corridor, grab the Bacta tank on the right, then swiftly turn around and raise your lightsaber. Several of Kota's men are entrenched in the hallway behind you. Carefully creep into the hallway, reflecting their fire back at them, then rip a panel from the wall.

Holding the panel in your Force Grip, direct the panel ahead of you so that it blocks the militia's blaster fire. When the panel is within tossing distance of Kota's men, launch it at them and knock them back. If the panel's impact doesn't destroy them, rush ahead and finish the job.

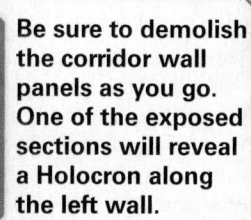

Be sure to demolish the corridor wall panels as you go. One of the exposed sections will reveal a Holocron along the left wall.

At the corridor's end, use the Force to blast through the locked door. The next area is another hangar bay. At the far end is a transport ship with an extremely accurate gun. Enter the bay and immediately dash left to gain cover. The ship's gun will easily cut through your Health bar, and the hangar bay is swarming with militia troops. Once again, you must destroy enough militia troops to deplete the Militia Troops bar at the screen's bottom.

21

Dash along the bay's edge, avoiding the ship's fire, until you reach the hangar's rear. Grab the Bacta tank, then raise your lightsaber to deflect incoming fire from the troops on the ground. Wait for the ship to take off before relinquishing your cover. Once the ship is gone, either slash through the militia troops or use your Force Grip to pick them up and toss them through the hangar portal into space.

Finally, after eliminating most of the militia troops, run to the room's right side to find another gun turret. As before, rip the gun from its support and use it to finish cleaning the hangar bay of all Rebel scum.

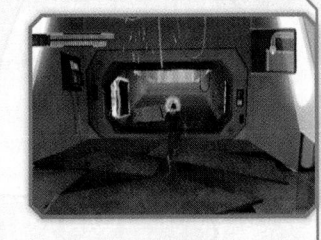

Before leaving the bay, hop atop a crate, then double-jump onto the large balcony along the rear wall. Grab the Holocron on the balcony, then inspect the two rooms on the bay's far left side. They are crawling with stormtroopers but also contain another Holocron and a Bacta tank.

After a little bit of coaxing, the last of Kota's men reveals his general's location on the construction ship. Master Kota is in the construction ship's control room. Grab any remaining Bacta tanks in the bay, then storm into the corridor on the room's right side.

The entry to the corridor has a green Health Holocron; you can't miss it. Grab your Health Holocron and trek into the hallway where more of Kota's men wait.

Inside the short bending hallway is a small barrel with a blinking detonator. Retrieve it and carefully hurl it up the small flight of stairs at the enemy soldiers waiting to ambush you. The force of the explosion clears out most of the militia, leaving only a handful of men for your lightsaber. Approach them carefully, guard up, and slice through them when you're within striking distance.

Go up the steps and dash farther into the hallway. When you encounter another group of Kota's men, burn them with your Force Lightning, then pummel their fallen bodies with debris from the busted wall panels.

Just beyond the next flight of stairs—this one leading down—several more militiamen wait for you. Slowly walk up to the steps and lure them toward you. When the men reach the top of the stairs, turn toward them and unleash a Force Push. This inflicts major damage, and the impact from the surrounding debris will help finish them off.

Just beyond the flight of steps is an exposed electrical field obstructing the path down the corridor. Wait for the electricity to begin dissipating, then Force Dash past the dying field. When you pass the electrical field, raise your lightsaber and block the fire from the gun turret down the hall.

Stop at the bend in the hall, just before running headlong into the turret, and use a busted wall panel to demolish the gun. Force Grip the panel and move it toward the gun. As you do, use it as a shield. When the panel is close enough to the gun, let it fly.

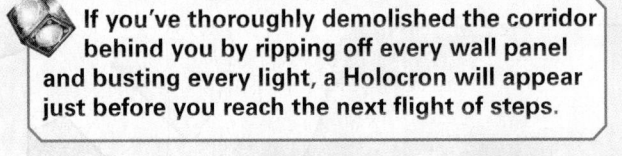

If you've thoroughly demolished the corridor behind you by ripping off every wall panel and busting every light, a Holocron will appear just before you reach the next flight of steps.

Dash past the now-destroyed turret and into the next room. A fierce battle rages above the room's ground floor. Stormtroopers and militia exchange fire on one of the tall room's platforms.

While on the tall room's bottom floor, turn left and unleash a Force Push to knock back the militia fighter behind the large crate. Rush him while he's on the floor and slash through him as he gets up. With the first soldier down, sneak up on his partner and run your 'saber through him. He'll be watching the room along the left wall, so Force Dash up to him from behind and get the drop on him.

Now turn on the soldier on the room's right side and fry him with Force Lightning. Grab the Bacta tank in the room's far right corner, then hop on the elevator platform on the room's left side. Don't bother trying the platform on the right; the battle busted it.

As soon as you step on the platform, it begins carrying you upward. Unfortunately, it comes to a screeching halt halfway up the tall room, just as another platform arrives with a squad of stormtroopers. Get off the elevator platform and head into the walkway. Raise your 'saber while walking toward the militia troops on the left, then Force Push them backward.

With one group of soldiers disabled, dash around the catwalks, slicing through the stormtroopers. If the militia get back up and catch you in their cross fire, pick up the Bacta tank on the catwalk's far left side before turning your blade on them.

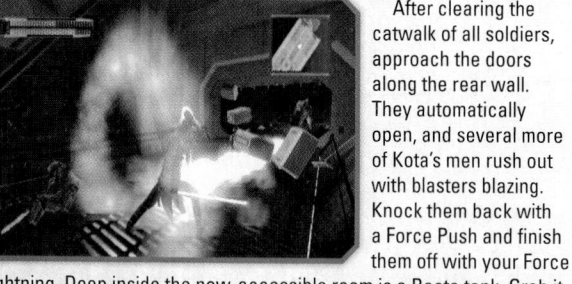

After clearing the catwalk of all soldiers, approach the doors along the rear wall. They automatically open, and several more of Kota's men rush out with blasters blazing. Knock them back with a Force Push and finish them off with your Force Lightning. Deep inside the now-accessible room is a Bacta tank. Grab it if necessary, then return to the catwalk where the two groups of soldiers were previously engaged in battle.

Walk onto the platform the stormtroopers used earlier and ride it up to the next level.

Wait for the elevator to reach the next level, then step off briefly (you must step off and then back on to make the platform move again). Immediately step back onto the elevator so that it begins taking you back down; however, instead of riding it back to the catwalk, jump off and out toward the room's center. You'll land on a floating structure containing a Holocron. Grab it, then jump back onto the elevator platform and take it all the way back up. On the top level, leave the elevator and pick up the Force Holocron on the bridge ahead.

Dismount the elevator and approach the bridge. Either dash at the troops and slash them to ribbons or simply lift them with your Force Grip and toss them over the bridge's side.

JEDI KNOWLEDGE

There's no use trying to jump onto the center structure as you ride the platform upward the first time. You can't jump off as it moves upward, only downward.

Run into the corridor, just beyond the bridge, and engage another group of militia troops. Begin by demolishing the corridor walls and tearing off the panels. Fire the busted panels at the troops in the hallway and dash to a set of steps. Stand your ground here and reflect the militia's fire back at them. When a militia saboteur rushes at you, block his attack and counter with a combo.

Storm up the steps and fire another piece of debris at the soldiers in your way. By now, the path into the next area should be clear. Dash into the next room and prepare for a tough battle. As you enter the hangar, a militia trooper manages to commandeer an AT-ST...and he turns its guns on you.

Quickly dash around the hangar's right side and take cover from the AT-ST's blaster fire. Luckily you're not alone in this fight. The stormtroopers realize that their enemy is in the AT-ST and also open fire on the mechanical menace. Let the stormtroopers' fire distract it before launching your own assault. Just as the AT-ST fires on the Imperial soldiers, come out of hiding and use your Force powers to launch barrels at it.

When the AT-ST turns and fires at you, use your lightsaber to reflect some of its fire back at it. Carefully approach the vicious vehicle and keep your view locked on it. Blast it with Force Lightning when you're close enough, then immediately retreat back into the shadows behind the large crates lining the hangar walls.

Wait for the AT-ST to turn its back to you, then rush out and unleash a lightsaber combo on its legs.

WOOKIEE WARNING

Be careful while you attack the AT-ST's legs. It can easily trample you and inflict damage.

Continue the hide-and-seek assault on the AT-ST until it attempts to squash you under its metallic foot. When it does, use your Jedi speed and immediately follow the onscreen prompts to block and counter the beast's attack.

If the AT-ST takes chunks out of your Health bar, dash into the bay's corner and pick up a Bacta tank. With your Health bar refreshed, return to the battle and continue chipping away at the AT-ST with your Force Lightning and counterattacks.

SITH WISDOM

You can shorten the battle and inflict even more damage on the metal monstrosity by tossing explosive barrels at it.

When the AT-ST's Health bar is almost entirely depleted, finish it off by following the final set of onscreen prompts. The final counterattack is too much for the AT-ST, and it finally succumbs to your might.

Before leaving the hangar, destroy all the electric towers in the room; a Holocron will appear on the ledge along the far wall.

Force Push through the hangar door on the right and dash into the next corridor. Stop in the hall just long enough to fry the troops in your way, then dash at them and crush them with a Force Push or two. Once the first batch of soldiers is gone, dash farther into the corridor.

Just before entering the next room, stop and face the entry. A lone stormtrooper waits for you on the door's other side and pelts you with grenades. Wait for him to launch a grenade, then immediately use a Force Push to bounce the grenade back at him.

Walk into the next room with your 'saber held high and reflect the militia's fire back at them. Get close to the soldiers at the room's center. When your blade is close enough, cut through them with a flurry of combos. If the militia manage to surround you before you can cut them all down, blast them away with a repulse attack and create some breathing room.

Grab the Bacta tank on your way out of the room, and head into the next area.

Before entering the next room, stop in the short dark hallway and locate the ledges above the doors. Double-jump onto the first ledge, then double-jump across the hall onto the second one and grab the Holocron. Finally, hop back down and go into the next room.

The next room contains several more of Kota's men. Approach them as you did the militia in the previous room; reflect their fire, then slash through them with a few quick combos. This time, however, don't immediately engage the men at the room's center. Instead, focus on the two soldiers flanking the doorway. If you ignore them, they can blast you from behind while you deal with their buddies.

When the first two soldiers are eliminated, dash to the room's center and destroy the rest of the squad.

In the room's far right corner is another grenade-tossing soldier. Launch his grenades back at him until he's out of your way. Once the room is clear, continue your hunt for Rahm Kota.

Saunter into the next hallway and Force Grip the explosive barrel atop the flight of steps down the hall. Launch it at the militiamen guarding the hall. If any soldiers survive, launch the other barrels at them and finish them off.

Kota is a full-fledged Jedi Master, so be ready to use your lightsaber skills carefully. Leap at the Jedi Master and attack him with a lightsaber combo. He'll probably block your attack and counter. If he does, either block his attacks by raising your lightsaber or press the Jump button while in midair to nullify his Force Push. Kota will often use Force Push to knock you back and create some distance between you and him, so stay on guard and press Jump to avoid taking damage when he does.

After climbing the second flight of stairs, turn right and face the next group of militiamen. They're lined up on the next set of steps and are itching for a fight. Give them one. Force Dash up to them and launch a Detonate attack. The initial impact will knock them away, but the following electric explosion should destroy most of them. Walk up to the remaining soldiers with your lightsaber in blocking position and finish them off.

Once you've reengaged Kota in battle, block his attacks and counter-attack with 'saber combos. After striking him a few times and whittling down a bit of his health, Kota will back away and blast you with another Force Push. As you reel from the blast, Kota will overconfidently taunt you. Ignore his verbal jabs and continue your attack.

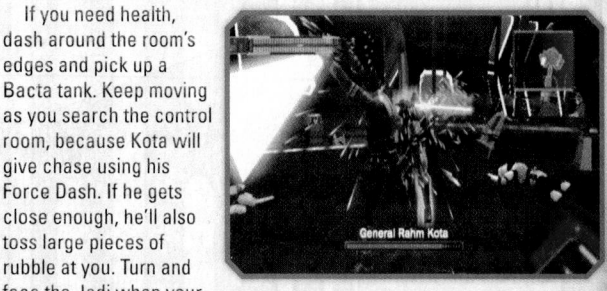

If you need health, dash around the room's edges and pick up a Bacta tank. Keep moving as you search the control room, because Kota will give chase using his Force Dash. If he gets close enough, he'll also toss large pieces of rubble at you. Turn and face the Jedi when your health is refilled. Let him catch up to you, then greet him with a thrown lightsaber to his face.

The final room before reaching Kota has two Holocrons. One is out in the open; the other is behind a control panel having an electrical problem. Wait for the electricity running through the panel to disappear, then jump into the crevice behind the panel and grab the Holocron.

Continue playing this game of cat and mouse, chipping away little bits of health with every battle. After you've chipped away one-fifth of his health, use your Force Lightning to blast the Jedi Master. This locks you in a Force battle with Kota. Follow the onscreen prompts to match the master's moves and reverse the electric current. The Force Lightning will send the Jedi flying to the control room's opposite side.

Go through the next door into the construction ship's control room, where you confront Kota. Your first test is nearly complete.

When Kota recovers, he'll charge and lock lightsabers with you. Once again, match the master's moves by immediately following the onscreen prompts and winning the lightsaber battle. Your victory sends Kota flying back just as before.

Jedi Master Rahm Kota

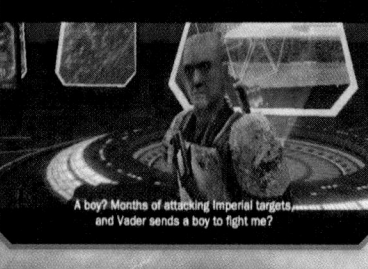

A boy? Months of attacking Imperial targets... and Vader sends a boy to fight me?

Apparently, Kota wasn't expecting to see you. The look on his face reveals disappointment. His attacks on the Imperial shipyards weren't meant to get *your* attention, but rather your master's. It doesn't matter; Kota doesn't need to be excited to see you in order for you to destroy him....

Rush the fallen Jedi and slash at him as he gets up. If he manages to get up before you reach him, stun him with Force Lightning and follow up with a lightsaber combo.

Eventually, Kota is able to get back on his feet and launch an attack of his own. When he does, block his assault and dash around the room until you find more Bacta tanks. Refill your health, then turn on Kota and blast him away with your Force Push. Dash at him as he staggers and follow up your attack with Force Lightning.

The closer you get to defeating him, the more aggressive Kota becomes. After he realizes you've depleted half his health, he brings the control room crumbling down around you. The explosions from the crumbling control room knock you around a little bit, but they don't do much damage. Launch another assault on Kota and blast him one more time with your Force Push. Follow it up with Force Lightning and lock him in another Force battle.

Once Kota has less than a fifth of health left, you can engage him in the final phase of your duel. When Kota's ready to fall, you'll gain the upper hand, and several more onscreen commands will appear. Follow them quickly and accurately to slash, electrocute, and toss Kota about the room. Just as he's about to be destroyed, he foolishly attempts to talk you out of defeating him. He rambles on about your future and how he sees only...himself?

It's too late. Your 'saber burns his eyes, and your final attack sends him flying out into space. Your first battle against a Jedi is victorious.

Just as before, match the onscreen prompts and defeat the Jedi Master at his own game. Follow up with lightsaber combos and deplete his health even more.

If Kota surrounds himself with Force Maelstrom, he'll unleash a repulse attack and send you to the room's opposite side. Back away, wait for him to release his repulse attack, then dash back at him with your lightsaber swinging.

TRIAL OF SKILL

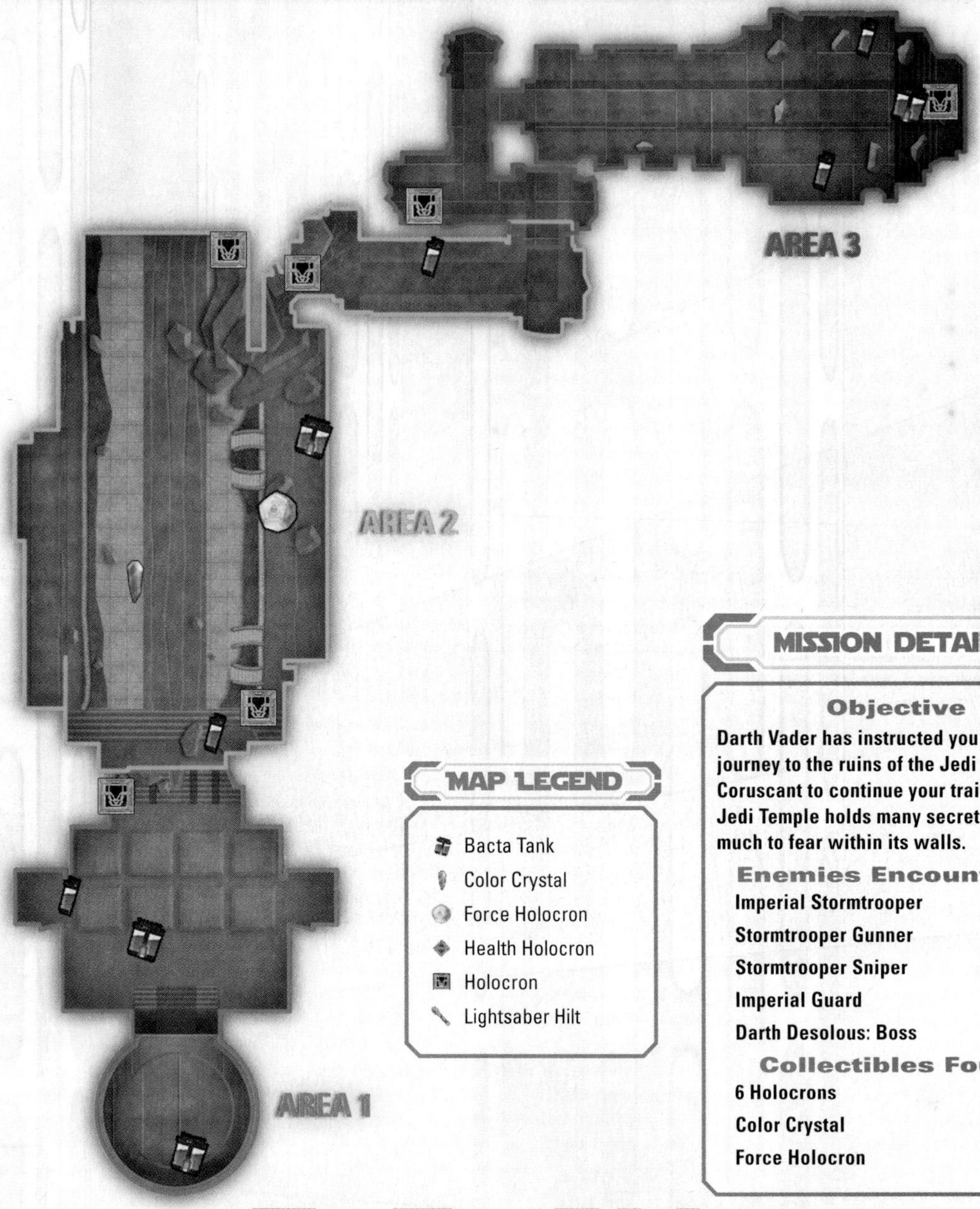

AREA 3

AREA 2

AREA 1

MAP LEGEND

- 🦐 Bacta Tank
- 🦴 Color Crystal
- 🔵 Force Holocron
- ✦ Health Holocron
- 🔲 Holocron
- 🗡 Lightsaber Hilt

MISSION DETAILS

Objective

Darth Vader has instructed you to journey to the ruins of the Jedi Temple on Coruscant to continue your training. The Jedi Temple holds many secrets; there is much to fear within its walls.

Enemies Encountered

Imperial Stormtrooper

Stormtrooper Gunner

Stormtrooper Sniper

Imperial Guard

Darth Desolous: Boss

Collectibles Found

6 Holocrons

Color Crystal

Force Holocron

The First Trial

You return to your master victoriously and deliver your trinket. As you approach Darth Vader, he steals Kota's 'saber from you and quickly draws the blade on you. Even though you delivered Kota's 'saber to Darth Vader, proving you can handle the Jedi on your own, your lack of focus concerns him, and he's not quite ready to unleash you on the galaxy yet. Your next trip is to the Jedi Temple on Coruscant.

You lack focus. You're easily distracted.

JEDI KNOWLEDGE

Having completed the previous mission, you'll unlock new Force powers, characters in Duel mode, and a combat crystal for your lightsaber. You can now execute the Ground Slam attack.

While on the *Rogue Shadow*, your transport ship and home in between missions, you can change your outfit, upgrade your Force powers, and even modify your lightsaber. Take this time to increase the strength of your Force Lightning and Force Push, then equip the Kaiburr lightsaber crystal.

You've unlocked a new lightsaber crystal!

Kaiburr Crystal.
When applied, this crystal allows the wielder to focus the Force to increase the strength of Push. Go to the Lightsaber Customization option in the Rogue Shadow to apply to your lightsaber.

Assault on the Jedi Temple

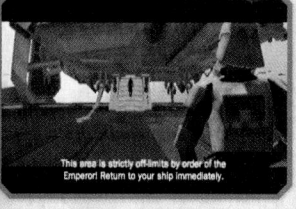

This area is strictly off-limits by order of the Emperor! Return to your ship immediately.

You arrive at the Jedi Temple only to find that the Emperor has deemed it off-limits. Several stormtroopers approach the *Rogue Shadow* to stop you as you disembark. Show them how foolish they are.

Raise your lightsaber and reflect the stormtroopers' fire back at them as you approach. Wait for the first two troopers to fall, then use your Force Grip to grab the third soldier from behind the rubble nearby. Choke the life from him.

Pick up the large piece of stone near the Temple entrance's right side and hurl it at the Imperial soldier near the right wall. Several more stormtroopers rush out from beyond the pillared entrance ahead. Stay near the *Rogue Shadow* and continuously hurl rubble at the attacking soldiers until you destroy them all.

Dash past the Temple's entry pillars and slash through the two stormtroopers waiting to attack. Once they're down, three more troopers rush out from the Temple's main entrance; one of them has a laser-guided gun. You can't reflect his blasts, so don't bother raising your guard. Instead, rush at him and use your Ground Slam attack, then follow up with two short combos to take out his partners.

Before entering the Temple, use your Force powers to remove the large rock on the Temple entrance's left side and collect the Holocron hidden in front of the partially collapsed entrance.

Grab the Bacta tank along the far left wall, then go into the Temple.

Inside the Jedi Temple is a whole battalion of Imperial guards. Cut the first one down with your lightsaber, then raise your guard to reflect the guards' blaster fire. Slowly creep into the Temple as the blaster fire bounces off your lightsaber. Slide between the pillars as you approach the troopers, and use the Temple's supports as cover.

Dash to the Temple's right side and use your Force Grip to rip the turret from its support. Turn it on the stormtroopers. Let the turret blast away while your lightsaber protects you. Once you've put down most of the soldiers, dash around the area and run your blade through the remaining soldiers on this side of the Temple. Several more soldiers are entrenched on the Temple's far side, but their blaster fire isn't as accurate from that distance, so take a moment to scour the area and pick up the Bacta tank on the far left end.

Destroy the Jedi statue near the left staircase to expose a color crystal. Grab it, then dash back down to the main Temple floor—a few more angry Imperial soldiers will have arrived by now. Toss your lightsaber at the stormtrooper sniper, then turn your attention to the other two soldiers. Use the rubble scattered on the floor as projectiles against the soldiers at the Temple's far end.

Once the coast is clear, you can scour the rest of the Temple for hidden Holocrons. Destroy the large Jedi statue in the Temple's far right corner and grab the Force Holocron hidden inside. Another Holocron is tucked away at the Temple's rear end, behind the fallen rubble. Pick it up before returning to the main Temple.

As you assault the Jedi Temple, use all of the debris to your advantage. The Pummel attack is extremely handy in this area.

Having collected all the hidden items in the area, continue your assault on the Jedi's sanctuary. Climb atop the debris in the Temple's far right

corner, and cut through the two Imperial soldiers perched high atop the concrete mess. Edge out to the end of the fallen concrete and double-jump to the area below. You'll land directly behind two more stormtroopers. Crush them with Detonate before they realize you're behind them.

Turn around and immediately unleash a Force Push on the troopers behind you. The blast sends three Imperial Guards and two stormtroopers flying down the hall. Focus your attention on the guards first. They can inflict major damage with a ground attack that knocks you down. Turn the tables on them and knock them off *their* feet with a Ground Slam attack. Finish them off with a swift lightsaber combo, then crush the remaining stormtroopers in the hall.

There's another Holocron hidden behind the crumbled corner of the Temple. After hopping down from the rubble, turn left and grab it.

Use Force Push on the large rocks blocking the next hallway on the left. The rocks tumble down, revealing a new passage and creating several projectiles to use against the next group of stormtroopers.

Destroy the large Jedi statue in the hall's niche to expose a Holocron.

Turn left into the next hall and use the available debris against the Imperial soldier on the right. Follow the path down the hall and into the large Temple room lined with Jedi statues. As you enter the room, your vision temporarily blurs and the room seems to sway for a moment.

Approach the Temple's rear. When you do, you're mysteriously surrounded by a red electrical current and tossed aside. It is no normal current, however, but a Force attack! Ironically, this is no Jedi attack, but rather a Sith assault. Your next opponent, Darth Desolous, emerges from the Temple's shadows.

Destroy Darth Desolous!

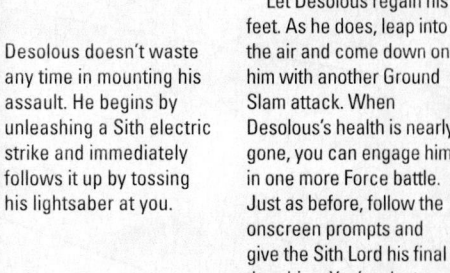

Desolous doesn't waste any time in mounting his assault. He begins by unleashing a Sith electric strike and immediately follows it up by tossing his lightsaber at you.

When Desolous lunges at you with his 'saber, raise yours to block his attack. Wait until he pulls away, then toss your lightsaber at him. Dash toward him and blast him with a Force Push attack. Rush him again as he lands and attack him with a blast of Force Lightning.

Shove Desolous back with a series of lightsaber combos. He's incredibly resilient and can quickly launch a counterattack. Don't let him regain the offensive! Instead, stay aggressive by slashing away and hitting the Sith scum with Ground Slam attacks.

Continue your attack until Desolous surrounds himself with a force field. If you stay close, he'll detonate the field and hurt you in the process. Back away and don't reengage him in battle until the field is destroyed. Once it's gone, rush him and slash away with more lightsaber combos.

If Desolous manages to get you in his clutches and attempts to choke you, use Force Push to knock yourself free and immediately attack him as you land. Slash away at your foe until he backs away. Dash to the Temple's rear and pick up a Bacta tank, then return to the fight fully healed.

After you whittle away half Desolous's health, you can engage him in a Force battle. Match the onscreen prompts to reverse the electric current and blast Desolous with his own Force attack. The blast knocks him off his feet, leaving him vulnerable. Rush him again and unleash some Force Lightning followed by a lightsaber combo.

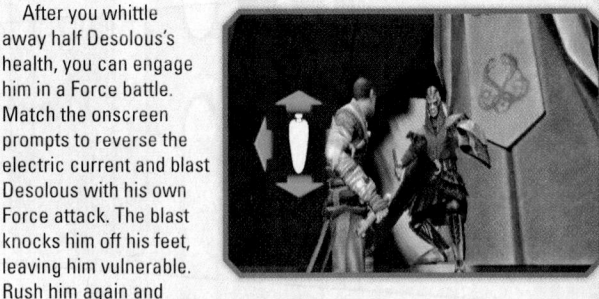

Let Desolous regain his feet. As he does, leap into the air and come down on him with another Ground Slam attack. When Desolous's health is nearly gone, you can engage him in one more Force battle. Just as before, follow the onscreen prompts and give the Sith Lord his final thrashing. You've destroyed a Jedi. Now you've destroyed a Sith as well.

My spies have located another Jedi.

Just as your battle against Darth Desolous comes to an end, PROXY arrives with a message from your master. Your next task will pit you against another Jedi, and this one is far more powerful than the rogue Jedi you faced earlier.

29

RAXUS PRIME

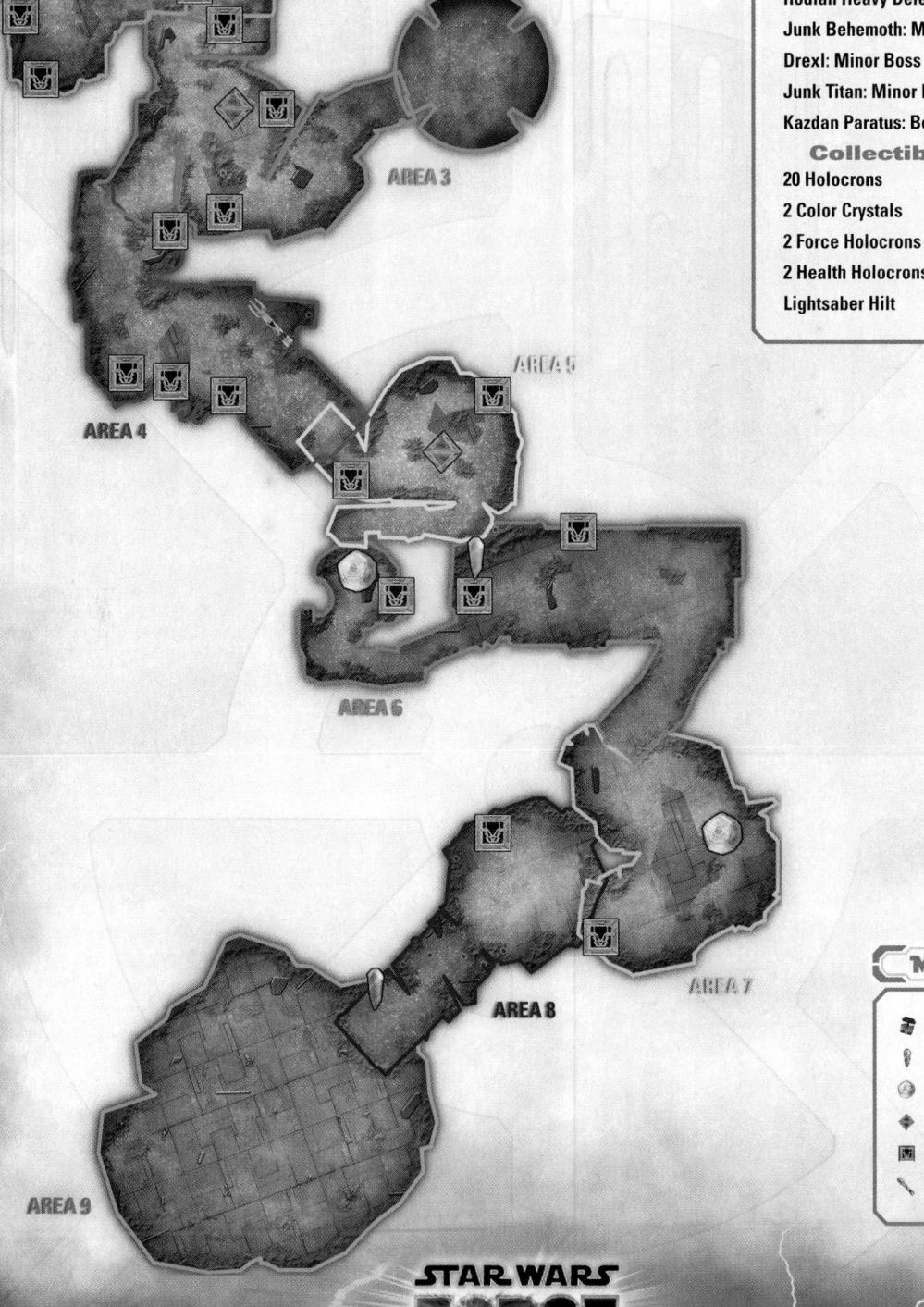

AREA 1

AREA 2

AREA 3

AREA 4

AREA 5

AREA 6

AREA 7

AREA 8

AREA 9

MISSION DETAILS

Objective

The Jedi Kazdan Paratus, who has been hiding since Order 66, has been located on the junk planet of Raxus Prime. Find him and destroy him.

Enemies Encountered

Junk Golem

Junkyard Dog Golem: Mechanical Monstrosity

Rodian Heavy Defender

Junk Behemoth: Minor Boss

Drexl: Minor Boss

Junk Titan: Minor Boss

Kazdan Paratus: Boss

Collectibles Found

20 Holocrons

2 Color Crystals

2 Force Holocrons

2 Health Holocrons

Lightsaber Hilt

MAP LEGEND

🜚 Bacta Tank

🕯 Color Crystal

◎ Force Holocron

◆ Health Holocron

▦ Holocron

⬈ Lightsaber Hilt

STAR WARS
FORCE
UNLEASHED

"Where All Droids Go to Die..."

Your hunt for Jedi Master Kazdan Paratus takes you to Raxus Prime, a world whose entire surface resembles the trash heaps and junkyards of Coruscant. From high above the planet, Paratus's home looks much like a Jedi Temple. Once you touch down, however, it is clear that this planet is extremely hostile.

Disembark the *Rogue Shadow*, then step on the elevator pad at the front of the landing area.

> Before getting on the elevator, walk up to the glowing wall panel on the landing area's front left side, and rip the panel off the wall. Pick up the exposed Holocron.

Take Out the Trash

The elevator takes you down to Raxus's metal-and-rubble-riddled corridors where several junk golem rise from the ground and attack. They're armed with blasters and carry shields. Reflect some of their fire back at them, then use Force Push to toss the creatures aside. Finish them off with a blast of Force Lightning before trekking deeper into the junkyard.

Several more junk golems and a large junkyard dog golem attack in the next area.

Lock on to the junkyard dog and focus your attacks on it first. Give it a shot of Force Lightning, then leap into the air and come down on it with a Ground Slam attack. This also knocks away the surrounding junk golems, allowing you to continue demolishing the large mechanical monstrosity. Slash away at it with lightsaber combos followed by Ground Slam attacks until it is destroyed.

After you destroy the junkyard dog, it's remnants create several more junk golems. Push them away with a Repulse attack and wait for them

to get up. As they do, unleash another Ground Slam to inflict even more damage. Turn any surviving junk golems into scrap metal with a final Force Push.

Scour the area and pick up a Bacta tank before pressing deeper into Raxus Prime. Follow the winding hallway past piles of trash, scrap metal, and disabled droids, and raise your lightsaber as you walk—as more junk golems rise from the ground and attack, your lightsaber will reflect their fire. Strike them down when you get close. If they surround you on all sides, use a Repulse attack to create some breathing room.

Once the junk golems are far enough away, activate your Dark Rage to increase your strength, then lunge at them with your 'saber swinging. With your Dark Rage active, it shouldn't take much more than a simple combo to finish the job.

> As you traverse the trash-riddled passages, stop and search the niche behind the holoprojector. Remove the broken panel and claim the Holocron lying behind it. Then, just a bit farther down the passage, another electronic panel hides a second Holocron. Destroy the panel and grab it.

Turn right into the next corridor and detonate the bomb in the hall to destroy the attacking junk golems. Follow up the bomb blast with one of your own, frying the remaining junk golems with Force Lightning.

The fight in the corridor heats up as another dog golem rises from the ground and rushes you. Activate your Dark Rage and counterattack with several lightsaber combos. Backtrack out of the corridor if the mechanical creature gets too close for comfort—tight spaces can make it harder to battle the overgrown beast.

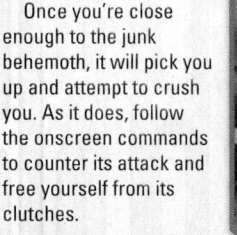

After you destroy the junkyard dog, claim the Holocron from behind the broken panel on the hall's right.

Use Force Push to bring down the obstruction at the corridor's end. Just beyond, a fierce battle rages as several junk golems blast away at rogue soldiers. In order to proceed, you must destroy enough junk golems to deplete the bar that appears at the screen's bottom. Activate Dark Rage and cut down the first few golems that attack. They don't take much while your Force powers enhance your strength, so use quick fluid combos to take them down.

Follow your Dark Rage rampage by detonating a nearby bomb and demolishing several more golems. After destroying the majority of the blaster golems, two more junkyard dogs appear. Separate the two clanging canines by locking on to one, attacking, then immediately dashing away. Let it give chase, then turn on it and use a Ground Slam attack.

SITH WISDOM

You can also use the blinking bombs to destroy the dogs a bit quicker. Back away from them and use your Force Grip to hurl the bombs at the beasts.

Behemoth Battle!

The demolition of the junkyard dogs gives rise to an even larger, more dangerous foe. The junk behemoth is a hulking brute of an enemy. Act quickly to minimize taking damage. Lock on to the behemoth and blast it with Force Lightning.

When it approaches you, leap into the air and come down on it with a Ground Slam. If it passes underneath you while you're airborne, distance yourself from it when you land and use blinking bombs to blow off small chunks of health.

Stay on the move when you're not attacking. The behemoth has a devastating ranged attack. It lashes out with both arms, using them like ball-and-chain-like weapons. Leap or dash away from its attacks and maintain a lock on the creature. As it's retracting its arms, dash toward it and slash at it with a lightsaber combo.

Once you're close enough to the junk behemoth, it will pick you up and attempt to crush you. As it does, follow the onscreen commands to counter its attack and free yourself from its clutches.

WOOKIEE WARNING

If you use Force Push attacks, the behemoth will simply brush them off and stomp you with its oversized feet.

Continue pounding away at the junk behemoth with Ground Slam attacks, and slowly whittle away at its health. When the lumbering litter is ready to fall, another onscreen prompt will flash. Follow the commands to finish the fight against the clanking creature.

A lone Rodian bandit survived the battle with the junk golems. When you approach to question him, he decides to be difficult. After some gentle coercing, the bandit drops the name of his boss, Drexl.

I don't want to die...

Before heading off to meet Drexl, remove the rubble along the right wall and grab the hidden Holocron. Then destroy all the crates and rubble in the area. Another Holocron appears near the center. Pick it up along with the Health Holocron that appears, then head off to meet Drexl.

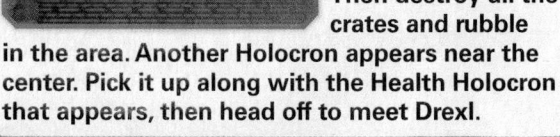

Walk up the ramp and follow the path into the next area. There you find the Rodian leader, Drexl. He's not impressed by your power but still offers to help you find Paratus—for a price. After a cutscene in which you show him why you can't be negotiated with, he coughs up Kazdan Paratus's location. The Jedi is hiding at Raxus Prime's temple.

STAR WARS
FORCE
UNLEASHED

On the Hunt

Resume your hunt for the Jedi in the area where you previously faced the junk behemoth (you're transported there after the cutscene above). There, several junk golems rise from the surrounding debris and attack. Raise your 'saber and block the blaster fire. Dash toward the far right wall and cut through the junk golem in your way. Grab a Bacta tank lying near the area's edge, then turn your lightsaber on the other walking piles of junk.

Hit the encroaching enemies with a Force Push, then follow it up with a Ground Slam attack. If the golems are close together, they'll take damage with one hit. Finish off the remaining golems by reflecting their fire back at them. If more golems pop up, dash back and forth, knocking them down and attacking as you go until they are no more.

Follow the path on the right and destroy the metal pillar next to the pipe with the steam jet. Grab the Holocron, then follow the path into the next area.

In the next area, cut through the first two golems that attack, then hurl the large pieces of scrap metal at the golems in the distance. The junk golems can suddenly leap out at you and attack, so either intercept their leaping attacks with pieces of trash or toss them back with a Force Push.

As the golems struggle to get up, dash toward them and destroy them with Force Lightning or a Ground Slam attack.

As you go left around the corner, continuously use your Force Grip to throw large pieces of debris ahead of you. Just before you reach the next door, a junkyard dog golem sprouts from the trash. Use the debris pieces to knock it back and keep it at a distance; as it stumbles backward, activate your Dark Rage and focus your Force power. Destroy the dog golem while you're enraged.

Pick up the Holocron inside the niche on the right wall. Destroy all the crates and rubble in the area to reveal two more Holocrons nearby. Check behind the demolished electronic panel and along the area's right edge. Look for the 'saber hilt on the left side just out of double-jump range.

As you approach the doorway, another junkyard dog golem appears. Lock on to it, activate your Dark Rage, and attack it with a lightsaber combo. Circle around the beast as it comes toward you, and attack as it moves past you.

After destroying the beast, use a Force Push to crush the door ahead and hop onto the elevator behind it.

SITH WISDOM

There is a Bacta tank on the platform to the elevator's right. Grab it before setting foot on the elevator.

Get off the platform, then dash down the passage. Activate your Dark Rage and crush the junk golems in your way. At the path's base, turn your lightsaber on the giant dog golems that appear.

When you emerge from the elevator, destroy the nearby crates. A Holocron appears atop the broken console on the right.

Use a Force Push to knock one back, then Force Grip the blinking bomb on the ledge above you. Toss it at one of the junkyard dog golems and blow it to bits. If that doesn't destroy it, hit it with a Detonate attack to finish the job. The blast from the bomb and Detonate attack should damage both dogs simultaneously. Once one is eliminated, the second should be easier to take down. Slash it with a lightsaber combo or two to take it out.

Turn right at the path's base and grab the Health Holocron in the corner.

Use a Force Push to bring down the blockage in your way, then venture deeper into the Raxus Prime tunnels.

Emerge from the cramped tunnels into an area where several more junk golems attack. The area is slightly less cramped than the tunnels, but not by much. Tight spaces make lightsaber attacks a bit more risky, as they leave you open for counterattack. Instead, raise your lightsaber to reflect their fire back at them. This will damage the golems without leaving you open.

If the golems get too close, shove them back with a Force Push and blast them with a shot of Force Lightning.

Demolish the surrounding area and crush every crate to reveal a Force Holocron and a regular Holocron. Grab them before moving on.

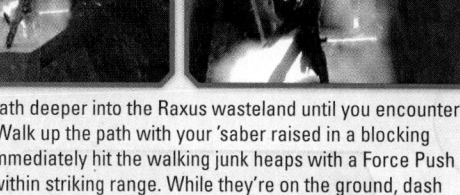

Follow the path deeper into the Raxus wasteland until you encounter more golems. Walk up the path with your 'saber raised in a blocking position, and immediately hit the walking junk heaps with a Force Push when they're within striking range. While they're on the ground, dash up to them and use a Ground Slam to turn the golems into scrap. If the golems manage to surround you, use Repulse to shove them away, then eliminate them with a sideways slash from your 'saber.

JEDI KNOWLEDGE

Use your Maelstrom attack to quickly dispatch surrounding Golems! The narrow corridors make lightsaber battle more difficult than usual, but Maelstrom actually turns the narrow corridors to your advantage!

The destroyed junk golems give rise to a junkyard dog. Unfortunately, the tunnel isn't the best place to face the giant junk heap. Back away and lure the junkyard dog golem toward you. As it rushes you, hit it with Force Push to knock it into the air. As it lands, dash toward it and hit it with a blast of Force Lightning. After you destroy the beast, it gives rise to several more junk golems. Make short work of them with a few Dark Rage–enhanced 'saber combos.

Behemoth Battle Redux

Continue following the Raxus Prime tunnels. As you move deeper into the tunnels, a junk behemoth rushes at you from the darkness. Wait for it to come careening toward you and leap over it when it gets near. Double-jump over the creature's head and land squarely behind it. Keep a lock on it and quickly hit it with your lightsaber.

Let the metallic monster get a hold of you. When it does, more onscreen prompts will appear. Quickly match the prompts to counter the monstrosity's attacks and chop off a bit of its health. Leap away from the behemoth when it cuts you loose, and gain some distance from it. When you're safely away, turn around and hurl blinking bombs at it.

Let the behemoth get close and fry it with Force Lightning. Its Health bar should be halfway depleted by now. Leap over the creature again, dash away to get some distance, then turn on it to blast it with bombs or debris.

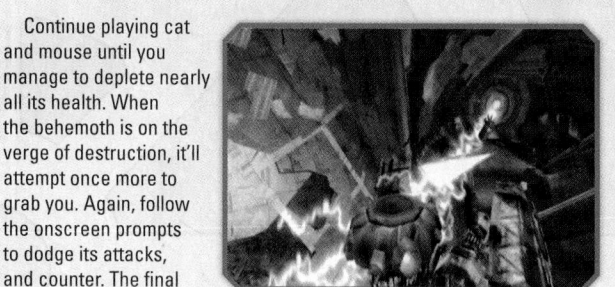

Continue playing cat and mouse until you manage to deplete nearly all its health. When the behemoth is on the verge of destruction, it'll attempt once more to grab you. Again, follow the onscreen prompts to dodge its attacks, and counter. The final exchange is too much for the monster, and the behemoth comes crumbling down.

With the monster gone, grab the Bacta tank at one end of the tunnel's end and the color crystal on the tunnel's opposite end. There's also a Holocron nearby.

34

The junk behemoth is gone, but a junkyard dog golem sprouts up from the surrounding rubble. Force it into a corner and pound away at it with Force Push and Force Lightning. After you destroy the overgrown grease gobbler, use a Force Push to bring down the rubble blocking the tunnel.

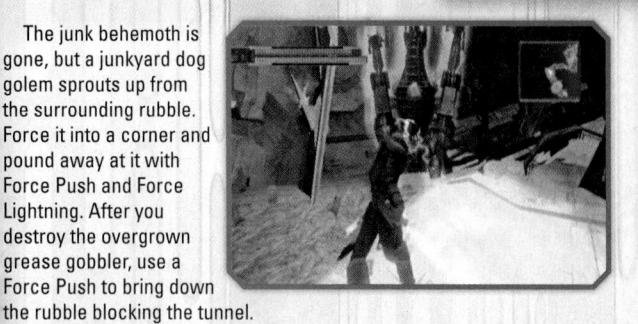

The Trouble with Drexl

In the next area, you find Drexl and more of his goons. While you've been hunting down Paratus, he's been doing some digging of his own. Somehow he's managed to discover that you're Vader's apprentice and, being a greedy Rodian, has decided to sell you to the Emperor. Of course, he's got to capture you first.

Drexl knows he's no match for you alone, so he's brought friends. Unfortunately for you, he is a formidable foe. Begin the battle with Drexl by hitting him and his squad with a Force Push.

While Drexl's pals are out of the fight, hit him with Force Lightning. He's surprisingly fast with the blade, so dash out of the way as soon as you've hurt him a bit, and immediately raise your lightsaber to defend. When he's done attacking, counter with your 'saber and double-jump away.

Continue to leap away from Drexl until you're far enough to safely turn around. Don't face him if he's hot on your heels. Turn around and use Force Grip to grab and toss the Rodian scumbag against the walls. Rush him as he's tumbling down the cliffside, and hit him with a Force Push to weaken him even more.

As soon as you reach the fallen bandit, slash away or use Ground Slam to damage him even further. If he manages to get up before you reach him, don't attack! Instead, raise your lightsaber to block and deflect his blade, then follow his attack with a counter of your own.

WOOKIEE WARNING

If you attempt to overpower the Rodian, he'll cut you like a block of Coruscant's finest cheese.

Wait until Drexl backs away, then use Ground Slam to knock him off his feet. Just as before, attack while he's down and leap away when he gets up.

Drexl's got a Ground Slam attack of his own, so keep moving. If he leaps toward you with his blade held high, leap into the air to avoid the shock wave from his Ground Slam.

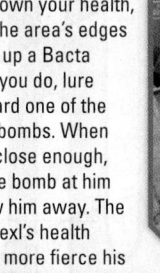

If Drexl manages to whittle down your health, dash to the area's edges and pick up a Bacta tank. As you do, lure him toward one of the blinking bombs. When he gets close enough, throw the bomb at him and blow him away. The lower Drexl's health gets, the more fierce his attacks will become. Continue to stay on guard and block his attacks. Lower your lightsaber only to counterattack and finish him off.

JEDI KNOWLEDGE

The battle with Drexl is one of the only boss encounters where you won't have to follow onscreen prompts to finish him off.

In spite of his defeat, Drexl still laughs maniacally while on the ground. A transport ship full of Rodian baddies attempts to sneak up on you. When you realize that he's got reinforcements on the way, you quickly jump into action and bring the ship down in a fiery blaze.

Climb the fallen rubble and grab the Force Holocron near the map's left edge.

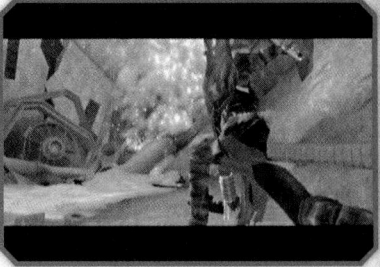

After climbing up the fallen rubble, explore the region ahead. Wait for more junk golems to pop up. Send them away with a Force Push and lock on to the junkyard dog golem that attacks. Lure it down to the lower area—where you fought and defeated Drexl—and pound away at it with Ground Slam and Force Push attacks.

With the dog destroyed, more junk golems show up looking for a fight. Use your lightsaber to turn their blaster fire on them and slowly approach them. As their fire reflects back and destroys them, the junk heaps fall one by one.

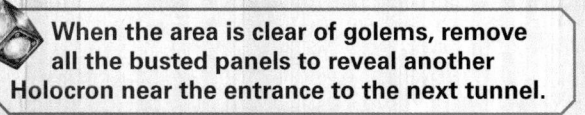

When the area is clear of golems, remove all the busted panels to reveal another Holocron near the entrance to the next tunnel.

Toss a blinking bomb through the next tunnel and blow up the junk golems in the following area. Rush in and take your 'saber to the remaining golems. If the junk golems leap out at you, hit them with your Force Push and send them hurtling back into the walls.

Don't proceed without thoroughly thrashing the area. Expose the hidden Holocron near the wall on the left.

You may be ready to continue the hunt for Kazdan Paratus, but two junkyard dog golems have other plans. Just as you're ready to move on, the two metal mutts rush and attack. Split them up. Double-jump over one dog, then lure it away. When you're far enough away from the dog, turn around and blast it with Force Lightning.

Just as you've done before, continue dashing away and turn only to relentlessly pound on the creatures. The dog golems eventually fall to your Force powers, leaving the area clear. Blast the obstruction out of the way and traipse through the now-exposed tunnel. As you go, collect a Bacta tank and the color crystal along the right wall.

Paratus and the Puppet

Just beyond the tunnel is Kazdan Paratus's hiding spot. Not only does the cowering Jedi have a small troop of junk golems to help him fight, but he also controls a giant junk titan. The fight against Paratus will have to wait until after you demolish his titan. Begin your assault by weakening it with a blast of Force Lightning.

The titan takes a vicious swipe at you with its giant axelike weapon. If it connects, you'll be sent flying back toward the battle arena's opposite end. As you fly back from his attack, press Jump to land on your feet safely.

Immediately upon landing, use a Force Push to keep the lesser golems at a distance. Keep a lock on the junk titan and focus all your energy on bringing it down quickly.

Double-jump to safety when the titan brings its axe down on you, and hit it with a Force attack while you're in the air. Move away from the lumbering titan, and hit it with debris as it ambles toward you. It's not nearly as fast as you, so you'll have plenty of time to turn around and hit it with projectiles. Do, however, stay nimble, as it can quickly reflect some of those thrown objects back at you.

Keep an eye out for blinking bombs littered about the area, and use them to chip away at the titan's Health bar. When you run out of bombs, resume your direct attack on the giant junk jalopy.

Watch for commands to pop up onscreen; quickly match them to lunge at Paratus's puppet and slash away at it. Be patient and precise in following the commands; if you make one false move, the titan will flick you like a flea and pounce on you.

SITH WISDOM

Don't bother trying to defeat all the junk golems fighting alongside the titan. In fact, you can even use them as ammunition for your titan target practice. As long as you keep moving, they don't pose a threat. The junk titan, on the other hand...

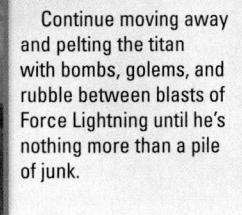

Continue moving away and pelting the titan with bombs, golems, and rubble between blasts of Force Lightning until he's nothing more than a pile of junk.

STAR WARS
THE FORCE UNLEASHED

When the junk titan comes crumbling down, Kazdan Paratus escapes into the dark blue haze of the cave arena. The pint-sized puppet master creates several large rock-shard pillars, and the fight begins! Dash right and collect a Bacta tank to refill your health.

Stalk the Jedi Master between the pillars and blast him with the Force. He'll continue scrambling for cover, so keep a lock on him and attack him relentlessly as he moves from pillar to pillar.

As Paratus scrambles away, zap him with Force Lightning and follow it up with a lightsaber combo. Paratus's slash attack can quickly knock you off your feet, so keep your guard up. When his dual-sabered weapon comes slashing down at you, leap backward to avoid its shock wave.

Stay on guard and block Paratus's vicious lightsaber attacks, which are more like a constant stream of lightsaber slashes rather than measurable combos; therefore, keep your lightsaber raised and wait for him to stop attacking. As soon as he does, counterattack.

After being deflected, the Jedi Master is a safe distance away. Watch for him to raise his weapon as if to threaten you, then hit him with a Force Push that knocks him back. Mount a quick offensive as he reels from your Force Push, and engage him in a lightsaber lock.

Match the onscreen prompts to counter Kazdan's attacks. By successfully doing so, you can thrash the little Jedi and slam him over and over against the cavern floor.

Once Kazdan realizes he is near defeat, he'll increase his attacks' ferocity. Follow him around and bring down the rocky pillars on his little Jedi head. Eventually, the Jedi's Force powers are no match for yours, and he falls to your 'saber.

AREA 3

AREA 2

AREA 1

MISSION DETAILS

Objective

Darth Vader has sent you once again to the Jedi Temple to test your abilities and build your knowledge of the Force. Beware what you find within the Temple; all is not what it appears.

Enemies Encountered

Imperial Stormtrooper

Stormtrooper Sniper

Imperial Guard

Darth Phobos: Boss

Collectibles Found

6 Holocrons

2 Color Crystals

Force Holocron

Health Holocron

Lightsaber Hilt

MAP LEGEND

- 🗃 Bacta Tank
- 🔮 Color Crystal
- ◉ Force Holocron
- ◆ Health Holocron
- ▦ Holocron
- 🗡 Lightsaber Hilt

STAR WARS
THE FORCE
UNLEASHED

"I Am Ready Now!"

My master, Kazdan Paratus is dead.

Then your training is almost complete.

With the defeat of Kazdan Paratus, your training is one step closer to completion. Darth Vader's training has been intense and often extremely arduous. Even now that you have beaten your most difficult enemy to date, Darth Vader still insists that the task did not sufficiently prove your power. Before the mission, Darth Vader did not expect you to defeat Paratus.

Now that the mission is complete, Kazdan Paratus is nothing more than "an outcast." Your next mission is to return to the Jedi Temple, where you must complete your Trial of Insight.

Return to the Jedi Temple

Your second trip to the Jedi Temple begins much like the first. Several Imperial troops are stationed near the familiar entrance. Immediately upon disembarking, dash toward the Imperial Guards and run your lightsaber through one of them. Follow the 'saber thrust with a short combo to hit the other guards nearby as well. The Imperial Guards are tough, so take them out first.

You can easily dispatch the other two soldiers after downing the Imperial Guards. Fry the guards with Force Lightning, then hit the small squad of troopers with a Ground Slam attack to finish them off.

SITH WISDOM

There is a large Bacta tank underneath the landing pad. Before entering the Jedi Temple, take the stairs flanking your ship to the area below and grab it.

Back on the landing pad, two stormtrooper snipers take aim at you as you come up the stairs. Don't let their laser-guided guns track you for too long; if they get a lock on you for even a second, they'll fire and inflict major damage. Rush them as you did the Imperial Guards and cut through them with your lightsaber.

Luckily, they're a lot easier to deal with than the Imperial Guards, so a few simple lightsaber combos should do the trick. If you keep moving and don't allow their lasers to lock on to you, the Imperial Guards won't be able to cause much damage.

Carefully creep inside the Temple and keep your lightsaber raised high in blocking position. Round the corner left into the main Temple room. As you go, grab the Bacta tank near the Temple entrance's right side, then use a Force Push to knock away the guards. You can also walk down the narrow Temple entrance with your 'saber in blocking position and simply let the guards blast themselves into oblivion.

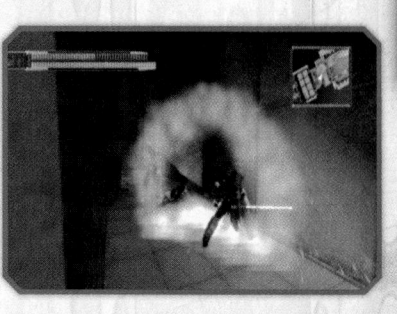

Inside the Temple, an entire battalion of stormtroopers waits for you with blasters ready. Walk in with your 'saber in blocking position and slowly slide to the main room's near left side. As you do, the troopers will slowly destroy themselves with their own blaster fire.

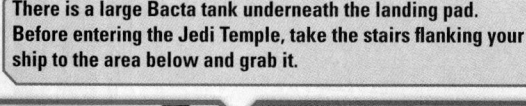

Slink down the Temple steps into the main room and double-jump onto the walkway along the left wall. An Imperial Troops bar appears at the screen's bottom. Grab the blue color crystal near the walkway's end, then focus on the troops behind you. Cut them down, edge up the walkway, then leap down when you see the gun turret below. Rip the turret from its supports, and lead it farther into the Temple room. Let the turret do most of the work so you can safely reflect fire back at the troops in the distance.

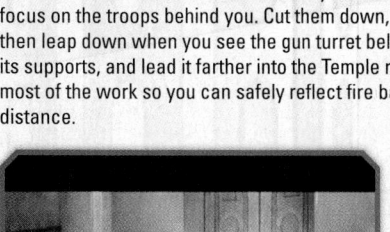

Just as you're destroying one of the last Imperial Guards in the main Temple room, a stormtrooper escapes through a door in the room's left side.

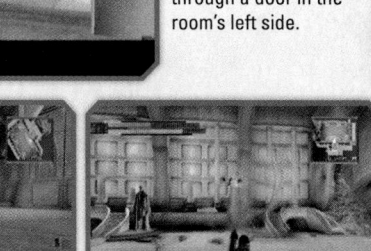

Unfortunately, the cowardly trooper leaves the door open behind him and more Imperial pests pour out. Rush up the steps toward the door and meet the troops head-on. Strike the first two soldiers with a Force Push, then pick them up and toss them to the other side of the room.

Imperial Guards are only dangerous while in close-quarters combat, so toss them as far as possible. If you can't knock both of them away, hurl one, then choke the other.

There are several collectibles in the main Temple room. Before giving chase and heading into the door on the Temple's left side, explore the small niche on the Temple's right side and grab a Force Holocron. Explore the room's rear and grab the green color crystal in the rear, right corner.

Next, remove the rubble near the right walkway's center to expose a Holocron. Leap over the fallen rocks at the Temple's far right end (just as you did on your last visit), and remove the small statue in the corner to reveal a Health Holocron. Finally, remove the fallen pillar at the walkway's end to expose one more Holocron before continuing.

Follow the stormtrooper that escaped and head into the hallway on the left. As you stalk the Jedi Temple halls, you hear a mysterious voice warning you to not be blinded by anger.

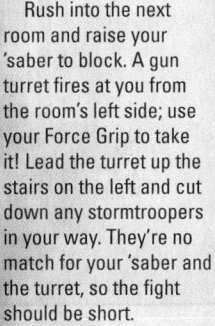

Rush into the next room and raise your 'saber to block. A gun turret fires at you from the room's left side; use your Force Grip to take it! Lead the turret up the stairs on the left and cut down any stormtroopers in your way. They're no match for your 'saber and the turret, so the fight should be short.

JEDI KNOWLEDGE

If the soldiers on the far left are too far to reach quickly with your lightsaber, use Pummel to pound them from afar.

Halfway up the steps are two snipers with laser-guided blasters. Rush them before they get a lock on you, and cut through them with a sideways 'saber slash. If one manages to escape your blade, grab him and toss him onto the area below.

Before turning left into the next area, turn right at the top of the steps and locate the Holocron atop the ledge in the distance. Double-jump onto the ledge to grab it.

Walk through the door on the steps' left and do away with the lone stormtrooper. Either slash him quickly or reflect his fire back at him. Even if you don't eliminate him first, a falling piece of rock will. With him out of the way, strafe into the hall while you're facing right.

Another stormtrooper waits to ambush you at the hall's bend. Hit him with a Force Push or toss the large rock that just crushed his comrade. Turn left at the bend and follow the hall until you reach a T-intersection. Cut down the soldier on the immediate left, then turn right and reflect the fire back at the guards at the hall's far end.

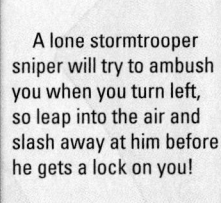

A lone stormtrooper sniper will try to ambush you when you turn left, so leap into the air and slash away at him before he gets a lock on you!

Confidently walk up the hall, reflecting fire as you go, until you reach an electrical field going haywire.

Wait for the field to calm, then leap onto the small crevice on the hall's right side. Grab the Holocron and immediately hop back down before the field electrocutes you.

Dash past the electric field and grab the small Bacta tank in the niche on the right; then remove the rubble blocking the hall on the right. A single Force Push should do the trick. If not, use your Force Grip to topple the rocks one at a time.

Follow the hall until it turns right. Stop just as you reach the corner and raise your guard. A blaster turret is at the hall's other end; it will open fire when you turn the corner. Reflect its fire back at it, then hit the two approaching Imperial Guards with a Force Push. That will

keep them out of your hair for a second while you focus on finishing off the turret.

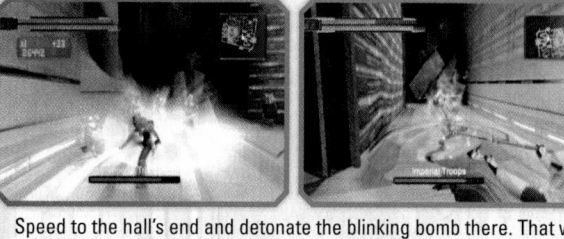

Speed to the hall's end and detonate the blinking bomb there. That will disable the turret and eliminate the stormtroopers near it.

With the turret destroyed and the trooper squad crippled, leap into the air and come down on the remaining Imperial soldiers with a Ground Slam attack. The Imperial Guards are incredibly resilient, so they'll take some more work. Continue hitting them with the Force and dashing away to safety until you destroy them.

SITH WISDOM

The cramped halls of the Jedi Temple are perfect for close-quarter combat attacks like Repulse.

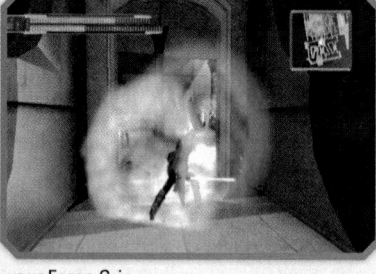

Before entering the next room on the left, stop at the doorway and unleash a vicious Force Push at the encroaching Imperial Guard. When he's down, rush in and take your lightsaber to the other Imperialists in the room. Turn back toward the fallen guard

and lift him into the air with your Force Grip.

Choke the final trooper until he's destroyed, then make a sharp left past the Temple library stacks.

Use the Force to remove the fallen rocks on the room's left side and grab the Holocron hidden underneath.

Hop over the fallen rocks and down onto the area below. Creep into the crevice created by the rocks and follow it to its end. When you emerge from the cracks, you'll be in a large partially destroyed room with more library stacks.

Face Your Fears

Inside, you spot Juno. She looks hurt, bent over as if in pain. When you approach, Juno leaps into the air and transforms in a blue puff of smoke. She's not Juno—it's Darth Phobos! Just as her name suggests, she feeds on phobias. Your fears give her strength.

When the battle with Phobos begins, she'll hit you with a lightsaber combo and a Force Push. Block her attacks and back away for a minute. She's extremely powerful and can use all of her powers in quick succession. She'll toss her dual-bladed lightsaber at you, follow it up with Force Lightning, and then knock you back with a Force Push before you know it.

Instead of being aggressive and lunging at the Sith, wait for her to rush at you and block her lightsaber attack. Blast her away with the Force and rush her as she's flying backward. When she lands, hit her with a quick 'saber combo and back away.

After you chop off a small chunk of her health, Phobos retreats into the shadows of the room. The screen becomes hazy and hard to see, so stay on guard as you explore the room. Phobos reappears in a blue puff and immediately rushes you. Block her attack and Force Throw her into the debris. Blast her with Force Lightning and engage her in a Force Lock. Match the commands onscreen to send her crashing into the stacks.

As the Sith scum tumbles backward, rush and shock her with Force Lightning. She gets up ready to fight, so slash at her with your 'saber and whittle her Health bar even more.

41

As you fight, keep an eye on the small tablets near the room's left. When destroyed, one of them reveals a Holocron. Grab it before you finish off Phobos or it'll be lost to you forever.

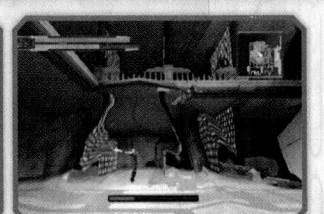

The closer you get to destroying Phobos, the more desperate she'll become. Eventually, she begins teleporting around the room while distorting your vision. Not only will she be harder to track, but the room will also become temporarily blurry, making it even tougher to get a lock on her. Let her teleport around the room while you dash to the room's end and grab a Bacta tank.

Wait for her to attack and expose herself before locking on to her again and mounting a counterattack. Phobos will also clone herself and double up on you. When she's cloned, lure both creatures toward you, slash them with a sideways strike, and leap into the air. Come down on them with a Ground Slam and destroy the clone quickly.

SITH WISDOM

Always press Jump when she uses her Repulse attack. You'll land safely on your feet and avoid taking damage.

Ignore Phobos's attempts to distract you when she transforms into Juno; maintain your assault. If you give in to your fear, she'll seize the opportunity and strike you down. Engage her in another Force Lock and hurl her into the library stacks once again. Dash toward her while you zap her with Force Lightning and immediately follow it up with a lightsaber combo.

Phobos's attacks won't change much when she nears defeat. She'll continue cloning herself and attack. She will keep dash attacking, so keep your block up when she's not directly in front of you. That way, she'll dash headfirst into your guard, allowing you to immediately counter. She will, however, increase the intensity of her Force attacks and lightsaber throws. To make matters worse, she'll link them into a vicious combo that can easily cut down your Health bar.

Stay on the move, dashing toward Bacta tanks, and stop only to raise your guard and counter. After you've blasted her back, engage her in a Force Lock and follow the onscreen commands to punish her.

WOOKIEE WARNING

Phobos's attacks are strong. If you throw your lightsaber to hurt her, you'll be defenseless to her attacks!

After several successful Force Locks, you can finally finish off the fiendish, fear-feasting freak. For your final attack, you must match the onscreen commands one more time and send her crashing through the library's stacks. The final trashing is just too much for her to handle; in a weak attempt to dissuade you from destroying her, she once again transforms into Juno. You ignore her pleas and run your 'saber through her chest, thus ending the confrontation with fear itself.

It is then that your master, Darth Vader, appears via PROXY to congratulate you on completing your test. Your next task is to face another Jedi. This time, it'll be a member of the former Jedi Council, Jedi Master Shaak Ti. You'll need to fully embrace the dark side to succeed.

You are ready to face a true Jedi now.

FELUCIA

MAP LEGEND

- 🔧 Bacta Tank
- ⚱ Color Crystal
- ⊙ Force Holocron
- ◆ Health Holocron
- ▦ Holocron
- 🗡 Lightsaber Hilt

AREA 7

AREA 6

AREA 5

AREA 4

AREA 8

AREA 2

AREA 3

AREA 1

MISSION DETAILS

Objective:

It is time to be tested against a true master. You must travel to Felucia and confront Shaak Ti, one of the last of the Jedi Council.

Enemies Encountered

- Felucian Warrior
- Felucian Shaman
- Felucian Blaster
- Rancor Beast: Minor Boss
- Shaak Ti: Boss

Collectibles Found

- 27 Holocrons
- 2 Color Crystals
- 2 Force Holocrons
- 2 Health Holocrons
- Lightsaber Hilt

"It Reminds Me of Callos."

Juno deftly pilots the *Rogue Shadow* toward the fertile planet of Felucia. The sensors pick up overwhelming signs of life on the planet, and Juno is reminded of her mission on Callos. There, she led her troops into battle and emerged victorious—but not before she, as part of the Imperial force, razed the planet and decimated it.

What was once a lush, green planet teeming with life is now a barren world. And it was because of her. Now, as she approaches Felucia, she's haunted by the destruction of an entire planet. You can sense it, no matter how deeply she buries her emotions.

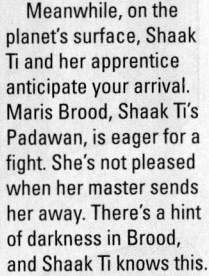

Meanwhile, on the planet's surface, Shaak Ti and her apprentice anticipate your arrival. Maris Brood, Shaak Ti's Padawan, is eager for a fight. She's not pleased when her master sends her away. There's a hint of darkness in Brood, and Shaak Ti knows this.

Felucian Fight!

You touch down on a large planet, which is so full of life that nearly everything on it seems to double as something else. Large mushrooms serve as platforms. Oversized flowers are landing pads for ships. As you speed away from the landing pad, you spy a few Felucian warriors perched high above you on large mushroomlike plants.

Proceed up the plant path until three Felucian warriors wielding blades confront you. They're extremely fast and adept with the blade, so stay on the move. The three warriors will attempt to surround you. If they do, use a Repulse attack to scatter them, then hit one with Force Lightning.

Leap away from the small Felucian mob and block your attacker's sword slashes. Counter with a combo, then send the warrior flying with a Force Burst.

Dash toward the tunnel up ahead and stop when you encounter a Felucian shaman. The plant-man is surrounded by a green glow and can grant other Felucians health. Similarly, once he's destroyed, he'll drop a Bacta tank to replenish *your* health. Stop just before you reach him and use your Force Choke to eliminate him.

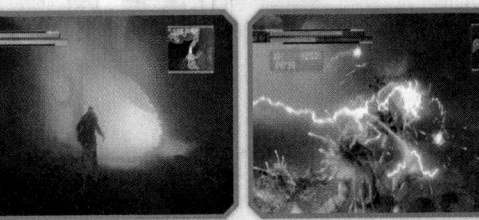

Venture into the cave with your lightsaber raised to block, and wait for a group of Felucian warriors to leap out from the darkness. Block their initial attacks, then use a quick combo to create some breathing room.

Back away from the warriors and hit them with Force Lightning. Remember, Felucians are extremely fast, so stay on the move or they'll swarm you in no time. Attack, then dash away to avoid getting surrounded in the cramped tunnel.

After you destroy the first group of Felucians, head deeper into the tunnel and attack the shaman with a quick 'saber combo. Shamans are not as tough as their warrior counterparts, so finish him off quickly. Grab the Bacta tank he drops and exit the tunnel into a wide open area full of vibrant plant life.

Pass up the holoprojector and prepare for a long battle. A Felucian Warrior bar appears at the screen's bottom—the only way to proceed is to defeat enough Felucians to deplete the bar completely. Force Push the first Felucian away, and use Repulse to disperse the other warriors as they surround you.

When only one Felucian remains, simply Force Choke him. Even though you've defeated the first squad, you still won't be able to proceed. Two Felucian blasters are waiting for you up ahead.

Dash up to them before they can lock on to you with their blasters, and strike them down with a sideways slash. As you attack the two Felucian warriors by the entrance to the next tunnel, a shaman and several more Felucian warriors appear behind you. Turn on the shaman after you finish off the other two warriors and replenish your Health bar with a Bacta tank. Then head up to the Felucian blaster hiding in the reeds on the right and slash him with a lightsaber combo.

After you clear the area, grab the Holocron just left of the holoprojector. It's hidden between several large trees and two bulbous plants. Follow the left wall until it ends in a small crevice hiding a Force Holocron. Grab it, then double-jump onto the area above the crevice. When you land, explore the base of the large reeds near the center and find a second Holocron. Finally, cut down the tree just left of the wrecked ship to expose a third Holocron, then enter the tunnel.

Inside the tunnel are more Felucians. Two shamans and several other warriors huddle up near the tunnel's end and wait for you to come trampling in. As soon as you spot the shaman's glowing green haze, hit the group of Felucians with a Detonate attack.

This will damage the squad just enough to make them easy picking when they get close. Allow the remaining Felucians to surround you, and hit them with Repulse to knock them away. You can then pick off the surviving Felucians with quick lightsaber combos.

Stop midway down the tunnel and use the Force to bust through the large glowing obstruction at the end.

Storm toward the Felucians on the other side of the now-destroyed glowing wall and hurl them back with Force Push. Use short, quick 'saber combos to slash away at their health and bring them down.

Follow the tunnel to its end and engage the Felucian warrior in combat. Strike him down with a 'saber combo and electrocute him with Force Lightning while he's on the ground. If he gets up, simply pick him up and throw him against the trees.

Upon exiting the tunnel, make a sharp right and grab the Holocron in the corner.

JEDI KNOWLEDGE

Felucian warriors are fast and furious! If they manage to surround you or overwhelm you with numbers, use Maelstrom to knock them all back and deal decent damage!

Follow the main path until two more Felucians stop you. Thrash them quickly and minimize damage incurred. If possible, destroy them from afar with Force Lightning or Force Push attacks. If they manage to reach you before you can swat them down from a distance, use Repulse to create some room, then blast them and take them out.

As you continue farther up the path, a large piece of scrap metal comes raining down on you. Though it narrowly misses you, there's no escaping the rancor beast that hurled it at you.

Rampaging Rancor!

The rancor beast comes barreling down on you, and you've nowhere to go!

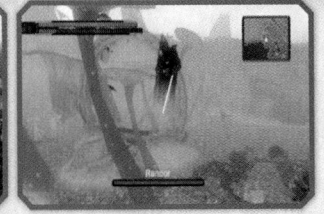

attack, dash away and lure it into the open. Avoid getting trapped along the area's edges! If the rancor manages to squeeze you against the wall, it'll keep you trapped and thrash you until you're history.

After you deplete the majority of the beast's health, engage it in a final confrontation. Match the onscreen commands to leap on top of it; then ram your lightsaber into its cranium and slash down its spine.

When the battle with the brute begins, release your lock on it! Your first battle with a rancor won't be easy, but if you maintain a lock on it, you'll limit the amount of room you have to dodge its attacks. You can still use the lock-on feature—in fact, you'll need to at times; just don't rely on it against these oversized brutes.

When the beast attacks, double-jump into the air and dash away from it. Land behind the rancor and streak far away. The lumbering beast isn't as fast as you, but its giant gait will allow it to catch you eventually. As you dash away, search the area's edges to find Bacta tanks and replenish your health to full.

Before leaving the area where you faced the rancor, scour the place for collectibles. There are three Holocrons here. Grab the Holocron hidden in the trees just left of the tunnel exit, then cut down all the trees to expose a Holocron near the next tunnel. The third Holocron is just off the path as you come around the corner after defeating the rancor.

WOOKIEE WARNING

The rancor isn't the only enemy you must worry about. A shaman and several other Felucian warriors are waiting for you near the next tunnel.

After the rancor fight, more Felucian shamans appear. Run your 'saber through them with a few lightsaber combos followed by a Force Lightning attack. They're not as tough as their warrior brothers, but they still pose a threat.

When the Felucian warriors arrive, use Force Slam to slash and slam them into the ground. Use the wide-open area to maintain a safe distance and not get surrounded by the attacking Felucians. Take them down one by one.

Once your health is full, turn around and face the approaching rancor. Pick up a rock or one of the exploding bulbous plants nearby and hurl it at the beast. Lure it toward you, then approach the shaman and his squad. Blast the Felucians with Force Lightning while the rancor gives chase. Hit the Felucians with a Ground Slam attack to knock them off their feet, then dash away immediately.

The rancor beast will trample the remaining Felucians while he chases you. Once again, turn and face the rancor and blast it with a shot of Force Lightning.

SITH WISDOM

If there are too many Felucians to handle, dash away and use the large exploding plants as projectiles. Their explosions are big enough to damage up to three Felucians at a time.

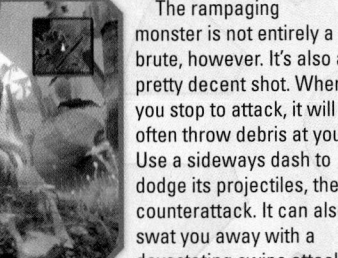

The rampaging monster is not entirely a brute, however. It's also a pretty decent shot. When you stop to attack, it will often throw debris at you. Use a sideways dash to dodge its projectiles, then counterattack. It can also swat you away with a devastating swipe attack, so stay swift. If you see its hand go up to swat, Force jump backward to avoid the attack.

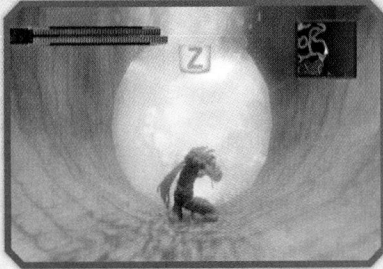

The next passage contains a system of tunnels. Follow the tunnel to the left and exit into the next area.

Continue dashing away from the rancor and turn only to temporarily lock on and electrocute it with Force Lightning. After your lightning

You can follow the right tunnel instead. Force Push through the thin membranes that separate the tunnel into different passages. Slash

Continued on Next Page

past the Felucian warriors in your way until you come upon a Holocron. Collect it, then backtrack to the entrance. This time, follow the tunnel left until you encounter another Holocron. Grab it and exit the tunnel into the next area.

You can navigate the tunnel system from one Holocron to the other, but it is much easier to backtrack to the beginning and take the second path.

Double Trouble

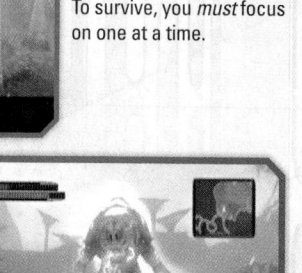

The next area is home to two large vicious rancors. To survive, you *must* focus on one at a time.

Hit the closest creature with a current of Force Lightning and immediately dash away before it reaches you. Remove your lock from the creature and run away before both can circle in on you.

As you move away from your enemies, search the area on the left and pick up the Health Holocron. The increased health will help during this battle.

Stay on the move. Draw one rancor away from the other by rapidly dashing toward it, luring it to attack, then running away. If you can do this while the other rancor is at a distance, you'll be able to split the two.

After you split the two beasts, approach the battle as you did with the previous solo rancor. Dash away, turn and attack, then run away again. If the two beasts manage to join up again, use large exploding bulbs to damage both with one shot before splitting them up again.

SITH WISDOM

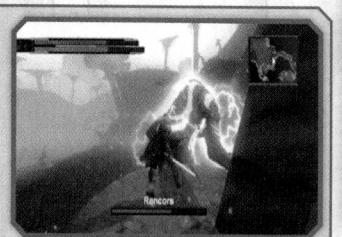

While you dash away, look for platforms along the surrounding walls. They're perfect perches to attack from.

WOOKIEE WARNING

Remember, these rancors are just like the other one you faced earlier, so they can throw things at you too. Now you'll have to dodge plants on two fronts.

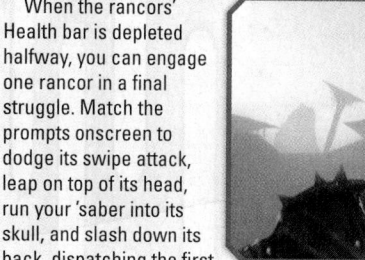

When the rancors' Health bar is depleted halfway, you can engage one rancor in a final struggle. Match the prompts onscreen to dodge its swipe attack, leap on top of its head, run your 'saber into its skull, and slash down its back, dispatching the first beast. Now the second one will be easier to focus on.

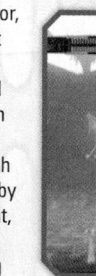

Lock on to the rancor, dash up to it, and hit it with Force Lightning. Release your lock and run away before it can hit you. Find another Bacta tank to replenish your health. If you go by a large exploding plant, hurl it at the rancor, then continue dashing away. After depleting the rancor's Health bar to less than one-quarter, you can finally eliminate it. Once again, follow the commands onscreen to unleash your final attack.

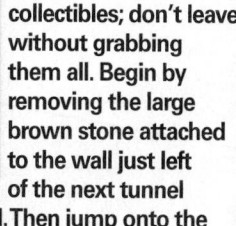

This area is rife with collectibles; don't leave without grabbing them all. Begin by removing the large brown stone attached to the wall just left of the next tunnel entrance to reveal a color crystal. Then jump onto the platform left of the color crystal to get a new lightsaber hilt. From the platform, dash across the area to the opposite corner and grab the Holocron in plain view.

Continued on Next Page

Now follow the left wall toward where you first encountered the rancors. When you come across another large brown stone attached to the wall, remove it and reveal a Holocron. Continue backtracking, hugging the left wall until you pass the tunnels through which you first entered the area. Pass the tunnel, still hugging the wall until you come across another Holocron near two large trees. Cut across to the area's center and remove the large bulbous stone there, exposing yet another Holocron. Grab it and approach the next tunnel entrance at the region's far end.

Approach your fallen foes and follow up your initial blast with a Ground Slam attack to take out the first few Felucians. When the Felucian shamans show up, shred them with swift 'saber strikes. If the lightsaber combos don't destroy both shamans, thrust one away and choke the other. When one is down, lift and choke the second.

Check the area just left of the tunnel exit and grab the Holocron. Then follow the left wall deeper into the area to find a second Holocron.

Finally, cut down the three reeds just in front of the next pathway to find a third Holocron.

Blast through the thin membrane and step into the next tunnel. Follow it to its end, past a holoprojector, and into a wide-open area full of lush plant life.

Run up the incline and fry the first Felucian you encounter. Pick him up and toss him at the other approaching Felucian as he storms down the path toward you. The first warrior perishes, but the second one will be down for only a bit. Pick him up and toss him over the cliffside on the left.

Two more Felucian warriors ambush you when you reach the incline's top. Greet them with a Detonate attack, followed by lightsaber slashes. If any survive your initial onslaught, use Force Choke to destroy them completely.

Search the area behind the large greenish blue mushroom stalks on the right to find some collectibles. Hug the right wall all the way to the far end of the area and grab a Force Holocron and two regular Holocrons. When you reach the area's opposite end, turn left and pick up the Holocron near the next tunnel entrance.

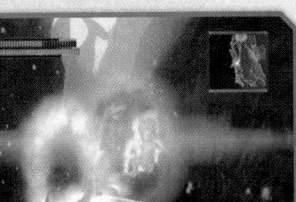

Follow the path and turn right at the incline's top. As you go, three more Felucian warriors leap out at you from the rock face on the right. Blast them back with Force Push to keep from getting surrounded, then pick them off one at a time with Force Lightning. If they manage to crowd you, use Repulse to make room, then attack. Farther up the path, several more Felucians come marching down. As they approach, grab them one by one and swiftly throw them against the wall on the left.

Blast down the membrane blocking the tunnel and lock on to the Felucians inside. One of them is carrying a blaster, so target him first. Zap him with Force Lightning, then dash at the duo and attack them with a sideways 'saber slash. They are the last two Felucians standing between you and the Jedi. When they're out of your way, speed to the tunnel's exit.

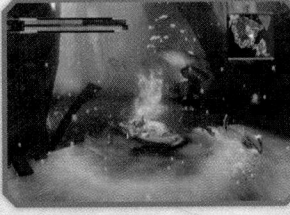

In the next area, you encounter the Jedi Master riding a rancor beast across the vibrant landscape. When she becomes aware of your presence, she sets off on the rancor, leaving you to contend with her Felucian warriors. Allow the Felucians to approach you and attack. As they get near, blast them away with a Detonate attack.

Strike them down as they get up, then approach the shaman at the next bend in the path. When all other Felucians are gone, crush the shaman with a Force Choke and grab the Bacta tank he leaves behind. Make another right at the next bend and encounter three more Felucian warriors. Use Repulse to avoid getting surrounded, and hit them with a burst of your Detonate power. You can now speed to the path's end to face Shaak Ti.

 Follow the path until you reach a slight bend to the left and stop. Remove the brown boulder from the corner on the right to expose a Holocron.

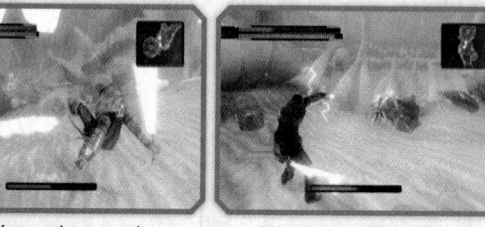 After you blast her a second time with your Force powers, increase your lightsaber attacks and corner her against the wall. Relentlessly attack her with your 'saber and finish with a Force thrust to knock her down.

The Last of the Council

You find the Jedi Master in front of a large open chasm containing a Sarlacc. She waits for you with her rancor beast at her side. Luckily for you, just as you approach for the final battle, one of the 10-story tentacles wraps itself around the rancor and drags it into the chasm.

That's when the battle begins! Immediately blast Shaak Ti with Force Push and send her flying back toward the chasm. Run up to her while you blast her with Force Lightning and immediately engage her in a lightsaber-lock battle. Match the onscreen prompts as they appear and overpower her!

 As soon as she lands from your initial attack, hit her again with another shot of Force Lightning to engage her in a Force Lock. Match the onscreen prompts and inflict more damage on the last of the Jedi Council. When she's had enough, she'll back away and let out a shrill scream for help.

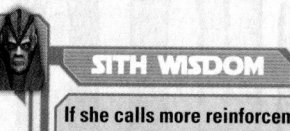 There is one Holocron in the battle arena, just right of where Shaak Ti appears. Grab it as you battle her.

Shaak Ti's reinforcements arrive immediately—five Felucian warriors and a shaman! Draw the Felucian warriors along with Shaak Ti and hit them all with a burst of the Force as they approach. The blast scatters the approaching enemies, granting you just enough room to dash into their ranks and slash away with a lightsaber combo.

Ignore Shaak Ti for a moment and focus your attacks on her lackeys. Draw them toward you and hit them with combos until no one but Shaak Ti remains. Slash at her with a quick combo and engage her in a Force Lock again.

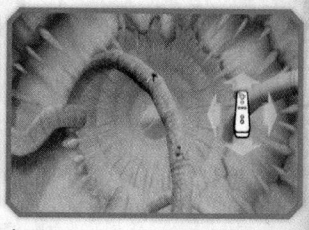

Shaak Ti's attacks are rather easy to avoid or counter. Her Force Push won't cause much damage as long as you jump while you're being tossed away, and her lightsaber dash attack can be easily blocked. Stay on the offensive and keep steady pressure on the Jedi. If you're constantly on the attack, she'll have little chance to counter.

When she creates a protective bubble around herself, she'll begin regenerating her health. Don't let her! The second her bubble appears, fry it with Force Lightning and stop her health regeneration.

SITH WISDOM

If she calls more reinforcements, target the shaman first. He can help Shaak Ti replenish her health.

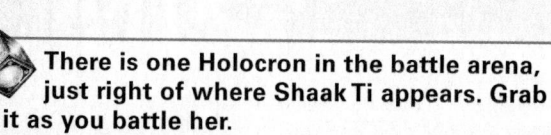

When Shaak Ti's Health bar is less than one-quarter, you can lock her in another Force battle. Match the commands onscreen to fry her and further deplete her health. After winning the Force Lock, follow it with a lightsaber combo and bring her to the brink of elimination. This triggers a final set of onscreen commands. Match the first few prompts to follow Shaak Ti as she attempts to escape.

Realizing that she's about to be destroyed, she leaps atop one of the overgrown tentacles whipping around in the background. Follow her onto the whipping tentacles and block her attacks. Continue following the prompts onscreen until you bring down the final member of the Jedi Council. As expected, the defeated Jedi attempts to dissuade you from dispatching her. Just as the Jedi before her, she tries convincing you that you could be so much more than a Sith Lord and Vader's puppet. Her words fall on deaf ears, and she falls into the chasm. Your job here is done.

49

VADER'S FLAGSHIP

MISSION DETAILS

Objective
Rejoin Darth Vader, challenge the Emperor, and fulfill your destiny.

Enemies Encountered
None

Collectibles Found
None

JEDI KNOWLEDGE
The following is not a standard walkthrough, as there is no player-controlled action during this chapter. In fact, this chapter is a bridge between Acts 1 and 2 of *Star Wars: The Force Unleashed* and, more importantly, is a bridge between the prequel trilogy and the original trilogy. During Act 1, you were tasked with hunting down Jedi in accordance with Order 66, thus bringing a tidy end to the first three episodes of the *Star Wars* saga. During Act 2, you'll take part in setting up the last three episodes of the saga.

"We Will at Last Control the Galaxy!"

Having just defeated Jedi Master Shaak Ti, you communicate your success to Darth Vader via PROXY. He seems pleased—about as pleased as Darth Vader can seem, at least—and commands you to rendezvous with him on his flagship.

You can now stand together against the Emperor...and destroy him!

Betrayal!

You fly back to Vader's flagship to discuss the next phase of your plan. Little do you know that the Emperor's spies have followed you! All of Darth Vader's efforts to keep you a secret from the Emperor have been wasted, as your identity has been discovered! Shortly after your arrival on the flagship, the Emperor's ship arrives. Only it was not Vader who summoned him...

Just as the Emperor enters the chamber, Vader runs his lightsaber into your back. You've been betrayed! Still alive, you plead with your master to let you live. What of your plans to destroy the Emperor together?

Still, the Emperor's hold on Lord Vader is stronger than the sound of your pleas. The Emperor issues Vader an ultimatum: either Vader destroys you to prove his loyalty or the Emperor will eliminate you both. Without hesitation, Lord Vader sends you through a glass pane and into the darkness of space...

"It Is Done."

Once the Emperor is satisfied that you're no longer a threat, he returns to his ship and departs. Little did he know that Vader's treachery is boundless. As he departed, the Emperor failed to notice a small droid zip out into space toward your lifeless floating body.

Moments later, the darkness begins to fade. You wake up to find yourself on an operating table—alive! Lord Vader salvaged your body and rebuilt you.

Now that the Emperor believes you're history, you can resume your path to fulfill your destiny. Only this time, you and your master must alter the plan. The Emperor's sudden arrival proves that he cannot be easily deceived. If you and Vader are to destroy him, you must divert his attention away from your machinations. Your new task is to provide a large enough distraction to keep the Emperor preoccupied. Lord Vader believes that only a rebellion could sufficiently distract the Emperor. Before you and Vader strike, you must raise an army. A rebel army. You must form a Rebel Alliance....

With your next task in hand, you rush to Juno's rescue and free her from captivity. Even in her weakened state, she's a better pilot than anyone else you can find. Besides, she's much more than a pilot to you.

Back on the *Rogue Shadow*, you remember something Rahm Kota said during your first encounter. He said that he saw himself in your future. If what he said was true, then he must still be alive! Your Rebel Alliance must start with him.

NAR SHADDAA

MAP LEGEND

- 🗜 Bacta Tank
- 🔹 Color Crystal
- ◉ Force Holocron
- ◆ Health Holocron
- 🖳 Holocron
- 🖊 Lightsaber Hilt

MISSION DETAILS

Objective

Betrayed! Darth Vader has betrayed you at the bidding of the Emperor. However, Vader has kept you alive to continue the secret plot against the Emperor. Find General Kota on Nar Shaddaa and enlist him in your cause.

Enemies Encountered

Rodian Grenadier

Gamorrean Axemen

Blaster-toting Human

Imperial Stormtrooper

Shadow Stormtrooper

Shadow Guard: Boss

Collectibles Found

10 Holocrons

Force Holocron

Health Holocron

Lightsaber Hilt

AREA 1

AREA 3

AREA 2

The planet of Nar Shaddaa is not as vibrant as Felucia, but it is teeming with life nonetheless. Unfortunately, the life here is drunk and angry. Somewhere among the scum and villainy of Nar Shaddaa is General Kota.

Disembark the *Rogue Shadow* and follow the path down into the bar.

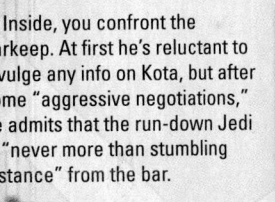

As you go, double-jump to grab the Holocron floating above the second arch along the path, then continue into the bar.

Inside, you confront the barkeep. At first he's reluctant to divulge any info on Kota, but after some "aggressive negotiations," he admits that the run-down Jedi is "never more than stumbling distance" from the bar.

JEDI KNOWLEDGE

Use the surrounding chairs, tables, and other debris to Pummel bar scum. If the bar's patrons attempt to surround you, use Maelstrom to make them hurt!

Bar Fight!

As soon as you get the information on Kota, the bar patrons turn on you. Having used your Force powers to interrogate the bartender, you've exposed yourself as a Jedi, and now your head will bring in a hefty bounty! Immediately use a sideways slash to cut through the surrounding scum. Clear a small path out of the riotous crowd and dash away to distance yourself.

When you're far enough away, turn around and face the crowd with your lightsaber in blocking position. Many of the blaster-toting bar rogues will shoot themselves and whittle down their own health. Locate the Rodian with the grenade launcher near the bar's rear and streak past the other rogues straight toward him. If you let him live too long, he'll blast you to bits; take him out first.

With the Rodian out of the fight, turn your blade on the human with the blaster. He's dangerous at any distance, so take him out. As you target him, two Gamorreans attempt to crowd you. Unleash a Repulse attack to knock them all down and finish off the human. When only the Gamorreans

remain, engage them in close-quarters combat and take them down with quick combos. If you want to dispose of them quickly, use Force Choke or simply toss them over the side of the bar's patio balcony. With the bar scum eliminated, the doors open into the next area.

Before leaving, remove all the poles from the tables with the holographic dancer to reveal a Holocron near the doorway.

Speed down the next walkway and double-jump over the final arch, grabbing the lightsaber hilt there. Pass the holoprojector at the walkway's end and proceed into the next barroom. There, several more ruffians hope to claim the bounty on your "Jedi" head. Walk into the room and lead with a Force Push to knock any scoundrels out of your way. Dash inside and gain a safe distance from the bar patrons.

Turn on the group of grubby rabble-rousers and hit them with your Sith Scorcher attack. The intensified electric blast will destroy some but not all of them. Follow your Scorcher attack with a lightsaber combo to cut down the remaining bandits. Leave the Gamorreans for last; they're tough but can only pose a threat at close range. If you're constantly on the move around the bar as you cut down the other rogues, you'll be safe from the Gamorreans' attacks.

As you fight in the bar, destroy the pole from the center table to expose a Force Holocron. Then explore the room's left side and remove the tables and chairs with a simple Force Push, revealing a Holocron. Pick it up and continue into the next area of Nar Shaddaa.

As you trek down the next walkway, you'll encounter a few blaster-carrying bandits. Hit the first two with a Force Push, then continue down the walkway and use the Force to toss the other scumbags over the walkway's side. When you reach the Rodian grenadier at

the walkway's end, either toss him over the side or use a Force Push to ricochet a grenade back at him.

Creep into the next room and raise your 'saber to block incoming fire. This two-story room has a large circular bar at the center. Circle around the bar and reflect as much blaster fire as possible before engaging in close-quarters combat.

When the Gamorreans in the room get close, dash past them and attack one of the Rodian bandits. Fry him with Force Lightning, then keep moving to avoid the Gamorreans' axes.

The Gamorreans are a heavy-set species, so Force Pushes aren't as effective as lifting them with the Force. Block their axe attacks and counter with combos of your own. When one is close enough to grab, pick him up with the Force and toss him into his partner to knock them both away.

With the bottom floor clear of all enemies, take the fight upstairs. Greet the two Gamorreans there with lightsaber combos, then hit them with a Sith Scorcher attack. Turn left at the top of the steps and assault the last two bandits with a Detonate attack to eliminate them quickly.

Once all your enemies have been eliminated, approach Kota as he slumps in his booth.

While you're on the second level, give the area a thorough thrashing. Remove the poles from the center of every table to make a Health Holocron appear at the top of the steps.

The run-down Kota is nothing more than a blubbering mess now. He's been drinking his troubles away and has seemingly given up on the Jedi

ways. Ever since you took his sight in your first battle, he's been on a downward spiral, even though he managed to salvage his life.

Kota's given up on fighting the Empire. As you try to convince him to fight the Empire, more bar scum arrive, itching for a fight. You must fight your way out of the Nar Shaddaa bars with Kota in tow.

Turn around to face them and lead your assault with a Force Push. Toss the first two enemies over the railing and down to the bottom floor. Then rush the other scoundrels and electrocute them with Sith Scorcher.

WOOKIEE WARNING

Watch out for the Gamorreans' ram attack. If you focus on one enemy too long or stay put, they'll ram you and send you flying toward the room's other side.

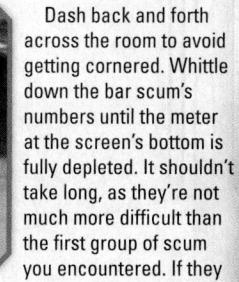

Dash back and forth across the room to avoid getting cornered. Whittle down the bar scum's numbers until the meter at the screen's bottom is fully depleted. It shouldn't take long, as they're not much more difficult than the first group of scum you encountered. If they do manage to surround you, simply hurl them away with Repulse.

Head back toward the stairs and destroy the Rodian at the top of the steps. Storm down the steps, picking up the Bacta tank as you go, and engage the enemies on the first floor. There aren't many and they're not as tough as the Gamorreans, so a simple Sith Scorcher or lightsaber combo should work. Head back toward your ship.

By now, the Imperial army has gotten word of what has transpired since you arrived on Nar Shaddaa, and several squadrons of stormtroopers have arrived to bring you down. When the door opens to the walkway, a small group of troopers greets you. Blast them off their feet, then pick each of them up and toss them over the walkway's side. At the walkway's end is another small troop. Walk up to them with your 'saber raised to reflect their fire, then burn them down with Sith Scorcher.

Confidently walk into the bar with your lightsaber in blocking position and circle around to the room's right. Locate the soldier near the room's right and strike him down. Pick up the Bacta tank, then use Force Push to thrash the remaining soldiers around the room. Use the tables, poles, and other objects in the room as projectiles and to shield you from the soldiers' fire.

Exit the room and follow the next walkway up to main bar. There aren't any enemies here, so don't worry about being careful. The next room, however, isn't as peaceful.

Shred the Shadow Guard!

When you enter the main bar, a Shadow Guard and a small group of stormtroopers ambush you. Blast the stormtroopers away, then lock on to the Shadow Guard. He's skilled in the ways of the Force and can easily break your Force Grip and hit you with a Force attack of his own. Luckily, you've got more weapons in your Force arsenal.

Attack him with a Sith Scorcher to begin depleting his Health bar. Dash away and lure him to the patio balcony, where you'll have more room to fight.

Let him approach you. When he hits you with a Force Push, jump to land safely on your feet, then counter with a combo.

Engage the Shadow Guard in a lightsaber lock, and match the prompts onscreen to slash him up and pound him with a Force Push. Your successful lightsaber-lock battle knocks off nearly one-quarter of his health.

Immediately follow up your blast with a shot of Force Lightning, then block his counter. He'll either dash toward you or toss his weapon at you, so raise your guard! Once you've blocked it, dash at him and cut him with a combo. After you deplete nearly half his health, the Shadow Guard creates a battalion of Shadow Troopers.

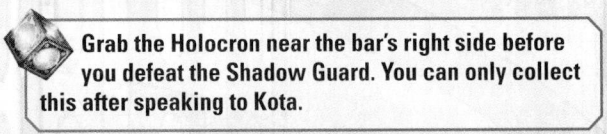

As soon as the Shadow Troopers appear, dash away to get some distance. Turn around when you can get them all in your view, and raise your 'saber to reflect their fire. Make them a priority when they appear. You can easily rush away from the Shadow Guard, but avoiding the Shadow Troopers' stream of fire will be harder to do. Hit the Shadow Troopers with Sith Scorcher to knock them out of the fight. More will appear periodically, but you can easily deal with them.

Grab the Holocron near the bar's right side before you defeat the Shadow Guard. You can only collect this after speaking to Kota.

Turn on the Shadow Guard and unleash a combo attack before dashing away again. If you're too close to him, he can easily pick you up and use a Force Choke. If he does, free yourself with Force Lightning. If more Shadow Troopers appear, leap into the air and come down on them with a Ground Slam attack to knock them off their feet. The attack should also knock the Shadow Guard back and inflict a decent amount of damage.

Continue to dash away from the Shadow Guard's attacks and turn only to blast him with Sith Scorcher. This attack severely depletes his Health bar and will hit any surviving Shadow Troopers that flank the bar's sides. When the group of enemies is bunched together, hit them with a Ground Slam to take them all out.

When the fight is over, Kota emerges half-drunk from behind the bar. He's still not convinced that you can fight the Empire and win, but he does know someone in the senate who could use your skills. He joins you... hesitantly.

Haha... Well, it's a fool's errand, boy. The Emperor's army is infinite.

TRIAL OF SPIRIT

AREA 4

AREA 3

AREA 2

AREA 1

55

MISSION DETAILS

Objective

Something is drawing you back to the Jedi Temple on Coruscant. Go there and find out if your instincts are true. You must prepare to confront your deepest fears.

Enemies Encountered

Imperial Stormtrooper

Stormtrooper Gunner

Imperial Guard

Jump Stormtrooper

Rogue Jedi: Boss

Collectibles Found

8 Holocrons

Health Holocron

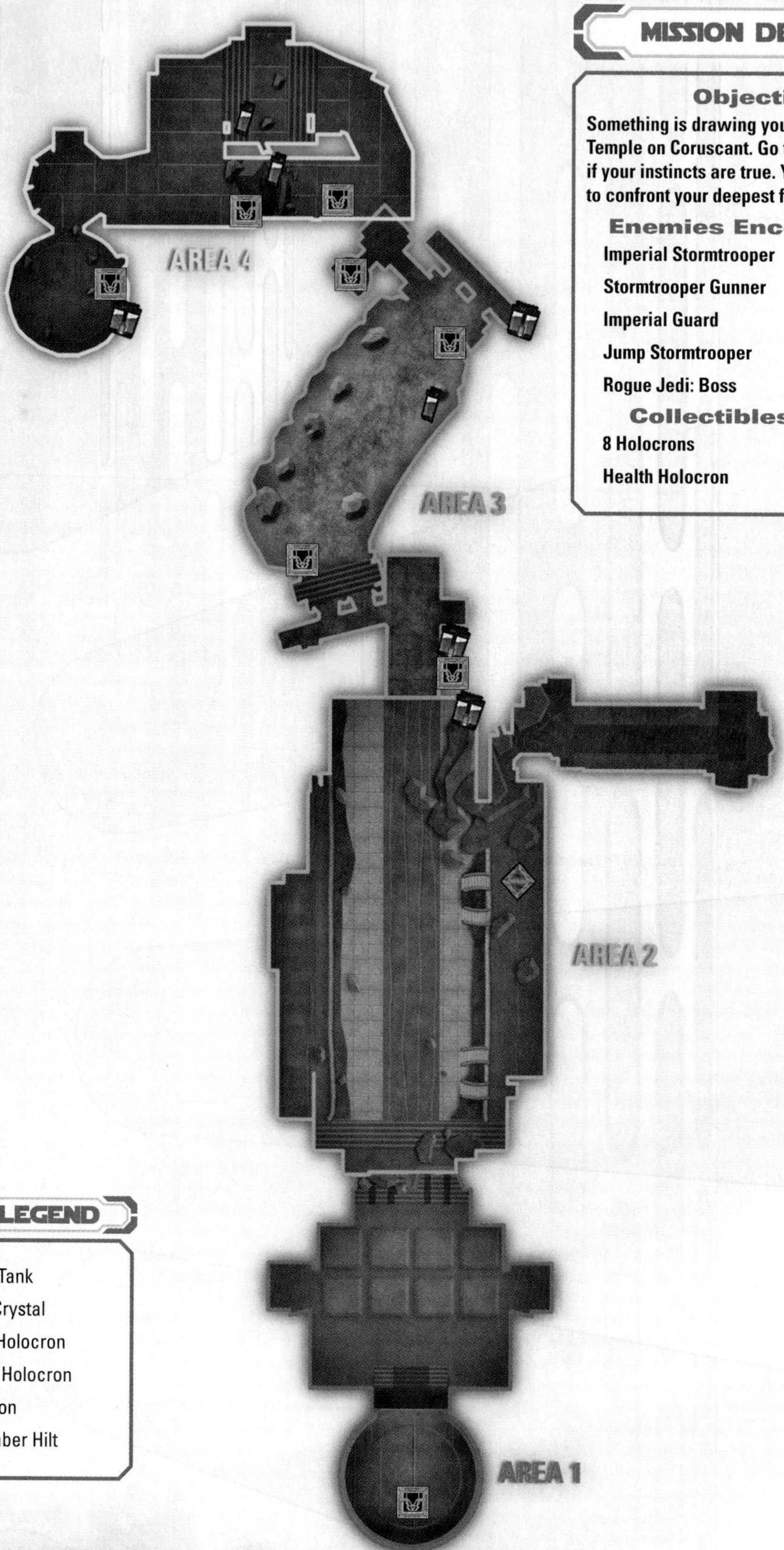

MAP LEGEND

- 🜲 Bacta Tank
- 🜚 Color Crystal
- ◉ Force Holocron
- ◆ Health Holocron
- 🝆 Holocron
- ✎ Lightsaber Hilt

Third Time Is the Charm

Your third trip to the Jedi Temple begins in the same way as the last two. Imperial Guards swarm the Temple entrance and feebly attempt to stop you from landing. As you disembark, a guard rushes out at you.

Hit him with Force Lightning. Fry him to a crisp, then chase down the other stormtroopers hiding near the Jedi statues. Slice them to ribbons, then go back up the steps to the Temple entrance.

> Search the area underneath the landing pad and grab the Holocron.

Nothing Is Sacred

Raise your lightsaber and slowly creep past the Temple pillars in front of the entrance. Reflect the enemy's fire and dash at them when you're close enough. Use Force Lightning to eliminate them quickly.

Rush past the pillars and rip the gun turret from its supports. Turn the turret on the remaining soldiers and clear the area of all hostiles.

Enter the main Temple as you have before, with your lightsaber raised. Speed to the Temple's right side and up the steps to the walkway on the Temple wall's right edge. Hold your position there and lure the guards toward you. As they come up the steps on either side of you, slash them down. Keep the higher ground to maintain a tactical advantage.

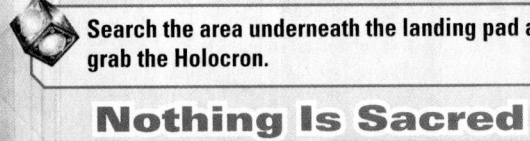

Allow the stormtroopers to reach you, and slash them with combos to take them down. If an Imperial Guard attempts to reach you, hurl him away. Take out all the weaker Imperial soldiers first and leave the tougher guards for last.

If the Imperial troops manage to pinch you on both sides, jump down to the main Temple floor, then go up one of the staircases to attack them

from behind. Just as you finish depleting the Imperial Troops bar at the screen's bottom, a stormtrooper escapes through the sliding doors at the Temple's rear.

Just because you depleted the Imperial Troops bar doesn't mean the Temple is completely clear. More Imperial Guards are entrenched near the far Temple wall. Approach them carefully and attack. Let them get close, then hit them with Repulse. Dispatch the small squad, then return to the walkway along the right wall. It'll provide protection from blaster fire and allow passage toward the Temple's far end.

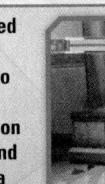

At the Temple's far end are three Jump Stormtroopers. Their jet packs make them extremely mobile as they hover above the ground. To make matters worse, their blasters are very quick and more powerful than normal blasters, and they carry flamethrowers. Approach them from the right walkway, using the railing as cover. Use Force Grip to hurl large chunks of debris at them.

Get close enough to reach them with your Force powers and either choke them or use Sith Scorcher to weaken them. When only one Jump trooper remains, leap out at him and strike him down with aerial assault attacks.

> Duck into the small alcove under the right walkway and grab the Health Holocron before proceeding.

Rush around the rubble at the Temple's rear to chase after the trooper that escaped earlier. As you round the corner, two Imperial Guards appear. Knock them away with a Force Push, then fry them with Sith Scorcher. There's a Bacta tank in a niche near the Temple door; grab it and head inside.

SITH WISDOM

If you're still in need of a Bacta tank after facing the two Imperial Guards, destroy the statue on the right just beyond the door. There is a tank inside the statue.

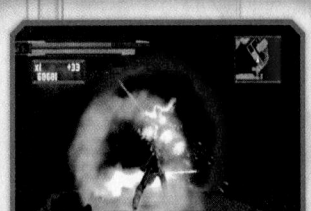

Use the Force to remove the toppled rocks at the passage's end and trek into the subterranean tunnel below.

Underground, turn right and stop just behind the large Jedi statue. Force Grip the statue to destroy it, then toss the large piece of stone at the stormtroopers in the distance. Aim carefully to get as many troopers as possible. If the first stone misses them, you can grab a second piece of the statue and try again.

Check the niche to the right of the steps beyond the statue and grab the Holocron.

Venture up the cavernous tunnel with your lightsaber in blocking position, and reflect the troopers' blaster fire. When an Imperial Guard attacks, pick him up with Force Grip and choke him. You may not be able to choke him completely; as your Force bar runs dry, toss him away to destroy him.

Just as before, grab the rubble nearby and toss it at the soldiers at the cavern's far end. Hold your position and allow the remaining guards to rush you from afar. When they get near, disperse them with a Ground Slam attack and retreat.

When the soldiers get up and rush at you again, hit them all with Sith Scorcher to finish them off. If any survive, use your Ground Slam until the cavern is clear.

With the cavern clear, examine the area behind the last sloping concrete support on the right. A Holocron is nestled just next to it. Grab it, then go up the stairs at the cavern's far end.

Turn left and go through the large hole in the wall. At the bottom of the steps, turn right and use a Force Push to remove the rubble blocking your path. Continue your trek deeper into the Temple's subterranean caverns.

Turn left at the top of the steps and immediately hit the troopers with Force Lightning. Leave the Imperial Guard for last, and keep him out of striking distance with your Force Push.

Remove the large stone in the corner to reveal another Holocron.

Continue down the pathway until you reach another trooper squad. Fry them with Sith Scorcher, then welcome the Imperial Guards with strong lightsaber combos. Let your Force meter replenish, and hit them with Force Lightning as well.

Round the corner up ahead and attack the three troopers in your way. One hit of Sith Scorcher should take them all out.

JEDI KNOWLEDGE

To take out these enemies from afar, use Force Pummel.

Follow the passage to the hall's end and turn left into the dead end. Remove the fallen pillar in the corner and claim the Holocron underneath. Backtrack to the stairs in the passage behind you.

At the top of the steps is a small chamber full of Imperial Guards. Don't rush in! Instead, stay just outside the archway and reflect their blaster fire back at them. If any try to rush out of the chamber and into the hallway, greet them with Sith Scorcher and take them out. Go through the now-empty chamber and into the elevator on the right.

Reunion

The elevator touches down, and you exit to find your master battling a familiar figure. The rogue Jedi seems familiar, but you can't place him. Apparently, you've arrived just in time, as the Jedi strikes down Darth Vader when you exit the elevator. You leap to your master's defense and engage the Jedi in battle.

The Jedi's techniques are similar to that of the Shadow Guard you faced earlier. Raise your 'saber to block the Jedi's lightsaber when he throws it; then attack him with Sith Scorcher.

Back away a bit and move the fight to the arena's center. When the Jedi comes at you, block his attack, then counter with a combo. When you engage him in a lightsaber lock, match the onscreen commands to slash the Jedi away. Follow him as he stumbles backward, and engage him in a Force Lock. Match the onscreen prompts to damage the Jedi even further.

After your attack, the Jedi attempts to strike you down with lightsaber combos. Block them, then hit him with a Ground Slam. If he tries hurting you with a Force Push, jump to avoid it, then reengage him in a Force Lock.

After successfully blasting the Jedi away, maintain your assault with Ground Slams and lightsaber combos. When he surrounds himself with a blue haze, back away to avoid his Repulse attack. Dash to the arena's left to get a Bacta tank before reengaging the Jedi in battle.

With your health refilled, return to the fight and finish off the Jedi. Leap over his Force attacks and land with Ground Slam attacks. Engage him in a final struggle and match the onscreen commands to destroy him once and for all.

Unfortunately, it is not until the Jedi lies dying on the ground that you realize who he is. His final words send shock waves of fear and regret through you. Just as his body fades, he says, "I'm sorry, son."

KASHYYYK

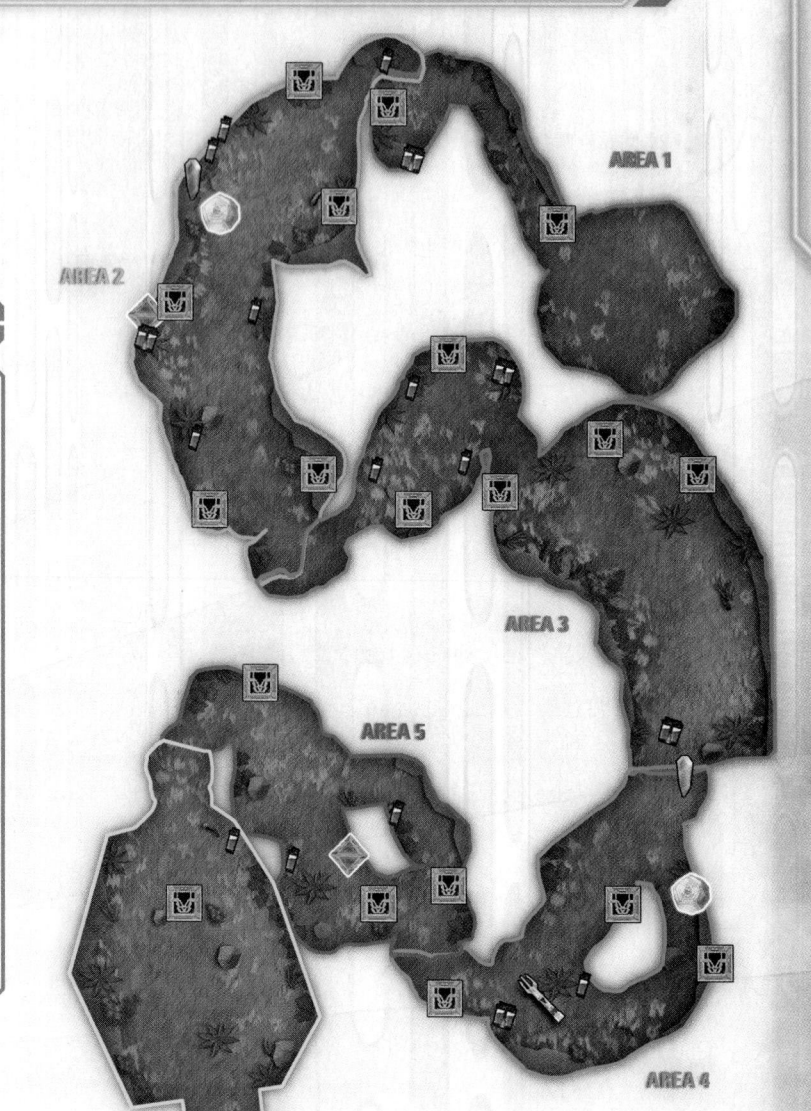

AREA 1

AREA 2

AREA 3

AREA 5

AREA 4

AREA 6

MISSION DETAILS

Objective

General Kota has been contacted by opponents of the Empire. To gain their help, you must investigate the Wookiee homeworld of Kashyyyk.

Enemies Encountered

Imperial Stormtrooper

Stormtrooper Gunner

Stormtrooper Sniper

Jump Stormtrooper

Shock Stormtrooper

AT-ST: Minor Boss

Ozzik Sturn: Boss

Collectibles Found

20 Holocrons

2 Color Crystals

2 Force Holocrons

2 Health Holocrons

Lightsaber Hilt

MAP LEGEND

🐟 Bacta Tank

🔹 Color Crystal

⊙ Force Holocron

◆ Health Holocron

▦ Holocron

🖊 Lightsaber Hilt

59

"We're Heading to Kashyyyk."

Back on the *Rogue Shadow*, General Kota's drunken stupor has started to wear off. As his haze begins to fade, one of his contacts in the Senate sends a communication. He doesn't say much other than the name of your new destination. Your next stop is Kashyyyk.

While you approach the planet, Kota remains tight-lipped about the purpose of your trip to Kashyyyk. He does mention that his contact in the Senate needs something from the Wookiee planet. If you get it, he might be persuaded to help you against the Empire. But the question still remains...

SITH WISDOM

Before touching down on Kashyyyk, upgrade your Force Lightning and Push powers to Level 3.

"Get What?"

There's only one way to find out what Kota's contact is after—explore Imperialized Kashyyyk. Leave the landing area and set off down the woody path. The planet is crawling with Imperial Guards, and they don't waste any time opening fire. Reflect their fire at them and slowly walk down the steps on the right.

If the stormtrooper snipers set their sights on you, dash away to keep them from locking on. Target the troops with the green fog around them first. They, like the Felucian shamans, regenerate their comrades' health. By taking them out first, you cripple the rest of the stormtroopers and leave them vulnerable to Force attacks.

After taking out the first squad of troopers, examine the crevice left of the steps to find a Holocron. If it's not already visible, send a Force Push in that direction to reveal it.

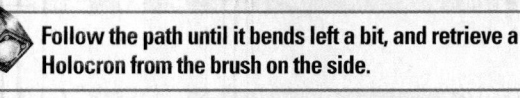

With the first squad gone, continue up the path until you encounter more troopers. Use Sith Scorcher to fry the first few, then pick up the other soldiers and toss them aside or at their comrades.

Follow the path until it bends left a bit, and retrieve a Holocron from the brush on the side.

Continue up the path toward the next group of enemies.

AT-ST Battle!

Unfortunately, the next group of enemies has one very large member. An AT-ST. Dash to the right and immediately grab the turret near the fire. Turn the turret on the soldiers behind you and take them out quickly. Let the turret do most of the work, and only use your lightsaber to finish off any remaining soldiers. As you cut down the troopers, stay mobile to avoid the AT-ST's blaster fire.

After you take out the ground forces, lock on to the mechanical beast and attack it with your electric Force powers. Stay behind the creature; as it stomps around, attack its legs with lightsaber combos.

SITH WISDOM

Examine the fire more closely to find a hidden color crystal in the flames. Grab it quickly to keep from getting burned and losing health.

Keep attacking the AT-ST's legs until you're prompted to match the onscreen commands. Slice away a large chunk of health from the metal monstrosity, then back away.

Get far enough away to launch another assault, and hit the creature with Detonate. Engage the walker one more time and trigger the onscreen commands again. This time you climb the creature and ram your lightsaber into its command center.

60

After you leap off the AT-ST, keep moving and use a series of Ground Slam attacks and leaping Force Lightning attacks to wear down the creature even further. After successfully completing another series of onscreen prompts, the creature comes crumbling down.

Round the corner just past the holoprojector on the left and greet the soldiers around the corner with a Detonate attack. Launch yourself at the next soldier with a lightsaber combo, then use Force Choke to eliminate enemies at a distance.

After you defeat the AT-ST, a Force Holocron appears to the fire's left. Also locate a Holocron at the base of the hill just at the bend and another underneath some bushes on the left, across from the fire and past the palm tree. Pick them up before you continue walking up the main path. Before exiting into the next open area after the narrow passage, Force Push the walls on the righ to reveal one more Holocron.

Walk up the path with your 'saber held high to deflect incoming fire and stop just as you reach the next area. Scorch the nearby enemies, then slowly pull the boulder on the left toward you, aim it, and hurl it at the troops ahead of you.

If you miss any soldiers, edge to the left, then cut down the trees nearby. Use them as projectiles on the remaining soldiers. Guide the tree trunks so they shield you from incoming fire before you unleash them on your enemy.

Nab the Holocron hidden behind the fallen tree trunks to the right of the red doors, then Force Push open the doors.

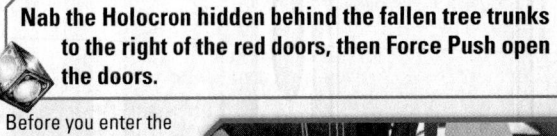

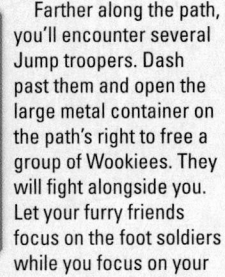

Farther along the path, you'll encounter several Jump troopers. Dash past them and open the large metal container on the path's right to free a group of Wookiees. They will fight alongside you. Let your furry friends focus on the foot soldiers while you focus on your floating flamethrowing foes. Hit the Jump troopers with Sith Scorcher, then toss them into the walls with your Force Grip.

Before you enter the next area, grab the turret and take it with you. The area beyond the red doors is full of Imperial troops. You must clear the area (and empty the Imperial Troop bar that appears at the screen's bottom) to continue. Allow your accompanying turret to mow down the majority of the soldiers in the immediate area. While it does, keep your lightsaber up to reflect the soldiers' fire.

Trek a little farther up and stop just before the blinking bombs on the ground. Let the soldiers near them open fire, then unleash Sith Scorcher to detonate the bombs and blow them up.

Leave the stormtrooper snipers at the rear for last. When only they remain, use Force Grip to pick up the blinking bombs littered about the area, then toss them at the soldiers from afar. Sprint at the soldiers and pummel them with lightsaber combos. Avoid the snipers near the area's right corner and leave them until last.

Leap into the air, double-jump toward them, then crush them with Ground Slam attacks.

WOOKIEE WARNING

Be careful when using Ground Slam attacks. If you land on a bomb, you'll blow yourself up too!

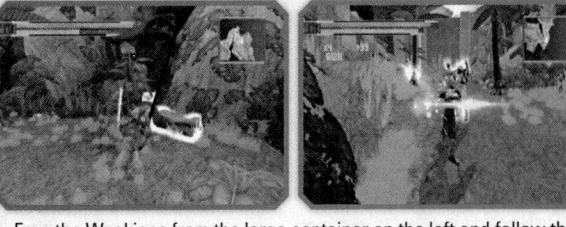

Free the Wookiees from the large container on the left and follow them up the hill. Use a Force Push to break down the trees and vines blocking the path ahead.

After defeating the first wave of enemies, several more troopers pour out of the room near the right corner. Back away from the Shock troopers and knock them away with Force Push attacks. As they reel back, toss rocks, boulders, and barrels at them until they're gone for good.

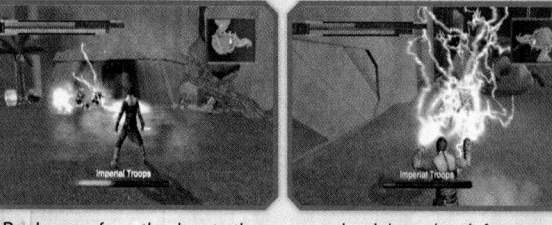

Back away from the door to the room on the right and wait for more soldiers to begin pouring out. When they come out, hit the waves of troopers with Detonate and take them out quickly. Stand your ground and hit the groups pouring out until they stop coming.

The final wave of soldiers is a group of Jump troopers. Lock on to them and hit them with Sith Scorcher attacks. Back away to avoid getting burned by their flamethrowers and get near only to hurl rocks and bombs or to fry them with Force Lightning. If their fire becomes too intense, raise your 'saber to reflect fire back at them, then grab one of the many Bacta tanks lying near the area's edges.

By defeating the final soldier here, you can now take the fight to the guards behind the red door. Force Push the door to bring it down, then wander deeper into the Kashyyyk jungle.

Remove the boulder on the right to expose a Holocron; grab it before the stormtroopers arrive.

When stormtroopers arrive, open fire with your electric Force powers and shock them. Let loose a Force Push on the other approaching troopers and shove the nearby debris at them.

This slows them down just enough for you to continue pelting them with other rocks, trees, and Force Lightning. Continue hitting the stormtroopers until they're no longer a threat, then follow the path to a turret. Take it and slowly move down the path with the turret by your side.

Move the small rock on the left, just before reaching the collapsed rocks ahead, and grab another Holocron.

SITH WISDOM

Immediately after entering the area, make a sharp left and grab the color crystal hidden in the plants.

Hop up the collapsed rocks to the next doorway. Just beyond the door is a fork in the road. On the left is a squad of Wookiees. To the right are stormtroopers and another large AT-ST. Storm down the right path to take out the AT-ST first. Scorch the metal monster as you approach it. Once you're close enough, assault its legs with lightsaber combos until it tries stomping on you. When it does, match the onscreen commands to counterattack and deplete a large chunk of its Health bar.

Back away when you land, and leap into the air for a Ground Slam. After slicing another chunk of health from the AT-ST, you can engage it in a final struggle. Match the onscreen commands to climb up the clanking creature and clean out the control cockpit to bring it crashing down.

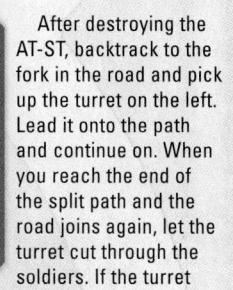

After destroying the AT-ST, backtrack to the fork in the road and pick up the turret on the left. Lead it onto the path and continue on. When you reach the end of the split path and the road joins again, let the turret cut through the soldiers. If the turret can't eliminate them all, grab the second turret at the road's end to finish the job.

At the beginning of the right-hand path, pick up the Force Holocron. Pass up the large pole on the right and stop where the path ahead bottlenecks. Remove the large stone on the left and pick up the Holocron underneath.

62

Reach another fork in the road and attack the soldiers down the right path. Hit them with a Ground Slam to demolish them and destroy the trees near the right edge.

 **The destroyed trees expose another Holocron nearby.**

Continue marauding down the Kashyyyk path. Fall in line behind the Wookiee forces and help them destroy their Imperial enemies. First lash out at them with Sith Scorcher, then follow it with Detonate attacks.

Make a left at the intersection in the road and backtrack a bit up the left path. Force Throw the Jump trooper toward the blinking bomb behind him, then unleash an Force Lightning burst to detonate the bomb and blow him up.

 **Backtrack up the right path to find a Health Holocron and a regular Holocron under a large mossy boulder.**

Resume your warpath down the trail and use the moss-covered boulders to smash the soldiers ahead. The rocks are large enough to block their incoming fire and smash several soldiers with one rolling swoop. Unfortunately, the snipers are out of reach.

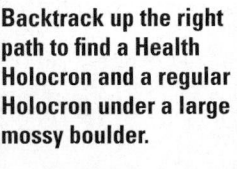

Dash toward them and pick them up with Force Grip. Toss them against the rock walls on the right. Farther up the path, you enter a large circular area containing several stormtroopers. Don't rush in! There are two large manned posts with troopers in them. Use the Force to topple the posts first. If you leave them standing, they'll waste you with blaster shots.

Take the turret just before entering the area and unleash it on the soldiers as you approach the guard posts. After toppling the posts, lock on to the Jump troopers. Use Sith Scorcher attacks and Ground Slams to knock away the other soldiers while you destroy the floating troopers. If they inflict too much damage, retreat to the path's right and pick up a Bacta tank before reengaging them in battle.

 **After bringing down the guard towers, a Holocron appears at the area's center.**

Having cleared the region of all stormtroopers, dash up the path on the right.

 **Keep your eyes peeled as you head toward the next area. A Holocron is hidden to the path's right. Use Force Push in this area to reveal the Holocron.**

Clash with the Captain!

The next area is no friendlier than any other part of Kashyyyk you've visited. Here, Captain Ozzik Sturn guards his prize with a superpowered AT-ST. This mechanical monster is not like the others you've faced thus far. It has backup shield generators as well as ground forces.

When the battle begins, lock on to Sturn's vehicle and use the Force to surround it with an electric surge. Back away from it and avoid its blaster fire. Circle around behind it and continue attacking it with Sith Scorcher and lightsaber combos.

Sturn quickly activates the backup shield generators and surrounds his machine in an impenetrable force field. When he does, don't waste any more energy on the AT-ST. Instead, locate the generator that is providing his shield—follow the stream from the AT-ST to the large circular generator  on the periphery and destroy it. To demolish it quickly, unleash every devastating attack you know. Hit it with lightsaber combos, Force Push, and Detonate attacks. As you attack it, keep the generator between you and Sturn.

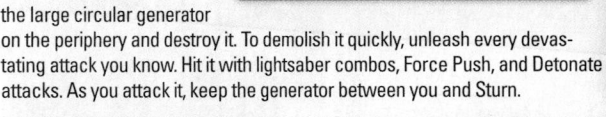

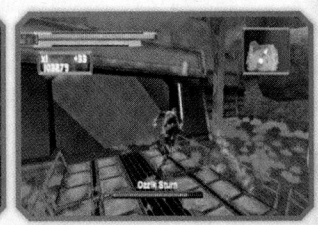

Stay on the move to avoid Sturn's attacks. If he lobs a blue grenade, leap into the air just as it detonates. The grenade will unleash a radial concussion wave that will knock you on your back immediately. You can block or dodge his blaster fire. As soon as you demolish the field

63

generator, resume your assault on the AT-ST. Hit it again with Sith Scorcher, Detonate, and lightsaber attacks.

Eventually, Ozzik activates another field generator. Just as before, dash behind it and destroy it quickly. If Sturn hurts you, speed over to the large structure in the corner and pick up the Bacta tank near the building's door.

WOOKIEE WARNING

Don't stand too close to the barrels near the building. One good shot from Sturn's device and they'll blow up, taking you with them.

After you destroy one of the generators, several of Sturn's men come pouring out of the nearby bunker to join the fight. Eliminate them quickly before they become a nuisance. Fry as many as you can with your electric Force attacks, then finish off the rest with quick combos.

With Sturn's men out of the way, resume your assault on his AT-ST. Target the active generator first. Once it's down, slash away at Sturn. If you're too far to reach the AT-ST, use one of the boulders nearby or an explosive barrel to hit the walker.

SITH WISDOM

Don't get ahead of yourself. You'll only waste time trying to destroy the generators while they're not in use. Only attack them while they provide Sturn a shield.

Move away from the area's center to grab Bacta tanks or to distance yourself from Sturn's men. His men fall easily, so take them out first when they appear.

After you destroy all the generators and Ozzik Sturn's AT-ST can take no more, the mechanical monster becomes scrap metal. Sturn, defeated and destroyed, lies helpless at your feet. Still, he's got something you need to fulfill your mission and your ultimate destiny. You run your lightsaber through the pitiful captain and enter the building in the corner.

Inside the building is what you've been after. It's not a thing, but a young woman named Leia Organa, whom Kota's contact is after! She must be of some importance. Rather than joining you on the *Rogue Shadow*, she decides to go her separate way. Still, she's free now and that was exactly what Kota's contact wanted.

DARK FELUCIA

AREA 1

AREA 6

AREA 2

AREA 5

AREA 3

AREA 4

65

MAP LEGEND

- Bacta Tank
- Color Crystal
- Force Holocron
- Health Holocron
- Holocron
- Lightsaber Hilt

MISSION DETAILS

Objective
Senator Bail Organa has vanished on Felucia. Go to Felucia and find him.

Enemies Encountered
Felucian Warrior

Felucian Shaman

Felucian Blaster

Imperial Stormtrooper

Stormtrooper Gunner

Stormtrooper Sniper

Jump Stormtrooper

Shock Stormtrooper

IT-O Interrogator Droid

Bull Rancor: Minor Boss

Maris Brood: Boss

Collectibles Found
13 Holocrons

Color Crystal

2 Force Holocrons

2 Health Holocrons

Lightsaber Hilt

JEDI KNOWLEDGE
Items marked on the map with a * can only be collected when you pass thorough that area a second time.

"Your Master Would Be Disgusted..."

Down on the Felucian surface, all is not well. Senator Bail Organa is being held captive by Jedi Master Shaak Ti's old apprentice, Maris Brood. Since her master's demise, Brood has become a dark, angry creature. She's resigned herself to giving in to the dark side, and she holds Organa as a prize for Darth Vader should he ever visit Felucia.

She tells Organa that if he attempts to escape, she'll feed him to her new pet—a monstrous bull rancor beast!

Return to Felucia

Immediately after disembarking on Felucia, pick up the Holocron underneath the *Rogue Shadow*.

Leave the landing area and hurry down the main path until you encounter a squad of rebels engaged in a firefight against Imperial Guards.

Let the rebels do most of the work here. They're well armed and more than capable of destroying the troopers. Still, wait for the Imperial Troops bar at the screen's bottom to be nearly depleted, then join the fight and help them finish off the stormtroopers.

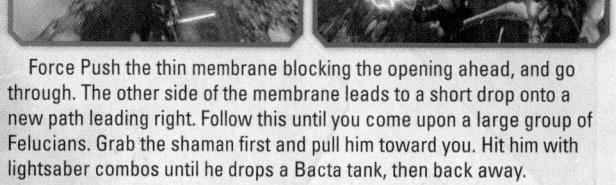

Pick up the Holocron near the rancor bones atop the small hill on the right before leaving the area.

Force Push the thin membrane blocking the opening ahead, and go through. The other side of the membrane leads to a short drop onto a new path leading right. Follow this until you come upon a large group of Felucians. Grab the shaman first and pull him toward you. Hit him with lightsaber combos until he drops a Bacta tank, then back away.

Lure the other Felucians toward you and stun them with Sith Scorcher. Keep them all on one side of you. Don't let any of them pass and attack from behind; if they do, you'll be pinched on both sides in tight spaces and will have a hard time getting loose.

Venture off the path and into a large, wide-open area. This is where you last fought the pair of rancor beasts.

Double-jump left as soon as you enter the wide-open area, and attack the Felucian Blaster perched atop the small ledge. Land a Ground Slam attack on the ledge and demolish the Felucian sniper! From here, leap into the air and execute another Ground Slam on the Felucians below, making sure to damage the shaman with your attack.

Rather than finish off the ground forces, double-jump away and execute another Ground Slam on the Felucian perched on the ledge along the opposite wall. This Felucian Blaster can pick you apart from up high. After eliminating him, go back down and use Sith Scorcher to finish off the remaining Felucians on the ground.

Before leaving the area, turn right and follow the right wall to its end. When you reach the large oddly shaped boulder along the wall, use Force Grip to remove it and expose a Holocron. Remove every stone from its base to reveal another Holocron on the ledge where the first Felucian sniper was perched. Grab both Holocrons, then take the path up to the next area.

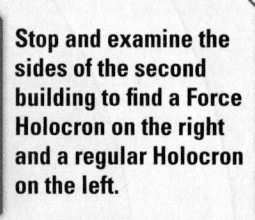

Storm up the path just left of where you entered the area and execute the three Felucians with a Sith Scorcher. Use a Force Push to bust through the red sliding doors at the path's top and proceed into the Imperial garrison.

Approach the group of troopers and hit them with Sith Scorcher. The attack leaves only two or three soldiers to contend with. Launch yourself at them with your lightsaber swinging. Use quick, short combos to take them out. If any Felucian warriors join the fight, fry them as soon as they appear.

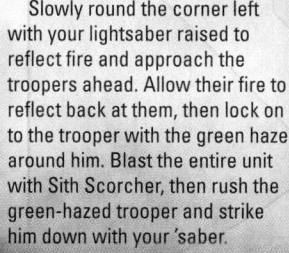

Stop and examine the sides of the second building to find a Force Holocron on the right and a regular Holocron on the left.

Follow the main path until you reach a small squad of troopers. Lock on to the blinking bomb at the next building's corner, and detonate it with Force Lightning. The explosion will destroy the majority of the troopers, leaving only a small handful for your lightsaber.

Slowly round the corner left with your lightsaber raised to reflect fire and approach the troopers ahead. Allow their fire to reflect back at them, then lock on to the trooper with the green haze around him. Blast the entire unit with Sith Scorcher, then rush the green-hazed trooper and strike him down with your 'saber.

STAR WARS THE FORCE UNLEASHED

> Jump onto the third building's roof, then double-jump onto the tower with the satellite dish on top. There, behind the dish, is another Holocron. Take it and hop back down to the main path.

Storm up the path and use a Force Push to destroy the IT-O Interrogator droid. Just up the path are more stormtrooper barracks. When the healing troopers come rushing out, leap into the air and hit them with Ground Slam attacks. Turn right and lock on to the IT-O Interrogator droid. Crush it with a combo, then turn back to the stormtroopers behind you.

Dash toward them as they get up, and slash furiously with quick combos and short bursts of Force Lightning. Wait for the next wave of enemies to pour out of the barracks, and greet them with Sith Scorcher attacks.

> Blow up the containers near the building's corner and pick up the Holocron that appears. Then hop atop the building and search the rear to find a Health Holocron.

Trek farther up the path and encounter another group of stormtroopers. Before they can get close enough to blast you, assault them with a Sith Seeker attack and electrocute them from afar. Reflect the fire of any surviving soldiers to eliminate them, then resume your journey deeper into the garrison.

JEDI KNOWLEDGE

The Imperial bunkers aren't as narrow as some of the Raxus hallways, but they do funnel enemies into small groups. Use Maelstrom to damage multiple enemies as they bunch together.

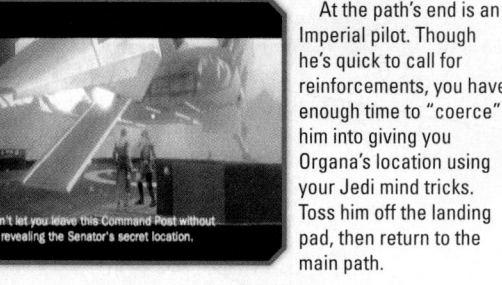

At the path's end is an Imperial pilot. Though he's quick to call for reinforcements, you have enough time to "coerce" him into giving you Organa's location using your Jedi mind tricks. Toss him off the landing pad, then return to the main path.

I won't let you leave this Command Post without revealing the Senator's secret location.

Backtrack through the garrison trail with your lightsaber raised high to reflect incoming fire, and launch Sith Seeker attacks at the men in your way. When you encounter a gun turret, take it and turn it on the soldiers. Stay out of reach of the Shock troopers' attacks, and let the turret do most of the work.

Speed past the third (now first) building and round the corner left, then right until you run into another trooper squadron. Stop and strike with Sith Scorcher attacks, then back away before the next wave of enemies comes rushing out of the nearby barracks.

Stay just out of reach of the stormtrooper waves by holding your position atop the hilly path. If they get past your Scorcher and Seeker attacks, use Repulse to create some breathing room.

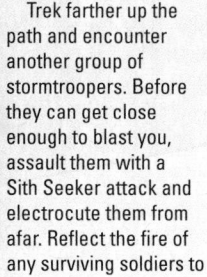

Hold your position and pummel away at the approaching guards until two snipers join the fight. When they do, double-jump over any enemies between you and the laser-toting guards, and pound them with Ground Slam attacks until they, and any surrounding soldiers, are destroyed.

Farther down the path is another turret. Grab it and lead it past the next group of soldiers to the garrison exit and back into the vibrant Felucian landscape.

Bully the Bull!

Back in the large wide-open area, you find Senator Organa...and Maris Brood. She claims to have fully embraced the dark side, then unleashes her bull rancor on you. Brood disappears into the Felucian landscape and leaves her pet behind to deal with you.

Unfortunately, this rancor is much more aggressive, speedy, and angry than any other rancor beast you've faced thus far. Don't lock on to the creature. Instead, immediately dash away from it and lure it into the area's center.

> Grab the Force Holocron near the right wall, then dash across the large arena to the bottom left to find a Health Holocron behind a small bulbous plant.

67

PRIMAGAMES.COM

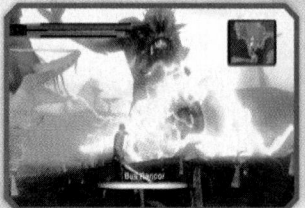

Once the bull rancor gets close enough, lock on to him and blast him with Sith Scorcher. He's deceptively fast, so immediately dash away after you shock him or be prepared to get swatted away by his large clawed paws. As you run away, locate a large boulder or a bulbous explosive plant to toss at the rancor as it gives chase.

Get out of its reach again, then turn around and attack with another Sith Scorcher. Continue dashing and slashing at the rancor until its health is depleted to nearly 75 percent.

After you deplete the rancor's health by 25 percent, head back toward the two ledges where the Felucian snipers were earlier. Double-jump onto a ledge and lure the rancor toward you. When it nears, back away a bit and get just behind the bend in the wall—stay just close enough to the edge to be able to attack the rancor, but far enough behind the bend so that it can't easily swipe you. Then repeatedly throw your lightsaber at the beast as it approaches the ledge.

Stand your ground as long as possible on the ledge and continuously attack the rancor with your lightsaber. If he manages to swipe you off the ledge, rush toward one of the many Bacta tanks by the arena's walls, then return to the sniper ledges.

Again, get just behind the bend in the wall and attack the rancor. This time, however, repeatedly zap the bullish beast with Sith Scorcher attacks. By now, the brute's health should be less than 50 percent. Hop down from the ledge and approach the rancor to trigger a final assault.

When you get too close, the beast picks you up and attempts to eat you. Match the onscreen commands to free yourself from the rancor's grip and counterattack!

You climb atop his back, slashing away, then leap from his tusk into his mouth where you cut your way out. Maris Brood's pet bull rancor is nothing more than a pile of bull bones now....

Approach the large triangular membrane blocking the path on the right and bust through it. Follow the trail until you come upon a small squad of Felucian shamans. Lift the first warrior into the air and toss him at the Felucians at the rear of the pack.

Rush down the path at the shamans and slash them with a lightsaber combo. Pick up the nearest shaman and toss him at the other to knock them both down. If they aren't destroyed yet, finish your assault with a Ground Slam or Sith Scorcher. With all Felucians out of the way, walk to the trail's end to a wide-open area full of plants and mushrooms.

The area at the trail's end has three Holocrons. The first is located behind the large brown mushrooms. The second and third are atop two large purple flowers—one just left of the next tunnel, the other on a plant just left of the three brown mushrooms.

SITH WISDOM

Before leaving, pick up the color crystal behind the plants across from the next tunnel.

Use a Force Push to destroy the thin membrane blocking the next tunnel and go through. Hit the two warriors in your way with Force Push, then destroy them with a Sith Scorcher attack. Once they're down, exit the tunnel and meet up with Maris.

The Battle with Brood...

Though she may have only been an apprentice, Maris Brood is highly skilled with her light-tonfas. As you enter her arena, she ambushes you from behind and hits you with a Force Push, knocking you flat on your face.

Begin the fight by hitting Brood with a Ground Slam attack. Knock her off her feet, then follow it up with Force Lightning. If she gets up before you can reach her, dash up to her and lash out with more Force Lightning. She'll engage you in a Force Lock, where you must match the onscreen prompts to reverse the Force current and lift her high into the air.

After slamming down Brood once, run up to her and hit her with a Force Push. She's knocked against a large plant and lands on her face. Unfortunately, before you can reach her, several Felucian warriors leap to her defense.

There's a Holocron along the left wall. Edge toward it as you fight and pick it up.

Use Repulse to knock away the surrounding Felucians and keep from being mauled on all sides. While the warriors are down, dash away from the group. Turn around to get them all in your view and attack with Sith Scorcher.

Once the Felucian warriors have had enough, Brood calls in her other reinforcement—another rancor beast! Luckily, this beast is far easier to handle than her bull rancor. Lock on to it as it approaches and scorch it with your Sith attack.

Double-jump away from the rancor when it attempts to swat you, and turn around to scorch it again when you land.

Continue jumping away and landing just long enough to hit the rancor with Sith Scorcher until it attempts squashing you under its palm. When it does, follow the onscreen commands and counter-attack! Do this one more time to defeat the rancor and resume your battle with Maris Brood.

When Maris returns, she has a full Health bar. This fight is not over yet....

Resume assaulting Brood with Ground Slam and Sith Scorcher attacks. When she engages you in a Force Lock, match the onscreen commands to reverse her electric attack and damage her with her own tonfas. When she lands back on the ground, launch at her with your lightsaber swinging.

Hit her again with Sith Scorcher, then activate your Maelstrom power. While you charge it, she'll be unable to attack you and inflict damage. Unleash your Maelstrom when Maris is close and send her back toward the arena's other side.

Use lightsaber combos while your Force meter recharges, then hit Brood one more time with Sith Scorcher or Sith Seeker. Once her health is below half, activate Dark Rage and unleash a series of powerful lightsaber combos.

Engage Brood in a lightsaber lock and match the onscreen commands to knock her backward. By now, she'll be close to defeat and will increase her tonfa attacks.

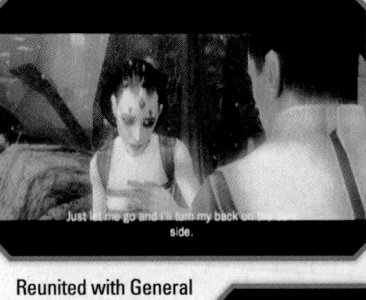

Block her attacks, activate Dark Rage, and counter with lightsaber combos. Accumulate just enough Force to unleash another Ground Slam and activate the final struggle. Match the onscreen prompts to follow Brood around the arena. You toss your lightsaber at her as you give chase, then lift her high into the air and toss her across the arena.

With Maris Brood under your lightsaber, it becomes clear that she can still be saved. Rather than strike her down for good, you decide to let her go.

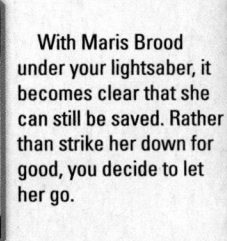

Reunited with General Kota, Senator Organa expresses his concerns over waging war against the Empire. Organa knows another Senator who has spoken out against the Emperor, but in order to rally troops, you must show them that the Emperor is vulnerable and must instill a sense of hope in the dissidents. Organa sets off to meet with his Senator comrades while you decide which Imperial facility to target first.

IMPERIAL RAXUS PRIME

MAP LEGEND

- Bacta Tank
- Color Crystal
- Force Holocron
- Health Holocron
- Holocron
- Lightsaber Hilt

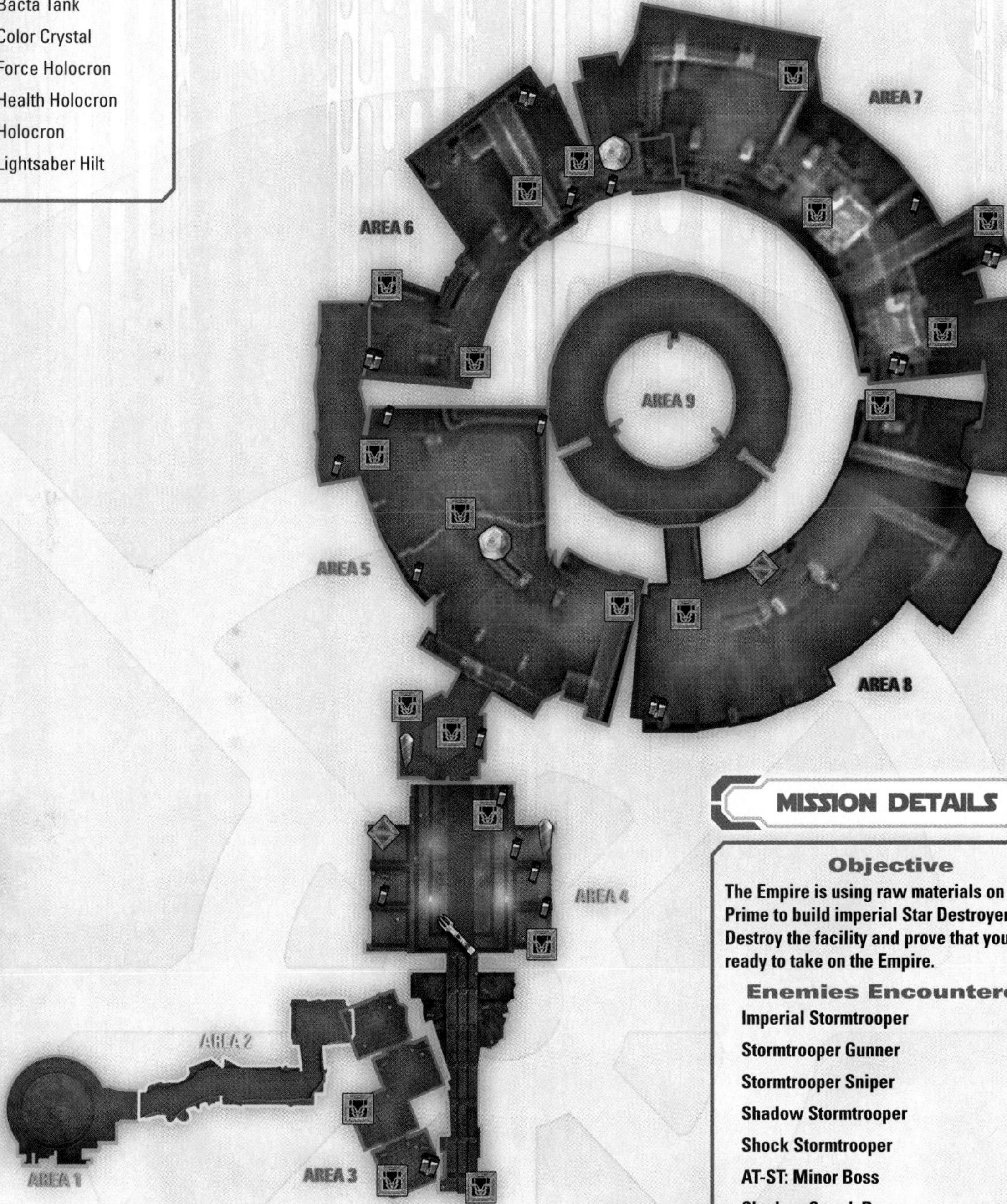

AREA 7

AREA 6

AREA 9

AREA 5

AREA 8

AREA 4

AREA 2

AREA 3

AREA 1

MISSION DETAILS

Objective

The Empire is using raw materials on Raxus Prime to build imperial Star Destroyers. Destroy the facility and prove that you are ready to take on the Empire.

Enemies Encountered

Imperial Stormtrooper

Stormtrooper Gunner

Stormtrooper Sniper

Shadow Stormtrooper

Shock Stormtrooper

AT-ST: Minor Boss

Shadow Guard: Boss

Collectibles Found

20 Holocrons

2 Color Crystals

2 Force Holocrons

2 Health Holocrons

Lightsaber Hilt

STAR WARS
THE FORCE UNLEASHED

"You Still Serve Me."

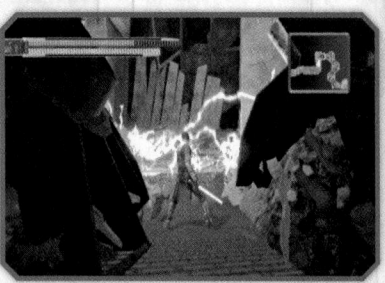

Back on the *Rogue Shadow,* you communicate your success with Darth Vader. Though he's satisfied with your progress, he senses conflict in you. Your feelings for your new allies grow while your allegiance to the dark side remains. Juno walks in on you while you seek Vader's counsel, and though she's disappointed in you for remaining loyal to him, she still remains loyal to you.

Perhaps she sees good in you still. Perhaps she sees through your cold exterior and sees the feelings you have for her. Regardless, she knows that sooner or later, *you* will decide the fate of the Rebellion, not Darth Vader. And when you do, she wants you to remember her struggles. For now, however, Darth Vader has given you the information you need to rally the Rebels. Your next target is the Star Destroyer construction facility on Raxus Prime....

Return to Raxus Prime

As you approach the planet, you're presented with a small problem. How exactly will you destroy the facility? Luckily, PROXY and Juno have a plan.

Your goal is to fight your way past the Imperial Guards and reach the large metal ore cannon. Once there, aim the cannon at the facility floating high above Raxus and let 'er rip!

Take the elevator down to the Raxus Prime main floor. Run down the debris-steam-jet-riddled hall until you reach a large trash blockage. Use a Force Push to take it down, then storm into the next area.

In the next passage, use Force Lightning to fry the stormtroopers. Creep ahead after taking out the first two troopers, and use the surrounding debris as projectiles against the enemies ahead. Toss the debris at the stormtroopers farther down the hall, and create a small traveling wall of trash.

Upon reaching the health-regenerating trooper in the next hall, use a Force Push to shove the trash at him and knock him down. Hit him with a lightning blast while he's down, then grab the Bacta tank he releases.

Dash to the hall's end and stop just before reaching a large circular room containing several Shock stormtroopers. Unleash a Sith Scorcher attack on the troopers, then rush in and follow up with a sideways slash. Dash away to let them get back up. When they bunch together, hit them with Detonate to finish them off. Get on the elevator and ride it up to the facility's next level.

The next level is crawling with Imperial Guards. Luckily the area is cramped, and they are all close together, making them easy targets. When the elevator stops, leap off it and hit the group of troopers with a Sith Scorcher attack. Pick up nearby troopers and toss them across the room to keep them from getting near you.

When the health-regenerating trooper gets near, use your Force Grip to lift him into the air, then choke him. Use short lightsaber combos to clear the room of any remaining troopers, then blast down the door on the other side.

Streak into the next room and hit the troops inside with a Force Push. Follow it up with a surge of lightning, then short 'saber strikes. If any health-regenerating soldiers remain, target them first before wiping out the rest of the Imperial squad.

The third room has a large blinking bomb near its entrance. Use it to blow up the Shock troopers and snipers near the entrance, then wipe out the remaining troops inside just as you did in the first two rooms. Lead with a powerful attack like Force Push or Sith Scorcher, and follow

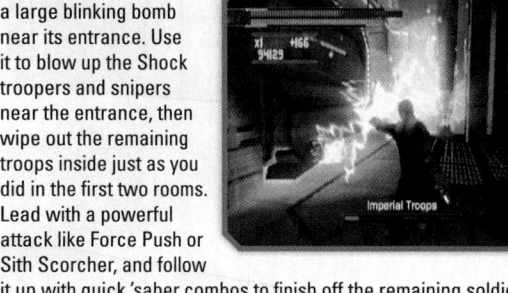

it up with quick 'saber combos to finish off the remaining soldiers.

> There is a Holocron near the room's far right edge. Pick it up after destroying the soldiers in the third room.

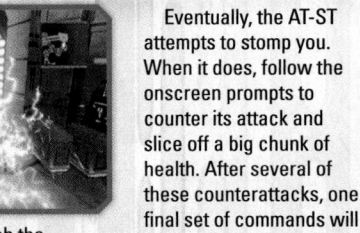

Blast down the door leading to the fourth room, and scorch the soldiers in your way. Slowly creep into the room with your 'saber in blocking position. Get close to the soldiers in the room's rear and slice through them with your lightsaber.

When the room is empty of all troopers, destroy the glowing wall panels along the right wall and expose another Holocron.

Approach the next hatch. As you do, several more stormtroopers come pouring through. Greet them with Sith Scorcher, then blast them away with Force Push. Rush into the room and detonate the explosive barrel near the far right corner.

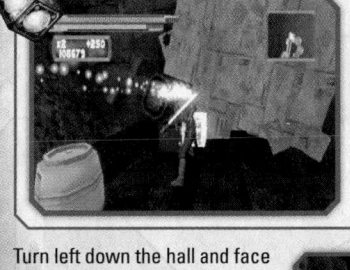

Turn right as soon as you enter this room, and destroy the small box to expose another Holocron.

Turn left down the hall and face off against three Shock troopers. Shove them back with Force Push, then lunge at them with several short combos. If they surround you, create some breathing room with Repulse, then burn them down with Sith Scorcher.

The next area is home to a large AT-ST. Begin your attack with a blast of Force Lightning, then speed past the mechanical monster. Release your lock on it so you don't face it as you run past, then pick up one of the many explosive barrels near the room's edge. Hurl the explosive canisters at the machine, then sprint away and get cover from its blaster fire.

Reflect the AT-ST's blaster fire as it approaches you, then sprint past it again when it gets too close. Turn around to toss exploding barrels at it, and hit it with another blast of Force Lightning. Continue hitting it and moving away before it can retaliate, and occasionally stop to slash at its legs from behind until its Health bar is almost completely depleted.

Destroy the two consoles by the door to open hatches above the empty AT-ST bays. Jump on the mechanical harness to reach the open hatches, and collect the two Holocrons, the Health Holocron, and the blue color crystal inside.

Eventually, the AT-ST attempts to stomp you. When it does, follow the onscreen prompts to counter its attack and slice off a big chunk of health. After several of these counterattacks, one final set of commands will appear onscreen. Follow them and demolish the machine once and for all.

SITH WISDOM

Leave the AT-ST room from the door you used to enter. Stack a few barrels with Force Grip to hop onto the small ledge high above the door you used to enter and grab the 'saber hilt and Holocron there.

Take the fight into the next room. Dash inside and target the health-regenerating soldier first. Slash through him with a few quick lightsaber combos, then double-jump onto the platform in the room's center. Double-jump again and come down on the soldiers atop the platform with a Ground Slam attack. While they're stumbling to get up, use Repulse to inflict some damage and detonate the nearby barrel.

Leap from the center platform onto the small ledge on the left and grab the color crystal before hopping back down onto the main floor. From there, speed around the center platform, knocking down enemies with Force Pushes as you go. Stop to slice them with 'saber attacks.

Remove the wall panels along the left side of the center platform to find two Holocrons.

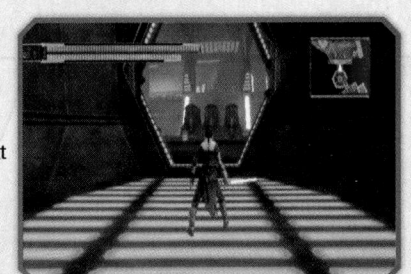

Set foot on the elevator platform and ride it to the facility's next region.

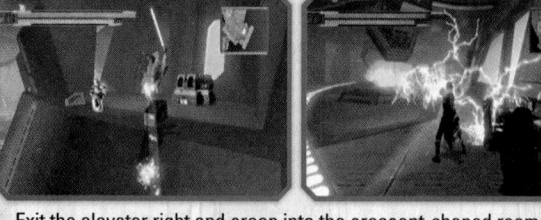

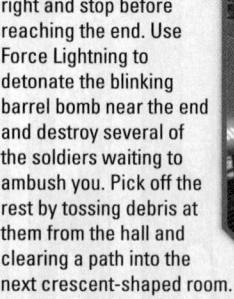

Exit the elevator right and creep into the crescent-shaped room with your 'saber held high. Knock away the soldier on the right, then dash to the room's far right corner. Hop onto the small control panel along the far wall, then double-jump onto the ledge high above you.

> **Stop to remove the small panel along the right wall and nab the Holocron, then turn around to follow the ledge left.**

Toss the soldiers in your way to the left, right over the ledge and onto the area below.

The ledge's end opens up to a large command center on the right. Turn right and use Sith Scorcher to fry the stormtroopers there. Pick up the remaining soldiers and toss them into the large reactors behind them. The explosion destroys the reactors and eliminates the soldiers at the same time.

There are several more Holocrons in the area. After clearing the area above, drop back down to the lower area and jump onto the connecting walkways between molten metal pits. Just behind the first walkway is a hidden niche containing a Force Holocron. Quickly hop into the molten metal, then hop onto the walkway containing the Force Holocron; grab it. Pick up the regular Holocron on the walkway's left end before returning to the fight. As you go, destroy all nine tanks in this area to expose another Holocron in front of the blue force field at the room's end.

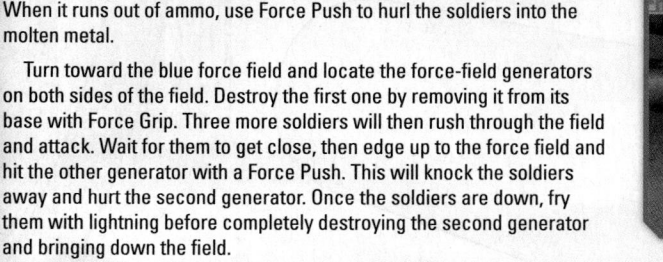

At the crescent-shaped room's far left end is a small stormtrooper squad. Take the gun turret on the left and let it rip through the soldiers. When it runs out of ammo, use Force Push to hurl the soldiers into the molten metal.

Turn toward the blue force field and locate the force-field generators on both sides of the field. Destroy the first one by removing it from its base with Force Grip. Three more soldiers will then rush through the field and attack. Wait for them to get close, then edge up to the force field and hit the other generator with a Force Push. This will knock the soldiers away and hurt the second generator. Once the soldiers are down, fry them with lightning before completely destroying the second generator and bringing down the field.

Follow the hallway right and stop before reaching the end. Use Force Lightning to detonate the blinking barrel bomb near the end and destroy several of the soldiers waiting to ambush you. Pick off the rest by tossing debris at them from the hall and clearing a path into the next crescent-shaped room.

As you exit, take the nearby turret with you. Lead it into the crescent room and let it cut through the first few enemies.

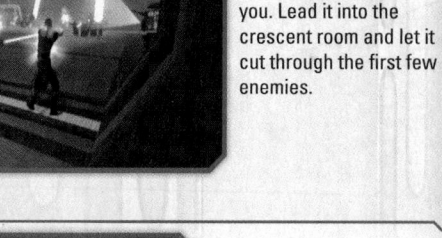

Move the stacked boxes on the left to find a hidden Holocron.

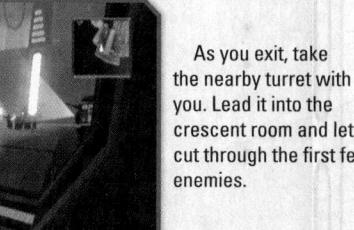

Go up the ramp on the left and turn right. Lift your lightsaber to reflect the incoming fire, then rip the turret from its supports. Allow the turret time to destroy the lone soldier.

Turn back around and Force Push the hatch on the left. Unleash a Sith Scorcher attack into the next passage to electrocute the troopers inside and detonate an explosive barrel. Follow your Scorcher attack with Detonate or Sith Seeker. Next, storm into the passage to clear it of any remaining soldiers with 'saber combos.

Blast down the door at the passage's end.

73

Begin your assault on the next group of stormtroopers by detonating the barrel on the next walkway's right edge. Stay on this walkway and use Force Grip to toss the soldiers down to the floor below. Survivors will attempt to rush back up the ramp on the room's left side.

Let some of the soldiers make it up the ramp and reach the walkway. When they do, leap down to the area below, take the nearby turret, and turn left toward the ramp. Slowly lead the turret across the room as it mows down more troopers. Finish clearing the room of all enemies by stalking around the large reactors with your 'saber in blocking position and using short lightsaber combinations when you're within striking distance.

With the room clear, destroy all eight wall consoles to destroy another Holocron near the blue force field.

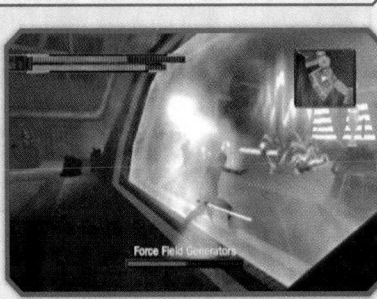

Use a few Force Pushes to destroy the force-field generators and bring down the blue field in your way. As you do, several Shock troopers will emerge from the hall beyond the field. Time your Force Pushes so they hit the generators and the attacking troopers simultaneously.

When the field is down, rush into the hall and push the soldiers into the passage on the left. Hurl the blinking barrel near the corner into the left passage and blow up the first few soldiers inside. Stalk deeper into the passage and hurl a second barrel at the soldiers near the hall's rear.

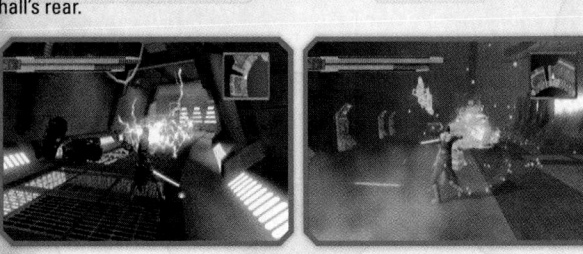

Walk down the passage with your 'saber in blocking position. Stop only to launch Detonate or Sith Seeker attacks, then continue stalking the soldiers down the hall.

Turn left at the hall's end and duck behind the door's left edge to avoid stormtrooper snipers. Wait for them to fire, then rush out of the hall and into the next crescent room. Pick up one soldier and toss him into the reactor behind him, then dash left to get the gun turret. Raise your 'saber after taking the turret and slowly edge to the right, letting the turret do your dirty work.

Double-jump into the air and land on the small walkway above the molten metal pit. Leap again and come down on the soldiers with a Ground Slam attack. From the walkway, double-jump to the right and land on the level above. Follow it left, deeper into the crescent room, and use explosive barrels to blow up the troopers with laser-guided guns.

Follow the walkway left to its end. Toss enemies over the left edge as you go and Force Push the door at its end.

At the top level's far right end is a Force Holocron. To find it, double-jump onto the top level from the small walkway below, then turn right instead of left. There is also a Holocron in the bottom level's far right corner. Drop down and pick it up before returning to the top level.

Speed into the hall and use Detonate to blow up the soldiers in your way. Use Sith Scorcher to burn down the remaining enemies, then blast through the door leading into the facility's next section. Creep out into the next area and fry the first wave of enemies that attacks.

Rush out into the large room, past the ramp on the left, and down the long hallway. Use Ground Slam attacks to destroy the troopers in your way, then toss the Shock troopers over the ledge.

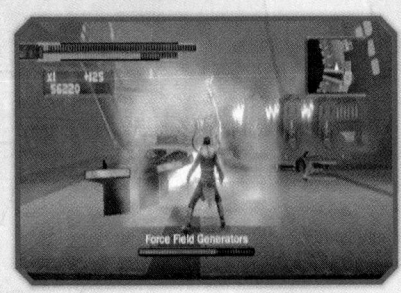

Hop down to the bottom floor and use more Ground Slam attacks on the stormtroopers near the blue force field. Throw the Shock troopers into the large reactors. Use Repulse attacks to keep them from surrounding you, and destroy the rest of the soldiers with lightsaber combos.

While on the bottom floor, backtrack and find the large niche on the room's left side. Move the crates near the rear of the niche and grab the Holocron.

Approach the blue force field and destroy the generators on both sides of the field. Turn right into the next passage and reflect the stormtroopers' blaster fire back at them. Detonate the explosive barrels in the hall to inflict damage on the gunners, then use their turret to finish them off.

Exit the hall right, into the final crescent-shaped room. Speed past the first few guards and double-jump onto the second-level walkway at the room's far end. Turn left and streak down the walkway. Pick up the turret. At the walkway's end, use Ground Slam attacks to destroy the remaining soldiers, then use a Force Push to bust down the door.

Destroy the force-field generators to bring down the blue field, then head onto the walkway with your 'saber in blocking position. Knock the troopers back with Force Push, and lift the closest soldier into the air. Choke him, then turn on the second trooper. Fry him with Force Lightning and proceed down the hall and into the facility's final room.

Shadow Guard, Round Two

In the final room, a Shadow Guard ambushes you as you communicate with Juno. Immediately hit him with Force Lightning followed by a Ground Slam attack.

Run into the hallway and unleash a Sith Seeker attack on the Shock trooper ahead. Scorch the enemies as they approach, then blast down the next door.

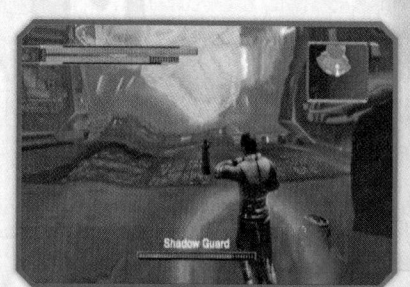

Move away from the Shadow Guard and hurl crates at him from afar. If he attempts to hit you with a Force Push, dodge it by dashing sideways, then double-jump toward him and come down on him with a Ground Slam attack. When he lands from the blast of your slam attack, hit him again with Force Lightning. Be quick and consistent with your attacks.

Dash away from him and let the guard give chase. When he gets close, turn on him and attack with swift 'saber combos. Engage him in a lightsaber lock, and follow the prompts onscreen to slice a chunk off his Health bar.

Fight past the first trooper and run to the next walkway's end; there, use one of the explosive barrels on the soldiers below. After blowing up a few troopers, hop down and take the turret near the force field. Turn it on the troopers as you slowly edge around the area.

When the Jump troopers appear, back up into the corner and lock on to one of them. Use Force Lightning to whittle its health, then finish it off with aerial attacks. After destroying the first Jump trooper, turn to another one. Toss every remaining explosive barrel to weaken it, then finish it off with Sith Scorcher. When only one floating flamethrower foe remains, use Force Choke to extinguish its flame.

If he tries choking you, use Force Lightning and Force Push to free yourself from his grip.

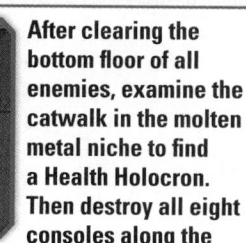

After clearing the bottom floor of all enemies, examine the catwalk in the molten metal niche to find a Health Holocron. Then destroy all eight consoles along the walls to reveal a Holocron near the force field.

Eventually, the Shadow Guard creates several Shadow Troopers to help him fight. Speed away from him and his cohorts and turn only to scorch the entire group. A single Sith Scorcher attack will annihilate most, if not all, of the Shadow Troopers. Once again, speed away from the Shadow Guard and pelt him with more debris until he is close enough to strike with your 'saber.

75

Maintain a lock on him as you leap away and avoid his attacks. When you land, hit him with quick combos. Blast him with Sith Scorcher, then dash away.

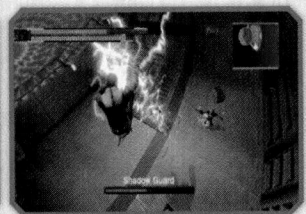

Once you're at a safe distance, lure him toward you. Wait for him to get close enough for a combo, then activate Dark Rage. Unleash a flurry of strong 'saber combos. As you attack, your Force meter will refill. Finish your fierce flurry of 'saber strikes with a Ground Slam attack, then move away to safety while the Shadow Guard is on his back.

After taking so much damage, the Shadow Guard will probably call on more Shadow Troopers. Leap into the air and use lightning attacks to fry them from above. By using consistent leaping attacks, you'll avoid taking direct damage and being surrounded.

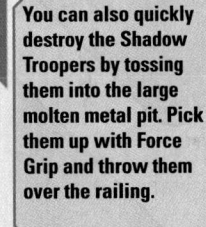
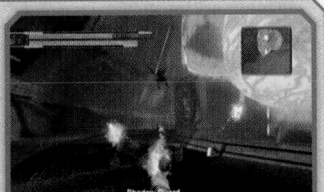
Stay on the move and continue picking away at the Shadow Guard's Health bar with Scorcher attacks, Ground Slams, and swift 'saber attacks. As he nears defeat, he'll begin using Force Lightning. When he does, lift your lightsaber to blocking position and absorb the lightning.

Finish the fight against the guard by repeatedly frying him with Sith Scorcher once his health is nearly 80 percent depleted.

With the facility completely in your control, you're finally free to fire a large glowing ball of molten metal at the shipyard floating high above Raxus Prime.

Unfortunately, one of the Star Destroyers docked at the floating facility pulls away before the explosion and heads toward the surface. Rather than let it get away, you rush out and use your Force Grip to bring the destroyer crashing down onto the planet's surface. Mission accomplished.

CLOUD CITY

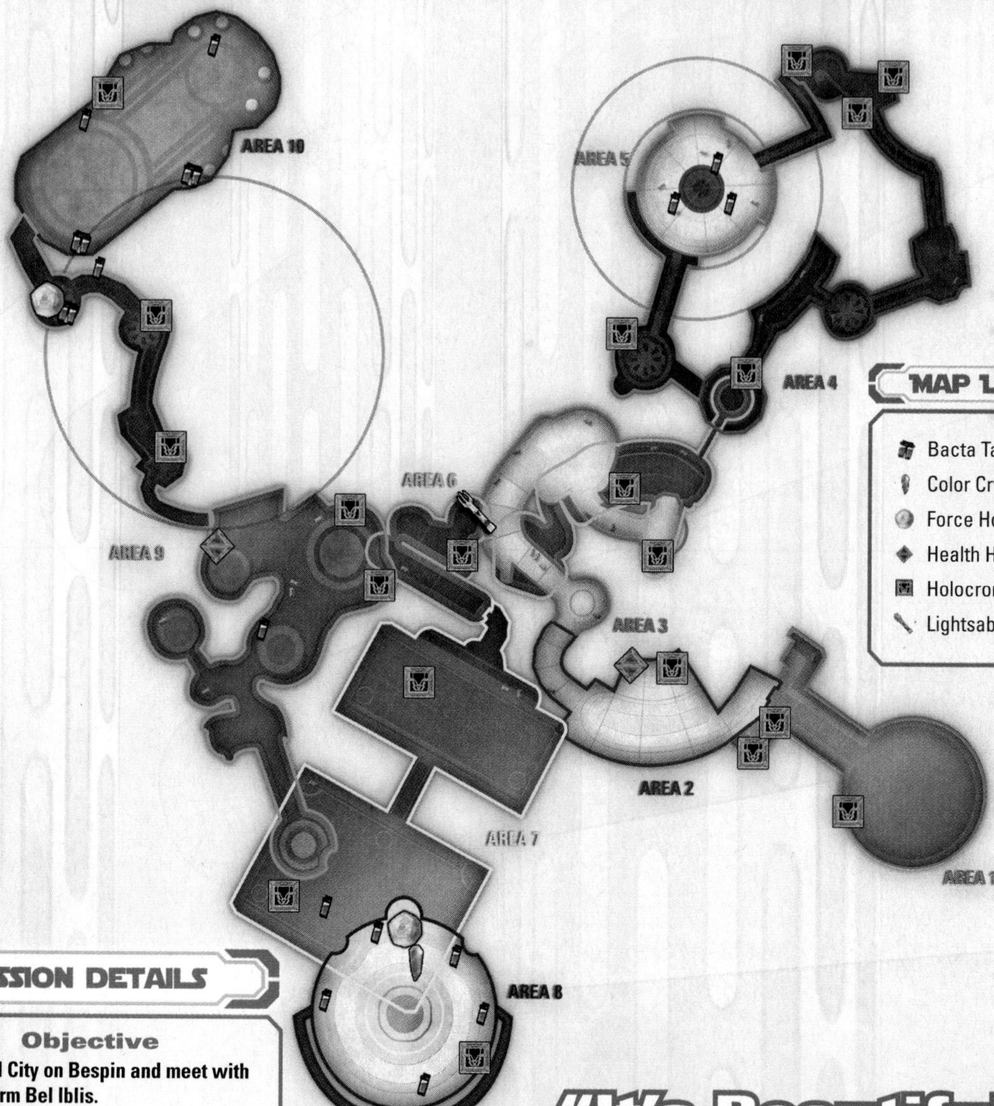

AREA 10

AREA 5

AREA 4

AREA 9

AREA 6

MAP LEGEND

- 🪣 Bacta Tank
- 💊 Color Crystal
- ◎ Force Holocron
- ◆ Health Holocron
- ▣ Holocron
- ⚔ Lightsaber Hilt

AREA 3

AREA 2

AREA 1

77

AREA 7

AREA 8

MISSION DETAILS

Objective

Go to Cloud City on Bespin and meet with Senator Garm Bel Iblis.

Enemies Encountered

Twi'lek Mercenary

Mandalorian Spy

Gran Grenadier: Grenade-tossing Bandit

Talz Medic

Whiphid Thug

Ithorian Smuggler

Kleef and H-TFU Droids: Minor Boss

Chop'aa and Minions: Boss

Collectibles Found

20 Holocrons

Color Crystal

2 Force Holocrons

2 Health Holocrons

Lightsaber Hilt

"It's Beautiful."

In the meantime, I've set up a meeting with another Imperial contact - Senator Garm Bel Iblis.

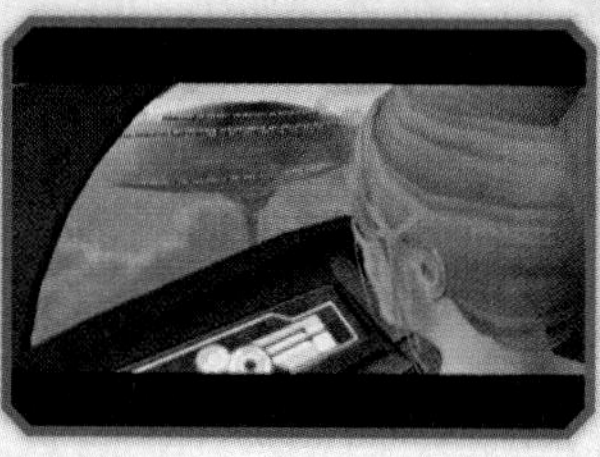

With word of your victories against the Empire spreading across the galaxy, it's time to contact the dissident Senators and organize a Rebel Alliance. General Kota decides to contact Senator Organa, but in the meantime you must travel to Cloud City to meet with another Senator.

Senator Garm Bel Iblis has absolutely no love for the Emperor and will surely join forces with you. In fact, Bel Iblis wants to discuss an alliance. In Cloud City, you'll need to contact the chief administrator, Lobot. He'll know where the Senator is. As you approach the floating city, you can see how beautiful it is. Unfortunately, there's something very ugly happening inside its walls.

Sky-High Fight

Immediately upon disembarking the *Rogue Shadow*, move the two barrels near the ship's front left to reveal a Holocron.

Follow the main walkway into the city. Inside you find Lobot engaged in battle with several Rebels. He says that the Senator is currently at the loading bay trying to negotiate with Chop'aa, the leader of the mercenaries on Cloud City. If you want to talk to the Senator, you must join the fight.

Backtrack out of the hall and make an immediate right. Blast the crates out of the way and grab the Holocron behind them. Then approach the protocol and astro-mech droids on the platform;
toss both over the side to reveal another Holocron near the city's entrance. With your Holocrons collected, go back into Cloud City.

Locate the Mandalorian spy down the hall on the left. As you approach him, toss the other mercenaries into each other to get them out of your way; keep your lightsaber up to reflect the blaster fire. Reach the Mandalorian and lock on to him. Fry him with Sith Scorcher, then destroy him with aerial attacks.

After beating the Mandalorian, examine the large circular niche on the room's right side. First, jump on top of the spire to get the Health Holocron. Then remove the small spire from the center and take the Holocron that appears.

Continue down the hall and Force Push the mercenaries out of your way. At the hall's end are two grenade-tossing Gran bandits. Use Force Push to bounce their grenades back at them and blow them up.

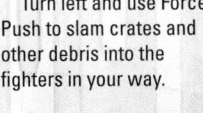

If you see a lighted spire, destroy it. Destroying every spire from here to the elevator will expose a Holocron on the elevator pad.

Turn left and use Force Push to slam crates and other debris into the fighters in your way.

Keep going down the hall until you see the next row of windows along the left wall. Stop and fire a Sith Seeker down the hall into the next area to destroy the criminals. The Sith Seeker may also bust a window or two. When it does, run into the large circular hallway and toss any remaining criminals out the broken window.

Once the hall is clear, a large hairy Whiphid thug and a Mandalorian come charging in. Lock on to the Mandalorian and dash past the Whiphid. Its charge attack is easier to avoid than the Mandalorian's assault, so take out the Mandalorian first. Scorch him, then hit him with aerial attacks as you avoid the Whiphid's rush attacks.

With the Mandalorian out of commission, pick up the Whiphid with your Force Grip. Throw your 'saber at him, then choke him. If he gets loose, shove him away with Force Push attacks and burn him with lightning.

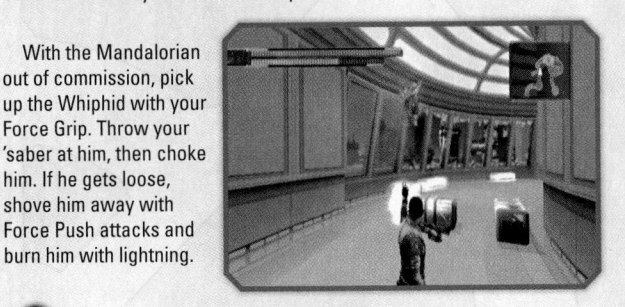

WOOKIEE WARNING

Don't bother trying to toss the Whiphid out the window. He's too large and cumbersome. If you try, he'll just keep coming at you.

Continue storming down the halls, dodging grenades. Reach another Gran grenadier and toss him out the nearest window. When the Whiphid thug rushes down the spiral staircase ahead, grab him before he reaches the floor and toss him out the window. This window is much bigger than the previous, so tossing the large lumbering creature won't be difficult this time.

Go up the spiral staircase and toss the two smaller mercenaries out the window. Lock on to the Talz medic and slam him with a quick Force Push, followed by several lightsaber combos.

SITH WISDOM

Before leaving the area with the spiral staircase, carefully creep out onto the small ledge just outside the busted windows. Follow it all the way left to find a lightsaber hilt.

Pick up the Bacta tank the Talz dropped, then turn left and go into the next hall. Pick up the Talz and toss him at the Gran grenadier at the hall's far end. If you miss the grenadier, use Force Push to bounce his grenades back at him.

At the hall's end, pick up the Ithorian smuggler near the elevator. While you have him in your grasp, choke him with your Force powers, then get on the elevator pad.

Exit the elevator and rush out with your lightsaber held high to reflect incoming fire. At the hall's end are two Twi'lek mercenaries; either Force Push them over the ledge or toss them over with Force Grip.

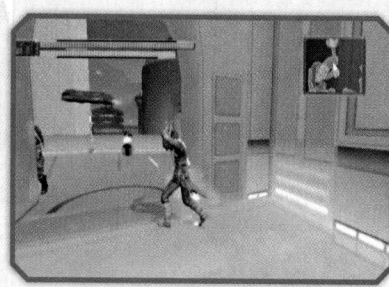

JEDI KNOWLEDGE

Enemies you toss over the ledge fall completely off Cloud City and will still release Force Points when they're destroyed.

Turn right as you exit the hall and take the fight to the three scumbags in the corner. Toss the two on the left over the edge, then bounce the grenadier's projectile back at him. When they're eliminated, turn left and lock on to the rushing Whiphid thug as he comes barreling down the red walkway. Dash away from him to avoid his attack and knock him back with a Force Push.

Scorch the overgrown hair ball, then hit him with 'saber combos. Finally, dash away and hit him with Force Lightning one more time to finish the job.

SITH WISDOM

From here on, the easiest way to eliminate enemies outdoors is tossing them over the ledges and letting them fall off Cloud City. However, not all enemies will be near ledges.

Walk down the long red walkway and into a small circular room containing another elevator. Take it down to the next level.

Exit the elevator and use several Force Pushes to destroy the pipes along the walls, revealing another Holocron.

Go through the large triangular doors and welcome the incoming Whiphid with a Sith Scorcher attack. Next, launch the beast back into the hall with Force Push. Hit him with a second Scorcher attack to destroy him, then turn to the other Whiphid down the hall.

Use Force Grip to throw him down the hall and into the next room. As he flies into the next large passage, launch a Sith Seeker attack to electrocute him. A third Whiphid thug waits in the next hall. Luckily, there are windows here. Pick up the third Whiphid from afar and toss him out the window before he can reach you.

Go down the hall and turn right at the bend. Enter the next small circular room and dash past the mercenaries. Take the turret at the room's rear and let it wipe them out. Make a left, go through the sliding doors, and emerge in the middle of a firefight between Chop'aa's thugs and Cloud City's security.

SITH WISDOM

Don't toss Talz enemies over the ledge. They'll drop Bacta tanks, so destroy them while they're *on* the platform; otherwise, you can kiss the Bacta tanks good-bye.

Mandalorian Melee!

Leap into the middle of the firefight and use a Ground Slam attack to knock enemies away from you. Sprint to the end of the large platform and turn on the thugs. Lift your lightsaber to reflect their fire at them, then lift the thugs one by one and toss them over the platform's side.

As you fight, one of Chop'aa's drop ships floats by overhead and opens fire on you. Block the blaster fire and pick up the Bacta tank before three more Whiphid thugs rush at you from the right walkway. Back up against the platform's end and let them come at you. Pick up each one as they approach, and toss them over the platform's side, letting them fall to their doom. If you try taking on all three at once, they'll just bounce you back and forth between them with their shoulder slam attacks.

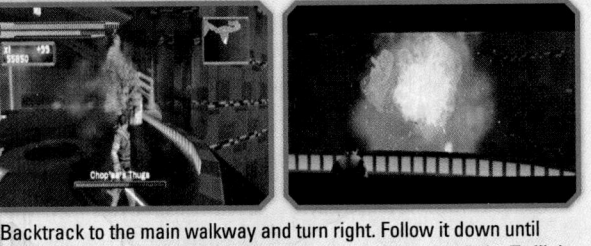
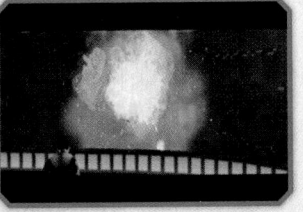

Backtrack to the main walkway and turn right. Follow it down until you encounter another group of Chop'aa's thugs. Force Push the Twi'lek mercenary, then lure the other three Whiphids onto the landing platform on the right. Double-jump over them to avoid getting hit, and lock on to the closest Whiphid when you land. Once again, toss them over the platform's side to dispatch them quickly.

After you destroy Chop'aa's thugs, Lobot arrives with good news: Senator Bel Iblis is eager to meet with you. He's waiting for you on the concourse.

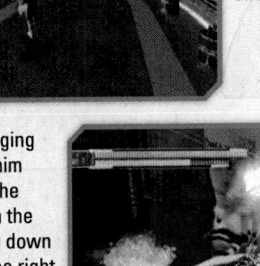

Make a right into another small room, go through the sliding doors, and turn left.

Pick up the charging Whiphid and toss him over the ledge on the right. Charge down the walkway and bring down the barricade on the right with a Force Push. Run across the bridge on the right to the large circular platform.

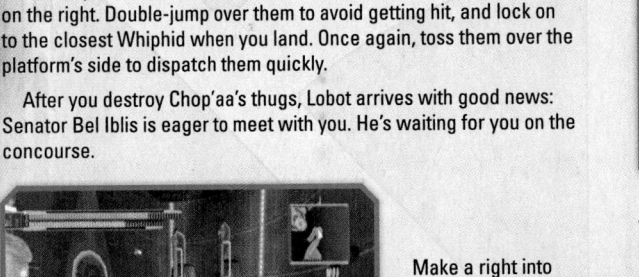

Chop'aa is not happy letting you run around Cloud City dispatching his thugs. He sends a group of Mandalorians to ambush you on the circular platform. Before you leave, you must destroy Chop'aa's flying friends.

Lock on to the closest Mandalorian and fry him with Sith Scorcher. Double-jump toward him, then come down on him with Ground Slam. Even though he's not on the ground, the Ground Slam's shock wave will knock him away.

Follow the Mandalorian as he sputters backward, and slash at him with an aerial attack. Maintain your lock on him as he flies about, and dash away or reflect incoming fire from other Mandalorian fighters.

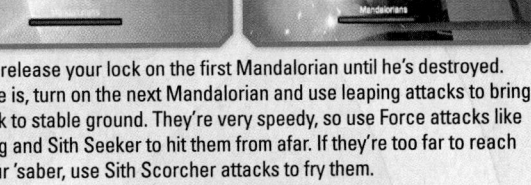

Don't release your lock on the first Mandalorian until he's destroyed. When he is, turn on the next Mandalorian and use leaping attacks to bring him back to stable ground. They're very speedy, so use Force attacks like Lightning and Sith Seeker to hit them from afar. If they're too far to reach with your 'saber, use Sith Scorcher attacks to fry them.

Grab them with Force Grip and slam them against the surrounding walls, then slash at them as they hover within your 'saber's reach.

WOOKIEE WARNING

Don't stand toe-to-toe with the Mandalorians! Their flamethrowers can engulf you quickly and cause major damage.

When only one Mandalorian is left, whittle down his health with a series of Sith Seeker attacks and Force Choke. Follow him around the platform, hitting him with aerial attacks until he's out of commission.

Cloud City Conflict!

With the Mandalorians gone, charge down the long red walkway on the platform's far end. Fire a Force Push ahead of you to knock away any mercenaries. Rush up the ramp leading into a small circular room. Enter with your lightsaber in blocking position, then turn left and take the nearby turret. Let it blast down the enemies in the room. Walk up the next passageway and into another small room.

Just as before, reflect the mercenaries' blaster fire back at them and wipe them out with Force attacks. Hop into the blue elevator and take it back up to the landing pad where you first encountered Chop'aa's drop ships.

This time, Chop'aa's mercenaries are waiting for you. Fortunately, Lobot's men are at your side, so you're not alone. Lock on to the attacking Whiphids and throw them over the walkway's side. Use Force Push to pound the Talz medics into the wall behind them, then knock them into each other with Force Grip.

Pick up the Bacta tanks the Talz medics drop, then go into the hallway through the door on the right.

After reaching the bottom of the steps, turn left and edge out onto the balcony behind the broken window. Make a right and pick up the Holocron at the balcony's end.

Another Mandalorian greets you at the bottom of the steps. Just as you set foot on the final step, he comes crashing through the window on the left. Fry him immediately with a Force Lightning blast, then leap into the air and hit him with aerial attacks.

Go through the next door and attack the Whiphid on the other side. Toss him overboard and continue down the walkway on the left. Stop when you see the Mandalorians speeding at you. Hit them all with Detonate or Sith Seeker, then turn left and go through the door.

At the hall's far end, to the left, are several more of Chop'aa's lackeys. As you slowly stalk them down the hall, use Force Push to bounce the grenadier's grenades back at the group. Destroy Chop'aa's thugs at the hall's end with Sith Scorcher, then advance into the plaza ahead. Lobot is waiting, but where is the Senator?

Senatorial Hunt

While you've been battling the criminal element in Cloud City, Senator Garm Bel Iblis was captured by a rogue named Kleef. To speak with the Senator, you must rescue him first.

Go down the steps on the right onto the plaza's lower level; toss the approaching scumbags over the side ledges. They can't fight if they're flying over the edge, so the battle with Chop'aa's thugs should be short and sweet.

Destroy all of the light props in the courtyard after the cutscene with Lobot to reveal a Holocron.

SITH WISDOM

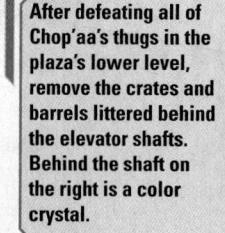

After defeating all of Chop'aa's thugs in the plaza's lower level, remove the crates and barrels littered behind the elevator shafts. Behind the shaft on the right is a color crystal.

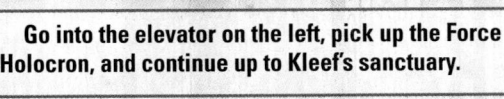

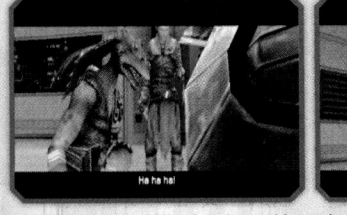

Go into the elevator on the left, pick up the Force Holocron, and continue up to Kleef's sanctuary.

When you find Kleef, he's working a large machine. He's not threatened by you or your 'saber. He picks up a blade and activates two large H-TFU droids.

Lead your assault with a Force Push and hit Kleef. Leap over his two clanking cronies and come down on Kleef with a Ground Slam. Lock on to him, then move away before he can run his blade through you.

Destroy the console to the elevator's left to reveal a Holocron.

Keep a lock on Kleef and dash away from his bodyguard droids' attacks to keep your distance. Engage him in melee combat to lure him away from his slower, lumbering protectors. Once you've isolated Kleef, use Sith Scorcher attacks to fry him and whittle down his health. When you see the robots' red lasers honing in on you, speed away to keep them from locking on.

If one of Kleef's robots manages to grab you, immediately follow the onscreen commands to avoid its attacks and flip it onto its back. While the machine is on the ground, speed toward Kleef and continue your assault.

Run away from the large droids and toward Kleef with your lightning attack leading the way. Fry Kleef every chance you get; it's the quickest way to whittle down the Gungan's health. When his bodyguards get close enough to strike, simply dash away. Lure Kleef away again and strike when he's far from his protectors.

After you've cut Kleef's Health bar to less than half, scorch his two clanging cronies. The attack will finally disable them, leaving you to deal with their Gungan leader one-on-one.

With his guards out of the way, deal with Kleef mano a mano. Increase your aggressiveness and hit him with Ground Slam attacks and strong 'saber combos. If he attempts to use a combo, block his attacks and counter as soon as he's done attacking. Activate Dark Rage and finish him off. Even though you've managed to take out Kleef, he doesn't give up the Senator's location. That information rests with Chop'aa. You've got one more stop to make.

Senatorial Rescue

Take the elevator back down to the plaza and exit. Here you can either speed past the enemies and into the elevator directly in front of you, or take on Chop'aa's thugs. For now, do the latter. Bounce the grenadiers' grenades back at them and toss the other rogues over the sides to dispatch them quickly. Leave the Talz medics for last, and take their Bacta tanks when they are destroyed.

Hop into the elevator and ride it to the next level. Exit the elevator and dispatch the two Twi'lek mercenaries quickly. Slam them into each other, then fry them with Sith Scorcher. Next, turn your attention down the hall and lock on to the Gran grenadiers hurling explosives at you from a distance. Bounce their explosives back at them until they, and the Talz next to them, are destroyed.

Exit the hall and locate the Whiphid thug in the pavilion on the right. Toss him over the edge, then dash right, into the winding pavilion. Lock on to the turret on the left and turn it on the other thugs nearby. Slowly creep right, around the pavilion, with your 'saber held high to reflect incoming fire.

Remove the barrels on the pavilion's far right to uncover a hidden Holocron.

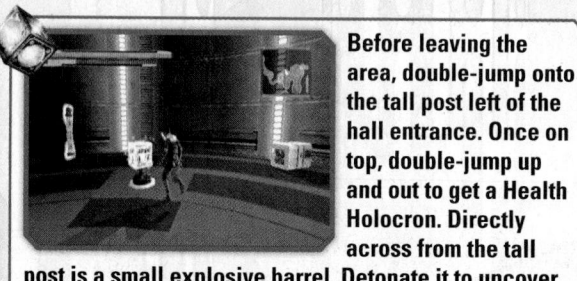

Snake around the pavilion, reflecting fire until you encounter several more Whiphids. They'll charge you all at once, so back away a bit, lure them into a wide-open area, and toss them over the ledges until they're all gone. If one manages to hit you with a shoulder slam, double-jump away to distance yourself from them, and lock on to them again to toss them to their doom.

Before leaving the area, double-jump onto the tall post left of the hall entrance. Once on top, double-jump up and out to get a Health Holocron. Directly across from the tall post is a small explosive barrel. Detonate it to uncover another Holocron.

Go down the long triangular hallway. Deflect incoming fire and launch Force Pushes at the thugs down the hall. Follow the winding hall until you reach another small group of enemies.

Lock on to the Talz and pull it near you. As it gets close, toss him aside. Turn to the other thugs and fry them all simultaneously with Sith Seeker. Once the other enemies are destroyed, turn back to the Talz and finish it off. Take its Bacta tank.

Destroy the barrels on the left to reveal another Holocron.

Farther down the hall are more thugs. Take their turret and unleash it on them while you block their fire. When the connecting room between halls is clear, take one of the blinking barrels nearby and direct it down the next passage at the group of thugs.

While in this room, remove the pipes on the left to expose a Holocron. Pick it up and return to the fight.

Sprint through the next passage, pick up the Force Holocron in the following small room, and Force Choke the Twi'lek rogue inside.

Turn left into the tunnel and go all the way through. Chop'aa is waiting.

Basilisk Battle

When you find Chop'aa, you see that he's got Senator Garm Bel Iblis with him. Two Mandalorians swoop in and join Chop'aa—he's not going to fight you alone. Lock on to one of the Mandalorians when the fight begins. Speed away from Chop'aa and attack one of the Mandalorians first.

Burn your flying foe with Force Lightning, then leap into the air and strike him down with aerial combos. Ignore Chop'aa while the Mandalorians buzz over your head. If he gets too close, knock him off his feet with a Ground Slam attack, then speed away (toward a Mandalorian) while he's on his back.

Remove the large spire on the room's left side to reveal a Holocron. Pick it up as you fight the Mandalorians.

Pursue the Mandalorians around the room, avoiding Chop'aa, and burn them down with Sith Scorcher and Sith Seeker attacks. Use those two attacks primarily, as they're high-damage and long-range attacks that you can unleash quickly. Dispatch the Mandalorians, then turn to Chop'aa.

attempt to squash you. As he floats overhead, stop just long enough for him to lock on to you. When he starts coming down, double-jump into the air and counter with Sith Scorcher. Several explosive barrels are scattered around the room. Hurl them at the basilisk whenever possible.

Continue dashing away, blocking his fire, and blasting him with Force attacks until the onscreen prompts appear. Match the commands and destroy the basilisk!

Clearly, Chop'aa isn't going to fight fair. So when his two Mandalorians are no longer in the battle, he calls in a very big friend to help him out. Suddenly, a large mobile battle suit touches down in front of you. Chop'aa hops in his basilisk and powers up. You're in for a tough fight.

As soon as Chop'aa is in his battle suit, hit him with Sith Scorcher and dash away. The basilisk has several devastating assaults. The first is a close-range smash attack where he reaches out with his hands and slams at the ground in front of you. If he connects, he'll knock you back several feet. Leap into the air to avoid this attack and scorch him once you're safely away.

Chop up Chop'aa!

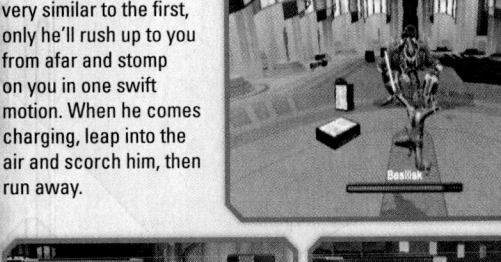

His second attack is very similar to the first, only he'll rush up to you from afar and stomp on you in one swift motion. When he comes charging, leap into the air and scorch him, then run away.

Chop'aa's Mandalorians are destroyed, and his basilisk is now a heap of burning metal, but he's not done with you yet. Chop'aa comes running out of the fire with his bo-staff, ready to attack.

Jump into the air and come down on Chop'aa with a Ground Slam attack, knocking him off kilter. Immediately blast him with Force Lightning. Launch him across the room with Force Push and chase him down. Don't let up on Chop'aa until he attempts to assault you. Leap away from his Ground Slam attack, then hurl him across the room again.

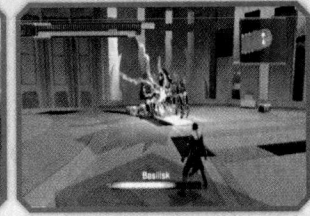

His third attack is a bit tougher to avoid. When the basilisk leaps into the air and hovers over you, he'll rain blaster fire on you. Raise your lightsaber to block his fire. Your 'saber won't reflect the blaster fire back; in fact, the force of his blasters will push you back, but at least you won't take much damage. Search the room's sides when he stops firing at you and pick up a Bacta tank.

Double-jump away from the basilisk to a safe distance. Unleash several Sith Seeker blasts to deplete his health and speed away as he gets close.

Aside from the Ground Slams, his attacks are all melee. Use standard lightsaber combos, well-timed blocks, and counterattacks to whittle his health. Activate Dark Rage and unleash several fierce combos on him. Chop'aa isn't as difficult to contend with as his basilisk, so don't back off. Keep your attacks aggressive.

Slash away at the rogue and stop only to blast him with Ground Slams and Force attacks. Chop'aa is no match for you and eventually succumbs to your skill. As Chop'aa lies defeated on the ground, Lobot and his men come rushing in just as you free the Senator.

WOOKIEE WARNING

Don't bother trying to hurt the basilisk with Ground Slam attacks. The shock wave will damage it, but it's too large to move. Use Repulse on the basilisk droid to temporarily stun it, leaving it open for you to attack.

Senator Bel Iblis has had enough of the Emperor. With threats against him and his family, he's ready to take action and join the Rebellion. You've got another ally. Next you'll need to meet with Organa and the other dissidents to discuss the next move.

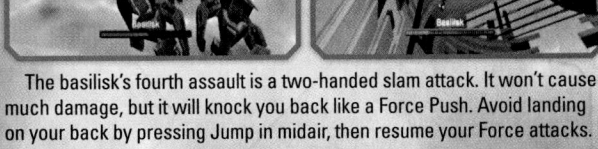

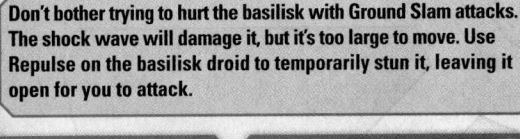

The basilisk's fourth assault is a two-handed slam attack. It won't cause much damage, but it will knock you back like a Force Push. Avoid landing on your back by pressing Jump in midair, then resume your Force attacks.

When you're close to destroying him, he'll use a new attack. Instead of floating about you and firing, he'll hover over you and then crash down in an

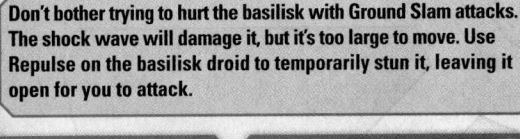

General Kota. I know. And I know about your plans for rebellion.

STAR WARS
FORCE
UNLEASHED

CORELLIA

Objective
You've contacted all the allies you can find who are opposed to the Empire. Now is the time to act. Go to Corellia and meet with them to plan a course of action.

Enemies Encountered
None

Collectibles Found
None

"One day, the galaxy will indeed be free."

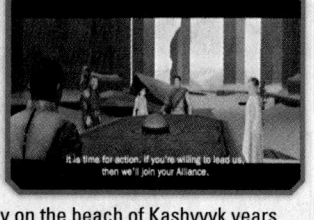

You've come a long way from that day on the beach of Kashyyyk years ago. Your journey began in Kashyyyk's warm, lush jungles, and now you're in the icy, snow-covered landscape of Corellia. You touch down on the planet and meet with your contacts.

Standing around the table are Senator Organa, his daughter, Senator Bel Iblis, Kota, you, and Mon Mothma. Everything has fallen into place, and the Rebel Alliance is taking shape.

You leap into the air with your 'saber raised, ready to strike down your master, but he's too quick. He uses the Force to hurl a table at you and knocks you out into the snowy Corellian mountain peaks. Vader confirms your greatest fears: he's been lying to you since the very beginning. He never planned to destroy the Emperor with you. You were just a tool to gather the Emperor's enemies together to destroy them all at once.

He picks you up and tosses you once more. This time you fall helplessly over the ridge and manage to hold on by your fingertips. Just when it seems you're about to slip and fall to your doom, Vader is attacked! A Jedi with shaggy brown hair and a full beard comes leaping out of the Corellian meeting room. It's Obi-Wan Kenobi!

Betrayal!

Just as Organa makes an official declaration of rebellion, the room begins to shake as if it's being bombarded with blaster fire. Everyone scatters as the meeting-room doors are blasted open and Darth Vader comes storming in. His men make short work of the Rebel soldiers guarding the Senators.

You've been betrayed again. Rather than allow the Rebellion to flourish and challenge the Emperor as planned, Darth Vader betrayed you and is taking the leaders of the Alliance as prisoners.

The battle doesn't last long. Kenobi strikes and Vader strikes back. A short exchange of flashing 'sabers ends with Vader's lightsaber running through Kenobi's chest. The Jedi Master falls to the floor. Kenobi's body disappears, revealing PROXY's fallen form. It wasn't the Jedi Master after all! It was your trusty PROXY droid all along.

Kota draws his lightsaber but is unable to do anything as Vader tosses him aside like a rag doll. It's up to you to save the Rebellion!

He knew that he was no match for Vader, but his surprise attack bought you enough time to safely drop down from the cliff's edge to a ledge along the cliffside. Juno swoops in to rescue you from the cliffside. Not all is lost.

DEATH STAR

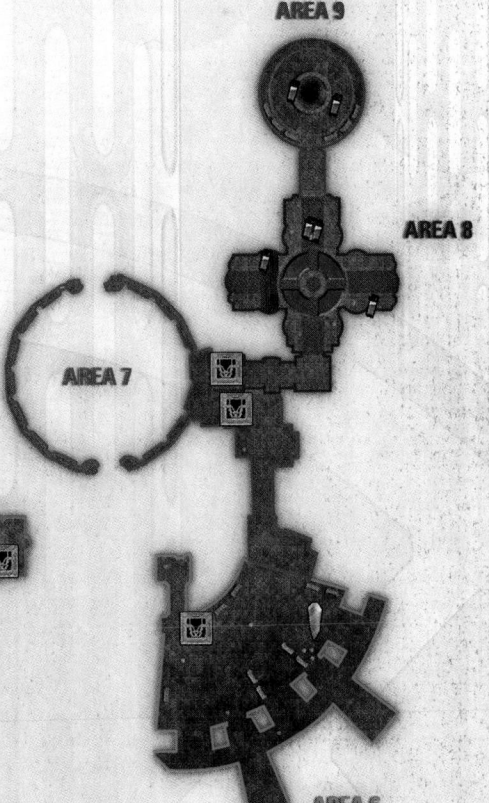

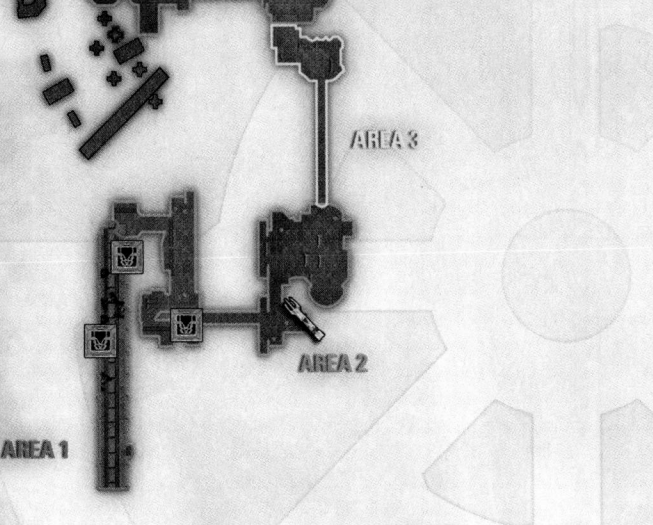

MAP LEGEND

- 🛁 Bacta Tank
- 🕯 Color Crystal
- 🔘 Force Holocron
- ◆ Health Holocron
- 🔲 Holocron
- 🗡 Lightsaber Hilt

AREA 9

AREA 8

AREA 7

AREA 5

AREA 6

AREA 4

AREA 3

AREA 2

AREA 1

MISSION DETAILS

Objective

Darth Vader has betrayed you again, revealing that he has always been loyal to the Emperor. The Emperor is preparing to execute your new allies—the future leaders of the Rebel Alliance. Launch an assault on the Death Star in search of the Rebels.

Enemies Encountered

Imperial Stormtrooper

Stormtrooper Gunner

Stormtrooper Sniper

Imperial Guard

Shadow Stormtrooper

Jump Stormtrooper

Shock Stormtrooper

IT-O Interrogator Droid

AT-ST: Minor Boss

Darth Vader: Boss

Collectibles Found

10 Holocrons

Color Crystal

Lightsaber Hilt

STAR WARS
THE FORCE UNLEASHED

"I've never been a Jedi before."

The *Rogue Shadow* is much quieter now without PROXY and General Kota on board. As you speed away from Corellia, Juno makes an eye-opening observation: Darth Vader betrayed you multiple times in spite of your loyalty. But now that he's taken the leaders of the Rebellion prisoner, the fate of the Alliance rests with you.

You decide to go after Darth Vader and rescue the Rebels. But first you must decide *where* to go. Juno pilots the *Rogue Shadow* while you sit in the navigator's seat meditating.

You've never been a true Jedi before, but somehow your meditation pays off. You see visions of Kota and a large space station still under construction. There's something wrong with General Kota....

You set course for the Outer Rim and find Vader's Death Star. Juno carefully navigates the *Rogue Shadow* into the Death Star and docks. You order her to raise the ship's cloak and orbit the space station just out of scanner range. Realizing that this might be the last time she sees you, she finally reveals her true feelings...with a kiss.

Assault on the Death Star

You disembark the *Rogue Shadow* by leaping off the ship and landing on a walkway far below. Charge down the walkway with your 'saber in blocking position. There are several stormtroopers ahead; they've got an elevated position, so they'll have an advantage. Block their incoming fire as you carefully approach. Blast the TIE fighter wings to create an explosion.

Double-jump onto the walkway above and hurl the troopers over the side to eliminate them quickly. Next, lock on to the Jump troopers. If you leave them unchecked, they'll blast you down in a matter of seconds. Hit them repeatedly with Sith Seeker and Sith Scorcher attacks to bring them down. Keep your block raised while your Force meter recharges after each Sith attack.

There are two Holocrons on the walkway. One is on the lower level behind the TIE wing racks. The other is on the lower-level walkway's opposite end. Pick them up before returning to the second-level walkway and getting on the elevator.

Ride the elevator at the hall's end to the next level of the Death Star. Exit the elevator and immediately hit the troopers with Sith Scorcher. They open fire on you as soon as you get off the elevator, so be quick! Dash to the room's left side to avoid the fire, then attack.

Your scorcher blast should eliminate all but one or two troopers. Wipe them out with short combos or choke attacks, then take the Bacta tank dropped by the health-regenerating trooper. Force Push through the hatch and head into the next section of the space station.

Grab the two troopers on the left and toss them through the window and into the large energy beam just beyond the walkway. Turn right and walk down the passage with your 'saber up to reflect blaster fire. Either scorch the enemies as you get near or toss them into the large beam to dispatch them quickly.

The stormtroopers in the Death Star are far more dangerous than any you've faced. They typically travel in large squads and open fire immediately. You'll need to destroy them as quickly and as easily as possible, so stick to Sith Scorcher, Sith Seeker, and Force Push attacks to get them out of the way.

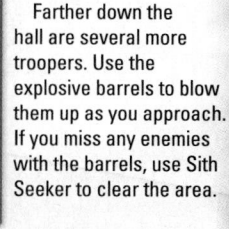

Farther down the hall are several more troopers. Use the explosive barrels to blow them up as you approach. If you miss any enemies with the barrels, use Sith Seeker to clear the area.

87

PRIMAGAMES.COM

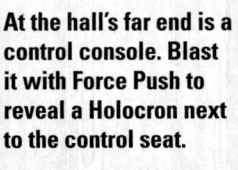

At the hall's far end is a control console. Blast it with Force Push to reveal a Holocron next to the control seat.

As soon as you emerge from the tunnel, burn the troopers with Sith Scorcher, then dash to the room's opposite side. Force Push the blaster-toting trooper in the corner and toss him aside. Demolish the health-regenerating trooper near the room's center with a series of Force Pushes, then run your lightsaber through the last guard.

Pick up the Bacta tank and use Force Push to knock down the hatch door in the room's top right corner. Just as before, immediately unleash a Sith Scorcher attack on the group of troopers waiting on the hatch's other side. Backtrack into the room to allow the troopers to give chase while your Force meter replenishes. When it does, turn around and fry them again with your lightning attacks.

Make a left across the long bridge into the station's next section. Wait until the energy beam deactivates before crossing. If you wait too long and it reactivates while you're on the bridge, you're toast.

Force Push the guards into the room's rear, then use Force Lightning to detonate the barrel and blow them up. Use a Force Push to demolish the wall on the right and pick up the 'saber hilt in the small room, then turn left and use the Force to blast down the next door.

There is another Holocron sitting near the control console in this room's far right corner. Grab it before crossing the bridge.

Creep to the right and get cover behind the corner. Raise your 'saber to block stray blaster fire, then use Force Lightning to burn nearby enemies from your covered position. Fry the first wave of troopers, then edge out and to the left.

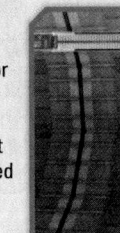

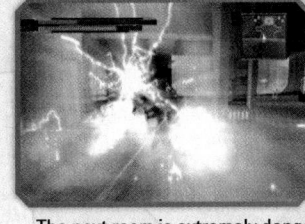

Leave the health-regenerating soldiers for last. Choke them, then take their Bacta tanks before entering the next room. Turn left and speed down the connecting bridge to the next area.

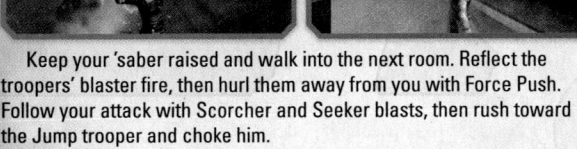

Keep your 'saber raised and walk into the next room. Reflect the troopers' blaster fire, then hurl them away from you with Force Push. Follow your attack with Scorcher and Seeker blasts, then rush toward the Jump trooper and choke him.

Make a right and lock on to the two Shock troopers. Hurl one across the room, then lock on to the second. Attack him with a strong lightsaber combo and choke him before the first trooper gets up. When the first Shock trooper gets near again, choke him as well.

WOOKIEE WARNING

Do not rush into the next room! You'll be instantly surrounded by several different types of troopers, who will destroy you in no time.

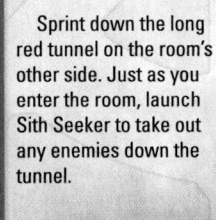

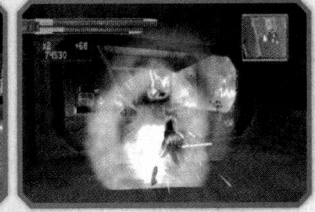

Sprint down the long red tunnel on the room's other side. Just as you enter the room, launch Sith Seeker to take out any enemies down the tunnel.

The next room is extremely dangerous. It is guarded by Jump troopers and contains Shock troopers, Imperial troopers, and stormtrooper snipers. Begin by locking on to the Jump troopers and frying them with Sith Scorcher. Use Force Push to separate them from the rest of the guards, and take them out quickly. As you battle the Jump troopers, the others will begin closing in on you. Dash to a safe distance, then turn your Scorcher attack on them.

Duck into the small room on the right and let your Force meter refill. When you're fully charged, dash out, slash through the first soldier on the left, and use Detonate attacks to clear the room of all remaining guards.

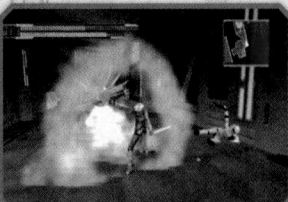

SITH WISDOM

While in this room, stay on the move! If you stand toe-to-toe with the soldiers, they'll cut you down instantly. Instead, stay mobile and block blaster fire when you're not moving. If you're close to the room's right side, hurl enemies into the large firing bay where the energy beam repeatedly ignites.

Approach the large blue force field on the room's far end and use Force Grip to destroy the generators on the other side. The force field comes down, and you're free to proceed, but Juno sends you a communication. The *Rogue Shadow* has been captured by the space station's tractor beam!

Use Force Push to destroy the two large cylindrical generators next to you, then Force Grip the explosive barrels nearby. Hurl the barrels at the generators across the large chasm to blow them up and free the *Rogue Shadow*.

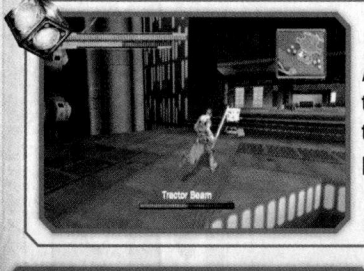

After bringing down the force field, grab the Holocron on the platform's far right.

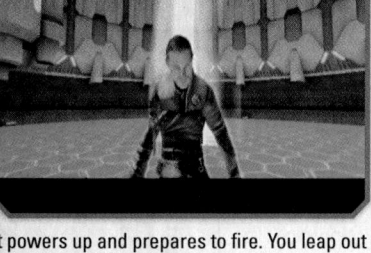

Your heroics don't go unnoticed. As soon as you free your ship, a TIE fighter comes zooming in on you, firing its blasters. You hurl explosive barrels at it and destroy it, but the explosion takes you down too. You fall several stories to a large green firing pad, just as it powers up and prepares to fire. You leap out of the way just in time to avoid being incinerated.

JEDI KNOWLEDGE

Instead of using explosive barrels to deactivate the tractor beam generators, Force Grip the TIE fighter as it zooms past. Hurl this at the generators to deactivate them!

The next room is just as dangerous as the previous one. Dash to the right and take cover behind the control console. Throw the Imperial soldiers behind the console at the other soldiers on the left, then dash out and unleash Sith Scorcher blasts on the remaining troopers.

Go into the passage on the left and launch a Detonate attack at the nearest group of troopers. Follow your Detonate attack as it travels down the hall, and Force Grip the nearest soldier. Toss him at the others and blast them all with Sith Seeker.

Stop halfway up the hall and destroy the control consoles on the left to reveal another Holocron; grab it and continue up the hall.

 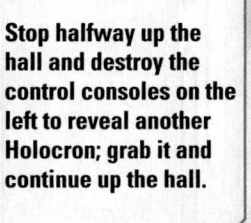

Stop just before entering the next room and raise your lightsaber; inside the room, reflect the soldiers' fire back at them, destroying them. At the room's entrance, slowly walk from left to right, allowing the soldiers to blast themselves down.

Allow the blaster fire to settle a bit, then unleash a series of Force attacks into the room. Use Force Pushes to bounce back incoming grenades, use Detonate attacks to hit approaching enemies, and use Sith Scorcher blasts to burn down multiple foes.

Enter the room and sprint right. Toss the explosive barrels at the soldiers at the room's rear. If the barrels don't destroy the soldiers, calmly walk up to them and hit them repeatedly with Force Push attacks to eliminate them.

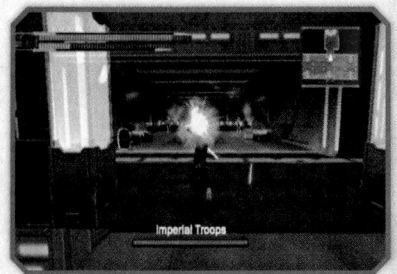

Wait for the energy beam on the right to stop, then speed across the bridge into the next room.

Just as you step off the bridge, stop and throw the barrel on the left at the soldiers near the room's far end. Edge right as you move forward and reflect blaster fire at the second batch of Imperial troops. Hit them with Sith Seeker, then edge back to the room's left side as you continue moving forward.

Move around the room with your 'saber held high, and let the remaining Imperial troops blast themselves down. When only the health-regenerating troopers remain, dispatch them with lightsaber combos and take the Bacta tanks they drop.

After defeating the Imperial troops, a pair of Jump troopers swoop in and open fire on you. Dash away and lure one away from the other so they can't gang up on you. Turn on the trooper in pursuit and fry him! Turn on the other one and blast him away with Force Push, then continue your assault on the first trooper. When the first one falls, turn your full attention on the second and finish him off.

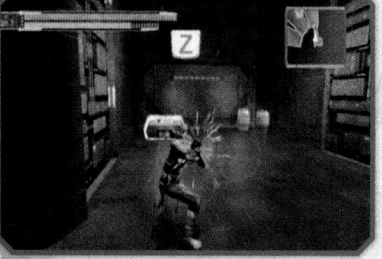

After you clean the room of all Imperial filth, examine the control console on the far right. Pick up the Holocron and get on the elevator.

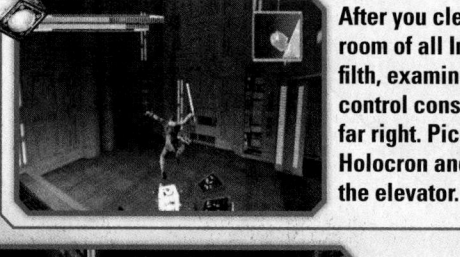

Ride the elevator to the next level. Exit the elevator and blast down the hatch door ahead.

Death Star Brawl!

Just behind the hatch door is a large room full of Imperial troops. In order to proceed into the next room, you must destroy every guard inside. Run in and hit the troops with Force Pushes to split them up. Then launch a Sith Seeker attack at them.

Lock on to the closest trooper and grab him. Throw him at the other troopers in the room, then launch a Detonate attack at him. Speed to the room's far end and blow up the barrel on the right. The explosion should take out nearby troopers, leaving only two or three in the room's far left corner.

Pick them up and toss them over the walkway to the right. When you do, the force field blocking the entrance to the next room disappears.

Walk into the next room with your 'saber blocking incoming fire; edge to the left. Take out the first two guards here with quick lightsaber combos, then dash to the far right corner. Leap into the air and hit the soldiers behind the console with Ground Slam attacks until they're eliminated. Stay behind the consoles for protection, and hurl the nearby soldiers over the walkway's side.

After you eliminate all the ground-bound troops, four Jump troopers zoom into the fight. Dash away from them, toward the room's far end. Turn around and lock on to the nearest flying guard and reflect his fire back at him. Slowly approach him as you sneak behind the consoles on the right.

Get within striking distance and activate Sith Scorcher to burn him down. Back away with your 'saber reflecting fire, and edge toward the other Jump troopers. Lure one away as you did before, then turn on him and blast him with Scorcher attacks. Play cat and mouse with the last two troopers, being careful not to get surrounded, and take them out.

The next room contains an all-too-familiar enemy. A large clanking AT-ST lurks here, ready to open fire when you enter. Run into the room and make a sharp right. Double-jump onto the platform high above you, and use the explosive barrels as bombs against the machine.

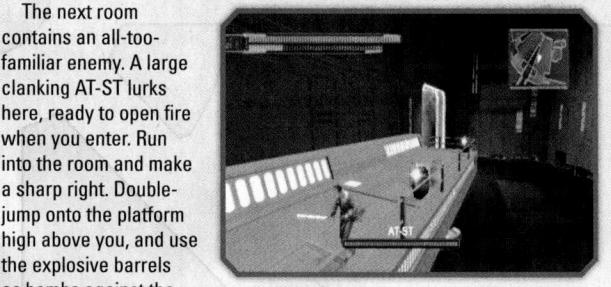

JEDI KNOWLEDGE

On the platform at the far end of the bay is a color crystal. Get it before you defeat the AT-ST, or lose it forever.

Dash around the room, avoiding the AT-ST's blaster fire, and repeatedly hit it with lightning attacks. Whittle its health down to less than half before getting near it. When it tries stomping on you, follow the onscreen commands to counterattack and slash at it.

When you land, sprint out of the way, then blast it again with Sith Scorcher. Follow the final set of prompts to climb atop the machine; slash it, then crush it with the Force.

With the hoards of Imperial troops and the AT-ST out of the way, you're free to continue searching the space station. Shove the first two troopers back down the hall, then hit them all with Force Lightning. Streak down the hall, fry the snipers at the end, and finish them off with 'saber combos.

Make a right at the hall's end and go into the next passage. Turn left and launch a Force Push down the hall to knock your enemies off their feet. Follow this with a Detonate or Sith Seeker attack, then sprint down the hall.

Throw the troopers into each other and strike them down with lightsaber combos as they try getting up. If they manage to gain their feet and surround you, knock them away with Repulse. Sprint to safety while the troopers are down; scorch them once your Force meter is replenished. Continue hitting them with Force Lightning until they're gone for good.

Examine the area behind the console at the passage's far left end. Pick up the Holocron and turn right.

Make a right around the corner and toss the trooper over the side of the next catwalk. Hop onto the elevator on the right, and take it all the way up. Exit the elevator and unleash Force Lightning on the approaching troopers. Follow the walkway to its end to conclude your journey.

The Reckoning

You reach the Emperor's room in the space station to find he's interrogating the founders of the Rebel Alliance. He paces back and forth as Vader stands by and watches his master. The Emperor, sure of himself and his power, insists that the Rebellion will fail. But he fails to see what Kota is immediately aware of—you.

You storm into the Emperor's control room with your lightsaber ready, but the Emperor leaves his dirty work to Darth Vader. It's time to confront your former master. Darth Vader calmly charges toward you and hurls you back with a Force Push.

When you get up, lock on to Vader and hit him with Force Lightning. Engage him in a Force Lock and follow the onscreen prompts to knock him into the air and slam him down into the ground. The slam momentarily stuns Vader. Rush at him and strike him with powerful lightsaber combos while he's dazed.

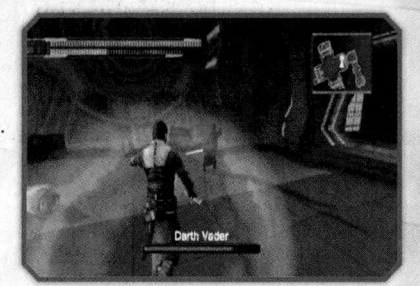

Darth Vader will raise his 'saber to block and counterattack as soon as he's out of his daze, so back away and raise your 'saber to do the same. Block his attack, then counter with quick, short combos. As you attack, activate Dark Rage to inflict more damage with lightsaber combos. If he tries blasting you backward with Force Push, jump in midair to land on your feet.

When your Force meter is replenished, knock Vader back and lunge at him. Come down on him with a Ground Slam to knock him back even farther, then blast him with Force Lightning attacks. This engages him in another Force Lock. Follow the onscreen commands to knock him into the air and slam him onto the ground. Rush him while he's dazed, and slash him with combos until he recovers.

If Vader picks you up with Force Grip, free yourself with Force Push. If he blasts you with Force Push, jump to land on your feet.

91

There are two Bacta tanks on opposite sides of the room. As you fight, dash back and forth between the two platforms and pick them up when you've taken too much damage. Engage Vader in another Force Lock and slam him into a stupor again. Follow up with 'saber combos as before, then block and counter his attacks.

If Vader successfully dodges your attacks, hit him with Ground Slam to knock him away, then engage him with lightsaber combos. Continue whittling Darth Vader's health like this until he's nearly defeated.

When Vader's health is almost gone, several more prompts appear onscreen. Match them to dodge Vader's attacks and launch him into the air. Continue following every onscreen prompt and thrash your former master around the room until he's nothing more than a tattered suit on a broken man.

Your final attack sends Vader flying into a chamber at the room's rear. There, the Emperor prepares to execute the leaders of the Rebel Alliance. You've got other plans, though.

A Choice

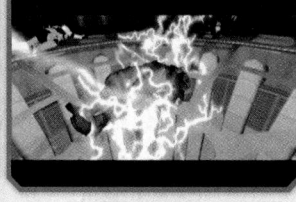

As you stand over Darth Vader's body with your 'saber drawn to his neck, the Emperor's scratchy voice urges you to do it. Destroy Vader and you'll rightfully take his place by the Emperor's side.

General Kota tries to keep you from striking down Vader and finally crossing completely to the dark side, but the Emperor stops him. Suddenly, things change. Vader is still at your feet, but the Emperor is destroying Kota! You have a choice: Eliminate Vader and take your place by the Emperor's side, or defeat the Emperor to free the Rebels.

What will you do?

Rather than give away the two possible endings, the following section provides tips on how to defeat the Emperor and Darth Vader. You must choose which side to align yourself with. Will you join the light side by defeating the Emperor and freeing the Rebels, or will you join the dark side by destroying Darth Vader and taking his place next to the Emperor?

Tips for Defeating the Emperor

- Though the Emperor wields a lightsaber, his attacks are primarily Force power–focused. Standard lightsaber combos won't be as effective as Force attacks against him.
- Stay on the move and leap over his Force Lightning blasts.
- The most effective attack against the Emperor is a Ground Slam. Use it to knock him off his feet and hurl him to the room's opposite side.
- After he's missed you with Force Lightning, use your own lightning attacks like Sith Scorcher and Sith Seeker to damage him.
- If you can't jump out of the way in time, raise your lightsaber to absorb his Force Lightning attacks.
- After successfully defeating the Emperor in a Force Lock, hit him with Ground Slam attacks to do the most damage.
- Jump to avoid getting knocked off your feet by his Force Push attacks.
- Watch out for flying objects! The Emperor will throw large pieces of debris at you every chance he gets.

Tips for Defeating Darth Vader

- Vader relies less on the Force than the Emperor. The majority of his attacks are lightsaber attacks.
- Keep your lightsaber in blocking position at all times to block his 'saber slashes.
- As soon as he stops swinging his 'saber, counter his attacks with 'saber combos.
- Don't rely too much on one attack. Mix up your lightsaber combos with Force Pushes, lightning strikes, and Ground Slam attacks.
- Use your strongest lightsaber combo after successfully defeating Vader in a Force Lock.
- Stay mobile and avoid standing toe-to-toe with him.
- If he corners you against a wall, double-jump to leap over him, then hit him with Ground Slam.

DUEL MODE

Duel mode is a one-on-one fighting mode where you and a friend can reenact some of the *Star Wars* saga's most memorable lightsaber battles. Pit Anakin Skywalker and Obi-Wan Kenobi against each other or restage the famous Darth Maul battle against Qui-Gon Jinn! With a combined 27 Jedi and Sith characters from the *Star Wars* universe, you can relive or rewrite the *Star Wars* saga! The following pages detail all nine stages of Duel mode, plus the 27 characters and their individual stats.

WII WONDERS

Duel mode is a Nintendo Wii exclusive mode!

Battle Rules

The basics of battle are simple. Pick the number of matches (from one to five) and the time limit for each match. Whoever wins the designated amount of matches first is the victor. As you battle, however, there are several key factors that help sway the tides of war.

Scattered throughout the arenas listed below are several Force Ups. These icons grant the user special abilities. By collecting them during battle, you can gain a temporary advantage over your opponent and possibly swing the fight in your favor.

| Increased Force damage | Increased lightsaber damage | Invincibility (you cannot take damage) | Unlimited Force power | Summon reinforcements |

Aside from the Force Ups, you can also attain a special state in Duel mode that allows you to turn the battle in your favor. Become Force Unleashed by dealing damage to your opponent, collecting Force Ups, and taking damage. Once Unleashed, your Force meter becomes unlimited, and your Force powers function at their maximum. Some arenas also have special interactive objects that glow red only while you're Unleashed.

Battle Arenas

In Orbit—TIE Construction Yard

The TIE Construction Yard is one of the most dangerous battle arenas. Players new to Duel mode will need time to adjust to the large hole in the arena's center, while expert duelers will make frequent use of the arena's plentiful explosive barrels.

Though this arena isn't multi-leveled like the others, you can still jump atop the TIE wing crates to gain an advantage over your opponent. While Unleashed, grip one of the TIE fighters shooting out of the arena's center hole and hurl it at your foe.

Coruscant Jedi Temple

The Jedi Temple on Coruscant may have once been sacred, but now it lies in ruins and has become a perfect place for dueling. With rubble lying around and crumbling statues half-standing at nearly every corner of the Temple, there is no shortage of things to throw at your rival.

Make ample use of the Temple's main floor while dashing to and fro during battle. Once Unleashed, however, lure your opponent to the second-level walkway along the Temple's far wall. There, you can use Force Push to hurl your opponent through the wall and into the Coruscant air traffic outside!

SITH WISDOM

Arenas with large holes like this are great for one-hit victories. If you're fast enough, you can either Force Push or Force Throw your enemy into the pit and take a quick and easy victory.

Raxus Prime Junkyard

What better place for a battle arena than the junkyards of Raxus Prime? Pieces of metal, chunks of destroyed droids, and concrete slabs serve as the weapons of choice. Though there aren't many explosive objects to toss, there are plenty of items with which to crush an enemy. You can even throw the metal grates covering the center lava pit.

Most useful, however, is the stream of molten metal running around the arena's exterior. Pick up your enemy and toss him into the stream. When Unleashed, grab the dilapidated platform at the arena's center and bash it over your opponent's head.

Geonosis Colosseum

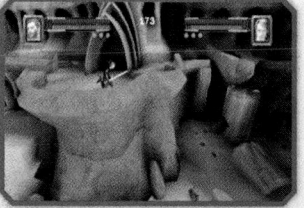

The Geonosis Colosseum is a large U-shaped arena. The center area has a large balcony where players can engage in close-quarters combat. Use the small niches in the balcony and the two lower levels to trap opponents and unleash Force attacks and strong lightsaber combos.

The crumbling execution pillars at the center of the bottom floor are great makeshift projectiles, but the best weapon in the arena is the tall pillar on the bottom floor's far left side. When Force Unleashed, grab the pillar with Force Grip and hurl it at your enemy.

Kashyyyk Wookiee Village

The Kashyyyk battle arena is simple, well rounded, and deceptively challenging. The only multilevel area is a small platform on the left. Lure enemies into close-quarters combat here and make effective use of the Force Ups littered nearby.

The challenging aspect of this arena is trying to activate your Force Unleashed mode while dealing with the Wookiee flying assault vehicle. Wait for the vehicle to swoop in over the arena's center, then finish filling your Unleashed meter (by damaging your opponent, collecting a Force Up, or taking damage) to activate Force Unleashed mode and crash the vehicle over your rival's head.

Bespin Carbonite Chamber

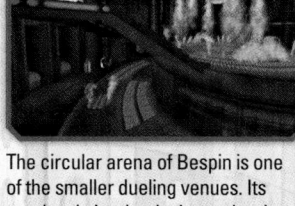

The circular arena of Bespin is one of the smaller dueling venues. Its two-level circular design makes it great for fighters who like to deal damage and dash away before they're counterattacked. The lower level makes for tight close-quarters combat, and the second level's center platform continuously releases spurts of steam that make it difficult to fight there and not take damage.

Time your attacks so that you knock your enemy into the carbonite pit at the platform's center, dealing major damage. Double this damage by dumping your enemy into the carbonite pit, then destroying the overhead carbonite emitter while Unleashed!

Hoth Battlefield

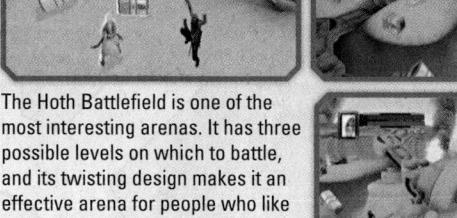

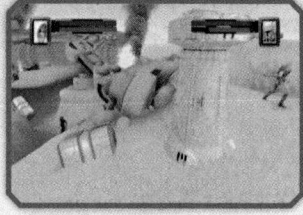

The Hoth Battlefield is one of the most interesting arenas. It has three possible levels on which to battle, and its twisting design makes it an effective arena for people who like to evade and counterattack. Sweep under the fallen walker's legs or leap atop its steely stomach.

When an enemy gives chase, turn on them and toss them into the fire for quick damage. Once you're Unleashed, rip off the fallen walker's bottom panel and swat your rival with it.

JEDI KNOWLEDGE

Battle purists will like the empty ditch at the map's far right side. Here, no Force Ups appear and the battle is determined solely by who is better with the 'saber or the Force.

STAR WARS THE FORCE UNLEASHED

Tatooine—Ben's Hovel

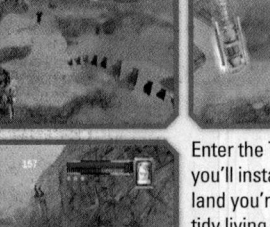

Enter the Tatooine battle arena and you'll instantly recognize whose land you're fighting on. The tiny, tidy living quarters are befitting the spartan lifestyle of one of the only surviving Jedi. Obi-Wan Kenobi's hovel makes for a great dueling place for fighters interested mostly in technical lightsaber combat. Sure, you can Force Throw the speeder at your foe or attempt to impale your enemy with the metal structure on the right, but aside from that, the arena is relatively empty of explosives, throwable objects, and land hazards.

In fact, the sole real land hazard is only a threat while you're Unleashed. While Unleashed, lure your opponent to the arena's right side and bring the large cliff side crashing down on his head with one swift Force Push.

Felucia—Sarlacc Pit

As far as simple arenas go, the Sarlacc Pit is the best. With a simple, circular, three-level design, you can run in any direction and come full circle in a matter of seconds. What makes this level unique, however, is its lethality. With every step, you encounter one of the Sarlacc's many razor-sharp teeth. Grip one with the Force and slash your enemy with it.

Better still, whittle down your enemy's health, then Force Throw him into the center of the Sarlacc Pit! Your enemy will fall straight into the beast's mouth and be chewed into a pulp!

Character Profiles

JEDI KNOWLEDGE

For detailed histories of all these characters, refer to the "Cast" chapter of this guide. The characters in this section are listed in the order they appear on the Duel mode character selection menu.

The Apprentice

Fighter Stats
Lightsaber Power: Medium
Force Lightning Power: Medium
Force Grip: Medium
Force Push: Medium

Profile
A powerful, almost primal Force wielder, Darth Vader's secret apprentice has been trained by the Sith's Dark Lord to hunt down the last of the galaxy's Jedi. Vader has spent years personally training the apprentice in the ways of the Sith, but no other Imperials—including the Emperor—know of his existence. It is Vader's hope that the apprentice will one day fulfill a dark destiny, standing at Vader's side as they confront and destroy the Emperor together....

The Apprentice: Light Training Gear

Fighter Stats
Lightsaber Power: Medium
Force Lightning Power: Medium
Force Grip: Low
Force Push: High

Profile
This combatant is the secret apprentice in light training gear.

The Apprentice: Kento's Robes

Fighter Stats
Lightsaber Power: High
Force Lightning Power: Medium
Force Grip: Medium
Force Push: Medium

Profile
This combatant is the secret apprentice in Master Kento's (his father's) robes.

The Apprentice: Corellian Flight Suit

Fighter Stats
Lightsaber Power: Low
Force Lightning Power: Medium
Force Grip: Medium
Force Push: High

Profile
This combatant is the secret apprentice in a Corellian flight suit.

The Apprentice: Bounty Hunter Disguise

Fighter Stats
Lightsaber Power: Medium
Force Lightning Power: Medium
Force Grip: Medium
Force Push: Medium

Profile
This combatant is the secret apprentice in a bounty hunter disguise.

The Apprentice: Ultimate Good

Fighter Stats
Lightsaber Power: Low
Force Lightning Power: Medium
Force Grip: Medium
Force Push: High

Profile
Having walked the path of the dark side as Darth Vader's slave, the secret apprentice turned on his master and the Emperor. Though he failed to crush the dark side once and for all, he made the ultimate sacrifice: He gave his life so that the Rebel Alliance might survive.

The Apprentice: Industrial Explorer Outfit

Fighter Stats
Lightsaber Power: Medium
Force Lightning Power: Medium
Force Grip: Low
Force Push: High

Profile
This combatant is the secret apprentice in an industrial explorer outfit.

The Apprentice: Jungle Combat Gear

Fighter Stats
Lightsaber Power: High
Force Lightning Power: Medium
Force Grip: Medium
Force Push: Low

Profile
This combatant is the secret apprentice in jungle combat gear.

The Apprentice: Sith Robes

Fighter Stats
Lightsaber Power: Low
Force Lightning Power: High
Force Grip: Medium
Force Push: Medium

Profile
This combatant is the secret apprentice in Sith robes.

The Apprentice: Heavy Training Gear

Fighter Stats
Lightsaber Power: Medium
Force Lightning Power: Medium
Force Grip: Medium
Force Push: Medium

Profile
This combatant is the secret apprentice in heavy training gear.

The Apprentice: Ultimate Evil

Fighter Stats
Lightsaber Power: Medium
Force Lightning Power: Medium
Force Grip: Low
Force Push: High

Profile
Faced with a critical choice, the secret apprentice faltered. Rather than save his friend Rahm Kota, he gave in to his hatred and destroyed his old master, Darth Vader. When he realized what he'd done, he regretted his decision and turned his 'saber on the Emperor. Unfortunately, it was too late. The Emperor struck him down. When he woke up, the secret apprentice had been rebuilt into a symbol of ultimate evil.

Qui-Gon Jinn

Fighter Stats
Lightsaber Power: Medium
Force Lightning Power: Low
Force Grip: Low
Force Push: High

Profile
In spite of the Jedi Council's many warnings and hesitation to allow Anakin Skywalker to enter into Jedi training, Qui-Gon Jinn took him under his wing and began teaching him the ways of the Force.

After Darth Maul destroyed Qui-Gon Jinn, Skywalker's tutelage fell into the hands of Jinn's former apprentice, Obi-Wan. Qui-Gon Jinn, though departed, found a way to commune with the living from the realm beyond.

Obi-Wan Kenobi

Fighter Stats

Lightsaber Power: Medium

Force Lightning Power: Medium

Force Grip: Low

Force Push: High

Profile

Obi-Wan Kenobi was one of the most gifted of the remaining Jedi. Taught by Qui-Gon Jinn and master to Anakin Skywalker and Luke Skywalker, Kenobi was an instrumental figure in the war against the Empire. Before the issuing of Order 66, Kenobi single-handedly defeated the Empire's most feared and destructive figure, General Grievous.

Unfortunately, it was his compassion that spared Anakin Skywalker and allowed the Emperor to resurrect him as Darth Vader.

Anakin Skywalker

Fighter Stats

Lightsaber Power: Medium

Force Lightning Power: High

Force Grip: Medium

Force Push: Low

Profile

Obi-Wan trained Anakin in the use of the Force, but then-Chancellor Palpatine recognized Skywalker's potential and began secretly grooming him to become his own apprentice. Anakin was torn between his loyalty to the Jedi Order and Palpatine, who promised that Anakin could prevent the demise of those he loved by mastering the power of the dark side.

Skywalker eventually discovered that the Chancellor was a Sith Lord but was left behind at the Jedi Temple when Mace Windu and other Jedi set out to arrest Palpatine. Anakin recklessly left the Temple, arriving at Palpatine's quarters just as Mace Windu was about to destroy the Chancellor. He lashed out to protect the Chancellor, ensuring Windu's demise. The Chancellor claimed that Anakin had now become a Sith Lord, and dubbed him...

Darth Vader

Fighter Stats

Lightsaber Power: Medium

Force Lightning Power: Low

Force Grip: High

Force Push: Medium

Profile

The personification of evil and fear, Darth Vader is Emperor Palpatine's relentless enforcer. Although seemingly loyal to the Emperor, Darth Vader harbors much anger toward his master and secretly plots to overthrow him. As part of his plan, Vader has taken a young apprentice, corrupting the boy and training him in the ways of the dark side, all with the promise that one day they will destroy the Emperor together.

Young Luke Skywalker

Fighter Stats

Lightsaber Power: Medium

Force Lightning Power: Low

Force Grip: Low

Force Push: Very High

Profile

If any one character represents the original *Star Wars* trilogy, it is Luke Skywalker. As beloved as he is dynamic, Luke Skywalker's rise from a simple farm boy to a powerful Jedi helped sway the war against the Empire and ultimately put an end to Darth Vader and the Emperor.

However, it was not his rise as a Jedi that most defined him, but the struggle against his inner demons as he fought to avoid taking his father's path to the dark side. After realizing that Anakin Skywalker, his father, was not dead, but instead the monstrous Darth Vader, Luke was thrown into great turmoil. Would he reunite with his father and become a Sith Lord? Would he bring his father back from the dark side? Would he slay his own father and take his place next to the Emperor? In the end, Luke's inner strength would help him save his father's soul and bring an end to the Empire.

Jedi Luke Skywalker

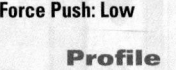

Fighter Stats

Lightsaber Power: Medium

Force Lightning Power: Low

Force Grip: Low

Force Push: Very High

Profile

This combatant is Luke Skywalker in his Jedi outfit.

Mace Windu

Fighter Stats

Lightsaber Power: High

Force Lightning Power: Low

Force Grip: Medium

Force Push: Low

Profile

Second only to Master Yoda on the Jedi Council, Mace Windu was one of the most respected and powerful Jedi before the issuing of Order 66. Had it not been for Anakin Skywalker's betrayal, Windu might have actually defeated Lord Sidious before Sidious could solidify his hold on the galaxy.

Shaak Ti

Fighter Stats

Lightsaber Power: Medium

Force Lightning Power: Low

Force Grip: Low

Force Push: High

Profile

A hero of the Clone Wars, Master Shaak Ti is one of the last surviving members of the Jedi Council. Shaak Ti is a Togruta, a humanoid species from the planet Shili. She is accurate and agile when moving and fighting in bustling crowds.

Shaak Ti has since become a respected Felucian chieftain, commanding tribes of Force-sensitive natives. She is dedicated to teaching them to control their burgeoning abilities and prevent the barbaric warriors from slipping to the dark side.

Darth Maul

Fighter Stats
Lightsaber Power: High

Force Lightning Power: High

Force Grip: Medium

Force Push: Low

Profile
Darth Maul was a relentless Sith warrior who employed the powers of the dark side to serve Darth Sidious, who would later become Emperor. A master of the double-bladed lightsaber, Maul remains a symbol of fear and Sith power.

Count Dooku

Fighter Stats
Lightsaber Power: Medium

Force Lightning Power: High

Force Grip: Medium

Force Push: Low

Profile
Count Dooku is a former Jedi Master who was seduced by the dark side. Dooku was instrumental in bringing about the rise of the Empire and spearheading the Clone Wars.

Asajj Ventress

Fighter Stats
Lightsaber Power: High

Force Lightning Power: Medium

Force Grip: Medium

Force Push: Low

Profile
Ventress was one of Dooku's dark acolytes. She began her Jedi training as a child but quickly gave in to her dark side when her master was destroyed.

Rahm Kota

Fighter Stats
Lightsaber Power: High

Force Lightning Power: Medium

Force Grip: Low

Force Push: Medium

Profile
Master Rahm Kota is a tough, grizzled Jedi Master. In one-on-one combat, Kota generally adopts a defensive stance, using his lightsaber skills and mastery of the Force to protect himself until he can launch a devastating counterattack. He often uses the Force to hurl debris or repel his enemies, and he can throw his lightsaber with unerring accuracy.

Aayla Secura

Fighter Stats
Lightsaber Power: Medium

Force Lightning Power: Medium

Force Grip: Low

Force Push: High

Profile
Aayla Secura was a skilled Jedi and general during the Clone Wars.

Mara Jade

Fighter Stats
Lightsaber Power: Medium

Force Lightning Power: Medium

Force Grip: Medium

Force Push: Medium

Profile
Throughout the course of her life, Mara Jade was many things. She first experienced the Force at the Emperor's side as his Hand. Later she married Luke Skywalker and gave birth to their son, Ben. After becoming a Master, Mara Jade trained her niece in the ways of the Jedi.

Darth Phobos

Fighter Stats
Lightsaber Power: Medium

Force Lightning Power: Medium

Force Grip: Medium

Force Push: Medium

Profile
Darth Phobos is a Sith Lord skilled in the ways of the Force. She preys on her opponent's fear and turns it against them during battle. Not only is she skilled with a lightsaber, but her mind tricks can fool a person into thinking she is someone else.

Maris Brood

Fighter Stats
Lightsaber Power: Medium

Force Lightning Power: High

Force Grip: Medium

Force Push: Low

Profile
Originally trained as a Jedi, Maris Brood's anger and fear of Darth Vader corrupted her, and she eventually fell prey to the dark side.

Although she is undisciplined and emotional, Maris is a skilled combatant. She is quick and agile, and has mastered a unique lightsaber fighting style that relies on rapid strikes. She has also learned to use the Force to mask herself and become invisible to the naked eye. She uses this ability to vanish for short periods of time before suddenly ambushing her opponents with a vicious attack.

SITH SECRETS

The following pages were ripped from secret scrolls known only to the Sith. They reveal the locations of all Holocrons and color crystals, and how to obtain all unlockables.

Holocron and Collectible Locations

The Holocrons and collectibles are listed in order as you progress through the level. Use that knowledge to identify specific locations listed below.

Prologue

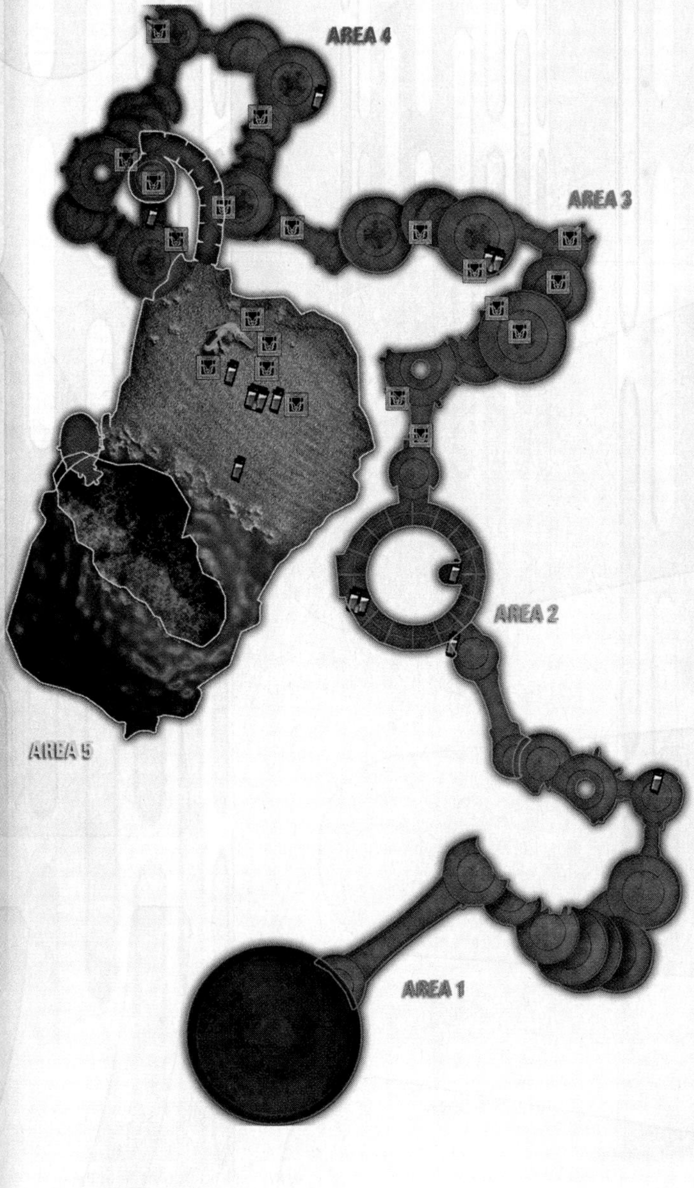

AREA 4

AREA 3

AREA 2

AREA 1

AREA 5

HOLOCRONS

- [ ] **Holocron 1:** Appears automatically as you cross the third long bridge at the start of Area 3.
- [ ] **Holocron 2:** Already visible on the left side of Area 3 immediately after crossing the bridge .
- [ ] **Holocron 3:** Appears on the platform in Area 3 after removing the small metal spire at the platform's center.
- [ ] **Holocron 4:** Hidden behind the large cylinder on the platform's left in Area 3.
- [ ] **Holocron 5:** Hidden in the middle of Area 3, just below walkway level on the right-hand side near the second pontoon, before the platform with blue lights.
- [ ] **Holocron 6:** Detach the small metal spire on the far end of the circular platform with blue lights. The Holocron will appear in the middle of Area 3.
- [ ] **Holocron 7:** On the left side of the crashed ornithopter near the end of Area 3.
- [ ] **Holocron 8:** Behind the large cylinder on the platform's left side, near the end of Area 3.
- [ ] **Holocron 9:** Appears after detaching the four metal base objects prior to reaching the bridge in Area 4.
- [ ] **Holocron 10:** On the platform's left side, after crossing the bridge into Area 4.
- [ ] **Holocron 11:** Detach the pipes near the start of Area 4 to reveal this Holocron.
- [ ] **Holocron 12:** Holocron appears after detaching the small metal base on the platform of Area 4.
- [ ] **Holocron 13:** On the path's left side, when approaching the elevator tunnel in Area 4.
- [ ] **Holocron 14:** Behind the holoprojector near the entrance to the elevator tunnel in Area 4. Reveal the Holocron by detaching the metal base on the floor.
- [ ] **Holocron 15:** On the elevator pad in Area 4.
- [ ] **Holocron 16:** In the ship wreckage on the left side of the beach in Area 5.
- [ ] **Holocron 17:** Amidst pipes on the beach's left side (Area 5), past the wreckage.
- [ ] **Holocron 18:** In Area 5, on the left-hand side of the beach near some tree roots, behind the Wookiee turret.
- [ ] **Holocron 19:** Near the tree root on the beach in Area 5.
- [ ] **Holocron 20:** Inside the crashed dropship on the beach in Area 5.

99

PRIMAGAMES.COM

TIE Construction Yard

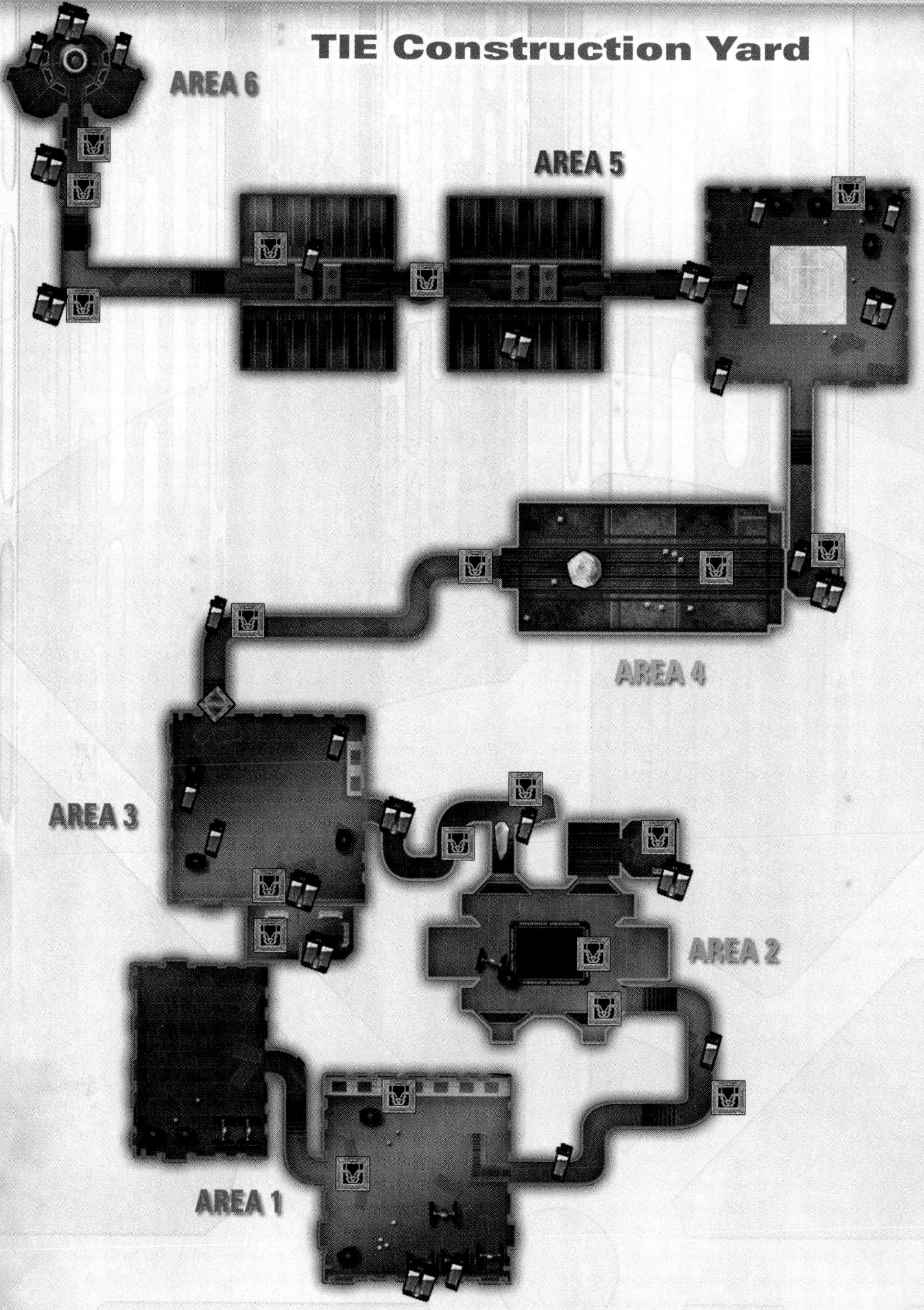

AREA 6

AREA 5

AREA 4

AREA 3

AREA 2

AREA 1

HOLOCRONS

- ❏ **Holocron 1:** Break the lights and rip off all the wall panels in the first corridor to make this appear after the first cutscene (Area 1).
- ❏ **Holocron 2:** In Area 1, stack objects to jump onto the upper platform on the hangar bay's far left side.
- ❏ **Holocron 3:** In the corridor leading to Area 2; reveal it by ripping off the wall panel on the right before reaching the console by the first small window.
- ❏ **Holocron 4:** Inside the storage container on the second level of Area 2.
- ❏ **Holocron 5:** Blast down the hatch to the room on Area 2's second level. The Holocron is inside the room.
- ❏ **Holocron 6:** On top of the large TIE wing crate on the way to Area 2's third level.

- ❏ **Holocron 7:** Beside the burning rubble in the corridor leading out of Area 2.
- ❏ **Holocron 8:** Behind the left wall's panel in the corridor leading out of Area 2.
- ❏ **Holocron 9:** Stack objects to jump onto the upper platform in Area 3.
- ❏ **Holocron 10:** Hidden behind the console with an electrical trap on the left of Area 3.
- ❏ **Holocron 11:** In the corridor leading out of Area 3, floating above the second set of steps.
- ❏ **Holocron 12:** Break the lights and rip off the wall panels in the corridor leading out of Area 3. The Holocron appears at the corridor's end.

STAR WARS
THE FORCE
UNLEASHED

HOLOCRONS CONTINUED

- ❑ **Holocron 13:** After riding the first elevator up to Area 4, inside the room with the red hatch door.
- ❑ **Holocron 14:** Sitting atop floating TIE wing machine at the center of Area 4. Double-jump onto the moving TIE wing to reach it.
- ❑ **Holocron 15:** Break all red electro-towers in Area 5 to reveal the Holocron in the far right corner of the upper platform.
- ❑ **Holocron 16:** Jump onto the small ledge above the walkway connecting the two large rooms in Area 5.
- ❑ **Holocron 17:** In the far right corner of the second large room in Area 5.
- ❑ **Holocron 18:** At the corridor's bend leading out of Area 5.
- ❑ **Holocron 19:** When the door opens to Area 6, defeat all 90 enemies in the level to reveal the Holocron.
- ❑ **Holocron 20:** Smash the central console's glass in the corridor before reaching the final battle. The Holocron is behind the console.

COLLECTIBLES

- ❑ **Health Holocron 1:** At the long hallway's start, leading out of Area 3.
- ❑ **Force Holocron 1:** At the walkway's start, high atop Area 4 as you get off elevator pad.
- ❑ **Green Color Crystal:** Atop the stairs in the corridor leading out of Area 2.

Trial of Skill

AREA 3

AREA 2

AREA 1

HOLOCRONS

- ❑ **Holocron 1:** Remove the large piece of rubble by the Temple entrance to reveal the Holocron in Area 1.
- ❑ **Holocron 2:** Sitting in the bottom right corner of the main Temple room in Area 2.
- ❑ **Holocron 3:** In the corner, behind some fallen rubble at the main Temple room's far end (Area 2).
- ❑ **Holocron 4:** Hidden behind the crumbled top-right corner of the main Temple room (Area 2). Leap over the rubble and turn left on the other side.
- ❑ **Holocron 5:** Hidden inside the third statue in the Area 3 hallway.
- ❑ **Holocron 6:** Hidden behind the Sidious statue in Area 3.

COLLECTIBLES

- ❑ **Force Holocron 1:** Inside the Jedi statue in Area 2's far right corner.
- ❑ **Purple Color Crystal:** Inside the Jedi statue near the left staircase in Area 2.

Raxus Prime

AREA 1

AREA 2

AREA 3

AREA 4

AREA 5

AREA 6

AREA 7

AREA 8

AREA 9

HOLOCRONS

- ☐ **Holocron 1:** Destroy the panel in Area 1's far left corner to reveal the Holocron behind it.

- ☐ **Holocron 2:** Far back end of Area 1, behind the *Rogue Shadow*.

- ☐ **Holocron 3:** On the rear wall of Area 2, behind the large brown cylinder after entering the area with the junkyard dog golem.

- ☐ **Holocron 4:** Destroy all crates in Area 2 to reveal the Holocron along the far right wall.

- ☐ **Holocron 5:** Behind the holoprojector near the end of Area 2; remove the large piece of scrap metal to reveal it.

- ☐ **Holocron 6:** Destroy the panel at the path's bend, near Area 2's end. The Holocron is behind the broken panel.

- ☐ **Holocron 7:** Make an immediate right after entering the passage in Area 3. The Holocron is behind the busted panel, before reaching the trash wall that requires Force Push.

- ☐ **Holocron 8:** In the same area with the first junk behemoth, to the left of the destroyable crates, there is a vertical panel to destroy. The Holocron appears after destroying that panel.

- ☐ **Holocron 9:** Break all crates in Area 3 during battle with the junk behemoth.

- ☐ **Holocron 10:** After meeting with Drexl, defeat the golems and go up the path. Remove the tall piece of metal in the niche on the left side to reveal the Holocron.

- ☐ **Holocron 11:** Break all crates in Area 4 to reveal the Holocron, near the area's right edge, behind the busted panel.

- ☐ **Holocron 12:** Along Area 4's right edge, behind the large curving piece of metal rubble.

- ☐ **Holocron 13:** In the niche on Area 4's right, just before reaching the large hatch doors; break the panel to reveal.

- ☐ **Holocron 14:** Break all crates in Area 5. The Holocron will appear near Area 5's entrance.

- ☐ **Holocron 15:** This Holocron is behind the rubble leaning on the left wall as you descend the walkway in Area 5.

HOLOCRONS CONTINUED

- Holocron 16: Break all crates in Area 6; the Holocron will appear on the left-hand side.
- Holocron 17: Near the left corner of the tunnel where you encounter the junk behemoth in Area 6.
- Holocron 18: Along the left wall of the junk behemoth tunnel; remove the tall metal object to reveal it (Area 6).
- Holocron 19: After defeating Drexl, go up to the next area. Defeat the junkyard dog golems, then remove the metal object in Area 7's far left corner.
- Holocron 20: To reveal the Holocron, break all the crates in Area 8 immediately after passing the holoprojector but before facing the two junkyard dog golems.

COLLECTIBLES

- Health Holocron 1: Break all the crates in Area 3 after battling the junkyard dog golem.
- Health Holocron 2: In Area 5.
- Force Holocron 1: Break all crates in Area 6.
- Force Holocron 2: Near the center of Area 7.
- Orange Color Crystal: In Area 6 near Holocron 17.
- Purple Color Crystal: Near the end of Area 8 on the left-hand side.
- Lightsaber Hilt: On the small platform on the left hand side of Area 4 before the elevator. Stack objects to reach it.

Trial of Insight

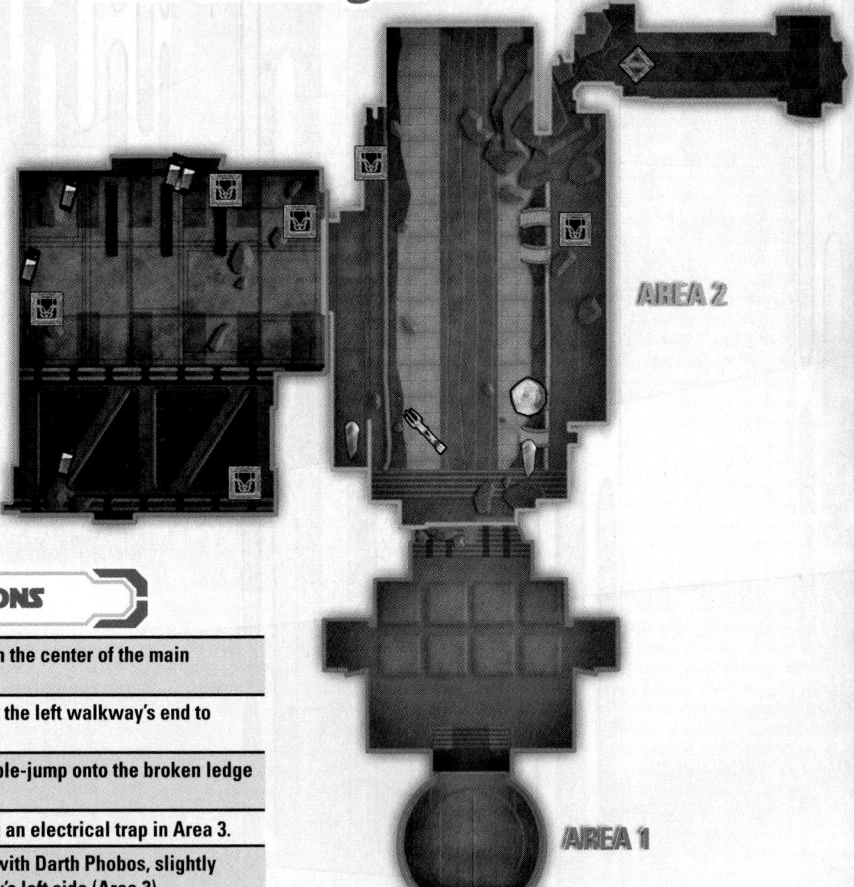

AREA 3

AREA 2

AREA 1

HOLOCRONS

- Holocron 1: Hidden inside the rubble in the center of the main Temple's right walkway (Area 2).
- Holocron 2: Remove the fallen pillar at the left walkway's end to expose the other Holocron in Area 2.
- Holocron 3: After entering Area 3, double-jump onto the broken ledge on the room's far right corner.
- Holocron 4: Sitting atop the ledge with an electrical trap in Area 3.
- Holocron 5: Before entering the room with Darth Phobos, slightly hidden behind the rubble on the library's left side (Area 3).
- Holocron 6: Hidden inside the broken pillar on the left side of the lower level during the battle with Darth Phobos (Area 3).

COLLECTIBLES

- Health Holocron 1: Inside the statue behind the fallen rocks at the Temple's far right end (Area 2).
- Force Holocron 1: In the small niche on the Temple's near right side (Area 2).
- Blue Color Crystal: In Area 2 at the far left walkway's end.
- Green Color Crystal: In the bottom right corner of Area 2, behind pillars and rubble.
- Lightsaber Hilt: Amidst the rubble in the main Temple room's bottom left corner (Area 2).

Felucia

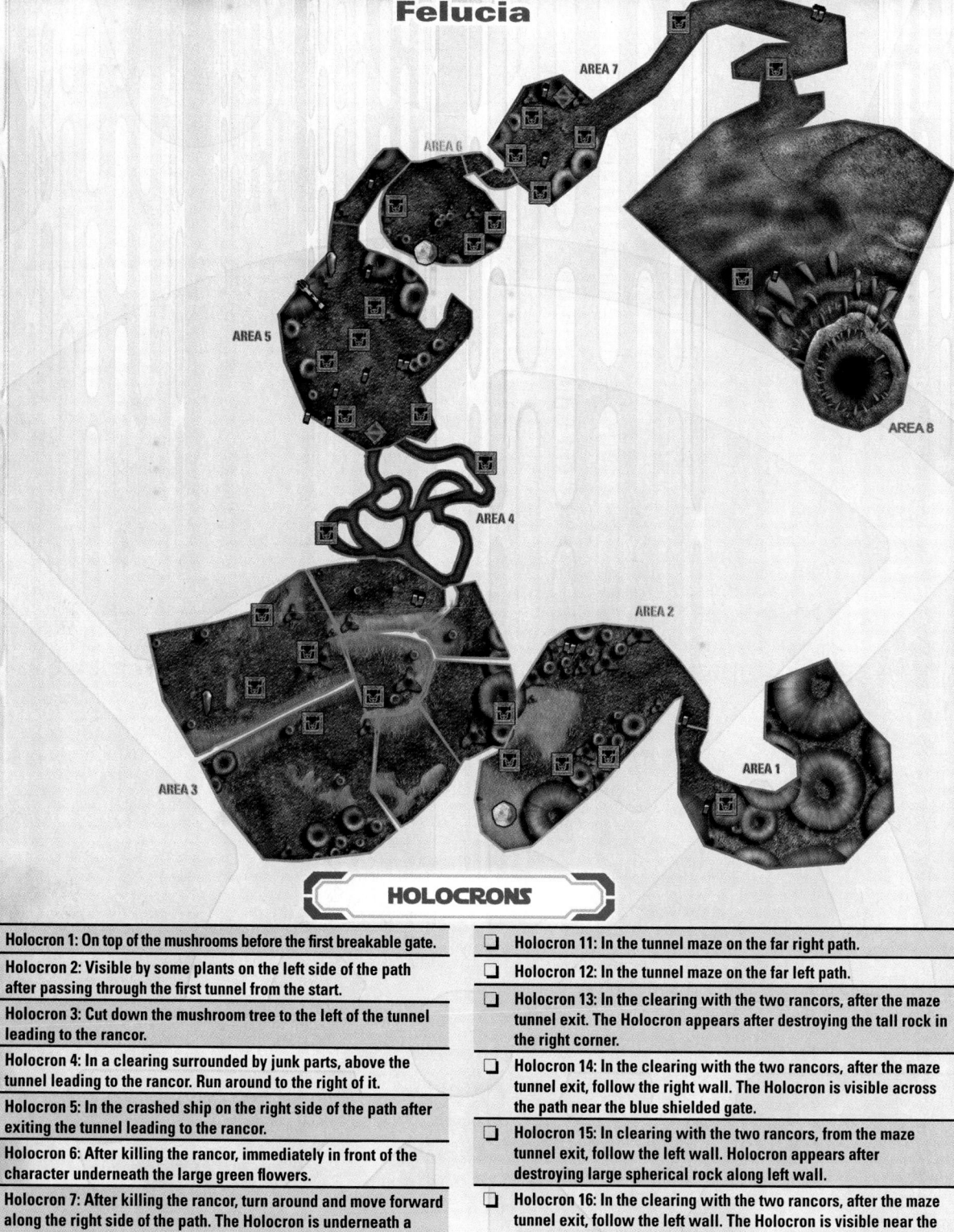

AREA 7

AREA 6

AREA 5

AREA 8

AREA 4

AREA 2

AREA 1

AREA 3

104

HOLOCRONS

- **Holocron 1:** On top of the mushrooms before the first breakable gate.

- **Holocron 2:** Visible by some plants on the left side of the path after passing through the first tunnel from the start.

- **Holocron 3:** Cut down the mushroom tree to the left of the tunnel leading to the rancor.

- **Holocron 4:** In a clearing surrounded by junk parts, above the maze tunnel leading to the rancor. Run around to the right of it.

- **Holocron 5:** In the crashed ship on the right side of the path after exiting the tunnel leading to the rancor.

- **Holocron 6:** After killing the rancor, immediately in front of the character underneath the large green flowers.

- **Holocron 7:** After killing the rancor, turn around and move forward along the right side of the path. The Holocron is underneath a large green flower.

- **Holocron 8:** After killing the rancor, turn around, move forward along left side of path. Holocron is visible at the end of the path near purple mushrooms.

- **Holocron 9:** After killing rancor, move forward slightly to the right near the two destroyable mushroom trees. The Holocron appears after destroying those trees.

- **Holocron 10:** After killing the rancor, move immediately towards the three large green flowers. The Holocron is underneath a small circular rock under the middle large green flower.

- **Holocron 11:** In the tunnel maze on the far right path.

- **Holocron 12:** In the tunnel maze on the far left path.

- **Holocron 13:** In the clearing with the two rancors, after the maze tunnel exit. The Holocron appears after destroying the tall rock in the right corner.

- **Holocron 14:** In the clearing with the two rancors, after the maze tunnel exit, follow the right wall. The Holocron is visible across the path near the blue shielded gate.

- **Holocron 15:** In clearing with the two rancors, from the maze tunnel exit, follow the left wall. Holocron appears after destroying large spherical rock along left wall.

- **Holocron 16:** In the clearing with the two rancors, after the maze tunnel exit, follow the left wall. The Holocron is visible near the left wall just past a large destroyable rock.

- **Holocron 17:** Destroy the single large rock in the middle of the clearing with the two rancors to make the Holocron appear.

- **Holocron 18:** In the Felucian village with the large green pillars, the Holocron is visible behind the first green pillar on the right wall.

- **Holocron 19:** In the Felucian village with the large green pillars, the Holocron is visible behind the last green pillar on the right wall near the blue gate.

HOLOCRONS CONTINUED

- **Holocron 20:** In the Felucian village with the large green pillars, the Holocron is on top of the purple mushroom near the blue gate.
- **Holocron 21:** In the second part of the Felucian village after the first cutscene with Shaak Ti, the Holocron is visible between the first and second green pillars along the left wall.
- **Holocron 22:** In the second part of the Felucian village after the first cutscene with Shaak Ti, the Holocron is visible between the third and fourth green pillars along the left wall.
- **Holocron 23:** In the second part of Felucian village after the first cutscene with Shaak Ti, the Holocron appears after destroying the lone mushroom tree along the right wall.
- **Holocron 24:** In the second part of the Felucian village after the first cutscene with Shaak Ti. The Holocron appears after destroying the pair of mushroom trees by the cluster of three large pillars at the bottom of the ramp.
- **Holocron 25:** Halfway up the path toward Shaak Ti, along the left side, the Holocron appears after destroying two mushroom trees.
- **Holocron 26:** Near the end of the path leading to Shaak Ti, a Holocron appears after destroying the lone rock on the right side of the wall.
- **Holocron 27:** On the right side of the wall during the Shaak Ti fight.

COLLECTIBLES

- **Health Holocron 1:** On the far left side of Area 5.
- **Health Holocron 2:** On the left side of Area 7, near Holocron 23.
- **Force Holocron 1:** On the far left side of Area 2.
- **Force Holocron 2:** In Area 6, near Holocron 18.
- **Purple Color Crystal:** Remove the large brown stone attached to the wall just left of the next tunnel entrance of Area 5.
- **Red Color Crystal:** Inside a small rock after turning left after the rancor fight in Area 3.
- **Lightsaber Hilt:** On the platform across from the purple color crystal.

Nar Shaddaa

AREA 1

AREA 3

AREA 2

HOLOCRONS

- **Holocron 1:** Floating over the second arch of the bridge in Area 1.
- **Holocron 2:** On the left corner of the main bar entrance. Destroy all tables to reveal it (Area 1).
- **Holocron 3:** Appears near the exit door to Area 1 after defeating all enemies.
- **Holocron 4:** On the left-hand side of Area 2; destroy the table to reveal it.
- **Holocron 5:** Knock over all the tables in Area 2 to expose the Holocron.
- **Holocron 6:** Jump onto the first arch of the bridge leading out of Area 2.
- **Holocron 7:** On the second floor of Area 3, past Kota.
- **Holocron 8:** Appears on the lower level of Area 3 after breaking all chairs on the upper level.
- **Holocron 9:** In front of the stairs in Area 3. The Holocron appears after meeting with Kota, destroying all wall panels, and defeating the final wave of enemies in Area 3.
- **Holocron 10:** In front of the bar (after speaking to the bartender) while fighting the Shadow Guard in Area 1.

COLLECTIBLES

- **Health Holocron 1:** Atop the steps in Area 3 after removing all the poles from the tables.
- **Force Holocron 1:** Atop the table in Area 2.
- **Lightsaber Hilt:** Atop the arch before entering Area 2.

Trial of Spirit

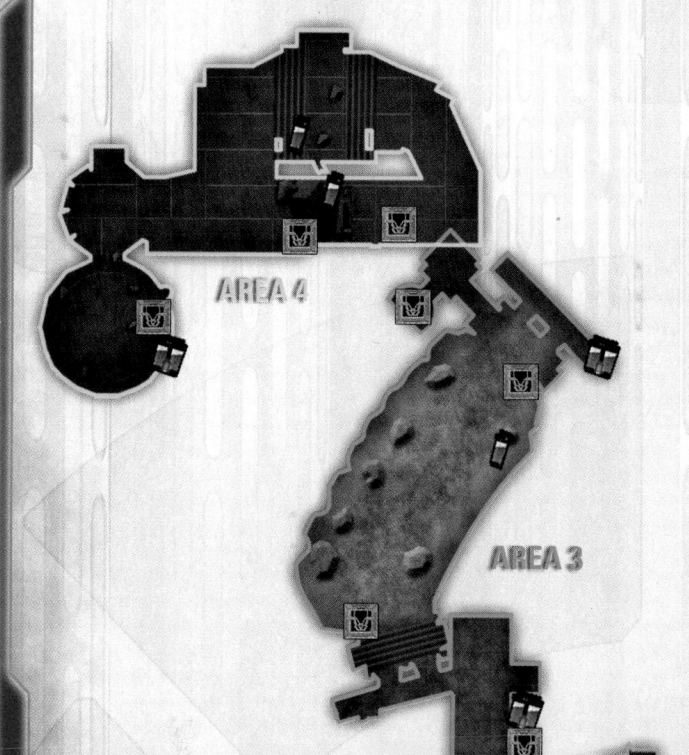

AREA 4

AREA 3

AREA 2

AREA 1

HOLOCRONS

❏ **Holocron 1:** In the area below the *Rogue Shadow* landing pad (Area 1).

❏ **Holocron 2:** Hidden behind the statue on the right as you enter Area 3.

❏ **Holocron 3:** Hidden to the left of the first set of steps in Area 3.

❏ **Holocron 4:** On the right, next to the large stone support near the end of Area 3, before reaching the second set of steps.

❏ **Holocron 5:** On the left, before entering Area 4. Pick up the Holocron before removing the collapsed rubble with Force Push.

❏ **Holocron 6:** On the left immediately after entering Area 4; remove the large fallen pillar to reveal it.

❏ **Holocron 7:** On the left before going up the steps to the elevator room in Area 4; remove the rubble to reveal it.

❏ **Holocron 8:** On the right behind the fallen pillar while fighting the rogue Jedi in Area 4.

COLLECTIBLES

❏ **Health Holocron 1:** Under the small alcove, near the steps on the right side of Area 2.

Kashyyyk

HOLOCRONS

- ☐ Holocron 1: On the ground to the right after exiting the *Rogue Shadow*. Force Push the plants on the right of the steps to reveal it.
- ☐ Holocron 2: Behind the vines, on the left side near the end of Area 1 after passing the first gun turret.
- ☐ Holocron 3: Under the rock on the right-hand side as you enter Area 2, just left of the palm tree.
- ☐ Holocron 4: On the left-hand side of Area 2, across from the burning rubble; pick it up after defeating the AT-ST.
- ☐ Holocron 5: On the right-hand side of Area 2 before exiting the narrow passage; Force Push the small green plant to reveal it.
- ☐ Holocron 6: Behind the plant on the right-hand side of Area 2 just before you reach the door barricade.
- ☐ Holocron 7: On the left, near the second Wookiee cage in Area 2; remove the fallen tree to reveal it.
- ☐ Holocron 8: Behind the tree root on the path's right side, before reaching the Lambda Shuttle section gate entrance (Area 3).
- ☐ Holocron 9: Under the rock on the left-hand side of the Lambda Shuttle section. Pick it up after defeating the Imperial troops (Area 3).
- ☐ Holocron 10: Inside the rock on the right-hand side after exiting the Lambda Shuttle section (Area 3).
- ☐ Holocron 11: Cut the warped tree trunk on the path's left side immediately after exiting the Lambda Shuttle area.
- ☐ Holocron 12: After the shuttle area, progress forward along the left wall. The Holocron appears under a rectangular rock after destroying a plant along the left edge of the path.
- ☐ Holocron 13: After the shuttle area, reach the path junction and take the left path into the protected area. Force Push the wall on the left-hand side after the first Wookiee barricade and the Holocron will appear.
- ☐ Holocron 14: Under a large grey rock on the left side of the right path after defeating the AT-ST. (Area 4).
- ☐ Holocron 15: Near the end of Area 4, under the rock on the area's left hand side where the two paths rejoin.
- ☐ Holocron 16: Exit the narrow passage at the beginning of Area 5. Send a Force Push toward the small plant across from the palm tree to reveal it.
- ☐ Holocron 17: Appears after destroying a plant, at the point where the two paths reconnect, on the left side of the path between a palm tree and the checkpoint droid. This is just past the second AT-ST fight.
- ☐ Holocron 18: Behind the vines on the right at the end of Area 5.
- ☐ Holocron 19: Destroy all watchtower posts to make it appear at the entrance to the bunker (Area 6).
- ☐ Holocron 20: Hidden behind the vines on the right side of the path leading to the bunker (Area 6). Force Push the left wall of the path to reveal it.

COLLECTIBLES

- ☐ Health Holocron 1: Under a large rock on the right side of Area 2, after the first Wookiee cage.
- ☐ Health Holocron 2: Behind the vines on the left path's right side, near the start of Area 5.
- ☐ Force Holocron 1: Appears in Area 2 after defeating the AT-ST.
- ☐ Force Holocron 2: Just after the fallen tree bridge in Area 4.
- ☐ Red color crystal: Inside the fire after battling the AT-ST in Area 2.
- ☐ Orange Color Crystal: Immediately left after entering Area 4.
- ☐ Lightsaber Hilt: Just after the fallen tree bridge in Area 4, on the ground between the two guard towers.

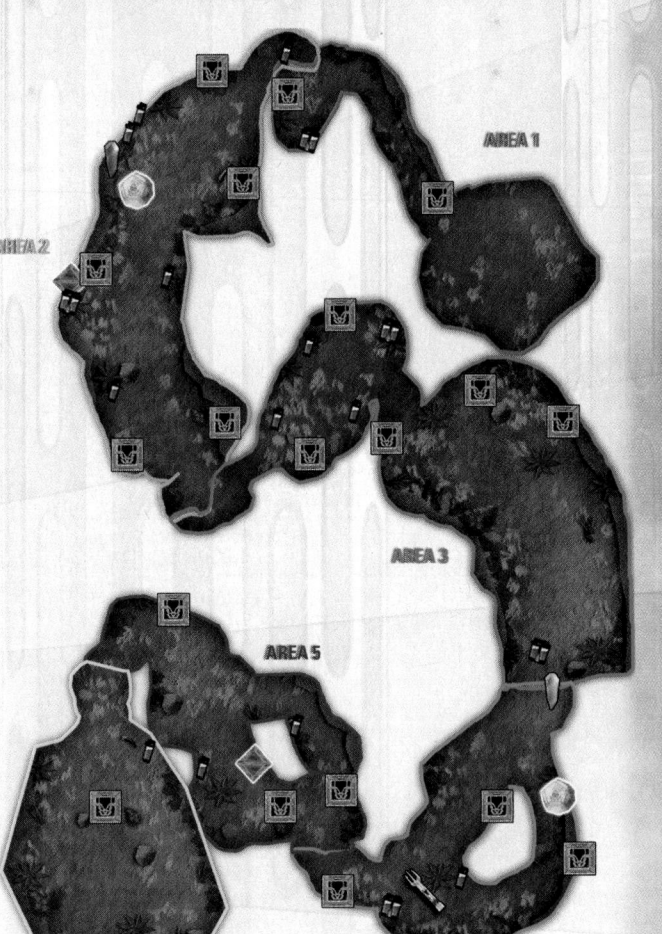

AREA 1

AREA 2

AREA 3

AREA 5

AREA 4

AREA 6

Dark Felucia

AREA 6

AREA 2

AREA 5

AREA 3

AREA 4

HOLOCRONS

☐ **Holocron 1:** At level start, the Holocron is visible on the ground behind the *Rogue Shadow*.

☐ **Holocron 2:** At level start, the Holocron appears after destroying the left side bone near the skull tunnel.

☐ **Holocron 3:** After the cutscene plays of rebels fighting stormtroopers, move left toward the other rancor skull. The Holocron is visible behind the rock pillar.

☐ **Holocron 4:** In the area with rebels fighting stormtroopers, move toward the right side near the rancor rib cage. The Holocron appears after destroying the farthest rib on the right side.

☐ **Holocron 5:** The Holocron is visible near the rancor skull to the right of the first blue gate.

☐ **Holocron 6:** After destroying the first blue gate and continuing along the path, the Holocron appears on top of a mushroom on the left side of the wall immediately after the checkpoint droid.

☐ **Holocron 7:** Upon entering the Imperial camp, the Holocron is visible on the left side of the second bunker next to the wall.

☐ **Holocron 8:** In the Imperial camp, the Holocron is on top of the third bunker near the radar dish.

☐ **Holocron 9:** In the Imperial camp, the Holocron appears after destroying the small tank to the right of the fourth bunker door.

☐ **Holocron 10:** In the Felucian village with large green pillars, the Holocron appears near the fourth green pillar on the right wall.

HOLOCRONS CONTINUED

☐ **Holocron 11:** In the Felucian village with large green pillars, the Holocron appears on top of the purple mushroom near the green pillars on the right wall.

☐ **Holocron 12:** In the Felucian village with large green pillars, the Holocron appears on top of the purple mushroom between a green flower and the blue gate.

☐ **Holocron 13:** In the Maris Brood fight, the Holocron appears along the left wall near the large green pillar.

COLLECTIBLES

☐ **Health Holocron 1:** On the roof behind the third Imperial barracks in Area 4.

☐ **Health Holocron 2:** In the bottom left of Area 3 behind a small bulbous plant, after backtracking out of Area 4.

☐ **Force Holocron 1:** On the side of the first Imperial barracks building in Area 4.

☐ **Force Holocron 2:** Near the right wall of Area 3, after backtracking out of Area 4.

☐ **Green Color Crystal:** Behind some plants across from the tunnel leading into Area 5.

☐ **Lightsaber Hilt:** Just past the beginning of Area 3 when you visit it the second time.

STAR WARS
THE FORCE
UNLEASHED

Imperial Raxus Prime

HOLOCRONS

❑ **Holocron 1:** In Area 3, third room on the right. Destroy the console to reveal it.

❑ **Holocron 2:** To the right of the hatch doors leading to Area 4. Destroy the crates to reveal it.

❑ **Holocron 3:** On the immediate right as you enter Area 4. Destroy the console to reveal it.

❑ **Holocron 4:** Behind the docked AT-ST on the right in Area 4.

❑ **Holocron 5:** Appears after destroying the vertical pipes near the doorway.

❑ **Holocron 6:** On the left side of the center platform in Area 5. Remove the first wall panel to reveal it.

❑ **Holocron 7:** Appears after removing the wall panel from the central structure.

❑ **Holocron 8:** On the right end of the second level walkway in Area 5. Remove the wall panel to reveal it.

❑ **Holocron 9:** Appears after destroying the small console near the edge of the lava on the ground floor.

❑ **Holocron 10:** Appears near the force field after all electric reactors have been destroyed in Area 5.

❑ **Holocron 11:** Underneath some crates near the ramps in Area 6. Immediately turn left after entering Area 6.

❑ **Holocron 12:** Behind the pillar on the second level walkway of Area 6. Turn right at the top of the ramp.

❑ **Holocron 13:** Remove all wall consoles in Area 6 to make it appear near the force field exit.

❑ **Holocron 14:** In Area 6, room two, behind the pillar on the second level walkway.

❑ **Holocron 15:** In the first room, behind the ramp to the second level of Area 7.

❑ **Holocron 16:** On the left of the passage connecting the two rooms in Area 7.

❑ **Holocron 17:** In the niche on the lower level of Area 7. Remove the control console on the left side to reveal it.

❑ **Holocron 18:** Destroy all electric generators in Area 7 to make it appear near the force field.

❑ **Holocron 19:** On the right side of the second level in Area 8.

❑ **Holocron 20:** Destroy all eight wall consoles to make it appear near the force field.

COLLECTIBLES

❑ **Health Holocron 1:** In the far left corner of Area 4. Double-jump up the empty AT-ST docking bay on the right to reach the second level of Area 4.

❑ **Health Holocron 2:** On the walkway inside the niche with the molten metal in Area 8.

❑ **Force Holocron 1:** On the walkway inside the niche with the molten metal in Area 5.

❑ **Force Holocron 2:** At the end of the second-level walkway in Area 6.

❑ **Blue Color Crystal:** In the top right corner of Area 4. Double-jump up the empty AT-ST docking bay on the left to reach the second level of Area 4.

❑ **Red Color Crystal:** Atop the ledge on the wall of Area 5.

❑ **Lightsaber Hilt:** On the ledge high above the entrance to the AT-ST bay in Area 4. From the second level of Area 4, creep out to the ledge, then double-jump and dash toward it.

AREA 7

AREA 6

AREA 9

AREA 5

AREA 8

AREA 4

AREA 2

AREA 1

AREA 3

Cloud City

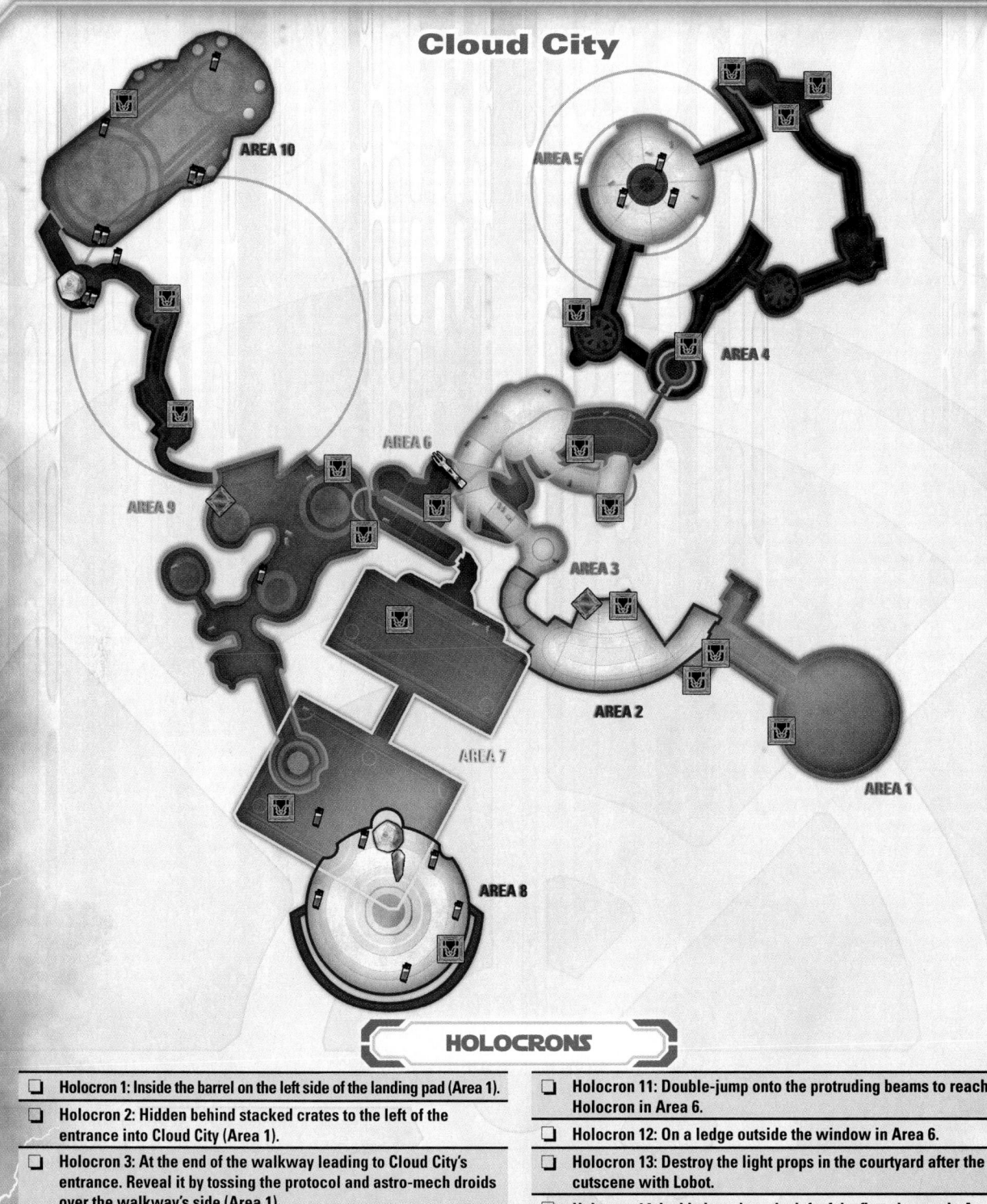

AREA 10

AREA 5

AREA 4

AREA 9

AREA 6

AREA 3

AREA 2

AREA 1

AREA 7

AREA 8

HOLOCRONS

- ❏ **Holocron 1:** Inside the barrel on the left side of the landing pad (Area 1).
- ❏ **Holocron 2:** Hidden behind stacked crates to the left of the entrance into Cloud City (Area 1).
- ❏ **Holocron 3:** At the end of the walkway leading to Cloud City's entrance. Reveal it by tossing the protocol and astro-mech droids over the walkway's side (Area 1).
- ❏ **Holocron 4:** Inside the large circular niche on the right in Area 2.
- ❏ **Holocron 5:** Outside the blue elevator.
- ❏ **Holocron 6:** Remove the pipe on the right wall of the small circular room after riding the second elevator.
- ❏ **Holocron 7:** High atop the second landing platform in Area 4; double-jump onto the large pipe, and edge out to the pipe's end.
- ❏ **Holocron 8:** Inside the barrel on the second landing platform in Area 4.
- ❏ **Holocron 9:** On the far left wall inside the curved room at the end of Area 4.
- ❏ **Holocron 10:** Inside the first circular room in Area 5.

- ❏ **Holocron 11:** Double-jump onto the protruding beams to reach the Holocron in Area 6.
- ❏ **Holocron 12:** On a ledge outside the window in Area 6.
- ❏ **Holocron 13:** Destroy the light props in the courtyard after the cutscene with Lobot.
- ❏ **Holocron 14:** Inside barrels to the left of the first elevator in Area 7.
- ❏ **Holocron 15:** To the right of the elevator immediately upon entering Area 8.
- ❏ **Holocron 16:** Inside the barrel on the plaza's far right side in Area 9.
- ❏ **Holocron 17:** Inside the barrel to the right of the turret guarding the tunnel entrance in the Area 9 plaza.
- ❏ **Holocron 18:** After entering the long tunnel in Area 9, remove the pipe on the left side of the first big room in the tunnel.
- ❏ **Holocron 19:** Remove the pipe on the left in the second connecting circular room near the end of Area 9.
- ❏ **Holocron 20:** Inside the farthest statue on the right in Area 10.

STAR WARS
FORCE
THE UNLEASHED

COLLECTIBLES

- ❏ **Health Holocron 1:** To the left of the first circular niche after entering Cloud City (Area 2). Double-jump from atop the spire to reach it.
- ❏ **Health Holocron 2:** High atop the entrance to the tunnel in Area 9; double-jump onto the post to reach it.
- ❏ **Force Holocron 1:** In the elevator shaft leading to Area 8.
- ❏ **Force Holocron 2:** In the circular room near the end of Area 9.
- ❏ **Blue Color Crystal:** Hidden inside crates behind the second elevator of Area 7.
- ❏ **Lightsaber Hilt:** On the ledge outside the window in Area 6.

Death Star

HOLOCRONS

- ❏ **Holocron 1:** Next to the crashed TIE fighter on the bottom level of Area 1. Jump up to the second level, then drop back down to the lower level.
- ❏ **Holocron 2:** On the bottom level of Area 1, at the far end near the fire.
- ❏ **Holocron 3:** Behind the control console at the far end of Area 2. Pick it up before turning left and crossing the bridge through the firing beam tube.
- ❏ **Holocron 4:** In the corner, by the console in Area 4. Pick it up before crossing the next bridge across the firing tube.
- ❏ **Holocron 5:** At the end of Area 4, near the large tractor beam cylinders. Pick it up after deactivating the blue force field.
- ❏ **Holocron 6:** On the left at the midpoint of the long hallway in Area 5, inside the control console.
- ❏ **Holocron 7:** Behind the semicircular console near the end of Area 5. Pick it up before getting on the elevator.
- ❏ **Holocron 8:** On the ledge on the immediate left in the first room with Imperial guards in Area 6. Stack crates to reach it.
- ❏ **Holocron 9:** Behind the console in Area 7, at the long walkway's end.
- ❏ **Holocron 10:** After getting off the elevator in Area 8; destroy the console on the right to reveal it.

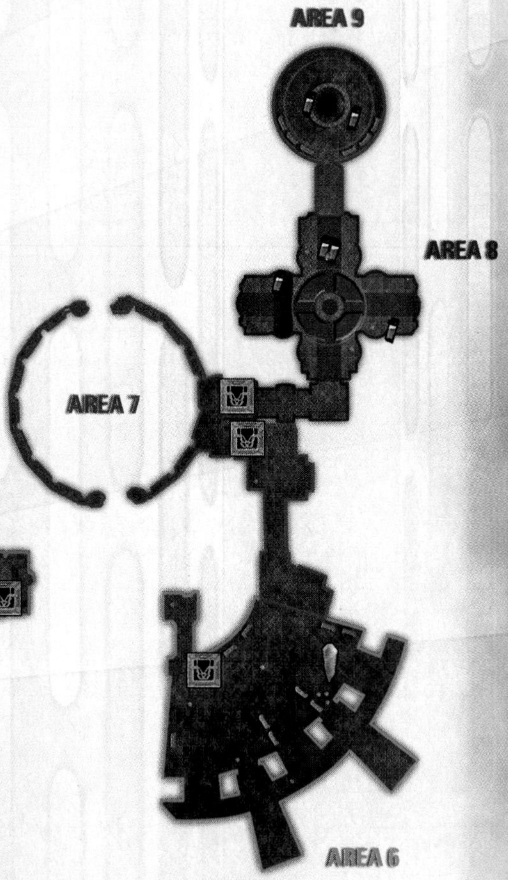

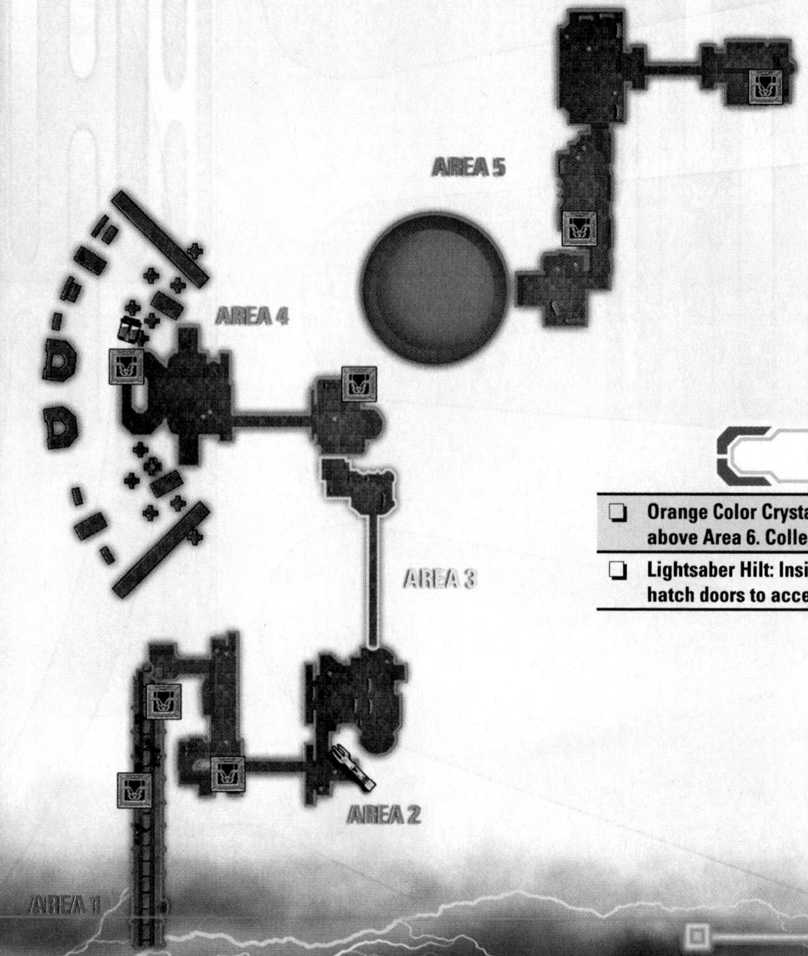

AREA 9

AREA 8

AREA 7

111

AREA 5

AREA 4

AREA 3

AREA 6

COLLECTIBLES

- ❏ **Orange Color Crystal:** At the platform's end on the left wall, high above Area 6. Collect this before defeating the AT-ST.
- ❏ **Lightsaber Hilt:** Inside the sealed room in Area 2. Force Push the hatch doors to access the room on the right.

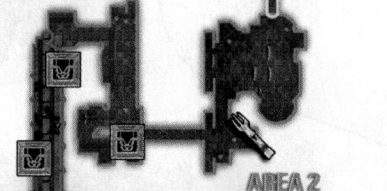

AREA 2

/AREA 1

PRIMAGAMES.COM

Level Unlockables

TIE Construction Yard

- ❏ Ground Slam Force power
- ❏ Kaiburr combat crystal
- ❏ Character—Duel Mode

Trial of Skill

- ❏ Dark Rage power
- ❏ Asajj Ventress character—Duel Mode
- ❏ Qixoni combat crystal
- ❏ Heavy training gear

Raxus Prime

- ❏ Pummel power
- ❏ Darth Maul character—Duel Mode
- ❏ Blaster Block lightsaber hilt

Trial of Insight

- ❏ Maelstrom power
- ❏ Darth Phobos character—Duel Mode
- ❏ Count Dooku character—Duel mode
- ❏ Opila combat crystal
- ❏ Light training gear

Felucia

- ❏ Sith Barrage Force power
- ❏ Shaak Ti character—Duel mode

Vader's Flagship

- ❏ Sith Scorcher Force power
- ❏ Luke Skywalker, Jedi Knight character—Duel Mode
- ❏ Blaster Block ability enhanced
- ❏ Sith robe costume

Nar Shaddaa

- ❏ Power Slam Force power
- ❏ Mace Windu character—Duel Mode

Trial of Spirit

- ❏ Sith Seeker Force power
- ❏ Force levels unlocked (upgrade Force powers two more levels)
- ❏ Kento's robe costume
- ❏ Mara Jade character—Duel Mode

Kashyyyk

- ❏ Obi-Wan Kenobi character—Duel Mode
- ❏ Blaster Block ability enhanced
- ❏ Dragite combat crystal
- ❏ Corellian flight suit costume

Dark Felucia

- ❏ Maris Brood character—Duel mode
- ❏ Firkrann combat crystal
- ❏ Jungle combat gear costume

Imperialized Raxus

- ❏ Qui-Gon Jinn character—Duel Mode
- ❏ Damind combat crystal
- ❏ Raxus Prime survival gear costume

Cloud City

- ❏ Bounty hunter disguise costume

Death Star

- ❏ Ultimate Good character—Duel Mode
- ❏ Ceremonial Jedi Robes Costume
- ❏ Ultimate Evil character—Duel Mode
- ❏ Sith stalker costume

JEDI KNOWLEDGE

Unlocking the Ultimate Good and Ultimate Evil characters depends on which side you choose in your final battle.